DEMOSTHENES OF

AND THE FALL OF CLASSICAL GREECE

IAN WORTHINGTON

DEMOSTHENES OF ATHENS AND THE FALL OF CLASSICAL GREECE

OXFORD
UNIVERSITY PRESS

OXFORD
UNIVERSITY PRESS

Oxford University Press
Oxford University Press is a department of the University of Oxford.
It furthers the University's objective of excellence in research,
scholarship, and education by publishing worldwide.

Oxford   New York
Auckland   Cape Town   Dar es Salaam   Hong Kong   Karachi
Kuala Lumpur   Madrid   Melbourne   Mexico City   Nairobi
New Delhi   Shanghai   Taipei   Toronto

With offices in
Argentina   Austria   Brazil   Chile   Czech Republic   France   Greece
Guatemala   Hungary   Italy   Japan   Poland   Portugal   Singapore
South Korea   Switzerland   Thailand   Turkey   Ukraine   Vietnam

Oxford is a registered trademark of Oxford University Press in the UK and certain other countries

Published in the United States of America by
Oxford University Press
198 Madison Avenue, New York, New York 10016

Library of Congress Cataloging-in-Publication Data
Worthington, Ian.
Demosthenes of Athens and the fall of classical Greece / Ian Worthington.
p.   cm.
Includes bibliographical references and index.
ISBN 978-0-19-993195-8 (hardcover : alk. paper); 978-0-19-026356-0 (paperback : alk. paper)
1. Demosthenes. 2. Statesmen—Greece—Biography.
3. Orators—Greece—Biography. I. Title.
PA3952.W67   2012
885'.01—dc23
[B]   2012005787

1 3 5 7 9 8 6 4 2
Printed in the United States of America on acid-free paper

Contents

Preface

In a book about Demosthenes published over seven decades ago, Werner Jaeger commented that "no one who hopes for the unanimous applause of his readers ever does well to take a politician for his hero." If Demosthenes was a hero he was certainly a flawed one. However, my intention is to take into account differing interpretations of his policies and motives and, in offering new insights into these, present as well-rounded a portrait of Demosthenes as possible, set against the history of not only Athens but also Greece and Macedonia. Whether this will generate any applause remains to be seen.

Demosthenes was one of ancient Greece's most influential figures. His political career spanned three decades, during which Athens clashed with Philip II of Macedonia, and his city as well as Greece lost their independence. His resolute defiance of Philip earned for him a reputation in antiquity and throughout the ages as one of history's outstanding patriots. He is also universally regarded as Greece's most distinguished orator, given the rhetorical style and power of his surviving speeches. Yet the odds against the sickly child, who suffered several physical and speech impediments and an interrupted education becoming as powerful as he did, were great. His story is certainly one of triumph over adversity.

Born in 384 and orphaned at the age of seven, Demosthenes was swindled by guardians out of the lion's share of his father's considerable estate so that when he came of age he, his sister, and their mother faced financial hardship. Demosthenes' afflictions prevented him from attending the same type of schools and gymnasium as other boys of his age. However, he imposed a brutal training regimen on himself to overcome his speech deficiencies—famously including speaking with pebbles in his mouth and running up and down hills to solve breathing problems. As a young man he indicted his guardians, winning his lawsuits convincingly, but recouping little of what his guardians had squandered. His victories opened the door to a brilliant and highly lucrative career as a speechwriter.

Ambitious, in the mid-350s he began to deliver domestic and foreign policy speeches. He was at first heckled because of his delivery, and a string of failures almost ended his political career. Then the rising power of Macedonia under Philip altered his career prospects as much as it would Greek history. His speeches calling the Athenians to arms against Philip, delivered over the period 351 to 339, elevated him to great political prominence: from the mid-340s he dictated Athenian foreign policy. His refusal to compromise with Philip culminated at the battle of Chaeronea in 338. Demosthenes fought in the Greek ranks, the phrase "good luck" emblazoned on his shield. However, victory, and with it control of Greece, went to Philip. The Macedonian king was assassinated in 336, and in 334 his son and successor Alexander III left for Asia destined to topple the Persian Empire and become Alexander the Great. Demosthenes was far less politically active in this period. After an abortive Greek revolt following Alexander's death in 323 he committed suicide in 322 at age sixty-two.

Demosthenes was also a great orator as the rhetorical style of his surviving speeches proves. He wrote in a style that could be vivid, emotional, rousing, sobering, sarcastic, or bitter according to the occasion, as the quotations from his speeches in the following chapters demonstrate. Among other things, he brought a sense of dramatic immediacy to his speeches by resorting to imaginary dialogue when, for example, he was critical of Athenian indifference to Philip: "'Is Philip dead?' 'No, by Zeus, but he is sick.' What difference does it make to you? Even if something were to happen to him, you would soon create another Philip, if this is how you apply yourselves to the situation" (*Philippic* 1.11). He was a master of the rhetorical device known as *ethopoiia* or characterization, making characters in his speeches come alive (as politicians do today) to provoke a deliberate response from his audience. For example, even today we feel sympathy for the abused arbitrator Demosthenes described as "a poor man, inexperienced, but otherwise not a scoundrel and actually quite honest" (*Against Meidias* 83). We cannot help but be swayed by Demosthenes' harsh staccato attack on his great enemy, the orator Aeschines: "You taught school, I was a student; you conducted initiation rites, I was initiated; you served as a public scribe, I attended the Assembly; you played bit parts on stage, I sat in the audience; you were hissed offstage, I was hissing. All your policies helped the enemy; mine helped our country" (*On the Crown* 235).

Demosthenes' patriotic appeals to the glorious deeds of the Athenians' ancestors, arguably the most touching and inspiring of all the Greek orations, stir our hearts as they must have done his fellow citizens: "But you were not wrong, no, you were not, Athenians, to take on danger for the sake of the freedom and safety of all—I swear by your forefathers who led the fight at Marathon, by those who stood in the ranks at Plataea, by those who fought aboard ship at Salamis and Artemisium, and by the many other brave men who lie in the public tombs, all of whom the city buried, deeming them all equally worthy of the same honor" (*On the Crown* 208).

This book is not about Demosthenes the orator because other books on this subject make another treatment superfluous. Included among them are L. Pearson, *The Art of Demosthenes* (Meisenheim am Glan: 1976) and especially D. M. MacDowell, *Demosthenes the Orator* (Oxford: 2009). However, I discuss aspects of Demosthenes' rhetorical style when relevant to a particular argument he was advancing, and the extensive quotations in translation from his speeches not only sum up their main points but also illustrate his rhetorical mastery.

It has been well over a century since A. Schaefer's monumental, three-volume *Demosthenes und seine Zeit*[2] (Leipzig: 1885–1887), which despite its age still remains a valuable resource for Demosthenes' life and speeches. It has also been almost a century since Sir A. W. Pickard-Cambridge's *Demosthenes and the Last Days of Greek Freedom* (London: 1914), published, coincidentally, in the series *Heroes of the Nation*. Since then there have been, to give a few examples, G. Clemenceau's *Démosthènes* (Paris: 1926), P. Cloché's *Démosthène et la fin de la démocratie athénienne* (Paris: 1957), P. Carlier's *Démosthène* (Paris: 1990), and G. A. Lehmann's *Demosthenes von Athen: Ein Leben für die Freiheit* (Munich: 2004). More focused studies have included W. Jaeger's *Demosthenes: The Origin and Growth of His Policy* (Berkeley and Los Angeles: 1938; repr. New York: 1977), H. Montgomery's *The Way to Chaeronea* (Oslo: 1983), R. Sealey's *Demosthenes and His Time, A Study in Defeat* (Oxford: 1993), and my own edited *Demosthenes: Statesman and Orator* (London: 2000), not to mention a mountain of scholarly articles. There is now a commentary on Plutarch's life of Demosthenes by A. Lintott, *Plutarch: Demosthenes and Cicero: Oratory and Political Failure* (Oxford:

2012), which I found out about too late to incorporate properly into the present book.

In all that time the pendulum of Demosthenes' political reputation has swung to the extremes. He has been lauded as Greece's greatest patriot, courageously and steadfastly defying the imperialism of Philip, and condemned as an opportunist who misjudged situations and contributed directly to the end of Greek freedom. In this new biography I aim to determine which of these two people he was: self-serving cynic or patriot—or arguably a combination of both.

All dates are BC except where indicated.

Acknowledgments

I am very grateful to one of the best editors I have ever had the pleasure to work with, Stefan Vranka at Oxford University Press. Not only was he always enthusiastic about this book but also he made a number of comments and suggestions on an earlier draft that greatly improved the final version. Sarah Pirovitz at the same press was a godsend in patiently answering my questions, especially the technology ones, and in obtaining the permissions for the illustrations. I thank the copyeditor for his many valuable stylistic suggestions and everyone at the press who helped steer this book to publication. Also on matters of style, I am very grateful to Keith Goldsmith, who improved the earlier chapters more than I care to admit.

I am indebted to Professor Jeremy Trevett for sending me the proof copy of his translation of Demosthenes' speeches 1–17 in advance of its publication in the University of Texas' Oratory of Classical Greece series. Literally the day after I delivered my book to the publisher, I learned that Professor Andrew Lintott had completed a translation of Plutarch's life of Demosthenes with commentary in the Clarendon Ancient History series. Although I could not properly incorporate it into this book, I am grateful to him for sending me parts of it in advance of its publication.

I thank my own institution for awarding me a Research Council Research Leave grant for 2011–12, which allowed me to complete this book and get to work on the next ones.

I have learned much from friends and colleagues, too numerous to mention, over the years and I thank them for that and their support, in

xii Acknowledgments

particular Joseph and Hanna Roisman, Tim Ryder (who first introduced me to Demosthenes when I was an undergraduate at the University of Hull and has probably regretted it ever since), Todd
Schachtman (those nightcap margaritas hit the spot), Nick Sekunda,
and Peter Toohey.

Finally, my gratitude as always to my wife and children—at least for
the times they let me work in peace.

Ian Worthington
University of Missouri
May 2012

List of Illustrations and Maps

Demosthenes' Life
The Main Events

359 Death of Perdiccas III of Macedonia in battle against the Illyrians; Philip II becomes king; begins military reforms.

358 Philip defeats Illyrians and Paeonians and makes alliance with Thessaly to secure his borders; unites Upper and Lower Macedonia.

357 Athens declares war on Philip over Amphipolis; Athenian campaign in Euboea, on which Demosthenes served as a volunteer syntrierarch.

356 Birth of Alexander, son of Philip and Olympias of Epirus, future Alexander III (the Great); outbreak of the Social War, a revolt of Athenian allies in the Second Athenian Confederacy.

355 Outbreak of the Third Sacred War against Phocis; Social War ends in allied victory at the Battle of Embata; Athens is financially exhausted; Demosthenes' court speeches *Against Androtion* and *Against the Law of Leptines* elevate his reputation.

354 Demosthenes' first (surviving) political speech, *On the Symmories (Navy Boards)*; Philip ends his siege of Methone to free his coastline of Athenian influence, during which he is blinded in one eye.

353 Philip intervenes in Thessaly, but defeated by Onomarchus of Phocis; Demosthenes' political speech *On Behalf of the Megalopolitans* and court speech *Against Timocrates*.

352 Battle of the Crocus Field in Thessaly at which Philip defeats Onomarchus of Phocis; Philip elected archon of Thessaly; Athenian troops led by Nausicles at Thermopylae block Philip, who returns to Pella; Philip campaigns in Thrace against Cersebleptes; Demosthenes' court speech *Against Aristocrates*.

351 Philip returns from Thrace, warns Olynthians to stay loyal to him, and takes action against Athens; Demosthenes' political speeches the first *Philippic* and *On the Freedom of the Rhodians*.

350 Philip campaigns in Paeonia and Illyria and invades Epirus; Demosthenes' political speech *On Organization*.

349 Philip invades the Chalcidice; breaks off campaign to intervene in Thessaly; Demosthenes' political speeches the first and second *Olynthiacs*.

348   Philip returns to the Chalcidice; Demosthenes' political speech the third *Olynthiac*; disastrous Athenian involvement in Euboea; fall of Olynthus; Meidias assaults Demosthenes at the Dionysia; Philip proposes peace with Athens; Philocrates recommends embassy to Philip but is indicted, defended by Demosthenes, and acquitted; Aeschines, Demosthenes' bitter opponent, debuts in the Assembly.

347   Demosthenes serves on the Boule (347/6); possibly marries; indicts Meidias; Demosthenes' court speech *Against Meidias*.

346   First and second embassies to Philip (on which Demosthenes serves) to negotiate peace; Peace of Philocrates ends war between Philip and Athens over Amphipolis; Phocian commander Phalaecus surrenders Thermopylae to Philip, and Phocis surrenders to him to end the Third Sacred War; third and fourth embassies to Philip (on which Demosthenes does not serve); Philip receives the two Phocian votes on the Amphictyonic Council and is elected President of the Pythian Games; Demosthenes' political speech *On the Peace*.

345   Demosthenes indicts Aeschines for professional misconduct (*parapresbeia*) on the second embassy to Philip, but Aeschines successfully blocks him with his speech *Against Timarchus*.

344   Philip sends Python of Byzantium to Athens to alter the Peace of Philocrates; Demosthenes' political speech the second *Philippic* persuades people to reject Philip's proposals.

343   Philocrates impeached in Athens for treason and flees; Demosthenes brings Aeschines to trial for *parapresbeia* on the second embassy to Philip; Demosthenes' court speech *On the False Embassy* and Aeschines' *On the False Embassy*; Aeschines is acquitted; Philip's possible plot to burn the Piraeus dockyards.

342   Philip conquers Thrace and intervenes on Euboea; Athenian Diopeithes' activities against Macedonia in Thrace anger Philip

341   Philip protests formally about Diopeithes; Demosthenes' political speeches *On the Chersonese* and the third and fourth *Philippics*.

340   Demosthenes crowned in the Theatre of Dionysus for his services to the people; Philip returns to Thrace; Philip's letter to Athens, possibly declaring war; Demosthenes' last surviving political speech *To Philip's Letter* calling for war; Philip besieges Perinthus and Byzantium and captures the Athenian grain fleet; Athens declares war on Philip; Demosthenes proposes further reform of the trierarchy.

339   Outbreak of the Fourth Sacred War against Amphissa; Philip seizes Elatea to control Thermopylae; Demosthenes effects alliance between Athens and Thebes against Philip; Demosthenes receives his second crown.

338   End of Fourth Sacred War; Battle of Chaeronea between Philip and the Greeks gives him mastery of Greece and ends second war with Athens; settlements with Greek states that opposed Philip, including end of Second Athenian Confederacy; delegates from Greek states summoned by Philip to Corinth to hear his plans for a Common Peace; Demosthenes delivers the funeral oration (*epitaphios*) to eulogize the Athenian dead at Chaeronea.

337   Second meeting of all Greek states (except Sparta) at Corinth; Common Peace sworn to and League of Corinth formally constituted with Philip as hegemon; his plan to invade Asia endorsed by Greeks.

336   Death of Demosthenes' daughter; Philip sends advance force to Asia Minor; assassination of Philip (July); Ctesiphon proposes another crown for Demosthenes, but Aeschines indicts him; Alexander succeeds to the throne as Alexander III (future Alexander the Great); revolt of the Greeks crushed by Alexander to reestablish Macedonian hegemony of Greece.

335   Revolt of Thebes; Alexander demands surrender of several anti-Macedonian Athenian politicians including Demosthenes, but relents.

334   Alexander invades Asia; Battle of the Granicus River (Alexander's first victory over Persian army); Demosthenes sends letters to Persians encouraging them to defeat the king.

333   Battle of Issus (the first time Darius III and Alexander fight; Alexander defeats the Persian army, calls himself Lord of Asia).

331 War of Agis III of Sparta; Demosthenes dissuades the Athenians from taking part in it; Battle of Gaugamela (the second time Darius III and Alexander fight; Alexander defeats the Persian army, Persia falls to him).

330 Antipater defeats the Spartans at the Battle of Megalopolis, in which Agis is killed; the Crown trial: Aeschines prosecutes Ctesiphon for proposing a crown for Demosthenes in 336; Demosthenes' court speech *On the Crown* and Aeschines' *Against Ctesiphon*; Demosthenes is acquitted; Aeschines leaves Athens and establishes a school of rhetoric on Rhodes.

324 Alexander issues his Exiles Decree; the Harpalus affair; Demosthenes proposes acceptance of Alexander's deification; Demosthenes and other men are accused of taking bribes from Harpalus.

323 Demosthenes is tried for corruption, found guilty, and flees into self-imposed exile; Alexander the Great dies in Babylon (June); Greeks revolt from Macedonian rule in the Lamian War; Hyperides delivers the funeral oration to eulogize the Athenian dead in the first year of the Lamian War; Demosthenes pardoned and recalled to Athens.

322 Antipater defeats the Greek coalition forces at the Battle of Crannon, ending the Lamian War; Athenian punishment includes abolition of direct democracy and a property requirement for citizenship; Antipater demands anti-Macedonian politicians who fled Athens; Hyperides is caught and executed; Demosthenes commits suicide on Calaura (Poros), aged sixty-two; survived by his wife and two sons.

Speech Numbers and Titles

References to speeches by all orators in this book are by their number only. The following is a list of the numbers and titles of the speeches cited in this book for ease of reference (spurious speeches are listed under the name of the orator in whose corpus they have survived).

Aeschines
1 *Against Timarchus*
2 *On the False Embassy*
3 *Against Ctesiphon*

Andocides
1 *On the Mysteries*

Demosthenes
1 *Olynthiac 1*
2 *Olynthiac 2*
3 *Olynthiac 3*
4 *Philippic 1*
5 *On the Peace*
6 *Philippic 2*
7 *On Halonnesus*
8 *On the Chersonese*
9 *Philippic 3*
10 *Philippic 4*
11 *Reply to Philip's Letter*
12 *Philip's Letter*

Quotations and Abbreviations

Quotations from the following ancient writers are taken from these translations (translations of other ancient writers are specified in the notes):

Aeschines:
C. Carey, *Aeschines* (Austin: 2000)

Demosthenes:
J. Trevett, *Demosthenes, Speeches 1–17* (Austin: 2011)
H. Yunis, *Demosthenes, Speeches 18 and 19* (Austin: 2005)
E. M. Harris, *Demosthenes, Speeches 20–22* (Austin: 2008)
D. M. MacDowell, *Demosthenes, Speeches 27–38* (Austin: 2004)
Ian Worthington, *Demosthenes, Speeches 60 and 61, Prologues, Letters* (Austin: 2006)

Diodorus:
C. L. Sherman, *Diodorus Siculus 16.1–65*. Loeb Classical Library Vol. 7 (Cambridge: 1952; repr. 1971)
C. Bradford Welles, *Diodorus Siculus 16.66–95*. Loeb Classical Library Vol. 8 (Cambridge: 1963; repr. 1970)

Hyperides:
Ian Worthington, C. Cooper, and E. M. Harris, *Dinarchus, Hyperides, Lycurgus* (Austin: 2001)

Justin:
R. Develin and W. Heckel, *Justin. Epitome of the Philippic History of Pompeius Trogus* (Atlanta: 1994)

xxiv   *Quotations and Abbreviations*

Plutarch, *Demosthenes*:
Ian Scott-Kilvert, *Plutarch, The Age of Alexander*. Penguin Classics
(Harmondsworth: 1973)

[Plutarch], *Moralia*:
H. N. Fowler, *Plutarch's Moralia*, Loeb Classical Library Vol. 10
(Cambridge: 1936; repr. 1969)

**The following frequently cited modern works are abbreviated in
the notes as follows:**

Blass, *attische Beredsamkeit*[2]	F. Blass, *Die attische Beredsamkeit*[2], 3 vols. (Leipzig: 1887–1898)
Carlier, *Démosthène*	P. Carlier, *Démosthène* (Paris: 1990)
FGrH	F. Jacoby, *Die Fragmente der griechischen Historiker (The Fragments of the Greek Historians)* (Berlin/Leiden: 1926–)
Jaeger, *Demosthenes*	W. Jaeger, *Demosthenes: The Origins and Growth of His Policy* (Berkeley and Los Angeles: 1938; repr. New York: 1977)
Lehmann, *Demosthenes*	G. A. Lehmann, *Demosthenes von Athen: Ein Leben für die Freiheit* (Munich: 2004)
MacDowell, *Demosthenes*	D. M. MacDowell, *Demosthenes the Orator* (Oxford: 2009)
Pickard-Cambridge, *Demosthenes*	A. W. Pickard-Cambridge, *Demosthenes and the Last Days of Greek Freedom* (London: 1914)
Schaefer, *Demosthenes*[2]	A. Schaefer, *Demosthenes und seine Zeit*[2], 3 vols. (Leipzig: 1885–1887)
Sealey, *Demosthenes*	R. Sealey, *Demosthenes and His Time: A Study in Defeat* (Oxford: 1993)
Worthington, *Philip*	Ian Worthington, *Philip II of Macedonia* (New Haven and London: 2008)

FIGURE 1 Roman copy of the bronze statue cast by Polyeuctus of Demosthenes of Athens.

MAP I Greece

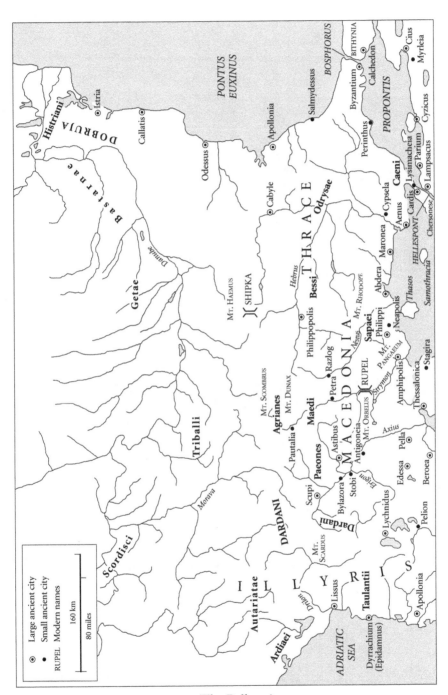

MAP 2 The Balkan Area

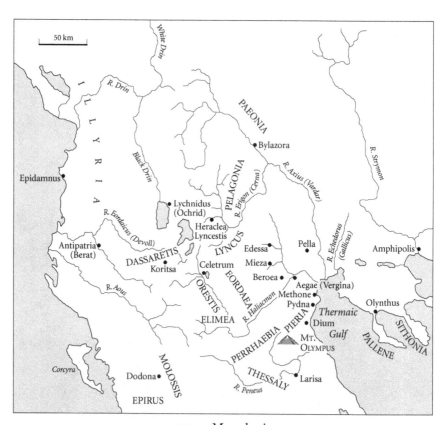

50 km

White Drin

R. Drin

ILLYRIA

PAEONIA

Bylazora

R. Axius (Vardar)

R. Strymon

Black Drin

PELAGONIA

R. Erigon (Cerna)

Epidamnus

R. Eordaicus (Devoll)

Lychnidus
(Ochrid)

Heraclea
Lyncestis

LYNCUS

R. Echedorus
(Gallicus)

Antipatria
(Berat)

DASSARETIS

Koritsa

Celetrum

Edessa

Pella

Amphipolis

R. Aous

ORESTIS

EORDAEA

Mieza

Beroea

Aegae (Vergina)

Olynthus

SITHONIA

ELIMEA

R. Haliacmon

Methone

Pydna

Thermaic

Corcyra

MOLOSSIS

PERRHAEBIA

PIERIA

Dium

Gulf

PALLENE

Dodona

MT.
OLYMPUS

Larisa

EPIRUS

THESSALY

R. Peneus

MAP 3 Macedonia

I

Preamble

"Politicians and Heroes"

WITH THE PHRASE "good luck" boldly emblazoned on his shield, Demosthenes of Athens stood resolutely with his fellow Greeks against King Philip II and the formidable Macedonian army on the plain of Chaeronea in Boeotia.[1] It was August of the year 338.[2] Demosthenes and the Athenian contingent on the left flank of the allied line faced the indomitable Philip himself, while at the other end of the Macedonian column his son, the future Alexander the Great, prepared to engage the famed Theban Sacred Band. The battle was the inevitable culmination of Philip's imperialistic policy, which had more than doubled the size and population of his kingdom from his accession in 359. Over the years, he had involved himself diplomatically and militarily in the affairs of Greece and had twice been at war with Athens, the most powerful polis (city-state) on the mainland. Aware of the danger Philip posed to Greek autonomy, Demosthenes had risen to great political prominence by doggedly pursuing an anti-Macedonian policy for more than a decade, despite considerable opposition, and relentlessly exhorting his fellow Athenians to oppose Philip before it was too late. He had finally succeeded in effecting a coalition of Greek states that now, in 338, forced Philip to stake everything on a pitched battle. To the victor went the prize of Greece.

---

[1] Plutarch, *Demosthenes* 20.2, [Plutarch], *Moralia* 845f.
[2] On the battle, see Chapter 10 pp. 248–251.

The victor was Philip—"for the whole of Greece this day marked the end of its glorious supremacy and of its ancient independence," solemnly declared the ancient writer Justin.[3] Philip imposed Macedonian hegemony over Greece, thereby ending the autonomy the Greeks had proudly enjoyed for centuries. Greece then remained under the control of different foreign powers until 1829, when the eight-year-long Greek War of Independence (or Greek Revolution) threw off Turkish domination, and in 1832 was recognized as an independent and free nation. The battle of Chaeronea was therefore a watershed in Greek history as it was in Demosthenes' political career, evincing the failure of his anti-Macedonian strategy. Eight years later, in 330, his bitter opponent Aeschines, an "abominable, deformed little clerk,"[4] accused him of never serving Athens' best interests and cited Chaeronea as proof.[5]

Yet Demosthenes boldly rebutted Aeschines' charge at this time, insisting that his policy was the right one because he had proposed it to preserve Greek autonomy and democracy. That it failed was not his fault but that of fate and even of the people, who did not implement it until it was too late. Chaeronea, Demosthenes rhetorically argued, was still a triumph for the Greeks because they had fought and died there for the noblest of causes, thereby emulating their glorious ancestors who fought to the death in the Persian Wars:[6]

> But you were not wrong, no, you were not, Athenians, to take on danger for the sake of the freedom and safety of all—I swear by your forefathers who led the fight at Marathon, by those who stood in the ranks at Plataea, by those who fought aboard ship at Salamis and Artemisium, and by the many other brave men who lie in the public tombs, all of whom the city buried, deeming them all equally worthy of the same honor. . . . Rightly so, for they all performed the task required of brave men, and they each met with the fortune conferred on them by god.

In the generation after Demosthenes' death, the Athenians commissioned an expensive bronze statue of him, which they set up in the agora (marketplace) for all to see.[7] The statue that exists today is a Roman

---

[3] Justin 9.3.11.

[4] Demosthenes 18.209.

[5] In his speech in the famous Crown trial: see Chapter 13.

[6] Demosthenes 18.208.

[7] The statue was sculpted in 288: Plutarch, *Demosthenes* 30.5, [Plutarch], *Moralia* 847a, c, 850f, Cicero, *Brutus* 286.

copy and portrays a mature, noble man who is pensively gazing into the distance (Figure 1). Its hands are missing, but they are said to have grasped papyrus rolls that represented the great speeches he delivered.[8]

Demosthenes' unremitting stance against the tyranny of Philip assured his posthumous reputation,[9] and history has called him Greece's supreme patriot.[10] His political success is all the more remarkable given his poor upbringing and the physical and speech defects that afflicted him in his youth. At the age of seven, he was orphaned and entrusted to the care of unscrupulous guardians who squandered his family's estate.[11] He was unevenly educated but nevertheless resolved to become an orator, and when he was old enough he sued his guardians. He was spectacularly successful in court but received little compensation. Still, his victory enabled him to commence a career writing law court speeches for clients, from which he amassed a tidy fortune. Politics coaxed him from that career, though he struggled hard and long to overcome a lisp, an inability to pronounce certain letters properly, and a shortness of breath that caused problems speaking long sentences.[12] Among other things, he was said to have practiced speaking with pebbles in his mouth to improve his diction and run up and down hillsides reciting speeches to enunciate better.[13]

In the mid-350s, Demosthenes gave his first political speeches, discussing foreign and financial affairs, to the Athenians (Chapters 4–5). They were unsuccessful and by 349 his political career appeared spent. In that year, however, he turned to focus exclusively on the threat Philip posed to Athens, thereby ending his string of failures and turning his career around (Chapter 6). A decade later he was the most politically influential politician in Athens and the most renowned of its

---

[8] On the statue and its restored hands on the Vatican statue, see further, Chapter 15 pp. 337–338.

[9] C. D. Adams, *Demosthenes and his Influence* (London: 1927), Carlier, *Démosthène*, pp. 277–304, C. Cooper, "Philosophers, Politics, Academics: Demosthenes' Rhetorical Reputation in Antiquity," and P. E. Harding, "Demosthenes in the Underworld: A Chapter in the *Nachleben* of a *Rhetor*," in Ian Worthington (ed.), *Demosthenes: Statesman and Orator* (London: 2000), pp. 224–245 and 248–257, respectively, Lehmann, *Demosthenes*, pp. 220–228, L. Pernot, *L'Ombre du tigre: Recherches sur la réception de Démosthène* (Naples: 2006).

[10] See, for example, A. W. Pickard-Cambridge, *Demosthenes and the Last Days of Greek Freedom* (London: 1914), G. Clemenceau, *Démosthènes* (Paris: 1926), Jaeger, *Demosthenes*, P. Cloché, *Démosthène et la fin de la démocratie athénienne* (Paris: 1957).

[11] On his youth and later indictments of his guardians, see Chapter 2.

[12] Plutarch, *Demosthenes* 11.1.

[13] Plutarch, *Demosthenes* 7.6, [Plutarch], *Moralia* 845d.

FIGURE 2. The reconstructed face of Philip II from the remains of the skull found in what is probably his tomb at Vergina. The blinded right eye is consistent with his wound at the siege of Methone in 354.

orators—not to mention one of the richest men in the city when he died by his own hand in 322.[14]

The story of Demosthenes is also the story of Philip II, on whose activities Demosthenes' political career depended until the king was assassinated in 336 (Figure 2). Philip turned Macedonia from a political, military, and economic backwater into one of the superpowers of the ancient world in a reign of little over twenty years (359–336).[15] He did so by combining diplomacy, military brilliance, and deceit, not to mention moving with a speed and determination that left the Greeks breathless. His achievements, not least in creating the most dynamic and forceful army of the classical period, permitted his son Alexander the Great (r. 336–323) to conquer the Persian Empire and expand his father's empire from Greece in the west to India in the east.

Despite his influence in public affairs, little is really known of Demosthenes' personal life. The principal sources are the gossipy and at

[14] Demosthenes' suicide: Chapter 15.

[15] See my *Philip II of Macedonia* (New Haven and London: 2008). Overlap with this book is inevitable, but I have tried wherever possible to minimize it.

times sensational biography that Plutarch wrote of him in the first century AD and the short account of his life and work that is one of the "Lives of the Orators" in the *Moralia*, a sweeping collection of jejune philosophical writings that are attributed to Plutarch. To these works can be added some of Plutarch's other biographies, such as those of Alexander the Great and the general Phocion. Plutarch's biography of Demosthenes, however, provides the most information. It is part of his "parallel lives" of prominent Greeks and Romans, in which he paired a Greek with his Roman "equivalent."[16] Demosthenes' ideals and values, his background, the means by which he attained power and wealth, his exile and triumphant return home, the manner of his death, and his rhetorical skill made Cicero the obvious parallel. As Plutarch says of the two men, "if there should be a contest between nature and fortune, as it might be between two sculptors, it would be difficult to decide which had produced the more complete resemblance, the one in shaping their characters and the other their destinies."[17]

Plutarch, however, was a biographer, not a historian, who was for the most part more interested in telling stories than getting to the truth of a matter. His later anecdotal material must be treated with caution. For example, his description of the extreme methods to which Demosthenes subjected himself in order to improve his speaking ability and delivery, while certainly entertaining to readers, may only have a kernel of truth to them.

Other writers also contribute information on Demosthenes' life and activities, such as the contemporary and judgmental Theopompus of Chios. He wrote a *Philippica* (*History of Philip*) in fifty-eight books in the late 330s and early 320s, which today exists only in fragments, and is critical of both Philip and Demosthenes.[18] There were also writers in the fourth century who wrote histories of Athens, the so-called *Atthides*, but their works also exist only in fragments.[19] A valuable body of contemporary evidence is a large number of inscriptions that pertain to political, military, and social matters, many of which are Athenian.[20]

[16] D. A. Russell, *Plutarch* (London: 1973), T. Duff, *Plutarch's Lives* (Oxford: 1999); cf. C. Pelling, *Plutarch and History* (London: 2002).

[17] Plutarch, *Demosthenes* 3.5.

[18] G. S. Shrimpton, *Theopompus the Historian* (Montreal: 1991) and M. A. Flower, *Theopompus of Chios* (Oxford: 1994).

[19] See, for example, P. E. Harding, *Androtion and the Atthis* (Oxford: 2001).

[20] See the collection in P. J. Rhodes and R. Osborne (eds.), *Greek Historical Inscriptions, 404–323 BC* (Oxford: 2003).

Then there are the much later narrative histories of Philip and Alexander the Great by Diodorus Siculus (first century BC), Quintus Curtius Rufus (first century AD), and Arrian (second century AD), as well as Justin's epitome (written between the second and fourth centuries AD) of a first-century BC account by Pompeius Trogus.[21] Ancient commentators on Demosthenes' speeches, especially the grammarian Didymus Chalcenterus and the rhetorician Dionysius of Halicarnassus (both alive and working in the first century BC), also supply information.[22] Dionysius also wrote an essay titled *On the Admirable Style of Demosthenes* to illustrate why he believed Demosthenes was the best of the Greek orators. In the fourth century AD, another rhetorician, Libanius, wrote introductions (*hypotheses*) to Demosthenes' speeches, in which he furnished details of the orator's life,[23] as did the ninth-century Patriarch of Constantinople, Photius, in his enormous collection of classical works, the *Bibliotheca*.[24]

The most important set of sources for Demosthenes are his own speeches. In the corpus of his surviving works there are sixty political and forensic speeches, as well as six letters written during a period of exile in 323 and over fifty rhetorical openings (*prooimia*) to political orations. Some of the speeches attributed to him are spurious and were composed by other orators but happened to be included in his corpus.[25] Of the other contemporary orators who impart information on Demosthenes, the most important are Aeschines (his embittered political adversary), Dinarchus, Hyperides, and Lycurgus.

---

[21] Diodorus: K. Sacks, *Diodorus Siculus and the First Century* (Princeton: 1990); Curtius: E. Baynham, *The Unique History of Quintus Curtius Rufus* (Ann Arbor: 1998); Arrian: A. B. Bosworth, *From Arrian to Alexander* (Oxford: 1988); Justin: J. C. Yardley, *Justin and Trogus: A Study of the Language of Justin's Epitome of Trogus* (Toronto: 2003).

[22] See C. A. Gibson, *Interpreting a Classic: Demosthenes and His Ancient Commentators* (Berkeley and Los Angeles: 2002), with P. E. Harding, *Didymos: On Demosthenes* (Oxford: 2006), R. Sealey, "Dionysius of Halicarnassus and Some Demosthenic Dates," *REG* 68 (1955), pp. 77–120, and R. Lane Fox, "Demosthenes, Dionysius, and the Dating of Six Early Speeches," *Class. & Med.* 48 (1997), pp. 167–203.

[23] C. A. Gibson, "The Agenda of Libanius' Hypotheses to Demosthenes," *GRBS* 40 (1999), pp. 171–202.

[24] Photius 490a–495a; cf. Carlier, *Démosthène*, pp. 321–324.

[25] The forensic speeches numbered 45, 46, 49, 50, 52, 53, and 59 are by Apollodorus, son of Pasion; the political speech numbered 7 is by Hegesippus; the speaker of 17 is unknown. See further, Chapter 2 p. 28.

The speeches present problems as source material because oratory was not history. The speakers' aim was to persuade a political gathering or a jury to vote in their favor and therefore their emphasis was less on content and more on performance. Since speeches were likely revised after oral delivery, Demosthenes and other orators were free to include material in these later versions that they had earlier disregarded or not even thought of, and they could adapt arguments in light of those of their opponents to strengthen their own.[26] For example, there were instances where Demosthenes simply lied about Philip's aims or about Aeschines' character. Indeed, the enmity that Demosthenes and Aeschines had for each other motivated each of them to distort accounts of political debates or events to upstage the other.[27]

It would appear perverse to label Demosthenes a hero, as W. Jaeger intimated in his study,[28] although in 1914 Sir A. W. Pickard-Cambridge's biography was published in a series titled *Heroes of the Nation*. That was then. Nowadays a more critical approach may be considered for the man who arguably ushered in two millennia of domination for Greece.[29] Yet Jaeger goes on to say that Demosthenes' story should not be seen as one of failure because he had the right intentions in opposing Philip.[30] Therefore did Demosthenes, as he himself contends, oppose Philip for

[26] Ian Worthington, "Greek Oratory, Revision of Speeches and the Problem of Historical Reliability," *Class. & Med.* 42 (1991), pp. 55–74 and "History and Oratorical Exploitation," in Ian Worthington (ed.), *Persuasion: Greek Rhetoric in Action* (London: 1994), pp. 109–129, and R. D. Milns, "The Public Speeches of Demosthenes," in Ian Worthington (ed.), *Demosthenes: Statesman and Orator* (London: 2000), pp. 207–209; cf. M. Golden, "Demosthenes and the Social Historian," ibid., pp. 159–169.

[27] See most recently J. Buckler, "Demosthenes and Aeschines," in Ian Worthington (ed.), *Demosthenes: Statesman and Orator* (London: 2000), pp. 114–158; cf. C. Tuplin, "Demosthenes' *Olynthiacs* and the Character of the Demegoric Corpus," *Historia* 47 (1998), pp. 276–320.

[28] Jaeger, *Demosthenes*, p. 1, quoted on prelim p. vii.

[29] G. L. Cawkwell, "Demosthenes' Policy after the Peace of Philocrates I and II," *CQ²* 13 (1963), pp. 120–138 and 200–213, and "The Crowning of Demosthenes," *CQ²* 19 (1969), pp. 163–180, Sealey, *Demosthenes and His Time: A Study in Defeat*, passim (for example, "the life of Demosthenes and the history of Demosthenic Athens are a story of failure," p. 3), and T. T. B. Ryder, "Demosthenes and Philip II" and J. Buckler, "Demosthenes and Aeschines" in Ian Worthington (ed.), *Demosthenes: Statesman and Orator* (London: 2000), pp. 45–89 and 114–158, respectively (Demosthenes' switching policy for his own ends).

[30] Cf. Clemenceau, *Démosthènes*, p. 10, Sealey, *Demosthenes*, p. 219.

the "right" reasons, and should blame for his failure be attached not to him but to an apathetic citizenry that allowed Philip to evolve into an unstoppable force?[31] Was he indeed Greece's greatest patriot, or did he cynically exploit the danger of Philip for his own political agenda, capitalizing on his rhetorical prowess to uphold a policy that ruined his city and Greece? What made him tick and how did he see himself?

Certainly, as the work of an ambitious young man working to make a name for himself in politics, his early speeches were self-serving. The critical Theopompus claimed that Demosthenes was fickle (*abebaios*) and inconsistent in his politics, presumably because he needed to pander to public favor and so establish support, although Plutarch disputed his opinion.[32] However, his later speeches evidence less self-interested motives in opposing Philip as he steadily expanded into Greece and moved ominously closer to Athens. "Intention" is potentially the most objective means to assess Demosthenes' career and his role in Greek history—and that is the intention of this book.

---

[31] Demosthenes 18.63, 66–68, 192–195, 199, 206, 245–246, 270–275.

[32] Quoted in Plutarch, *Demosthenes* 13.1–2, who says that Demosthenes' policy was obvious from the outset and he stayed true to it, even giving his life for it (quoted Chapter 15 p. 340); cf. Flower, *Theopompus of Chios*, pp. 139–140.

2

Demosthenes,
Son of Demosthenes

D EMOSTHENES WAS BORN in a town (deme) named Paeania, about a dozen miles east of Athens, the principal city of Attica, an area of roughly 900 square miles (Map 1).[1] Paeania today is a suburb of Athens, with a population of about 13,000 people. Part of the Hymettus mountain range, about ten miles in length and several miles wide, lies between Paeania and Athens, which in antiquity made travel between the two difficult and time-consuming. The people living in Paeania would have made the journey to Athens only when they had to—for example, farmers selling their produce and artisans their crafts, given the importance of Athens as an urban market, as well as men attending political meetings and fulfilling military and civilian obligations.[2]

Little is known about the place in Demosthenes' time. It was one of the bigger towns of Attica because it sent some eleven representatives to Athens to serve on the influential political council the Boule (see below)—a larger number then the majority of other towns.[3] Since

---

[1] [Plutarch], *Moralia* 844a. Paeania actually was comprised of two demes, Lower and Upper: J. S. Traill, *Demos and Trittys* (Toronto: 1986), D. Whitehead, *The Demes of Attica* (Princeton: 1986), p. 385. I am grateful to Professors J. Roy and N.F. Jones for e-mail exchanges about Paeania.

[2] Cf. N.F. Jones, *The Associations of Classical Athens* (New York: 1999), pp. 82–122.

[3] For example, see Whitehead, *Demes of Attica*, pp. 23, 24, 142, 152, 216–217, 370.

most of Attica's rural population lived in nucleated settlements, Paeania would have been home to a mixture of aristocratic and ordinary families as well as some metics (resident aliens).[4] All of these groups were engaged in a variety of occupations, but the bulk of the population was likely to have been farmers, growing grain, olives, and grapes. Some men were probably pastoralists, raising sheep to sell their wool and tending goats and perhaps pigs.

Demosthenes' family was an aristocratic one and may have been related to a local priestly clan.[5] Priests of local temples and cults were highly esteemed and played an important role in civic life. His family was counted among the *plousiotatoi* or richest of families in Athenian society,[6] but unlike other such families it did not own agricultural land, which for Greeks was a visible indicator of wealth. Its net worth was therefore not so readily apparent, but its members performed liturgies or public services for the people (see below), thereby attesting to its financial status.[7] Athenians did not collect personal income taxes but relied on business taxes and tariffs to meet expenses. In emergencies they resorted to levying an extraordinary tax or *eisphora*, which only the richest citizens grudgingly paid.[8] Since the Athenians' normal revenues

---

[4] Whitehead, *Demes of Attica*, p. 84.

[5] Plutarch, *Demosthenes* 4.1: "Demosthenes' father, who bore the same name, was of a good [noble] family." On the connection to the priestly clan of the Bouzygae, see E. Badian, "Harpalus," *JHS* 81 (1961), p. 34 n. 134 and "The Road to Prominence," in Ian Worthington (ed.), *Demosthenes: Statesman and Orator* (London: 2000), p. 12, P. Mackendrick, *The Athenian Aristocracy 399–31 B.C.* (Cambridge: 1969), p. 69 n. 33, based on arguing that all those men living in Paeania whose names began with Demo- were related, at least until Demosthenes senior's time. That does not necessarily follow, given how widespread the prefix was: see J. K. Davies, *Athenian Propertied Families* (Oxford: 1971), p. 114; cf. MacDowell, *Demosthenes*, pp. 14 n. 2 and 17. Officials with religious duties in Paeania: Whitehead, *Demes of Attica*, pp. 142, 197.

[6] Note the contrast of this word to *penetes* (poor) at Demosthenes 20.18 (cf. 18.104), and see also Davies, *Athenian Propertied Families*, pp. 9–14. Children whose parents were both Athenian citizens were likewise citizens, regardless of where in Attica they were born.

[7] Demon, his uncle, was a trierarch (Davies, *Athenian Propertied Families*, p. 115), as was Aphobus, his cousin (Demosthenes 27.14), for example. For Demosthenes the orator's own liturgies, see Demosthenes 21.153–167 (down to 347), Davies, *Athenian Propertied Families* pp. 135–137.

[8] On public finances, see M. H. Hansen, *The Athenian Democracy in the Age of Demosthenes*[2] (Norman: 1999), pp. 260–264. On the *eisphora*: R. Thomsen, *Eisphora* (Copenhagen: 1964), M. Christ, "The Evolution of the *eisphora* in Classical Athens," *CQ*[2] 57 (2007), pp. 53–69.

did not always meet demands, the richest members of society were called on to fund very expensive items of state expenditure (called liturgies) or engage in other public contributions. Liturgies were both military and civilian and included maintaining a trireme for a year, providing a chorus for a performance at a festival, and helping to fund Athenian competitors at the Olympic Games. They were at first voluntary, but by the fourth century were compulsory for the wealthiest citizens.[9] In a speech of 354, Demosthenes claimed that there were at least sixty liturgies performed annually, but the actual figure was almost double that.[10]

Demosthenes' family history is unknown until the time of his grandfather Demomeles, who may have been an architect.[11] Demomeles had two sons, Demon (probably the eldest) and Demosthenes (the father of our orator), as well as a daughter (probably his middle child).[12] Demosthenes senior was born around 420. At some point he moved to open a manufacturing establishment in Athens, perhaps with money from his father. A "factory" or "plant," conjuring up images of mass production lines and large numbers of employees, is too modern a term for the cottage-type industries that were typical of Athens. He employed thirty-three slaves to make knives and twenty to make couches or beds. Despite the substantial sums of money he had in banks and lent out to people, he was sneeringly nicknamed "cutler" because he was involved in manual labor despite being an aristocrat.[13]

In the first half of the 380s Demosthenes senior married a lady named Cleobule. They had a son Demosthenes (the orator) and a daughter whose name we do not know. There was something suspect, however, about Cleobule's family background.[14] Her father, Gylon of

---

[9] On liturgies, see further, P. Wilson, *The Athenian Institution of the Khoregia: The Chorus, The City and the Stage* (Cambridge: 2000), J. K. Davies, "Demosthenes on Liturgies: A Note," *JHS* 87 (1967), pp. 33–40, B. Jordan, *The Athenian Navy in the Classical Period* (Berkeley: 1975), pp. 61–73.

[10] Demosthenes 20.21. On the range and number of liturgies, see Davies, "Demosthenes on Liturgies: A Note," pp. 33–40.

[11] There is reference to his designing a bridge at Eleusis in 421 in *IG* i² 81, 16–17 (the name is partly restored): see Davies, *Athenian Propertied Families*, p. 114; cf. Carlier, *Démosthène*, p. 36.

[12] Davies, *Athenian Propertied Families*, pp. 115–119.

[13] Plutarch, *Demosthenes* 4.1 from the contemporary (and hostile) writer Theopompus.

[14] Demosthenes 28.14. Aeschines 3.171–172 talks of her father's treacherous activities, which cast doubt on the legitimacy of his children. Plutarch, *Demosthenes* 4.2, questions whether her background was suspect.

Cerameis, was condemned to death for treason, but the penalty seems to have been reduced to a fine because Demosthenes later mentioned he paid off a debt.[15] Gylon had been a garrison commander in the allied town of Nymphaeum in the east of what is now the Crimea (Map 2). In the late fifth century, Nymphaeum defied Athens and made an alliance with the rulers of the region, the Spartocids, who were at the time enemies of Athens. Gylon was accused of encouraging or even brokering Nymphaeum's new alliance.

Gylon's punishment was severe because Nymphaeum was in the Chersonese, an area strategically vital to Athens because of its position on the grain route from the Black Sea (Pontus Euxinus). The Athenians were as dependent on imported grain to feed the population as some modern countries are on oil to function—as Demosthenes remarked, "we rely on imported grain more than all the rest of mankind. The grain brought here from the Pontic district is about equal to that arriving from all other sources overseas."[16] These other sources included islands like Lemnos, Imbros, and Scyros in the Aegean, the island of Euboea off eastern Attica, Sicily, and Egypt. However, it was the Pontic grain that the Athenians coveted most, and they were prepared to go to war over it if need be.[17]

After his sentence was passed, Gylon fled into a self-imposed exile in Scythia. The Spartocid rulers allowed him to live there, during which time he married a wealthy Scythian lady, who bore him two daughters, Cleobule and Philia. Gylon's daughters were not Athenian citizens, however, since his wife was Scythian. In 451 Pericles had introduced a law in Athens that both parents had to be Athenian citizens for their children to share in citizenship and enjoy full judicial and political rights.[18] Previously, only one parent had had to be an Athenian. Thus, in Gylon's day only marriages between Athenians were recognized as legitimate, and bastards (*nothoi*) were not permitted to be citizens.

Yet clearly their son Demosthenes (the orator) was considered a citizen as he had a lengthy political career. The explanation for this is

[15] Demosthenes 28.1–3; cf. Aeschines 3.171–172, Davies, *Athenian Propertied Families*, p. 121, Carlier, *Démosthène*, p. 36.
[16] Demosthenes 20.31. See also Lysias 28.6. See further, A. Moreno, *Feeding the Democracy: The Athenian Grain Supply in the Fifth and Fourth Centuries BC* (Oxford: 2007).
[17] P. Hunt, *War, Peace, and Alliance in Demosthenes' Athens* (New York: 2010), pp. 35–39.
[18] [Aristotle], *Athenian Constitution* 26.3.

that Pericles' citizenship law was temporarily suspended during the Peloponnesian War (431–404) then reinstated in 403.[19] Gylon thus married his Scythian wife at a time when only one parent needed to be a citizen for the couple's children to be deemed legitimate. Also in 403, the Athenians issued a general amnesty, under which Gylon could return to Athens and not have to pay his fine. He did pay it, perhaps in an attempt to appease the people because of his earlier treachery.[20]

Mud sticks though, and Demosthenes intimated that Gylon could not shake off his earlier reputation,[21] potentially affecting the chances of his daughters marrying into good families. Perhaps he used his wife's wealth to attract suitable husbands for his daughters, for Philia married the well-to-do Demochares and Cleobule married the equally well-off Demosthenes senior. Having a father-in-law with a "record" might also account for Demosthenes senior taking little if any part in political life (including performing liturgies), despite his social standing.[22] His son Demosthenes, then, was a citizen by the skin of his teeth, so it is hardly any wonder that later his opponents in court denigrated his family lineage. In 330, Aeschines, for example, called Demosthenes a Greek-speaking barbarian and in 324 Dinarchus taunted him about his "Scythian mother."[23]

The exact year of Demosthenes' birth is not known, but it was either 385 or 384.[24] The Athenians reckoned their chronology by archon years, an archon being one of the annual chief officials in the city's administration. One of them was called the eponymous archon because he gave his name to the year of his office. Demosthenes was born in the archonship of Dexitheus, which was 385/4—the Athenian year ran from the roughly the middle of our July in one year to the middle of July the following year (thus 385/4 ran from mid-July 385 to mid-July 384).[25] In some of his later speeches, Demosthenes stated that he was seven when his father died, that he lived in the care

---

[19] Demosthenes 57.30.

[20] Since his wife was wealthy, he may have used some of her money to pay the fine: Badian, "Road to Prominence," p. 13.

[21] See the embarrassed passage at Demosthenes 28.1–2.

[22] Cf. Sealey, *Demosthenes*, p. 96.

[23] Aeschines 3.172, Dinarchus 1.15.

[24] On the controversy surrounding the actual year, see Davies, *Athenian Propertied Families*, pp. 123–126.

[25] [Plutarch], *Moralia* 845d. Hyperides 5.22, delivered in 323, refers to him as over sixty, which would also put his birth year in either 385 or 384.

of guardians for ten years,[26] and that he came of age (turned eighteen) in the last month of the archonship of Polyzelus.[27] That was 367/6, so subtracting eighteen puts Demosthenes' birth in June or July 384.[28]

Demosthenes senior's business did well in Athens, for when he died from an illness in 376 he was worth the considerable sum of fifteen talents.[29] Before his death, he had drawn up provisions to take care of his widow, his son Demosthenes (who was by then about seven), and his daughter (who was probably five).[30] The children were entrusted to the care of relatives, his nephews Aphobus (the son of his sister) and Demophon (the son of Demon, his brother) and a longtime family friend, Therippides of Paeania. Demosthenes senior also arranged husbands for his wife and daughter. Under Athenian law a father decided on a husband for his daughter and a husband could arrange for his wife to marry another man after he died. Aphobus (whose name means "Fearless") was to marry his widow and receive a dowry of 8,000 drachmas. They were to live in the family house until Demosthenes junior came of age. The daughter was promised in marriage to Demophon when she became of marriageable age at fourteen or fifteen, but he was to get a dowry of 12,000 drachmas immediately. Therippides was given 7,000 drachmas as an

---

[26] Demosthenes 27.4, 6, but see Davies' reservation, *Athenian Propertied Families*, pp. 123–125.

[27] Demosthenes 30.15. The coming of age or *dokimasia* is controversial, as it could refer to someone in his eighteenth year or after he turned eighteen: Davies, *Athenian Propertied Families*, pp. 125–126, M. Golden, "Demosthenes and the Age of Majority at Athens," *Phoenix* 33 (1979), pp. 25–38; cf. MacDowell, *Demosthenes*, p. 18.

[28] Cf. Lehmann, *Demosthenes*, pp. 30–31 (384); Carlier, *Démosthène*, p. 35, is noncommittal ("de 384 à 380"). However, in a speech of 347, Demosthenes states he was at that time thirty-two years old, thus giving us 379 for his birth (21.154). That year can be disregarded because it contradicts the majority of the evidence favoring 385 or 384. On the problems with the text, see D. M. MacDowell, *Demosthenes: Against Medias (Oration 21)* (Oxford: 1990), pp. 370–371. On dates in Demosthenes' early life, see also Sealey, *Demosthenes*, pp. 245–248.

[29] Demosthenes 27.9–1; cf. Plutarch, *Demosthenes* 4.3. On ancient coinage, see Appendix. He may even have been among the wealthiest men in Athens: E. M. Burke, "The Looting of the Estate of the Elder Demosthenes," *Class. & Med.* 49 (1998), pp. 46–47, details his assets.

[30] Plutarch, *Demosthenes* 4.3, [Plutarch], *Moralia* 844a.

interest-free loan for ten years until Demosthenes turned eighteen.[31] Demosthenes later related the anecdote that his dying father detailed all his decisions to everyone at his bedside while the young son sat on Aphobus' knee.[32]

Demosthenes senior's stipulations were recorded in a will, but the guardians ignored it. The marriages did not take place nor did they manage the estate properly.[33] Demochares, who was married to the widow's sister Philia (and so was Demosthenes junior's uncle), at some point accused Aphobus of not following the terms of his will despite keeping the dowry. Demochares' intervention plausibly suggests that he took the widow and her children into his own house to look after them. If so, he would have been all the more aggrieved with Aphobus for keeping the 8,000 drachmas.[34] Certainly, Aphobus never married the widow, for he later married the daughter of Philonides of Melite. The guardians were alleged to have squandered the family estate to the extent that when Demosthenes reached his majority at eighteen it was apparently worth only a talent.[35] Why they acted as they did is not properly known. Greed is certainly one explanation. On the other hand, there was "significant ideological diversity" among wealthy men in the fourth century, and they may also have scorned Demosthenes senior for making his money from business activities or even for not investing his wealth in land but in liquid assets.[36] Since his net worth was therefore harder to estimate, he may have performed fewer liturgies than his wealthy peers. In stealing and mismanaging his estate, the guardians therefore might have been getting their own back—for themselves and the city.[37]

---

[31] Demosthenes 27.4–5, 46; cf. 29.43, 45.

[32] Demosthenes 28.15–16.

[33] Demosthenes 27.13–15.

[34] On this, see MacDowell, *Demosthenes*, pp. 19 and 33.

[35] Demosthenes 27.4; cf. Davies, *Athenian Propertied Families*, pp. 132–133, Lehmann, *Demosthenes*, p. 46 (skeptically).

[36] Burke, "Looting of the Estate of the Elder Demosthenes," pp. 45–65; the quotation is on p. 60; cf. E. M. Burke, "Early Political Speeches of Demosthenes: Elite Bias in the Response to Economic Crisis," *Class. Ant.* 21 (2002), pp. 165–194.

[37] Against this view, as even Burke, "Looting of the Estate of the Elder Demosthenes," p. 65 n. 85, notes, is that Demosthenes said nothing of ideological prejudices or behavior in his speeches against his guardians.

THE YOUNG DEMOSTHENES

Demosthenes was often sickly as a boy and suffered from several physical afflictions. These included a speech impediment,[38] which may have
led to his childhood nickname of Batalus.[39] In addition to being the
name of an effeminate flute player and bawdy poet, the word meant
"stammerer" and was a slang term for the anus.[40] Demosthenes' speech
deficiency and weak disposition might have caused him to appear
effeminate, hence the nickname, which seems to have been given him
by his enemy Aeschines.[41] Another of his afflictions was a lisp, for which
he was nicknamed Argas, a composer of vulgar and unpopular songs,
whose own speaking problem "offended the ears of his listeners."[42]
Finally, Demosthenes apparently suffered from a shortness of breath
that made him pause frequently and caused his audience to lose track
of what he was saying.[43]

   The guardians went to some trouble to ensure that Demosthenes
received an education. Because his weak physique prevented him from
going to a regular school or a gymnasium for physical exercise like
other boys they hired private tutors for him.[44] That would explain why

---

[38] See H. Holst, "Demosthenes' Speech Impediment," *Symbolae Osloenses* 4 (1926), pp.
    11–25.

[39] Plutarch, *Demosthenes* 4.5, [Plutarch], *Moralia* 847e. See also Holst, "Demosthenes'
    Speech Impediment," pp. 11–25, G. Lambin, "Le surnom *Batalos* et les mots de cette
    famille," *Revue de Philologie* 56 (1982), pp. 249–263, H. Wankel, *Demosthenes: Rede für
    Ktesiphon über den Kranz* (Heidelberg: 1976), pp. 888–891.

[40] On this, cf. Demosthenes 18.180.

[41] Aeschines 1.126 says that Demosthenes' nurse used to call him Batalus as a pet name;
    at 1.131 and 2.99 Aeschines calls Demosthenes a coward and a homosexual. On the
    term, cf. Hermippus, *FGrH* IVA 1026 F 53. Note that Demosthenes 18.180 spells
    the word with a double t—Battalos—although whether this changes the meaning is
    unknown. The word is also associated with the fifth-century general and turncoat
    Alcibiades, so it may have been a common one rather than one merely meant to
    evoke Demosthenes.

[42] Plutarch, *Demosthenes* 4.8.

[43] Plutarch, *Demosthenes* 6.4.

[44] Demosthenes 27.6 (private tutors). Plutarch, *Demosthenes* 4.4–5; cf. Demosthenes
    18.257 (sickly disposition). On Demosthenes' youth, see further, Schaefer, *Demos-
    thenes*[2] 1, pp. 261–289 and 303–313, Blass, *attische Beredsamkeit*[2] 3.1, pp. 10–25,
    Carlier, *Démosthène*, pp. 35–55, Sealey, *Demosthenes*, pp. 96–98, Badian, "Road to
    Prominence," pp. 9–15, Lehmann, *Demosthenes*, pp. 29–39.

he did not work out at a gymnasium when he was an adult, unlike his peers, preferring to see the arena of the courts and the Assembly as his training ground.[45] His guardians did not always pay these tutors so his schooling had its interruptions.[46] Demosthenes would have grown up without friends, which may explain a lack of social grace as an adult, something his opponents used against him. For example, they claimed that he used to dress in women's clothes and go to taverns, which were frequented by the lower classes,[47] although he was a teetotaler.[48]

Everything seemed to conspire against the young Demosthenes. He was being swindled out of his family fortune; his guardians cared little for him; he was lonely, physically unfit, and in ill health; and he was ridiculed for his disabilities, which were no fault of his own. The odds at the time of his excelling as an orator and rising to great political heights would have been very long indeed. However, his life changed dramatically one day in 366 when he persuaded a tutor to take him to court to hear a defense speech by Callistratus of Aphidna, one of Athens' most influential politicians and the most brilliant orator of the time.[49] Callistratus was accused of allowing Athens' traditional enemy Thebes (in Boeotia) to seize the town of Oropus on the northeast border of Attica and Boeotia, thereby compromising Attica's security.[50]

Plutarch related the story that Demosthenes had to be smuggled into the court because he was still underage and had to sit where he could not be seen. In Athens, trials were held in the open air. There was no judge as there is today, and juries were comprised of several hundred men (who had to be over the age of thirty) depending on the type of case. Further, the prosecution and defense were expected to conduct their own cases. Trials were often noisy affairs, more like Prime Minister's Question Time in the British House of Commons

---

[45] On this point, see M. Golden, "Demosthenes and the Social Historian," in Ian Worthington (ed.), *Demosthenes: Statesman and Orator* (London: 2000), pp. 172–174, drawing attention to the parallel between athletic and rhetorical exercise and Plutarch's use of athletic terminology and analogies to demonstrate that "Demosthenes was the equal of any athlete" (p. 173).

[46] Demosthenes 27.46, Plutarch, *Demosthenes* 4.3.

[47] [Plutarch], *Moralia* 847e–f.

[48] Demosthenes 6.30, 19.46, [Plutarch], *Moralia* 848c.

[49] Plutarch, *Demosthenes* 5.1–4; [Plutarch], *Moralia* 844b has it that Demosthenes heard Callistratus in the Assembly.

[50] Xenophon, *Hellenica* 7.4.1, Diodorus 15.76.1.

than the sober silence of today, as prosecutors and defendants incited the jury to react to their speeches, making use of a rhetorical technique called *thorubos* ("raising an uproar").[51] Spectators at the trial were also vocal, their reactions to speeches and testimony perhaps influencing the jurors when they cast the vote.[52] Jurors often disregarded the actual points of law and were swayed by the speakers' rhetorical abilities, and since at least private trials lasted less than a day procedure was rushed.[53]

Plutarch's account of Demosthenes' attendance at Callistratus' trial raises a problem about his age. Demosthenes should have turned eighteen in 366, making him old enough to attend a trial legally and not have to sit somewhere out of sight. Perhaps, then, he was still in his eighteenth year when the trial took place.[54] On the other hand, Plutarch mistakenly connected this suit with an earlier one involving Callistratus.[55] Either way, Callistratus easily won his case, and in doing so inspired the young Demosthenes to become an orator, for when he "saw [Callistratus] being escorted by a huge following and congratulated on all sides, he was seized with a desire to emulate his fame."[56] Demosthenes' decision may well have been self-serving because he saw in Callistratus' victory the means to seek revenge on his guardians, which he could obtain only through the courts. Certainly he admired Callistratus' oratorical skills, for he heaped praise on him in speeches he gave in 343 and even as late as 330.[57]

Demosthenes now abandoned all his other studies to focus exclusively on rhetoric. There were a number of rhetorical schools in Athens, the best known being that of Isocrates. There is a tradition that because Demosthenes could not afford him he turned to another orator, Isaeus,

[51] V. Bers, "Dikastic Thorubos," in P. Cartledge and F. D. Harvey (eds.), *Crux: Essays Presented to G. E. M. de Ste. Croix on his 75th Birthday* (London: 1985), pp. 1–15.

[52] A. Lanni, "Spectator Sport or Serious Politics? οἱ περιεστηκότες and the Athenian Lawcourts," *JHS* 117 (1997), pp. 183–189.

[53] [Aristotle], *Athenian Constitution* 67.1: four private suits were judged in one day and one public case; cf. Aeschines 3.197.

[54] The story that Demosthenes was being taught at the time by Plato but interrupted the "class" to attend the trial perhaps lends weight to his being too young to attend it legally: Hermippus, *FGrH* IVA 1026 F 60.

[55] MacDowell, *Demosthenes*, p. 20.

[56] Plutarch, *Demosthenes* 5.1–4.

[57] Cf. Demosthenes 18.219, 19.297, 24.135.

for help, especially as he specialized in inheritance cases.[58] The story that Plato taught Demosthenes appears unlikely, given the philosopher's dislike of rhetoric.[59] It made sense anyway for Demosthenes to seek out Isaeus because inheritance law was complex and his opponents were older and more experienced in judicial matters than him. In inheritance cases the jury numbered 401,[60] and Demosthenes could not afford to appear before them with a weak or flawed case.

Regardless of where citizens were living when they came of age, they were registered in the towns of their birth. Demosthenes at age eighteen was therefore officially registered in his deme of Paeania by a fellow demesman (perhaps a relative) called Philodemus.[61] He could now vote in the Assembly and lodge prosecutions and he was also required to enroll in a two-year program of ephebic training (a form of military conscription).[62] He also came into full control of what remained of his estate, so Aphobus returned the family house to him and he and Therippides handed back 3,100 drachmas and the various slaves who forged knives in the family business.[63] Demophon, however,

---

[58] On his supposed teachers, see Plutarch, *Demosthenes* 5.5–7 and [Plutarch], *Moralia* 844b–c. Isaeus is the best attested. It is hard to accept the story at [Plutarch], *Moralia* 844c that Demosthenes kept Isaeus in his house for four years while he learned to imitate his speeches! The identity of Demosthenes' teacher is controversial because of the disagreements in the sources: Schaefer, *Demosthenes*[2] 1, pp. 282–288, 303–313 and Blass, *attische Beredsamkeit*[2] 3.1, pp. 11–25. On Isocrates, see S. Usher, *Greek Oratory: Tradition and Originality* (Oxford 1999), pp. 118–126 and especially 296–323, and T. Papillon, "Isocrates," in Ian Worthington (ed.), *Blackwell Companion to Greek Rhetoric* (Malden: 2007), pp. 58–74. On Isaeus, see Usher, *Greek Oratory: Tradition and Originality*, pp. 127–170.

[59] Schaefer, *Demosthenes*[2] 1, pp. 310–313 and 320–324, L. Pernot, *L'Ombre du tigre: Recherches sur la réception de Démosthène* (Naples: 2006), pp. 21–60; cf. MacDowell, *Demosthenes*, pp. 21–22, 408–409, H. Yunis, *Taming Democracy: Models of Political Rhetoric in Classical Athens* (Ithaca: 1996), pp. 237–277. See above (Callistratus' trial) with note 54.

[60] [Aristotle], *Athenian Constitution* 53.3.

[61] Demosthenes 30.15 (his *dokimasia* or enrolment), Aeschines 2.150 (Philodemus). Philodemus later became the father-in-law of Aeschines, Demosthenes' arch political and personal enemy (Aeschines 2.150–152), which must have been embarrassing for Demosthenes; cf. Badian, "Road to Prominence," pp. 14–15. Registering in the birth town: Whitehead, *Demes of Attica*, p. 95.

[62] [Aristotle], *Athenian Constitution* 42.1 with P. J. Rhodes, *A Commentary on the Aristotelian Athenaion Politeia* (Oxford: 1981), ad loc.

[63] Demosthenes 27.6; cf. 37.

did not return anything. Demosthenes still intended to sue them but first undertook his duty as an ephebe. His case against his former guardians would not go to court until two years later, in 364, in the archonship of Timocrates.[64]

TAKING ON THE GUARDIANS

Demosthenes targeted Aphobus first, probably because he had most clearly reneged on the will's provisions by not marrying his widowed mother while keeping her dowry. Under Athenian law, two disputants could have their case settled by either private arbitrators (chosen by both parties) or public (state) arbitrators. At Aphobus' request, he and Demosthenes went before private arbitrators. When they appeared to favor Demosthenes, however, Aphobus withdrew from the procedure before they rendered their formal decision, as he was entitled to do.[65] The two men then went to a public arbitrator, who decided there were enough grounds to refer the case to court.

Aphobus worked hard to foil Demosthenes' indictment. Initially, he tried to bankrupt him by forcing him to finance a trireme for a year—known as the trierarchy, this was one of the various liturgies that wealthy men were expected to bear. It was an enormous financial burden, costing two talents to build and equip a trireme and one talent per month to maintain it.[66] Therefore in 357 the law of Periander grouped twelve hundred of the richest citizens into twenty *symmories* (navy boards) to help spread out its costs.[67] Some of these men were not as wealthy as others but they all paid the same amount of money.[68] If, however, someone nominated for a

[64] Demosthenes 30.15, 17. See also Plutarch, *Demosthenes* 6.1, [Plutarch], *Moralia* 844c–d, with Schaefer, *Demosthenes²* 1, pp. 288–291.

[65] Demosthenes 27.1, 29.58.

[66] Hunt, *War, Peace, and Alliance in Demosthenes' Athens*, p. 34, quoting bibliography. On ancient coinage, see the Appendix.

[67] [Demosthenes] 47.21–23; cf. Demosthenes 14.16–17, with D. M. MacDowell, "The Law of Periandros about Symmories," *CQ²* 36 (1986), pp. 438–449. See also E. Ruschenbusch, "Die athenischen Symmorien des 4. Jh. v. Chr.," *ZPE* 31 (1978), pp. 275–284 and "Die Zahl der athenischen Trierarchen in der Zeit nach 340 v. Chr.," *Class. & Med.* 41 (1990), pp. 79–88, V. Gabrielsen, "Trierarchic Symmories," *Class. & Med.* 41 (1990), pp. 89–118. On the trierarchy in detail, see V. Gabrielsen, *Financing the Athenian Fleet: Public Taxation and Social Relations* (Baltimore: 1994).

[68] Demosthenes 21.154–155, 18.102.

trierarchy knew of another person equally well off or better able to pay the cost of the trierarchy, he could challenge that person with a procedure called *antidosis*. Aphobus now persuaded a friend named Thrasylochus, who owed 2,000 drachmas as his share of the trierarchy, to bring an *antidosis* against Demosthenes for the same amount.[69] If, as anticipated, Demosthenes did not have enough liquid capital to pay it, he would lose his civic rights and even suffer imprisonment until he paid it.

To ensure Demosthenes had enough money to cover his share, Thrasylochus went to his house to inspect it (as was his right), along with his brother Meidias, but Demosthenes would not admit them.[70] In his later speech against Meidias (of 347/6), however, Demosthenes more sensationally stated that the two men broke down the door, smashed some of the furnishings and used despicable language in front of his sister and mother:[71]

> First, they smashed in the doors to our rooms—as if they had already belonged to them as a result of the property exchange! Next, in front of my sister, who was still living at home then and was a young girl, they repeatedly shouted disgraceful words of the sort that men like this shout (no one could induce me to repeat to you any of the things they said), and they were uttering insults, speakable and unspeakable, at my mother, at me, and at all of us.

Thrasylochus' association with Aphobus implicated him in the break-in as well, which gave Demosthenes ammunition to use against Aphobus' character. For the moment, however, he mortgaged his house to pay Thrasylochus the 2,000 drachmas. Then he decided to charge Meidias before a public arbitrator for his conduct in front of his family.[72] Despite the seriousness of the charge Meidias failed to appear

---

[69] Demosthenes 28.17–18, 77–80. That the two conspired in this way: J. Roisman, *The Rhetoric of Conspiracy in Ancient Athens* (Berkeley and Los Angeles: 2006), pp. 45–47. On the *antidosis* procedure in more detail, see V. Gabrielsen, "The *Antidosis* Procedure in Classical Athens," *Class. & Med.* 37 (1987), pp. 99–114 and M. Christ, "Liturgical Avoidance and the *Antidosis* in Classical Athens," *TAPA* 120 (1990), pp. 13–28.

[70] Demosthenes 28.17.

[71] Demosthenes 21.77–79 (the quotation is from 79), a different version of events from what he gave here at 28.17: see D. M. MacDowell, *Demosthenes: Against Meidias* (Oxford: 1990), pp. 1–3 and 294–299; cf. Roisman, *Rhetoric of Conspiracy*, pp. 45–47, Badian, "Road to Prominence," p. 17.

[72] Demosthenes 28.17, 21.78–80, 154, with Badian, "Road to Prominence," p. 17, explaining the lack of mention of the forced entry in the present speech thus: "It seems that whoever wrote the speech wanted to stick to the barest essentials for the case."

before the arbitrator, who ordered him to pay 1,000 drachmas in damages to Demosthenes.[73] Meidias not only refused to pay but also successfully indicted the arbitrator for bias, who lost his citizenship.[74] Thus were laid the foundations of the enmity between Demosthenes and Meidias, which culminated in Demosthenes indicting Meidias in 348 for assaulting him (Chapter 7 pp. 156–162).

With all the challenges behind him, Demosthenes finally brought Aphobus to court.[75] He gave two speeches against him as was the custom in many private cases.[76] The first speech contained most of the details of the case, together with a detailed breakdown of his father's assets and annual income that had been squandered over the years.[77] The second speech rebutted charges Aphobus put forward in his defense speech that Demosthenes was in debt to the state and so was ineligible to indict people.

Against Aphobus[78]

Demosthenes began the first speech against Aphobus by reminding the jurors they were in court that day because Aphobus had betrayed his dying father's last wishes. The introduction of a speech typically served to gain the jury's goodwill and even pity, and Demosthenes secured both by asking the jurors to disregard the mistakes he will make from being young and inexperienced and presenting himself as someone wronged as a child (1–3):

---

[73] Demosthenes 21.76–81.

[74] Demosthenes 21.83–101, with MacDowell, *Demosthenes: Against Meidias*, p. 3 and ad loc. See Chapter 7 p. 160 for a quotation from this speech about the arbitrator.

[75] Schaefer, *Demosthenes*[2] 1, pp. 291–297, Blass, *attische Beredsamkeit*[2] 3.1, pp. 225–231.

[76] Speech 27 *Against Aphobus* 1 and Speech 28 *Against Aphobus* 2.

[77] See the detailed breakdown of the estate at Davies, *Athenian Propertied Families*, pp. 126–133; cf. Carlier, *Démosthène*, pp. 38–41, and MacDowell, *Demosthenes*, pp. 30–32. On ancient coinage, see Appendix.

[78] On the first two speeches against Aphobus, see Schaefer, *Demosthenes*[2] 1, pp. 291–297, Blass, *attische Beredsamkeit*[2] 3.1, pp. 199–205, MacDowell, *Demosthenes*, pp. 37–45, Usher, *Greek Oratory: Tradition and Originality*, pp. 172–178. See also D. Mirhady, "Demosthenes the Advocate," in Ian Worthington (ed.), *Demosthenes: Statesman and Orator* (London: 2000), pp. 186–191. Translation with notes: D. M. MacDowell, *Demosthenes, Speeches 27–38* (Austin: 2004), pp. 19–47; text with commentary: L. Pearson, *Demosthenes: Six Private Speeches* (Atlanta: 1973), pp. 29–54 and 103–164.

If Aphobus had been willing to do the right thing, men of the jury, or to refer the disputed questions to our relatives, there would have been no need of trial or proceedings . . . I am forced to try to obtain justice from him in your court. Now, I know, men of the jury, that it's not an easy matter to contend for the whole of my property against men who are competent speakers and also have powers of manipulation, when because of my youth I'm completely without experience of legal business. Nevertheless, although I'm at a great disadvantage, I have high hopes that I shall obtain justice in your courts . . . I request you, men of the jury, to give me a favorable hearing and, if you decide that I've been treated wrongfully, to give me the support I deserve.

Demosthenes then described his father's estate as well as the stipulations he had laid down in his will (4–12). The bewildering details, and especially the different figures coming one after the other toward the end, may have been deliberately overstated to exaggerate the extent of his guardians' swindling (9–11):

My father, men of the jury, left two workshops, each engaged in a not unimportant craft: one with thirty-two or thirty-three knife-makers, worth 5 or 6 minas each, or in some cases at least 3 minas, from whom he was getting a net income of 30 minas a year; the other with twenty bed-makers, who were security for a loan of 40 minas and who brought him a net income of 12 minas; also about a talent of silver, lent at a drachma, on which the interest amounted to more than 7 minas every year . . . Their total capital value amounted to 4 talents 5,000 drachmas, and the income from them to 50 minas a year. Besides those, he left ivory and iron used in the manufacturing and wood for beds worth about 80 minas, and dye and copper purchased for 70 minas; also a house worth 3,000 drachmas, and furniture, cups, gold jewelry, and clothes, my mother's trousseau, all of those together worth about 10,000 drachmas, and 80 minas in silver in the house. He left all that at home. In maritime assets, he left 70 minas on loan to Xuthus, 2,400 drachmas at Pasion's bank, 600 at Pylades', 1,600 with Demomeles son of Demon, and various loans of 200 or 300 amounting to about a talent. The total sum of this money comes to more than 8 talents 50 minas. You'll find if you check it that the grand total is about 14 talents.

Demosthenes then turned to supporting arguments, including his guardians' treatment of him, alleging that they failed to produce his father's will because it would prove they did not follow its terms (13–65). The will may have been lost after all this time or, more likely, Aphobus may have destroyed it. With no will to challenge his allegations,

Demosthenes could—and probably did—distort his facts and figures,[79] while emphasizing what damning evidence it would be (40):

> You would have still more exact knowledge if they'd been willing to hand over to me the will which my father left. It records, my mother tells me, all that my father left, and the property from which these men were to receive what was given to them, and instructions to lease the estate. When I ask for it, however, they acknowledge that a will was left, but they don't produce it. They do that because they don't want to reveal the size of the property which was left, and which they've plundered, and to conceal their possession of the legacies—as if they weren't going to be easily shown up by the facts themselves.

Demosthenes ended his speech by appealing for mercy, pointing out that his father would be "deeply grieved" if the jury found in favor of Aphobus (66–69). As a further appeal for pity he stated he was destitute, therefore if he lost his case he could not pay the one-sixth of what he is claiming to the defendant as the law demanded. In that event, he would suffer the loss of his citizenship (*atimia*).

There is no question that Aphobus was guilty as charged. In his defense speech, however, he argued that Demosthenes' description of his father's assets was inaccurate and that Gylon, Demosthenes' maternal grandfather, had died as a state debtor.[80] Since Gylon did not have any sons, but only two daughters, his daughters' sons-in-law therefore inherited his debt—in other words, Demosthenes (the orator) and his cousins. Consequently, Aphobus claimed Demosthenes was a state debtor and so could not bring his case against him.

Demosthenes delivered a second speech against Aphobus, which conformed to custom by being shorter. He immediately attacked Aphobus' "many big lies" (1), especially about Gylon. He claimed that Gylon had paid off his debt, reminding the jury that while he was a guardian Aphobus had never argued Demosthenes' estate was worth less and that he had concocted the idea that Gylon was a state debtor.[81] Demosthenes repeated arguments from his first speech, especially about Aphobus' failure to produce the will and all that his father had said from his deathbed, adding the detail that his father

[79] MacDowell, *Demosthenes*, pp. 41–42.
[80] Demosthenes 28.1.
[81] Demosthenes 28.1–4.

"placed me on Aphobus' knees" while he spoke (16). The jurors again condemned Aphobus. When he requested a fine of only one talent, they demanded he pay Demosthenes ten talents, the amount that he had claimed.[82]

AFTERMATH

Aphobus was not a man to give up easily. With the help of his brother-in-law Onetor he brought a charge of perjury (*dike pseudomarturion*) against Phanus, one of Demosthenes' supporting witnesses. If he could prove his charge, then Demosthenes' entire case against him would be rejected. Demosthenes gave a speech in Phanus' defense, which was technically a third speech against Aphobus.[83] The details of the case are not relevant here, but Phanus was probably acquitted.[84]

Since Aphobus had not paid his fine, Demosthenes could legally seize all of his property and belongings as recompense. To prevent that, and as a final insult to Demosthenes, Aphobus destroyed parts of his actual house and handed over his farm to Onetor, ostensibly in lieu of the dowry of his wife, Onetor's sister.[85] Demosthenes would now need to prosecute Onetor, the new owner, if he wanted to recover the money that Aphobus still owed him. He did take possession of the house and some slaves, but when he went to take the farm Onetor chased him away because Aphobus had given it to him. Undeterred, Demosthenes prosecuted Onetor under the legal procedure for eviction (*dike exoules*)

---

[82] Demosthenes 29.1, 8, 59–60, [Plutarch], *Moralia* 844d.

[83] Speech 29. There was a belief that this speech was spurious (see Blass, *attische Beredsamkeit*² 3.1, pp. 205–211), but it is now accepted as genuine: E. M. Burke, "A Further Argument on the Authenticity of Demosthenes 29," *CJ* 70 (1974), pp. 53–56, MacDowell, *Demosthenes*, pp. 45–53; cf. MacDowell, "The Authenticity of Demosthenes 29 (Against Aphobus III) as a Source of Information about Athenian Law," *Symposion* 1985 (1989), pp. 265–262.

[84] On the speech, see MacDowell, *Demosthenes*, pp. 45–53, Usher, *Greek Oratory: Tradition and Originality*, pp. 178–180. See also MacDowell, "Authenticity of Demosthenes 29 (Against Aphobus III)," pp. 265–262, Mirhady, "Demosthenes the Advocate," pp. 191–195. Translation with notes: MacDowell, *Demosthenes, Speeches 27–38*, pp. 48–66.

[85] On Demosthenes' belief that the two men cooked up this scheme to defraud him, see Roisman, *Rhetoric of Conspiracy*, pp. 22–27.

in 362 or 361. The two speeches he gave against Onetor survive,[86] in which he asserted that Aphobus and Onetor conspired to defraud him of what he was owed.[87] Although we do now know the outcome of the trial, Demosthenes ought to have won.

The speeches that Demosthenes gave against Therippides and Demophon have not survived. Plutarch reported that Demosthenes won all his cases against his guardians, but the amount of restitution he received from them was minimal, and he got nothing from Demophon.[88] Further, his house was still mortgaged to pay the 2,000 drachmas to Thrasylochus for the shared trierarchy. Still, Demosthenes, his mother, and his sister were far from being out on the street. He had the knife-making factory with its fourteen slaves, some cash reserves (the 3,100 drachmas from Aphobus and Therippides), and Aphobus' house and personal property. If he won his case against Onetor, he would also have acquired his farm. Later, his sister married her cousin Demochares' son Laches (perhaps their relationship developed from when she was living in his father's house).[89] They had a son, also named Demochares, who in 280/79 (forty years after Demosthenes' death) successfully persuaded the Athenians to set up a statue of his famous uncle.[90]

Demosthenes' case against his guardians brought him something that was more beneficial than financial redress—it gave him a reputation in Athens. He had spent three years doggedly bringing suits against his former guardians and his tenacity and their attempts to undermine him probably made the case a cause célèbre in a city where people talked about everything. Regardless of the extent of

---

[86] Speech 30 *Against Onetor* 1 and Speech 31 *Against Onetor* 2, on which see Schaefer, *Demosthenes²* 1, pp. 298–301, Blass, *attische Beredsamkeit²* 3.1, pp. 211–214, MacDowell, *Demosthenes*, pp. 53–57, Usher, *Greek Oratory: Tradition and Originality*, pp. 180–183. See also Mirhady, "Demosthenes the Advocate," pp. 195–198. Translation with notes: MacDowell, *Demosthenes, Speeches 27–38*, pp. 67–83; text with commentary: Pearson, *Demosthenes: Six Private Speeches*, pp. 57–72 and 165–203; commentary on Demosthenes 30: M. Kertsch, *Kommentar zur 30. Rede des Demosthenes (gegen Onetor I)* (Vienna: 1971).

[87] On the conspiratorial charge as a means to persuade the jurors, see in more detail Roisman, *Rhetoric of Conspiracy*, pp. 22–27, citing bibliography.

[88] Plutarch, *Demosthenes* 6.1, [Plutarch], *Moralia* 844c–d.

[89] [Plutarch], *Moralia* 847c.

[90] [Plutarch], *Moralia* 847a, c, 850f, Cicero, *Brutus* 286. Demochares' decree is quoted in Chapter 15 pp. 338–339.

Isaeus' help or even whether Isaeus had written the speeches for him,[91] it was Demosthenes who had successfully delivered them in court. Now in his early twenties, his recent court success permitted him to launch a career writing private (forensic) speeches for prosecutors or defendants.[92]

DEMOSTHENES' EARLY CAREER

Speechwriting or logography was a lucrative occupation. After his troubled childhood, Demosthenes probably wanted to make enough money to ensure that he would never find himself living as badly again. The Athenians were highly litigious, and multiple courts met on most days of the year to decide a variety of private and public cases.[93] The professional, specialized lawyers of today did not exist in ancient Greece, so regardless of the case it fell to the individual prosecutors and defendants to prepare their own cases. The system perhaps deterred men who lacked legal knowledge or even the self-confidence to stand before a jury of several hundred citizens. Hence the rise of the *logographoi* (speechwriters), who for a fee wrote a required court speech and probably dispensed legal advice to their clients.[94] Successful speechwriters quickly established a reputation, and the better ones (including Demosthenes) circulated copies of their speeches as means to increase their business.[95]

---

[91] Thus, in view of their content and style, 27, 28, and 30 may not be Demosthenic, but 29 and 31 are genuine: Badian, "Road to Prominence," p 17, citing bibliography.

[92] On this genre, see C. Cooper "Forensic Oratory," in Ian Worthington (ed.), *Blackwell Companion to Greek Rhetoric* (Malden: 2007), pp. 203–219.

[93] M. Christ, *The Litigious Athenian* (Baltimore: 1998).

[94] Thucydides 8.61.1 says that Antiphon in the later fifth century gave legal advice; since business before the courts increased in the fourth century, it is no leap of faith to see *logographoi* continuing to do the same. See also J. Sickinger, "Rhetoric and the Law," in Ian Worthington (ed.), *Blackwell Companion to Greek Rhetoric* (Malden: 2006), pp. 286–302, H. J. Wolff, "Demosthenes as Advocate: The Functions and Methods of Legal Consultants in Classical Athens," in E. Carawan (ed.), *The Attic Orators* (Oxford: 2007), pp. 91–115.

[95] Plutarch, *Demosthenes* 11.4 implies a revision process, and see further, Ian Worthington, "Greek Oratory, Revision of Speeches and the Problem of Historical Reliability," *Class. & Med.* 42 (1991), pp. 55–74; cf. "History and Oratorical Exploitation," in Ian Worthington (ed.), *Persuasion: Greek Rhetoric in Action* (London: 1994), pp. 109–129.

Today, speeches by only a fraction of the orators who must have
lived and worked in Classical Athens survive. In the first century BC,
scholars at Alexandria drew up a "Canon of the Ten Attic Orators,"
including orators of the late fifth to late fourth centuries BC.[96] The
compiler of this canon mistakenly included speeches by two other orators, Apollodorus and Hegesippus, in the selection of Demosthenes'
works.[97] Thus we have speeches by twelve orators, although not all
their speeches have survived. Demosthenes, for example, was credited
with writing either sixty-five or seventy-one speeches in total.[98] Of
these, only sixty-one were included in the canon (although, as noted,
he did not write all of them).[99]

Demosthenes' earliest private speeches probably dealt with family
property disputes because of his experience in his cases against his
guardians.[100] It was not long before he took on different cases in both
the private and public spheres. He amassed a tidy fortune from his
speechwriting work (and later also from his political career), as shown

[96] The list (which is not in chronological order of their lives) is: Antiphon, Andocides,
Lysias, Isocrates, Isaeus, Demosthenes, Aeschines, Hyperides, Lycurgus, and Dinarchus: see Ian Worthington, "The Canon of the Ten Attic Orators," in Ian Worthington (ed.), *Persuasion: Greek Rhetoric in Action* (London: 1994), pp. 244–263. On these
orators, see, for example, J. F. Dobson, *The Greek Orators* (London: 1919), G. Kennedy, *The Art of Persuasion in Greece* (Princeton: 1963), pp. 125–263, and Usher, *Greek
Oratory: Tradition and Originality*.

[97] The private (court) speeches numbered 45, 46, 49, 50, 52, 53, and 59 were written by
Apollodorus, son of Pasion. On Apollodorus and his speeches, see J. Trevett, *Apollodorus the Son of Pasion* (Oxford: 1992), MacDowell, *Demosthenes*, pp. 99–126; cf.
Blass, *attische Berdesamkeit*² 3.1, pp. 514–543, Usher, *Greek Oratory: Tradition and
Originality*, pp. 338–343. The symbouleutic (political) speech numbered 7 was composed probably by Hegesippus, on whom see Blass, *attische Beredsamkeit*² 3.2, pp.
111–121, MacDowell, *Demosthenes*, pp. 332–333, 343–346. The speaker of Demosthenes 17 is unknown: see Blass, *attische Beredsamkeit*² 3.2, pp. 121–126, MacDowell,
Demosthenes, pp. 379–381. Speech 12 is actually a letter written by Philip of Macedonia to the Athenians (to which Demosthenes replied in Speech 11). On the authenticity of Demosthenes' speeches, see further, Blass, *attische Beredsamkeit*² 3.1, pp.
47–63, Carlier, *Démosthène*, pp. 310–315, Sealey, *Demosthenes*, pp. 230–240.

[98] [Plutarch], *Moralia* 847e, Scholiast on Aeschines 2.18. On the transmission of Demosthenes' speeches, see Blass, *attische Beredsamkeit*² 3.1, pp. 47–63, Carlier, *Démosthène*, pp. 315–320, Sealey, *Demosthenes*, pp. 221–229.

See above, note 91.

They are discussed by MacDowell, *Demosthenes*, pp. 60–98, who makes the suggestion about Demosthenes' earlier cases on p. 60.

by his liturgies and the two houses he owned, one in Athens and the other in the Piraeus.[101] By the 350s, however, he was becoming increasingly involved in politics and by the 340s he dominated political life.[102] He therefore had less time and financial need to write speeches for others. In the 320s, when he played a less active role in public affairs, he may well have returned to his former profession.

DEMOSTHENES' SEXUALITY AND MARRIAGE

Demosthenes' later political opponent Aeschines would accuse him of being effeminate and a homosexual (*kinaidos*).[103] Aeschines claimed that Demosthenes had had a sexual relationship with a dim-witted youth named Aristarchus, who he had promised to turn into a great orator for payment, and that Demosthenes then used his power over Aristarchus to get him to murder a rival named Nicodemus.[104] Another time, when Demosthenes was married, he allegedly brought a boy named Cnosion into his house, which so infuriated his wife she had sex with him to spite her husband.[105] On yet another occasion he supposedly took advantage of a young boy, Aristion from Plataea, who he was allowing to live in his house.[106] How Demosthenes' sexuality was perceived may also explain why a curious didactic discourse called the *Erotic Essay* was attributed to him and was included in his corpus.[107] In this essay, which is utterly different from all of Demosthenes' other works and probably

---

[101] Aeschines 3.209, Dinarchus 1.69; see Davies, *Athenian Propertied Families*, pp. 133–137 on Demosthenes' wealth.

[102] For a balanced and well-presented survey of Demosthenes' career, see G. Kennedy, "The Oratorical Career of Demosthenes," in J. J. Murphy (ed.), *Demosthenes' On the Crown: A Critical Case Study of a Masterpiece of Ancient Oratory* (New York: 1967), pp. 28–47. Demosthenes as a speechwriter: Carlier, *Démosthène*, pp. 49–52, Lehmann, *Demosthenes*, pp. 48–58.

[103] Aeschines 1.181, 2.88, 2.151; cf. N. R. E. Fisher, *Aeschines, Against Timarchos* (Oxford: 2001), pp. 272–273.

[104] Aeschines 1.170–173, 2.148, 166; see also Demosthenes 21.104, 116–122, Dinarchus 1.30, 47.

[105] Aeschines 2.149, Athenaeus 593a. This Cnosion might also be the friend of Demosthenes named at Hyperides 5.13.

[106] Aeschines 3.162.

[107] Demosthenes 61, on which see Blass, *attische Beredsamkeit*[2] 3.1, pp. 358–360, MacDowell, *Demosthenes*, pp. 23–29. Translation with notes: Ian Worthington, *Demosthenes: Speeches 60 and 61, Prologues, Letters* (Austin: 2006), pp. 38–54.

not written by him, a young man named Epicrates is addressed by an older man (perhaps his teacher). He praises Epicrates' beauty and physical prowess, then urges him to ignore the sexual attention of other men and focus only on philosophy so that he will become a morally upright citizen.

The term homosexual cannot be used of ancient Greece in the same way as it is employed today.[108] Greek society did not stigmatize same-sex homoerotic relationships (whether between men or women) or, to use another modern term, bisexuality. However, Greeks frowned upon older men who took advantage of youths for their own sexual pleasure. Aeschines' anecdotes about Demosthenes' homosexual behavior involve younger boys, and so need to be treated with caution, not least because he gave them in court speeches, in which denigration of an opponent's personal life was a common rhetorical topos. Since Demosthenes did marry, he may have been openly bisexual,[109] in which case his lifestyle provided Aeschines with an opportunity to advance the claims he did based on the public perception of Demosthenes' sexuality. For the same reason, the *Erotic Essay* may have been considered Demosthenic because of Epicrates' youth and the attempt to save him from the lustful advances of men.

When Demosthenes married is unknown. He had three children, all born after 346,[110] so he may have married shortly before that year, making him close to forty years old. His wife was the daughter of a man named Heliodorus from the island of Samos.[111] Their first child was a daughter, who died in 336 aged ten and so did not reach adolescence.[112] After she died, Demosthenes and his wife had two sons, who survived his death in 322.

The status of Demosthenes' Samian wife has implications for the legitimacy of both their marriage and their children. Samos had belonged to the Athenians since their general Timotheus captured it from the Persians in 365.[113] After Timotheus' action, the Athenians sent various waves of settlers to Samos over the years that displaced the native population. If Heliodorus was a Samian, then Demosthenes'

---

[108] See the classic study of K. J. Dover, *Greek Homosexuality* (London: 1978).

[109] MacDowell, *Demosthenes*, p. 23.

[110] Demosthenes 21.187.

[111] Plutarch, *Demosthenes* 15.4, [Plutarch], *Moralia* 847c.

[112] Davies, *Athenian Propertied Families*, pp. 138–139.

[113] *IG* ii² 108, Isocrates 15.111–112, Demosthenes 15.9, Nepos, *Timotheus* 1.2.

marriage to his daughter meant that, under Pericles' citizenship law, their children were not citizens.[114] If, however, Heliodorus was one of the Athenian settlers, then he and his daughter were Athenians, making her marriage to Demosthenes legitimate. The matter cannot be properly resolved, but Heliodorus' daughter was described as a Samian lady, and other, biased writers claimed that Demosthenes had illegitimate children by a courtesan.[115] Perhaps the reason why it was Demosthenes' nephew Demochares (the son of his sister and her husband Laches) who proposed a statue for his uncle (see above) was because Demosthenes' sons were not citizens and so were debarred from proposing such honors.[116] If Demosthenes married when he was about forty, at which time he was the dominant person in Athenian politics, he may not have been concerned about the legitimacy of his family.

FROM THE COURTS TO THE ASSEMBLY

A career writing court speeches for others eventually lost its appeal for Demosthenes as he began to involve himself in the political life of the city. In particular, he was attracted to the Assembly, the "supreme democratic body" in the constitution,[117] which debated and voted on all matters of domestic and foreign policy.[118] Assemblies were held forty times per year or four times a prytany. The Athenian year had twelve months in it (see Appendix), but for administrative purposes the Athenians divided it into ten prytanies, so each prytany lasted about six weeks. Meetings of the Assembly began at dawn and lasted until dusk and were held on the Pnyx, a rocky outcrop close to the Acropolis (Figure 3a–c).

There was no break once the meeting began, so people brought their own food and a cushion to sit on to help them get through the long day. They worked through a prepared agenda, on which item any citizen could speak, addressing his peers from a *bema*, or rostrum. There

---

[114] Cf. Davies, *Athenian Propertied Families*, p. 138, and J. Cargill, "*IG* II² 1 and the Athenian Kleruchy on Samos," *GRBS* 24 (1983), p. 324.

[115] Athenaeus 13.592e–f, Dinarchus 1.71; cf. Demosthenes 21.187 and Aeschines 2.149.

[116] The suggestion of MacDowell, *Demosthenes*, p. 22.

[117] Aristotle, *Politics* 1299a1.

[118] See in detail M. H. Hansen, *The Athenian Assembly in the Age of Demosthenes* (Oxford: 1987).

was no actual time limit although speakers could be heckled if they were too verbose or said things with which their audience disagreed.[119] After the speeches and debate, the people voted on the item by a simple show of hands (*cheirotonia*) rather than by secret ballot as in the law courts.[120]

Several thousand male citizens over the age of eighteen attended Assemblies – in the later fourth century, there was room on the Pnyx for over 13,000 attendees.[121] Such large numbers made a precise count

FIGURE 3A. View from the Athenian Acropolis to the Pnyx rock, where the Assembly met; the auditorium area where the people sat and speaker's rostrum can be seen top right.

[119] For example, Demosthenes, *Prooimion* 4, 5, 26.1, 56.3.

[120] [Aristotle], *Athenian Constitution* 68 and 69, with Hansen, *Athenian Assembly in the Age of Demosthenes*, pp. 41–46. Aristotle, *Politics* 2.1270b27–28, 1271a9–10, considered *cheirotonia* a far better way of deciding matters than the Spartan Assembly, in which citizens shouted to vote.

[121] M. H. Hansen, "How Many Athenians Attended the Ecclesia?," *GRBS* 17 (1976), pp. 130–132, "The Athenian Assembly and the Assembly-Place on the Pnyx," *GRBS* 23 (1982), pp. 241–244, "Political Activity and the Organization of Attica in the Fourth Century B.C.," *GRBS* 24 (1983), pp. 227–238, *Athenian Assembly in the Age of Demosthenes*, pp. 12–19, but R. K. Sinclair, *Democracy and Participation in Athens* (Cambridge: 1988), pp. 114–119, argues for a lower level of attendance at Assemblies. On composition, see too Hunt, *War, Peace, and Alliance in Demosthenes' Athens*, pp. 39–48.

FIGURE 3B. The auditorium area of the Pnyx, looking back to the Acropolis; the speaker's rostrum is to the right.

FIGURE 3C. Looking from the top of the speaker's rostrum on the Pnyx over the Agora to modern Athens (the reconstructed Stoa of Attalus can be seen in the middle ground).

impossible, so presiding officials estimated the votes for and against a proposal.[122] The people sat with other members of their tribes in the semicircular auditorium area of the Pnyx, facing the *bema* (Figure 3b–c above). As Aristotle tells us, unlike the courts with their focus on justice, the Assembly concerned itself with matters of expediency that affected the city presently and in the future.[123] Political speakers employed a style of oratory known as symbouleutic.[124] Political speeches may not have been written down in advance as in the courts, although Demosthenes appears to have been an exception here.[125] His apparent practice of writing speeches before Assembly debates may explain why his political speeches are the only ones to have survived from classical Athens.[126] The surviving versions of his political speeches were likely not verbatim, however, but presented the thrust of what he spoke to the people.[127]

Demosthenes dominated the Assembly in the 340s, but he was also a member of another powerful body, the Boule (often referred to

---

[122] [Aristotle], *Athenian Constitution* 30.5, 44.3, with Rhodes, *Commentary*, ad loc.

[123] Aristotle, *Rhetoric* 1.3.1358b21–37.

[124] On this genre, see S. Usher, "Symbouleutic Oratory," in Ian Worthington (ed.), *Blackwell Companion to Greek Rhetoric* (Malden: 2007), pp. 220–235.

[125] See, for example, J. Trevett, "Did Demosthenes Publish his Deliberative Speeches?," *Hermes* 124 (1996), pp. 436–441.

[126] The surviving version of Andocides 3 *On the Peace with Sparta* of 392 may have been a political speech. Another reason may have to do with Demosthenes circulating his *prooemia*, over fifty rhetorical openings of speeches, on which see Ian Worthington, *Demosthenes: Speeches 60 and 61, Prologues, Letters* (Austin: 2006), pp. 55–98. Alexandrian scholars may well have included some political speeches in his corpus as examples of a complete oration: Ian Worthington, "Why we have Demosthenes' Symbouleutic Speeches: A Note," in F. C. Gabaudan and J. V. M. Dosuna (eds.), *Dic mihi, Musa, virum: Homenaje al profesor Antonio López Eire* (Salamanca: 2010), pp. 709–713. Yunis, *Taming Democracy*, p. 242, suggests Demosthenes wrote out his Assembly speeches because he had done so in the courts.

[127] M.H. Hansen, "Two Notes on Demosthenes' Symbouleutic Speeches," *Class. & Med.* 35 (1984), pp. 60–68: Demosthenes was exceptional in publishing several of his political speeches, but they do not accurately reflect what he delivered in the Assembly; contra R. Lane Fox, "Demosthenes, Dionysius, and the Dating of Six Early Speeches," *Class. & Med.* 48 (1997), pp. 167–168. Demosthenes himself published his speeches: Hansen, "Two Notes on Demosthenes' Symbouleutic Speeches," pp. 57–70, Sealey, *Demosthenes*, pp. 221–229, Yunis, *Taming Democracy*, pp. 241–247; they may have been collected after his death, perhaps by his nephew Demochares, and circulated: Trevett, "Did Demosthenes Publish his Deliberative Speeches?," pp. 425–441, R. D. Milns, "The Public Speeches of Demosthenes," in Ian Worthington (ed.), *Demosthenes: Statesman and Orator* (London: 2000), pp. 207–209.

as the Council). Composed of 500 men over the age of thirty who served for one year (reelection was possible only once), the Boule prepared the Assembly's agenda and advised it. Since the Boule met practically every day, it came to exercise other important political and judicial powers, including supervisory functions over various administrative boards or subcommittees that dealt with such things as public works, roads, and finances, and met with foreign embassies.[128] The 500 men were drawn from the ten tribes into which Cleisthenes had divided the Athenians in 508, fifty from each tribe. Because 500 was a large number, each tribe's fifty members served in an executive function for each of the ten prytanies into which the year was divided.

The Athenians believed that democracy was the best form of government.[129] From the middle of the fifth century Athens was a radical democracy, in which the people played a direct role in governing their state.[130]

---

[128] On the Boule, see in detail P. J. Rhodes, *The Athenian Boule* (Oxford: 1972). As many as two-thirds of the citizens may have served on the Boule, some of them twice: Hansen, *Athenian Democracy in the Age of Demosthenes²*, p. 249.

[129] For example, Herodotus 3.80.6 (mid-fifth century): "The sovereignty of the people has, firstly, the fairest name of all—equality before the laws; secondly, a popular government does none of the things a monarch does. In a democracy the magistrates are chosen by lot, and their conduct in office is subject to judicial scrutiny, and all resolutions are brought before the assembly" and Plato, *Republic* 8.558c (around 380): "'Democracy,' I replied, 'would have these qualities and others similar to them, and it would be, it seems, a pleasant kind of government, anarchic and motley, assigning a sort of quality to equals and unequals alike.'"

[130] Radical democracy was introduced by the legislation of Ephialtes in 462: [Aristotle], *Athenian Constitution* 25. On the democracy and its workings, see especially Hansen, *Athenian Democracy in the Age of Demosthenes²*; cf. Sealey, *Demosthenes*, Chapter 2, pp. 19–35, "The Athenians and their Environment," covering population, wealth, food supply, and the constitution, Sinclair, *Democracy and Participation*, and J. Ober, "Public Speech and the Power of the People in Democratic Athens," in J. Ober (ed.), *The Athenian Revolution. Essays on Ancient Greek Democracy and Political Theory* (Princeton: 1996), pp. 18–31; cf. "Power and Oratory in Democratic Athens: Demosthenes 21, *Against Meidias*," ibid. pp. 86–106. On the workings of the democracy and how people made their decisions using the evidence of Demosthenes' speeches, see H. Montgomery, *The Way to Chaeronea* (Oslo: 1983) and Hunt, *War, Peace, and Alliance in Demosthenes' Athens*. The speeches of the orators, especially those of Aeschines, tell us much about the ideals and practices of democracy: R. Lane Fox, "Aeschines and Athenian Politics," in R. Osborne and S. Hornblower (eds.), *Ritual, Finance, Politics: Athenian Democratic Accounts Presented to David Lewis* (Oxford: 1994), pp. 135–155; cf. Montgomery and Hunt cited above.

Only male citizens over the age of eighteen could vote in the Assembly, for women never had the franchise. The political society of Athens (those that could vote), then, consisted of a very small minority in relation to the whole society. Elected public officials had largely administrative duties in the city's economic, civil, and religious life because political power had come to rest on popular approval in the Assembly. In other words, ambitious men did not need to hold elected office to become politically influential. If they were adept speakers or *rhetores* (orators), they had only to persuade their peers in the Assembly to vote for them and so build up a political following.[131] That was why rhetoric as a formal art developed in tandem with democracy, enticing ambitious men to exploit it for their own political advancement.[132] The downside was that very often an Assembly was swayed not so much by the content of speeches (and thus the validity of propositions) but by the speakers' rhetorical performance.[133]

In ancient Greece, there were no organized political parties with different platforms, no party in power and opposition parties, no political manifestos, and no sets of diehard supporters committed to one party or program as there are today. The people voted for the policy of the man who delivered the best speech in the Assembly on the day. Politically ambitious individuals, however, still needed to court influential men, making the structure of Athenian political life

---

[131] On the socio-economic composition of the Assembly, see R. K. Sinclair, "Lysias' Speeches and the Debate about Participation in Athenian Public Life," *Antichthon* 22 (1988), pp. 54–66 and *Democracy and Participation*, pp. 119–134 (wealthier citizens preferred to go to the Assembly rather than the law courts); cf. J. Ober, *Mass and Elite in Democratic Athens: Rhetoric, Ideology and the Power of the People* (Princeton: 1989), pp. 122–138 and "Public Speech and the Power of the People."

[132] See further, Ian Worthington, "Rhetoric and Politics in Classical Greece: Rise of the *Rhêtores*," in Ian Worthington (ed.), *Blackwell Companion to Greek Rhetoric* (Malden: 2007), pp. 255–271. On the nature of rhetoric, see Kennedy, *Art of Persuasion in Greece*, pp. 3–25.

[133] Cf. P. E. Harding, "Rhetoric and Politics in Fourth-Century Athens," *Phoenix* 41 (1987), pp. 25–39. The number of speakers who proposed decrees in the late fifth and fourth centuries and who are known to have spoken consistently at Assemblies is relatively small: M. H. Hansen, "The Athenian 'Politicians', 403–322 B.C.," *GRBS* 24 (1983), pp. 33–55, "*Rhetores* and *Strategoi* in Fourth-Century Athens," *GRBS* 24 (1983), pp. 151–180, and "The Number of *Rhetores* in the Athenian Ecclesia, 355–322 B.C.," *GRBS* 25 (1984), pp. 123–155.

a personal one dependent on interpersonal relationships.[134] Over time some of them emerged as their own men in politics (as was the case with Demosthenes), but even then they collaborated on policy issues. The recently discovered fragment of a forensic speech, *Against Diondas* by the orator Hyperides, displays the same anti-Macedonian bias and championing of Demosthenes' policy toward Philip as in Demosthenes' *On the Crown* of 330 (Chapter 13), suggesting some collaboration between the two orators.[135] In 324, however, Demosthenes and Hyperides split over resistance to Alexander the Great (Chapter 15).

Demosthenes' earliest surviving political speech, *On the Symmories* (navy boards), was delivered in 354, when he was about thirty years old, and dealt with financial reform (Chapter 4). If he had been attending the Assembly since he was eighteen, he had probably already spoken in a debate before then. Indeed, he mentioned in a speech he gave to the Boule in 360 or 359, when he was awarded a crown for a trierarchy, that he had already addressed the Assembly.[136] Initially, his speech impediments and poor speaking style caused the Athenians to mock him when he spoke, and whatever he said was disregarded.[137] He was in

---

[134] See the seminal work in this area of R. Sealey, "Athens after the Social War," *JHS* 75 (1955), pp. 74–81 and "Callistratos of Aphidna and His Contemporaries," *Historia* 5 (1956), pp. 178–203, with his *Demosthenes*, passim; cf. for example J. Ober, *Mass and Elite in Democratic Athens* (Princeton: 1989), Carlier, *Démosthène*, pp. 28–34, C. Karvounis, *Demosthenes: Studien zu den Demegorien orr. XIV, XVI, XV, IV, I, II, III* (Tübingen: 2002), pp. 67–70.

[135] Speech: C. Carey, M. Edwards, and Z. Farkas, "Fragments of Hyperides' *Against Diondas* from the Archimedes Palimpsest," *ZPE* 165 (2008), pp. 1–19; for parallels between it and *On the Crown*, see p. 3, and see too M. J. Edwards, "Le palimpseste d'Archimède et le nouvel *Hypéride*," *Comptes Rendus de L'Académie des Inscriptions* (2010, II avril–juin), pp. 753–768.

[136] Speech 51, *On the Trierarchic Crown*: see MacDowell, *Demosthenes*, pp. 133–136; on p.136, MacDowell takes Demosthenes' reference to those who oppose what some men say in their public speeches (51.20) as "our first evidence of his entry into politics." On the other hand, Demosthenes might not be one of these critics; he could simply be denigrating his prosecutors by alleging their public policies are dangerous for the city.

[137] Plutarch, *Demosthenes* 6.3. Eunomus of Thriasia was said to have told Demosthenes he had the speaking ability of Pericles, but would never be as influential until he showed more courage before the people: Plutarch, *Demosthenes* 6.5. Demosthenes' admiration of Pericles' style: Plutarch, *Demosthenes* 9.2.

despair until a chance meeting one day with the comic actor Satyrus changed everything.[138]

PEBBLES IN THE MOUTH

Satyrus listened to Demosthenes complain that he worked harder than anyone else on his speeches yet could not hold the Assembly's attention. The two men went to Demosthenes' house, where Satyrus asked him recite a speech from a tragedy of Sophocles or Euripides. Satyrus then repeated the same speech back to Demosthenes, adding intonation and characterization that completely transformed it. His simple demonstration showed Demosthenes that standing up and speaking were not enough: delivery was everything. It became Demosthenes' principal stylistic feature.[139] When later in his career someone asked him "what was the first thing in oratory, he replied 'Delivery,' and what the second, 'Delivery,' and the third, 'Delivery'."[140] He built a study under his house where he spent two to three months at a time practicing his delivery and was said to have shaved one side of his head to force himself to stay indoors so as not be seen like that in public.[141]

Plutarch related several stories about how Demosthenes overcame his physical afflictions, although their veracity is suspect.[142] For example, he supposedly practiced speaking with pebbles in his mouth to overcome his lisp and enunciate more clearly—the letter "r" (so Cicero said) apparently caused him the most problem.[143] He ran up and down hillsides reciting speeches to strengthen and help his breathing techniques. To ignore distractions from noises around him, he practiced speaking

[138] Plutarch, *Demosthenes* 7.1–5; [Plutarch], *Moralia* 845a–b, has the same story, but instead of Satyrus the actor Andronicus helps out Demosthenes in this way.
[139] [Plutarch], *Moralia* 845b; cf. Cicero, *Brutus* 142. Cf. Schaefer, *Demosthenes²* 1, pp. 329–339, C. Cooper, "Demosthenes: Actor on the Political and Forensic Stage," in C. J. Mackie (ed.), *Oral Performance and its Context* (Leiden: 2004), pp. 145–161.
[140] [Plutarch], *Moralia* 845b.
[141] Plutarch, *Demosthenes* 7.6, [Plutarch], *Moralia* 845d.
[142] Plutarch, *Demosthenes* 11.1; see too Cicero, *de Oratore* 1.260–261. On the veracity of Plutarch's anecdotes, which were perhaps the product of a later peripatetic tradition to elevate Demosthenes' reputation by showing how hard he struggled, see C. Cooper, "Philosophers, Politics, Academics: Demosthenes' Rhetorical Reputation in Antiquity," in Ian Worthington (ed.), *Demosthenes: Statesman and Orator* (London: 2000), pp. 224–245.
[143] Cicero, *de Oratore* 1.260–261.

above the waves as they broke on the beach at Phalerum. Finally, because he had an awkward habit of shaking one shoulder when he spoke, "he put an end to the habit by fastening a spit or, as some say, a dagger from the ceiling to make him through fear keep his shoulder motionless."[144]

Demosthenes also closely studied the speeches of other orators, including Isocrates, Zethus of Amphipolis, and Alcidamas.[145] He analyzed them, we are told, for their use of language, style, and arguments, and reworked them to fit his own manner.[146] He was especially concerned with integrating illustrative examples from past history in speeches, which was the mark of an adept orator.[147] Thucydides' writing had a profound impact on him,[148] but his complex prose style did not lend itself to a spoken speech and is a likely reason why Demosthenes' early speeches failed.[149] Eventually he changed to a simpler style, which lent itself to oral performance.[150]

---

[144] [Plutarch], *Moralia* 844f.

[145] Plutarch, *Demosthenes* 5.7, [Plutarch], *Moralia* 844c.

[146] See D. J. Ochs, "Demosthenes' Use of Argument" and G. O. Rowe, "Demosthenes' Use of Language," in Murphy, *Demosthenes' On the Crown*, pp. 157–174 and 175–199, respectively.

[147] Isocrates 4.9–10; cf. 15. See further, Worthington, "History and Oratorical Exploitation," pp. 109–129 and M. Nouhaud, *L'utilisation de l'histoire par les orateurs attiques* (Paris: 1982); see also L. Pearson, "Historical Allusions in the Attic Orators," *CP* 36 (1941), pp. 209–229, S. Perlman, "The Historical Example, Its Use and Importance as Political Propaganda in the Attic Orators," *SH* 7 (1961), pp. 158–166, Milns, "Public Speeches of Demosthenes," pp. 214–215, and (somewhat dated now) C. R. Kennedy, "Demosthenes' Use of History," reprinted in Murphy, *Demosthenes' On the Crown*, pp. 145–156.

[148] Schaefer, *Demosthenes²* 1, pp. 320–324, Yunis, *Taming Democracy*, pp. 237–277.

[149] Plutarch, *Demosthenes* 6.3.

[150] On Demosthenes' style, see in detail Blass, *attische Beredsamkeit²* 3.1, pp. 63–198, G. Ronnet, *Étude sur le style de Démosthène dans les discours politiques* (Paris: 1951), L. Pearson, *The Art of Demosthenes* (Meisenheim am Glan: 1976), C. Wooten, *Cicero's Philippics and Their Demosthenic Model* (Chapel Hill: 1983), Usher, *Greek Oratory: Tradition and Originality*, pp. 171–278, and MacDowell, *Demosthenes*. On Demosthenes' use of rhetoric in his political speeches, see also Yunis, *Taming Democracy*, pp. 237–277. More generally, see Pickard-Cambridge, *Demosthenes*, pp. 17–28, C. Wooten, "Dionysius of Halicarnassus and Hermogenes on the Style of Demosthenes," *AJP* 110 (1989), pp. 576–588, L. Pearson, "The Development of Demosthenes as a Political Orator," *Phoenix* 29 (1975), pp. 95–109 and "The Virtuoso Passages in Demosthenes' Speeches," *Phoenix* 29 (1975), pp. 214–230, Kennedy, *Art of Persuasion*, pp. 206–236, Mirhady, "Demosthenes the Advocate," pp. 181–204 and Milns, "Public Speeches of Demosthenes," pp. 209–223.

Demosthenes' speeches were highly praised by ancient commentators on them, especially Didymus and Dionysius of Halicarnassus, as well as Plutarch.[151] Dionysius even said that Demosthenes' "forcefulness" (*deinotes*) was the most perfect form of oratory.[152] In the Roman era, Cicero described him as flawless and Quintilian as the "standard of oratory."[153] Cicero, in fact, was so taken with Demosthenes' mastery of language and style in his four *Philippics* that he modeled his famous speeches against Mark Antony on them, giving them the same title.[154]

Demosthenes was, however, criticized throughout his career for not speaking extemporaneously about anything.[155] Unlike in the courts, where the facts of a case were known in advance, speakers at Assemblies had to speak off the cuff much of the time because of the unpredictable direction a debate might take. They also had to be more adept at performance than their counterparts in the courts, who presumably could not successfully depart from their prepared speeches. Demosthenes, as noted, seemed the exception to the rule. He put forward various excuses to explain his reluctance to speak extemporaneously: the audience's noise unnerved him; he preferred to speak on a subject only after he had written a speech about it; and as a democrat he needed time to prepare speeches, whereas impromptu speakers ignored the best interests of the people and favored oligarchy.[156] Yet when foreign

---

[151] C. A. Gibson, *Interpreting a Classic: Demosthenes and his Ancient Commentators* (Berkeley and Los Angeles: 2002). On Didymus (whose commentary survives on Demosthenes 9–10, 12, and the start of 13), see P. E. Harding, *Didymos: On Demosthenes* (Oxford: 2006); cf. R. D. Milns, "Didymea," in Ian Worthington (ed.), *Ventures into Greek History: Essays in Honour of N. G. L. Hammond* (Oxford: 1994), pp. 70–88. On Dionysius of Halicarnassus (who was primarily concerned with dating Demosthenes' speeches), see R. Sealey, "Dionysius of Halicarnassus and Some Demosthenic Dates," *REG* 68 (1955), pp. 77–120 (general comments on him on pp. 77–80), R. Lane Fox, "Demosthenes, Dionysius, and the Dating of Six Early Speeches," *Class. & Med.* 48 (1997), pp. 167–203 (general comments on him on pp. 171–176).

[152] Dionysius of Halicarnassus, *Isaeus* 20; see also Schaefer, *Demosthenes*² 1, pp. 316–320.

[153] Cicero, *Brutus* 35, Quintilian 10.1.76.

[154] Wooten, *Cicero's Philippics and Their Demosthenic Model*, exhaustively discusses Demosthenes' and Cicero's styles, and the influence of the former on the latter.

[155] Plutarch, *Demosthenes* 8.3–7, 10.1; contra [Plutarch], *Moralia* 848c, that he delivered most of his speeches extemporaneously, but that is highly doubtful. Note [Plutarch], *Moralia* 848c: Epicles rebukes Demosthenes for always preparing his speeches.

[156] Plutarch, *Demosthenes* 8.5–7.

envoys visited the city Demosthenes spoke extemporaneously and well.[157] Still, he was more at home with prepared speeches, so much so that the orator Pytheas said that these "smelled of the lamp," meaning that he had been up so late the night before that people could still smell the lamp wax on him.[158] Even so, there were still speakers who got the better of him, such as the influential general Phocion. Whenever Phocion prepared to speak against him, Demosthenes exclaimed "here comes the chopper of my speeches."[159]

The turbulent history of Greece, especially in the second half of the fourth century, which saw the rise to power of Philip II in Macedonia, provided Demosthenes with the means to acquire great political power. To these events we now turn.

[157] Plutarch, *Demosthenes* 9.1. Demosthenes' ability to speak off-the-cuff and the manner in which he did so is studied at length in a series of articles by A. P. Dorjahn: "Demosthenes' Ability to Speak Extemporaneously," *TAPA* 78 (1947), pp. 69–76, "A Further Study on Demosthenes' Ability to Speak Extemporaneously," *TAPA* 81 (1950), pp. 9–15, "A Third Study on Demosthenes' Ability to Speak Extemporaneously," *TAPA* 83 (1952), pp. 164–171, "A Fourth Study on Demosthenes' Ability to Speak Extemporaneously," *CP* 50 (1955), pp. 19–193 and "Extemporaneous Elements in Certain Orations and the *Prooemia* of Demosthenes," *AJP* 78 (1957), pp. 287–296. See also Pearson, "Virtuoso Passages in Demosthenes' Speeches," pp. 214–230.

[158] Plutarch, *Demosthenes* 8.4–5.

[159] Plutarch, *Demosthenes* 10.4.

3

Greece and the
Awakening of Macedonia

THE FALL AND RISE OF ATHENS

In the fifth century Athens was one of the wealthiest cities in Greece and headed a powerful naval empire, the Delian League. Declining relations with Sparta, the other military powerhouse of Greece, led to their fighting each other in the Peloponnesian War, which lasted from 431 to 404.[1] The Athenians had the most resources at the start of the war and enjoyed some military successes in it, but were forced in the end to capitulate to the Spartans, who imposed humiliating terms on them, including the dismantling of the Delian League and the establishment of a pro-Spartan oligarchy. Thus ended the days of Athens as an imperial leader.

The Spartans dominated affairs in Greece until 371, a period called the Spartan hegemony,[2] during which Demosthenes was born and raised. The Spartans, however, were unpopular leaders who disregarded the rights of their allies and were especially anxious about the military power of Thebes, the principal city of Boeotia. In an attempt to cripple Thebes, they seized its Cadmea (acropolis) in 382, installed a garrison in the city, and exiled 300 leading citizens.[3] The Thebans

---

[1] On the war, see D. Kagan, *The Peloponnesian War* (London: 2003) and L. Tritle, *The Peloponnesian War* (Westport: 2004).

[2] For an overview of this period, see P. Cartledge, *Agesilaos and the Crisis of Sparta* (Baltimore: 1987) and C. D. Hamilton, *Agesilaus and the Failure of Spartan Hegemony* (Ithaca: 1991); cf. J. Buckler, *Aegean Greece in the Fourth Century BC* (Leiden: 2003), pp. 12–295.

[3] Diodorus 20.20, Xenophon, *Hellenica* 5.2.28–31, Nepos, *Pelopidas* 1.2.

rightly protested this high-handed action, but to no avail. Then in 371 a Theban army led by the generals Epaminondas and Pelopidas brought the Spartans to battle at Leuctra (in Boeotia) and defeated them.[4] The Spartan hegemony was thereby replaced by a period of Theban dominance, which lasted until 362.[5]

The Thebans intended to end Spartan influence in Greece for good, so in 370 they invaded the Peloponnese and liberated the helots (slaves) of Messenia (in the southwest Peloponnese), who had been the economic backbone of the Spartan state since the mid-eighth century.[6] They rebuilt their capital Messene in Messenia and made alliances with several Peloponnesian states, which rebelled against Sparta. These included the towns of Arcadia in the northern Peloponnese, which formed an Arcadian League, recalled exiles banished by Sparta, and built a new capital, Megalopolis.[7]

Athens' citizen population had suffered a catastrophic decline of between 45 and 75 percent as a result of the Peloponnesian War, and needless to say its military power had been greatly diminished.[8] Nevertheless, its people were resilient. Some democrats who had fled into exile at the end of the war returned in 403 and expelled the pro-Spartan oligarchy, allowing the people to restore their previous democratic constitution. Over the next years the Athenians began to rebuild their shattered manpower and economy.[9] They also entered into an agreement

---

[4] Cf. G. L. Cawkwell, "Epaminondas and Thebes," *CQ*² 22 (1978), pp. 254–278, V. Hanson, "Epameinondas, the Battle of Leuktra and the 'Revolution' in Greek Battle Tactics," *Class. Antiquity* 7 (1988), pp. 190–207, J. Buckler, "Plutarch on Leuctra," in J. Buckler and H. Beck (eds.), *Central Greece and the Politics of Power in the Fourth Century BC* (Cambridge: 2008), pp. 111–126.

[5] J. Buckler, *The Theban Hegemony* (Cambridge: 1980); cf. Buckler, *Aegean Greece*, pp. 296–350, 359–366, and "Alliance and Hegemony in Fourth-Century Greece: The Case of the Theban Hegemony," in J. Buckler and H. Beck (eds.), *Central Greece and the Politics of Power in the Fourth Century BC* (Cambridge: 2008), pp. 127–139.

[6] Diodorus 15.62.3–66.1, Plutarch, *Pelopidas* 24, *Agesilaus* 34.1–2, Pausanias 4.27.5–8; on Messene: Diodorus 15.66.2 fin; on Epaminondas' campaigns, as part of a general Peloponnesian policy, see Buckler, *Theban Hegemony*, pp. 70–102 (cf. 233–242).

[7] Diodorus 15.72.3–4, Pausanias 8.27.1–8); cf. Buckler, *Theban Hegemony*, pp. 108–109.

[8] P. Hunt, *War, Peace, and Alliance in Demosthenes' Athens* (New York: 2010), p. 11.

[9] Cf. E. M. Burke, "Athens after the Peloponnesian War: Restoration Efforts and the Role of Maritime Commerce," *Class. Antiquity* 9 (1990), pp. 1–13.

with their traditional enemies the Thebans because of Spartan unpopularity,[10] so much so that in the midwinter of 379/8 they helped the Thebans expel the Spartan garrison from their city.[11] Their action caused the Spartan general Sphodrias to ravage Attica's border and attempt to seize the Athenian port of the Piraeus, prompting the Athenians to issue an invitation to other Greek states to join them in a league against Sparta. Formed in 378/7, the Second Athenian Confederacy (or League) as it became known, boasted some seventy allies from all over the Greek world at its height.[12]

The end of Spartan dominance in Greek affairs also brought about a collapse in the friendly relations between Athens and Thebes. When Pelopidas was killed during a campaign in Thessaly in 364, Epaminondas found himself in sole control of Theban policy. Suspicious of the growth of Athens' power, he planned to build one hundred triremes to use against the Athenian fleet.[13] He also made diplomatic overtures to the Athenian allies of Chios, Rhodes, and Byzantium. Probably Byzantium, an especially important ally because of its strategic position on the Hellespont (Dardanelles), which lay on the grain route to Greece from the Black Sea, seceded from the Athenian confederacy.[14] When in

---

[10] See J. Buckler, "A Survey of Theban and Athenian Relations between 403–371 BC," in J. Buckler and H. Beck (eds.), *Central Greece and the Politics of Power in the Fourth Century BC* (Cambridge: 2008), pp. 79–84.

[11] Diodorus 15.25 ff., Xenophon, *Hellenica* 5.4.1 ff., Plutarch, *Pelopidas* 7, 14.1, [Plutarch], *Moralia* 596 ff., Nepos, *Pelopidas* 2–3. Chronology: G. L. Cawkwell, "The Foundation of the Second Athenian Confederacy," CQ^2 23 (1973), pp. 56–57.

[12] J. Cargill, *The Second Athenian League* (Berkeley: 1981), Sealey, *Demosthenes*, pp. 52–73, Cawkwell, "Foundation of the Second Athenian Confederacy," pp. 56–60 and "Notes on the Failure of the Second Athenian Confederacy," *JHS* 101 (1981), pp. 40–54, G. T. Griffith, "Athens in the Fourth Century," in P. D. A. Garnsey and C. R. Whittaker (eds.), *Imperialism in the Ancient World* (Cambridge: 1978), pp. 127–144, J. Buckler, "Sphodrias' Raid and the Evolution of the Athenian League," in J. Buckler and H. Beck (eds.), *Central Greece and the Politics of Power in the Fourth Century BC* (Cambridge: 2008), pp. 79–84. For the charter of the confederacy, see below.

[13] A number that was still numerically inferior to Athens' triremes, which in 357 numbered 283 (*IG* ii² 1611, 9 and 1613, 302), and may have been higher in the 360s. By 353/2, the Athenians had 349 ships (*IG* ii² 1613, 302), and 292 ships in 330 (*IG* ii² 1627, 266); see further, G. L. Cawkwell, "Athenian Naval Power in the Fourth Century," CQ^2 34 (1984), pp. 334–345, J. S. Morrison, "Athenian Sea-Power in 323/2 BC: Dream and Reality," *JHS* 107 (1987), pp. 88–97.

[14] Diodorus 15.79.1; cf. E. Badian, "The Road to Prominence," in Ian Worthington (ed.), *Demosthenes: Statesman and Orator* (London: 2000), p. 26.

the summer of 362 Epaminondas warned of moving the Propylaea (the monumental gateway to the Athenian Acropolis) to the Theban Cadmea,[15] signaling that he intended to subjugate Athens, the Athenians struck hard and fast. With the support of troops from Sparta, Elis, and Achaea, they engaged the Thebans in battle at Mantinea and defeated them, killing Epaminondas in the fighting.[16]

Thus, a little over forty years after the Athenians' massive defeat in the Peloponnesian War, the pendulum of power in Greece swung back in their favor. For the first few years of their confederacy they abided by the terms of its charter, which survives.[17] They swore oaths to respect their allies' rights and not to return to the unpopular practices of their fifth-century empire: levying a tribute, installing garrisons and governors in allied towns, and founding cleruchies (settlements of Athenian citizens that took over towns and territories displacing the native population). As time passed, however, the Athenians abused their oaths, among other things establishing cleruchies and levying a tribute, which they euphemistically named "contributions" (*syntaxeis*).[18] Eventually, in 356, a number of allies revolted in what is called the Social War, which ended in Athenian defeat and financial ruin the following year (see below). The league continued to exist, but it was a shadow of its former self.

For much of his childhood, then, Demosthenes lived under Spartan hegemony. He was about seven years old when the Athenians founded their confederacy in 378 and fourteen when the Spartan hegemony ended. As a young man he experienced firsthand the threat to Athens from Thebes as well as the role of Peloponnesian affairs in Athenian policy, and he was thirty on the outbreak of the Social War. The ambitions of Sparta and Thebes continued to be a source of concern for the Athenians as Demosthenes' early political speeches demonstrated (Chapter 5).

Demosthenes also experienced firsthand the rise to power in the Greek world of Macedonia, north of Mount Olympus (Map 3). In 359, when he was in his mid-twenties, Philip II became its king.

[15] Aeschines 2.105.
[16] Buckler, *Theban Hegemony*, pp. 213–219.
[17] See P. J. Rhodes and R. Osborne (eds.), *Greek Historical Inscriptions, 404–323 BC* (Oxford: 2003), no. 22 (pp. 92–105), citing bibliography.
[18] F. Mitchel, "The Assessment of the Allies in the Second Athenian League," *EMC* 3 (1984), pp. 23–37.

A mere two decades later, in 338, Philip defeated the Greeks in battle at Chaeronea, bringing an end to Greek autonomy.[19] Demosthenes eventually devoted all his energy to the danger Philip posed to Greece, which would bring him great political power and oratorical fame.[20]

MACEDONIA AND THE MACEDONIANS

Mount Olympus, the largest mountain in Greece (9,461 feet), was the border in antiquity between Macedonia and Greece. The Greeks called the Macedonians "barbarians" throughout the archaic and classical periods, a term that had nothing to do with their cultural tastes but simply indicated they did not speak Greek.[21] The Macedonians in fact were a civilized people whose craftsmen produced exquisite gold, silver, and bronze artworks, whose painters brilliantly decorated the walls of tombs, and whose superb mosaics easily rival any that the Romans produced (Figure 4).[22] The ethnicity of the ancient Macedonians is

---

[19] On his reign in detail, see N.G.L. Hammond and G.T. Griffith, *A History of Macedonia* 2 (Oxford: 1979), J.R. Ellis, *Philip II and Macedonian Imperialism* (London: 1976), G.L. Cawkwell, *Philip of Macedon* (London: 1978), N.G.L. Hammond, *Philip of Macedon* (London: 1994), Worthington, *Philip II* and *By the Spear. Philip II, Alexander the Great, and the Rise and Fall of the Macedonian Empire* (New York: 2014) (also comparing and contrasting him to Alexander the Great). For the focus on Philip as general and tactician, see R. A. Gabriel, *Philip II of Macedon: Greater than Alexander* (Washington: 2010). See also E. N. Borza, *In the Shadow of Olympus: The Emergence of Macedon* (Princeton: 1990), pp. 198–230 and R. M. Errington, *A History of Macedonia*, transl. C. Errington (Berkeley: 1990), pp. 38–91; a succinct yet thorough treatment is S. Müller, "Philip II," in J. Roisman and Ian Worthington (eds.), *Blackwell Companion to Ancient Macedonia* (Malden: 2010), pp. 166–185.

[20] Demosthenes and Philip: T. T. B. Ryder, "Demosthenes and Philip II," in Ian Worthington (ed.), *Demosthenes: Statesman and Orator* (London: 2000), pp. 45–89.

[21] Cf. Thucydides 2.80.5, Isocrates 4.3, Demosthenes 15.15, Dinarchus 1.24. On the origins of the word, cf. Strabo 142.28.

[22] See further, M. Andronikos, "Art During the Archaic and Classical Periods," and J. Touratsoglou, "Art in the Hellenistic Period," in M. B. Sakellariou (ed.), *Macedonia, 4000 Years of Greek History and Civilization* (Athens: 1983), pp. 92–110 and 170–191, respectively. See also C. L. Hardiman, "Classical Art to 221 BC," in J. Roisman and Ian Worthington (eds.), *Blackwell Companion to Ancient Macedonia* (Malden: 2010), pp. 505–521.

FIGURE 4. Early Hellenistic mosaic from Pella supposedly depicting a young Alexander the Great on a lion hunt.

controversial because of the nature of the evidence. There are no Macedonian written records, and the Greek sources are naturally biased.[23] On balance, however, the evidence supports a belief that the Macedonians were Greek, and so Greek-speaking.[24] They probably spoke a local dialect, which the other Greeks did not understand.[25]

[23] On the Greeks' perceptions of Macedonians as barbarians from the fifth century to the age of Alexander the Great, see E. Badian, "Greeks and Macedonians," in B. Barr-Sharrar and E. N. Borza (eds.), *Macedonia and Greece in Late Classical and Early Hellenistic Times* (Washington: 1982), pp. 33–51. See also now S. Asirvatham, "Perspectives on the Macedonians from Greece, Rome, and Beyond," in J. Roisman and Ian Worthington (eds.), *Blackwell Companion to Ancient Macedonia* (Malden: 2010), pp. 99–124.

[24] Summarized at Worthington, *Philip II*, pp. 216–219, quoting bibliography, to which add C. Karvounis, *Demosthenes: Studien zu den Demegorien orr. XIV, XVI, XV, IV, I, II, III* (Tübingen: 2002), pp. 261–286 and J. Engels, "Macedonians and Greeks," in J. Roisman and Ian Worthington (eds.), *Blackwell Companion to Ancient Macedonia* (Malden: 2010), pp. 81–98, citing bibliography.

[25] Cf. N. G. L. Hammond, "Literary Evidence for Macedonian Speech," *Historia* 43 (1994), pp. 131–142. As I have done elsewhere in my work, when I refer to "Greeks" in this book I mean the people who lived south of Mount Olympus, and when I refer to "Macedonians" I mean those living to its north. I do so only for the sake of convenience.

Before Philip came to the throne in 359, Macedonia was weak, disunited, and a political and economic backwater.[26] The kingdom was separated into two parts by the Pindus mountain range (Map 3). Upper Macedonia was to the west and Lower Macedonia, extending to the Thermaic Gulf, including the capital Pella, was to the east.[27] Lower Macedonia had a warm climate and, in contrast to much of Greece, rich, fertile soil and well-watered plains. These conditions allowed the people there to grow cereal crops, vegetables, grapes, and fruits, as well as to graze their sheep, goats, cattle, and horses. Upper Macedonia, the larger of the two parts, was an area of remote cantons where life was more a matter of survival. Here lived mostly nomadic peoples belonging to different tribes. Winters were harsh, so the people moved their flocks of sheep and goats and herds of cattle to different areas for pasture, including Lower Macedonia. The kingdom had abundant silver, gold, copper, iron, and lead deposits as well as dense forests of oak, pine, fir, and cedar.[28] The size of Macedonia's population is unknown, but an estimate puts the figure at the end of Philip's reign (who more than doubled Macedonia's size) at 500,000.[29] When Philip died, Macedonia consisted of modern Greece, the modern Republic of Macedonia, much of Albania, most of Bulgaria, and all of European Turkey.[30]

There was considerable dissension between the two parts of Macedonia, and the people of the upper part showed little loyalty to the king at Pella. Archelaus, a king who ruled from 413 to 399, had attempted

---

[26] Macedonia before Philip in a nutshell: Worthington, *Philip II*, pp. 220–225. In more detail: N. G. L. Hammond, *A History of Macedonia* 1 (Oxford: 1972) and Hammond and Griffith, *History of Macedonia* 2, pp. 3–200, Borza, *Shadow of Olympus*, pp. 3–197, Errington, *History of Macedonia*, pp. 1–38. See also S. Sprawski, "From the Bronze Age to Alexander I," and J. Roisman, "Classical Macedonia to Perdiccas III," in J. Roisman and Ian Worthington (eds.), *Blackwell Companion to Ancient Macedonia* (Malden: 2010), pp. 127–144 and 145–165, respectively.

[27] Thucydides 2.99.1–3. Nowadays, what used to be Lower Macedonia and the southern area of Upper Macedonia are in Greece, while the remainder of Upper Macedonia is in the independent Republic of Macedonia (previously Serbia, then Yugoslavia).

[28] E. N. Borza, "The Natural Resources of Early Macedonia," in W. L. Adams and E. N. Borza (eds.), *Philip II, Alexander the Great, and the Macedonian Heritage* (Lanham: 1982), pp. 1–20 and *Shadow of Olympus*, pp. 50–57.

[29] Ellis, *Philip II*, p. 34; cf. Hammond, *History of Macedonia* 1, pp. 12–18.

[30] On the early extent of Macedonia and its geographical expansion under later kings, including Philip, see C. G. Thomas, "The Physical Kingdom," in J. Roisman and Ian Worthington (eds.), *Blackwell Companion to Ancient Macedonia* (Malden: 2010), pp. 65–80.

FIGURE 5. Pella, the capital of Macedonia from 399.

to unite his kingdom, but had failed. He did, however, introduce a series of beneficial military and economic reforms and moved the capital from Aegae (modern Vergina) to Pella, several miles to Aegae's northeast (Figure 5).[31]

Aegae, however, continued to be the traditional venue for royal weddings and burials. Archelaus' achievements were quickly undone because of a rapid succession of dynastic problems that brought at least five kings to power in six years. Then in 393/2 Amyntas III, Philip II's father, succeeded to the throne by murdering his opponents.[32] He

[31] Thucydides 2.100.2: Archelaus "organized his country for war by providing cavalry, arms, and other equipment beyond anything achieved by all of the eight kings who preceded him." On the place for the new capital, see P. B. Faklaris, "Aegae: Determining the Site of the First Capital of the Macedonians," *AJA* 98 (1994), pp. 609–616. Identification of Aegae with Vergina: N. G. L. Hammond, *History of Macedonia* 1, pp. 156–157 and "The Location of Aegae," *JHS* 117 (1997), pp. 177–179. On Pella, see Worthington, *Philip II*, pp. 226–227.

[32] Diodorus 14.89.2; on Amyntas, see Hammond and Griffith, *History of Macedonia* 2, pp. 172–180, Borza, *Shadow of Olympus*, pp. 180–189, Errington, *History of Macedonia*, pp. 29–34. See further, W. S. Greenwalt, "Amyntas III and the Political Stability of Argead Macedonia," *Anc. World* 18 (1988), pp. 35–44.

ruled until 369, but at one point had to flee his kingdom because of an invasion by the neighboring Illyrian tribes to the northwest. Chaos continued to plague Macedonia even after his return, and his son Alexander II, who became king in 369, was assassinated the following year. Fortunately, in 365 Perdiccas III assumed the throne and created some stability in the country.

Added to the problems within Macedonia were those that came from outside it. Bordering tribes, especially those of the Illyrians to the northwest (in the western Balkan peninsula) and Paeonians to the north (in the Axius valley), who were more than a match for the poorly trained conscript army, raided Macedonia for livestock, crops, and possibly timber.[33] Various foreign states also interfered in Macedonia's domestic affairs, including Athens, Thebes, and, to Macedonia's east, Thracian kings and the Chalcidian League, headed by Olynthus (Map 2).[34] All of them at different stages in Macedonia's history supported pretenders to the throne, since they coveted, among other things, Macedonia's rich timber reserves.[35] In 437, the Athenians, for example, had founded the colony of Amphipolis, located on the border of Macedonia and Thrace and close to several trade and communication routes, to protect their access to timber (Map 2).

The king and an Assembly of male citizens exercised political power in Macedonia, but in practice the king ruled absolutely and did not need to heed the Assembly's decisions.[36] Always a warrior king who led the army in battle, he decided domestic and foreign policy, including waging wars and all fiscal matters. He was the final judge in cases of appeal and the chief priest, performing daily sacrifices for the continued well-being of the state. The most important duties of the Assembly were to judge treason cases and to acclaim the new king. On the latter occasions, the men dressed in full armor and clashed their spears on their shields.

---

[33] On the Illyrians, see J. Wilkes, *The Illyrians* (Oxford: 1995).

[34] A good overview of these problems is given by N. G. L. Hammond, *The Macedonian State* (Oxford 1992), pp. 89–99.

[35] E. N. Borza, "Timber and Politics in the Ancient World. Macedon and the Greeks," *Proceedings of the American Philosophical Society* 131 (1987), pp. 32–52.

[36] See further, C. J. King, "Kingship and Other Political Institutions," in J. Roisman and Ian Worthington (eds.), *Blackwell Companion to Ancient Macedonia* (Malden: 2010), pp. 374–391, citing bibliography.

There were many social, cultural, and political differences between the Macedonians and the Greeks.[37] The Greeks believed that their system of independent city-states, or poleis (polis in the singular), was the ideal type of political, economic, and social structure, and therefore anyone ruled by a king was ignorant. In practice, however the polis system had major flaws. The individuality of each city led to feelings of superiority over other poleis and even distrust of other Greeks. The poleis were unable to unite effectively, especially against a common foe, and more often than not were at war with each other. Philip cunningly exploited these weaknesses as he played off one city against another to dominate Greece.

The Macedonians practiced polygamy, which the Greeks deplored. Philip married seven times without ever divorcing a wife, his first six marriages being for political and military reasons—as one ancient writer states, he "made war by marriage."[38] Polygamy increased the chances of heirs to succeed the king,[39] but it also caused social problems and even dissension among the queens.[40] Philip's fourth wife Olympias (the mother of Alexander the Great) apparently hated his seventh and last wife (Cleopatra), and that marriage may have been a factor in his assassination in 336 (Chapter 11 pp. 269–270).

The Greeks' social snobbery is evidenced by their contempt of the Macedonians for drinking their wine neat (*akratos*). To Greeks, only "barbarians" drank their wine *akratos*; they themselves mixed theirs with water,[41] a practice that affected behavior at their symposia (drinking parties), which began with the attendees discussing politics, literature, and philosophy while eating and drinking mixed wine. Dancing girls performed, and as the evening wore on made themselves available sexually to the men. Macedonian symposia were far rowdier from the outset because of the unmixed wine. One writer claims that

---

[37] See further, N. Sawada, "Macedonian Social Customs," in J. Roisman and Ian Worthington (eds.), *Blackwell Companion to Ancient Macedonia* (Malden: 2010), pp. 392–408, citing bibliography.

[38] Athenaeus 13.557b–e for Philip's marriages.

[39] Cf. W. S. Greenwalt, "Polygamy and Succession in Argead Macedonia," *Arethusa* 22 (1989), pp. 19–45.

[40] See E. D. Carney, *Women and Monarchy in Macedonia* (Norman: 2000), pp. 23–27, 29–31; cf. Hammond, *Macedonian State*, pp. 31–36.

[41] For ratios (not always 50–50) and the strength of the wine (15–16 percent as opposed to the contemporary 12.5 percent), see J. Davidson, *Courtesans and Fishcakes* (London: 1997), p. 40.

the Macedonians "were drunk while they were still being served their first courses, and could not enjoy their food."[42] Demosthenes, who visited Philip at Pella in 346, complained that his court was teeming with drunkards and lowlifes and—conveniently ignoring the degeneracy of Athenian symposia when intellectual talk ended—accused everyone of all manner of debauchery:[43]

> [Their] drunken dancing is so vile that I shrink from describing it to you. And this is clearly true: for those men whom everyone drove away from here for being far more disgusting than conjurers, that public slave Callias and men of his stamp, pantomime actors of the ridiculous and poets of shameful songs, which they compose for their associates in order to raise a laugh—these are the men [Philip] loves and keeps about himself.

His picture is deliberately distorted because he wanted to present Philip in the worst light possible. Still, Philip was a ferocious drinker,[44] as was his son Alexander (the Great), who held drinking contests lasting days and then "would sleep without waking for two days and two nights."[45]

As a people, the Macedonians were like the warriors of Homeric society—tough, quick to fight, enjoying the company of women, and drinking heavily when the opportunity arose. Their rugged culture embraced all manner of exacting trials. For example, for a man to

[42] Ephippus, *FGrH* 126 F 1 = Athenaeus 3.120e. Macedonian symposia: R. A. Tomlinson, "Ancient Macedonian Symposia," *Ancient Macedonia* 1 (Institute for Balkan Studies, Thessaloniki: 1970), pp. 308–315, E. N. Borza, "The Symposium at Alexander's Court," *Ancient Macedonia* 3 (Institute for Balkan Studies, Thessaloniki: 1983), pp. 45–55, Sawada, "Macedonian Social Customs," pp. 393–399, F. Pownall, "The Symposia of Philip II and Alexander III of Macedon: The View from Greece," in E. D. Carney and D. Ogden (eds.), *Philip II and Alexander the Great: Lives and Afterlives* (Oxford: 2010), pp. 55–65.

[43] Demosthenes 2.19. Theopompus, *FGrH* 115 FF 163, 224–225 (Philip's court), 236, 282, makes heavy drinking part and parcel of Macedonian society. Demosthenes the teetotaler: Demosthenes 6.30, 19.46, [Plutarch], *Moralia* 848c.

[44] Theopompus, *FGrH* 115 F 282 (he often attacked an enemy when drunk, although this can hardly be true); cf. F 236.

[45] *Ephemerides*, *FGrH* 117 F 2b = Athenaeus 10.434b. These kings were not alcoholics in the modern sense of the term, but more like binge drinkers. On the misuse of the modern term "alcoholism," cf. Davidson, *Courtesans and Fishcakes*, pp. 147–148; on drinking in the ancient world, see pp. 36–69.

recline at a symposium while he ate and drank he had to have speared a boar without using a net. This custom probably evoked the slaying of the Erymanthian boar, one of the famous labors of Heracles, whom the Macedonians accepted as one of their ancestors. Another custom was that a Macedonian soldier wore a rope around his waist until he had slain his first opponent in battle, thereby encouraging him to fight harder to prove his courage. The king was no different from the rest of the men in these respects. It is little wonder that with customs like these boys were trained to fight, ride a horse, and hunt from an early age.

The Macedonians embraced their differences from the Greeks, in particular their hard-living, hard-drinking image, with gusto.[46] At the same time, Philip knew what the Greeks thought of his people, and that knowledge must have inflamed his dealings with them when he was king.

PHILIP AND THE AWAKENING OF MACEDONIA

Philip was born in either 383 or 382.[47] His father was Amyntas III and his mother Eurydice, a princess of the royal house of Lyncestis in Upper Macedonia.[48] They also had two more sons and a daughter. His father married a second time, to Gygaea, who bore him three sons and a daughter. All six sons were in line for the throne, but, as today, the eldest took precedence. Philip's two brothers reigned as Alexander II (369–368) and Perdiccas III (365–359). His half-brothers were never kings since Philip killed one of them as soon as he took the throne and the other two a decade later.

Little is known about Philip's youth because ancient writers were less concerned with him than with his more famous son, Alexander the Great. Only two, much later, narrative histories of Philip survive, one by the first-century BC Greek historian Diodorus Siculus (of Sicily) and the other by Justin, who sometime between the second and fourth centuries AD wrote an epitome (condensed account) of a first-century BC work by Pompeius Trogus.[49] Of contemporary writers, the

---

[46] J. M. Hall, "Contested Ethnicities: Perceptions of Macedonia within Evolving Definitions of Greek Identity," in I. Malkin (ed.), *Ancient Perceptions of Greek Ethnicity* (Cambridge: 2001), pp. 159–186.

[47] Pausanias 8.7.6, Justin 9.8.1.

[48] Diodorus 16.1.3.

[49] On the sources, see Worthington, *Philip II*, p. 210–215.

speeches of Aeschines and Demosthenes provide information about Philip, although those of his opponent Demosthenes are particularly biased.

Philip was brought up in traditional Macedonian fashion, learning to hunt, ride a horse, and fight at a young age. He was also taught to read and write, and he had a keen appreciation of not only his own but also Greek culture. He was an intellectual, who was courted by philosophers such as Speusippus, Plato's successor as head of the Academy, and he hired Aristotle to tutor his son and heir Alexander. Philip lived up to the expectations of a warrior king, always leading his army into battle, and suffering the loss of an eye, a shattered collarbone, and a nearly fatal wound to his leg that caused him to limp for the rest of his life. The reconstructed face from the skull fragments discovered in what is probably his tomb testifies to the life he led (Figure 2, p. 4). He was also blessed with extraordinary diplomatic and political prowess as well as brilliant strategic and tactical skills. Throughout his reign, his preference was to try to settle disputes with the Greeks by diplomacy rather than military action.[50]

Philip's education and indeed life were interrupted when from age thirteen to fifteen he was held as a hostage in Thebes.[51] However, he gained valuable insight into Theban military training while there, which proved beneficial to his military reforms and tactics when he became king. Philip returned home to Pella in probably 365, shortly after his brother Perdiccas III became king. Perdiccas appointed him governor of part of his kingdom, perhaps Amphaxitis, which stretched from the Axius to the Thermaic Gulf, with orders to defend it against Thracian and Paeonian invasions.[52] He was also married for the first

---

[50] Diplomacy versus military action: T. T. B. Ryder, "The Diplomatic Skills of Philip II," in Ian Worthington (ed.), *Ventures into Greek History: Essays in Honour of N. G. L. Hammond* (Oxford: 1994), pp. 228–257 and G. L. Cawkwell, "The End of Greek Liberty," in R. W. Wallace and E. M. Harris (eds.), *Transitions to Empire: Essays in Honor of E. Badian* (Norman: 1996), pp. 98–121. Military prowess: G. T. Griffith, "Philip as a General and the Macedonian Army," in M. B. Hatzopoulos and L. D. Loukopoulos (eds.), *Philip of Macedon* (Athens: 1980), pp. 58–77.

[51] In 368, Philip's brother Alexander II had been forced to call on the Thebans for help when another member of the royal house, Ptolemy, challenged his kingship. The Theban general Pelopidas supported Alexander as king, but to ensure his dependency on Thebes Pelopidas took Philip and other noble sons as hostages: Diodorus 15.61, 67.4, 16.2.2–3, Plutarch, *Pelopidas* 26.4–5, Justin 6.9.7, 7.5.1–3.

[52] Cf. Athenaeus 11.506f.

time, to Phila, the daughter of Derdas II of Elimeia, perhaps as part of a treaty to bind Macedonia and Elimeia closer together.[53]

In 359 Perdiccas III and 4,000 Macedonian soldiers were killed in battle against an invading Illyrian tribe led by its octogenarian chieftain Bardylis.[54] The Illyrians then advanced on Lower Macedonia while the Paeonians mobilized to invade Macedonia. In the confusion following Perdiccas' death, the king of western Thrace, Berisades, and the Athenians each supported pretenders to the throne since Perdiccas' son Amyntas was only a minor.[55] The Macedonian Assembly had the option of appointing Amyntas' twenty-four-year-old uncle Philip, given his military and administrative experience in Amphaxitis, as his regent. However, the severity of the threats facing Macedonia called for more drastic action. The Assembly therefore set Amyntas aside and acclaimed Philip as king, at which point the people swore their customary oath of allegiance to him.[56] Philip took no action against Amyntas, but to prevent possible opposition from his half-brothers he ordered their executions. Archelaus, probably the eldest, was killed, but the other two escaped his clutches for the moment.[57]

The four external threats to Macedonia were arguably the most serious the kingdom had ever faced, but Philip "was not panic-stricken by the magnitude of the expected perils, but, bringing together the Macedonians in a series of assemblies and exhorting them with eloquent speeches to be men, he built up their morale."[58] He knew he could not face all of them militarily so he decided to deal with each one diplomatically to buy time.[59] This would be a pattern in his dealings with opponents throughout his reign.

The Illyrians were the greatest menace, so Philip dealt with them first. He must have reached some sort of arrangement with them, for not only did they suddenly return home but also he married Bardylis' granddaughter Audata (his second wife).[60] The Illyrian chieftain perhaps

[53] Athenaeus 13.557c (from Satyrus). On Phila, see Carney, *Women and Monarchy*, pp. 59–60.
[54] Diodorus 15.71.1, 77.5, 16.2.4–5.
[55] Justin 7.5.8 calls him a *parvulus* (infant).
[56] Discussion at Worthington, *Philip II*, pp. 20–22.
[57] Diodorus 16.2.6, Justin 8.3.10; see also J. R. Ellis, "The Stepbrothers of Philip II," *Historia* 22 (1973), pp. 353–354.
[58] Diodorus 16.3.1.
[59] Justin 7.6.4–5. For Philip's actions in detail, see Worthington, *Philip II*, pp. 23–25.
[60] Athenaeus 13.557c; see further, Carney, *Women and Monarchy*, pp. 57–58.

anticipated that his new son-in-law would provide him with supplies without having to invade Macedonia again.

Philip then turned to the threat from the Paeonians and simply bribed them to abandon their campaign.[61] Presumably expecting that Philip would give them money whenever they decided to invade Macedonia, the Paeonians also returned to their homes. Philip also bribed Berisades of Thrace to abandon his pretender, who was executed.[62] For the moment he did not need to worry about further Thracian involvement in Macedonia because of disunity in Thrace itself. On the death of the Thracian king Cotys shortly before Philip became king, his three sons divided up Thrace among themselves. Berisades became king of the western part (from the Strymon river to Maroneia), Amadocus ruled the central part (Maroneia to the river Hebrus), and Cersebleptes the eastern part (Hebrus to the Chersonese).[63] These kings viewed each other suspiciously and had little interest in Macedonian affairs at this time.

In a matter of weeks, Philip had neutralized three of the dangers facing Macedonia. That left only the Athenians, whose pretender, a man named Argaeus, was a more serious threat than the Thracian-backed one.[64] He had landed at Methone on the Thermaic Gulf with 3,000 troops, intent on marching on Aegae. Here he hoped to find nobles who were against Philip becoming king and therefore sympathetic to his cause. How Philip dealt with Argaeus was a classic combination of diplomacy and deceit involving the Athenian colony of Amphipolis. In 424, during the Peloponnesian War, Amphipolis had defected from the Athenian empire, and from then on it resisted the Athenians' attempts bring it back under their control. When Perdiccas III installed a Macedonian garrison in the city to help protect it, the Athenians' chances of recovering their colony appeared even slimmer. They were backing Argaeus now not because they wanted to control Macedonia but because they were relying on him to return Amphipolis to them if his attempt were successful.

Philip withdrew the Macedonian garrison from Amphipolis, thereby encouraging the Athenians to think he was conceding any

---

[61] Diodorus 16.3.4.

[62] Diodorus 16.3.4, Justin 7.6.1–4.

[63] Threefold division of Thrace: Rhodes and Osborne, *Greek Historical Inscriptions*, no. 47, with commentary.

[64] J. Heskel, "Philip II and Argaios: A Pretender's Story," in R. W. Wallace and E. M. Harris (eds.), *Transitions to Empire, Essays in Honor of E. Badian* (Norman: 1996), pp. 37–56.

claim to it. The Athenians fell for the trick and ordered their soldiers to hold fast at Methone. Some of them nevertheless set out with Argaeus to Aegae but failed to find any support there. As they returned to Methone, Philip attacked them and captured Argaeus, who disappeared from history.[65] The king then sent a letter to Athens seeking an alliance and as a goodwill gesture he released the Athenian soldiers he had captured with Argaeus.[66] The Athenians were debating a request for an alliance from Olynthus, which considered that Philip posed a danger to its interests in the region. However, they turned down the Olynthians in light of Philip's offer and made an alliance with him, although they insisted that he not claim Amphipolis for himself.[67]

In less than a year, Philip had rescued Macedonia from four very real threats to its border security and internal stability. In the process, he displayed a masterful combination of speed, diplomacy, and deception, which set a pattern for his reign and which Demosthenes later contrasted unfavorably to the indifference of the Athenians and slowness of the Assembly in making its decisions.[68]

A NEW ARMY

Philip now embarked on an ambitious reform of the Macedonian military. While a hostage in Thebes he had lived in the house of the general and statesman Pammenes, a personal friend of the brilliant Epaminondas.[69] Despite his youth, Philip learned much of the strategy and tactics he later displayed when he was king, including shock tactics and combining infantry and cavalry in battle. He may even have trialed some of the military lessons he had learned to protect Amphaxitis when he was appointed its governor.

---

[65] Diodorus 16.3.5; cf. Demosthenes 23.121.

[66] Demosthenes 23.121, Diodorus 16.3.4, Justin 7.6.

[67] Theopompus, *FGrH* 115 F 42; cf. Demosthenes 1.8–9. See also Heskel, "Philip II and Argaos," pp. 50–51.

[68] Demosthenes 19.184ff., 227–228. See also Demosthenes 1.12–13, quoted in Chapter 5 p. 127.

[69] Diodorus 15.61, 67, 16.2.2–3, Plutarch, *Pelopidas* 18, 26.4–5, Justin 6.9.7, 7.5.1–3; cf. Plutarch, *Pelopidas* 26.5. On Philip in Thebes, see Worthington, *Philip II*, pp. 17–19. Philip's military reforms: Hammond and Griffith, *History of Macedonia* 2, pp. 405–449, Worthington, *Philip II*, pp. 26–32, Gabriel, *Philip II of Macedon*, pp. 62–92.

Philip's military reforms included new tactics, weaponry, and training. In battle the customary tactic was for the Greek hoplite infantry to attack the enemy line prior to a cavalry charge. Philip, however, trained his cavalry to assail the enemy flanks first to cause maximum disruption to them while his infantry—massed together in the various battalions that made up the phalanx—charged the enemy's center. The cavalry very often wheeled around behind the enemy line, thereby opening up gaps in it that the Macedonian infantrymen were able to penetrate.

Weaponry innovations included replacing the customary short infantry sword for stabbing with the deadly sarissa, a pike fourteen feet long with a pointed iron head, which needed both hands to wield it.[70] A small shield (*pelta*) that the infantryman carried was slung over his shoulder because he needed both hands for his sarissa. These long weapons were carried upright when the infantry were marching, and lowered, five ranks at a time, when the Macedonians engaged enemy soldiers and in jabbing motions impaled them (Figure 6). Philip was also responsible for innovations in siege machinery. In about 350, he formed an engineering corps that among other things developed the torsion catapult, replacing the mechanically drawn catapult.[71]

Philip intended his army to be self-sufficient. He taught his men to carry their own arms, armor, and food, as well as to forage for food in different terrains. He ended the old system of conscript farmers, who returned to their farms when campaigning ended, by making military service a full-time occupation, and introduced regular pay and even a promotion pathway that allowed men to rise from the ranks to more senior positions and a rewards system that included grants of land.[72] His army was thus composed of highly trained professionals, who were also able to train constantly and became highly feared within a few

---

[70] On the sarissa, see especially N. V. Sekunda, "The Sarissa," *Acta Universitatis Lodziensis, Folia Archaeologica* 23 (2001), pp. 13–41; see also N. G. L. Hammond, "Training in the Use of the Sarissa and Its Effect in Battle 359–333 BC," *Antichthon* 14 (1980), pp. 53–63.

[71] E. W. Marsden, "Macedonian Military Machinery and its Designers under Philip and Alexander," *Ancient Macedonia* 2 (Institute for Balkan Studies, Thessaloniki: 1977), pp. 211–223; cf. P. T. Keyser, "The Use of Artillery by Philip II and Alexander the Great," *Anc. World* 15 (1994), pp. 27–49, Gabriel, *Philip II of Macedon*, pp. 88–92.

[72] In 354, Philip divided the land of Methone among his men (Diodorus 16.34.5), and Alexander the Great gave land to his men (Plutarch, *Alexander* 15.4–6).

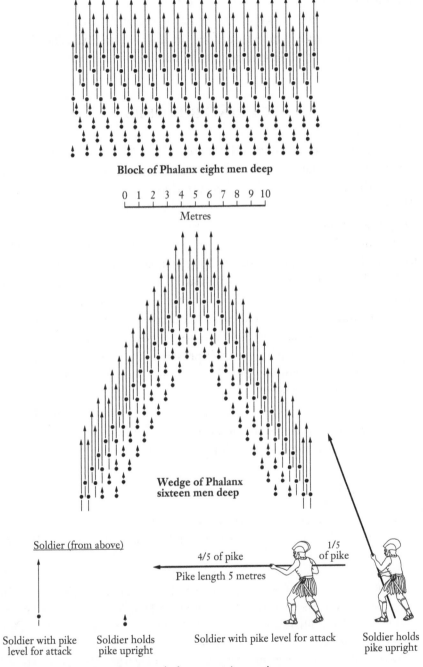

Block of Phalanx eight men deep

0 1 2 3 4 5 6 7 8 9 10
Metres

**Wedge of Phalanx
sixteen men deep**

Soldier (from above)

4/5 of pike

1/5
of pike

Pike length 5 metres

Soldier with pike
level for attack

Soldier holds
pike upright

Soldier with pike level for attack

Soldier holds
pike upright

FIGURE 6. The Macedonian phalanx carrying sarissas.

short years. When Philip began his reforms in 359 he could muster only 10,000 infantry and 600 cavalry.[73] On his death in 336 his army numbered 24,000 infantry and 3,000 cavalry.[74]

After only a year as king, Philip was sufficiently satisfied with his new army to lead it against the foes on his borders. Macedonia, the dormant giant of the Balkan peninsula, was about to be wakened.[75]

SECURING BORDERS

Philip did not intend to be at the mercy of the Illyrians and Paeonians for any longer than necessary. In the spring of 358 he marched first against the Paeonians, perhaps because they were not as formidable as the Illyrians, defeating them in battle (the details are unknown). His victory absorbed Paeonia into Macedonia, giving him a buffer between his northeast border and the tribes of the Danube as well as opening up for him the northern trade route along the Axius valley to Dardania.

Next he invaded Illyria, bringing Bardylis to battle somewhere in the vicinity of Lake Lychnitis (Ochrid) or Heraclea Lyncestis (Monastir).[76] The Macedonian infantry and cavalry routed the Illyrians, killing 7,000 of them including Bardylis.[77] Philip could now impose terms on the Illyrians, who were to abandon their presence in Upper Macedonia and withdraw to their own domains. He continued to face dissension from the Illyrians throughout his reign, prompting his military intervention.[78] Nevertheless, his victory over them allowed him to unite Lower and Upper Macedonia for the first time in the kingdom's history, and he followed it with the construction of new towns along his western

---

[73] Diodorus 16.4.3.

[74] Diodorus 17.17.5.

[75] The description of this sentence is that of Buckler, *Aegean Greece*, p. 387.

[76] See N. G. L. Hammond, "The Battle between Philip and Bardylis," *Antichthon* 23 (1989), pp. 1–9.

[77] Diodorus 16.4, Wilkes, *The Illyrians*, p. 120.

[78] A. B. Bosworth, "Philip II and Upper Macedonia," *CQ²* 21 (1971), pp. 93–105. On relations between Macedonia and Illyria, including Philip's reign, see W. S. Greenwalt, "Macedonia, Illyria and Epirus," in J. Roisman and Ian Worthington (eds.), *Blackwell Companion to Ancient Macedonia* (Malden: 2010), pp. 279–305. Justin 11.1.1–6 refers to the danger from "the Illyrians, the Thracians, the Dardanians, and the other barbarian tribes" when Philip was assassinated in 336. Demosthenes indicates dissent in *Olynthiac* 2 (of 349) among these men at being part of the Macedonian army: Pickard-Cambridge, *Demosthenes*, p. 152.

frontier and a more rigorous exploitation of the area's rich silver mines. Indeed, the unification of Macedonia was arguably his most outstanding achievement.[79] It permitted him to attract the loyalty of all Macedonians to Pella as the capital of Macedonia and introduce all his other reforms, especially those that benefited the economy.[80]

In the same year (358), Philip marched south into the bordering state of Thessaly. This large, fertile area was home to the finest horses in Greece, which Philip used for his cavalry. By this period, two cities dominated affairs in Thessaly: Larissa, which because of its control of the states of the inland plain headed a Thessalian League and had enjoyed close contacts with Macedonian kings for some time, and Pherae (Velestino), which dominated the coastal states because of its nearby harbor Pagasae (Volos). In the 370s, Pherae had wielded considerable dominance thanks to its ambitious ruler, Jason. Dubbed the greatest man of his age,[81] Jason was an imperialist who envisioned expanding Pherae's sphere of influence over all Thessaly as well as Epirus, Macedonia, and even Persia.[82] The ruling family of Larissa, the Aleuadae, procured the help of Alexander II of Macedonia and Thebes to resist Jason's attempts to take over their league. When Jason was assassinated in 370, the bitter enmity between Larissa and Pherae persisted as each one strove to control the whole of Thessaly.

Threats from Pherae led the Aleuadae in 358 to seek assistance from Philip.[83] He was quick to form an alliance with Larissa so as to protect his southern border and obtain Thessalian cavalry when

---

[79] Cf. J. R. Ellis, "The Dynamics of Fourth-Century Macedonian Imperialism," *Ancient Macedonia* 2 (Institute for Balkan Studies, Thessaloniki: 1977), pp. 103–114 and "The Unification of Macedonia," in M. B. Hatzopoulos and L. D. Loukopoulos (eds.), *Philip of Macedon* (Athens: 1980), pp. 36–47.

[80] Philip and the economy: Worthington, *Philip II*, pp. 7–8, 30, 33–34, 40, 45–48, 50, 78–79, 110, 117, 124, 135, 168–169, 196–197; see also N. G. L. Hammond, "Philip's Innovations in Macedonian Economy," *SO* 70 (1995), pp. 22–29. For an alternate view of Philip's economic program, see H. Montgomery "The Economic Revolution of Philip II—Myth or Reality," *SO* 60 (1985), pp. 37–47.

[81] Xenophon, *Hellenica* 6.4.28.

[82] Xenophon, *Hellenica* 6.1.11–12, 18, 4.28, Isocrates 5.119–120, Pausanias 6.17.9.

[83] On Thessaly in the fourth century, see H. D. Westlake, *Thessaly in the Fourth Century BC* (London: 1935; repr. Chicago: 1993) and M. Sordi, *La Lega Thessala fino ad Alessandro* (Rome: 1958). On Philip's involvement at this time, see G. T. Griffith, "Philip of Macedon's Early Intervention in Thessaly (358–352 B.C.)," *CQ²* 20 (1970), pp. 67–80 and C. Ehrhardt, "Two Notes on Philip of Macedon's First Interventions in Thessaly," *CQ²* 17 (1967), pp. 296–301.

needed. The alliance included his marrying a Larissan lady named Philinna (his third wife), who one year later bore him a son, Arrhidaeus.[84] Philip was always careful to preserve close relations with Larissa because Thessaly was an important ally throughout his reign.[85]

The following year, 357, Philip turned to the tribal kingdom of Epirus on his southwestern border.[86] Epirus was ruled by Arybbas, a member of the Molossian tribe, the strongest of the three tribes that dominated the country.[87] The two kings formalized an alliance, which included Philip's marriage to Olympias, the king's niece (and the daughter of the recently deceased previous king Neoptolemus I).[88] The following year she gave birth to a son, the future Alexander the Great.

In only two years Philip had unified Macedonia, initiated military reforms that revolutionized the army, and secured his northern, western, and southern borders. These were staggering achievements for any king, but even more so in such a short time. Now Philip prepared to deal with two powers that had plagued Macedonia: Athens and the Chalcidian League.

WAR WITH ATHENS

Regardless of the terms of his earlier agreement with the Athenians, Philip could not afford to return Amphipolis to them. It was located on his eastern border and on important trade and communication routes as well as being the gateway to rich mines at Crenides. The people of

---

[84] Athenaeus 13.557c, Justin 9.8.2, 13.2.11, and cf. Athenaeus 13.578a, Carney, *Women and Monarchy*, pp. 61–62.

[85] See S. Sprawski, "All the King's Men: Thessalians and Philip II's Designs on Greece," in D. Musial (ed.), *Society and Religions: Studies in Greek and Roman History* (Torun: 2005), pp. 31–49; see also Ryder, "Diplomatic Skills of Philip II," pp. 247–250, E. Badian, "Philip II and the Last of the Thessalians," *Ancient Macedonia* 6 (Institute for Balkan Studies, Thessaloniki: 1999), pp. 109–121. On relations between Macedonia and Thessaly, including Philip's reign, see D. Graninger, "Macedonia and Thessaly," in J. Roisman and Ian Worthington (eds.), *Blackwell Companion to Ancient Macedonia* (Malden: 2010), pp. 306–325.

[86] For a convenient history, see N. G. L. Hammond, *Epirus* (Oxford: 1967); see also W. S. Greenwalt, "Macedonia, Illyria and Epirus," in J. Roisman and Ian Worthington (eds.), *Blackwell Companion to Ancient Macedonia* (Malden: 2010), pp. 279–305.

[87] The other two were the Thesprotians and the Chaonians.

[88] Athenaeus 13.557c, Justin 7.6.10–12; cf. Diodorus 19.51.1, Carney, *Women and Monarchy*, pp. 62–67 and 79–81. Olympias in detail: E. D. Carney, *Olympias, Mother of Alexander the Great* (London: 2006).

Amphipolis now had second thoughts, however, about Philip's intentions toward them. In a speech delivered eight years later,[89] Demosthenes stated that two men from Amphipolis, Hierax and Stratocles, traveled to Athens to ask the people to "sail and take over the city."[90] Whether they represented the Amphipolitan government or were merely part of an anti-Macedonian faction is not known. Ultimately, it did not matter, for in the spring Philip besieged the city, neatly countering any Athenian opposition by sending a letter to the Athenians promising to hand Amphipolis over to them once it surrendered.[91] Naively taking him at his word, the Assembly conferred an official vote of thanks on him and ordered two envoys, Antiphon and Charidemus, to convey its decision to him.[92]

One of the more enigmatic events in diplomatic relations between Athens and Philip now follows. Demosthenes later accused Philip of breaking a "secret agreement" with the Athenians by which he would give them Amphipolis if they handed him their ally Pydna on the Macedonian coast.[93] Only the Assembly, however, could authorize this type of agreement, which could hardly have remained secret.[94] Demosthenes' lie was in order to highlight Philip's treachery because when Amphipolis fell to him after a short siege he did not hand it over to Athens. Likewise, Demosthenes' scornful comment that traitors within the city opened its gates to him was meant to downplay the king's success in taking a walled city.[95] Not that the people of Amphipolis were able to mount much of a defense. Philip attacked sections of the walls with battering rams while using scaling ladders on other parts of them.

---

[89] This is the earliest episode in Athens' relations with Philip that Demosthenes mentioned in any of his surviving speeches (1.8 and 2.6), as noted by T. T. B. Ryder, "Demosthenes and Philip II," in Ian Worthington (ed.), *Demosthenes: Statesman and Orator* (London: 2000), p. 45.

[90] Demosthenes 1.8; cf. Theopompus, *FGrH* 115 F 42 (who calls them envoys).

[91] [Demosthenes] 7.27, Demosthenes 23.116.

[92] Theopompus, *FGrH* 115 F 30; cf. Demosthenes 2.6.

[93] Theopompus, *FGrH* 115 F 30a–b, Demosthenes 2.6, 23.116, one of the "more disgraceful incidents in fourth-century Athenian policy, which is not devoid of them": Badian, "Road to Prominence," p. 20.

[94] See G. E. M. de Ste. Croix, "The Alleged Secret Pact between Athens and Philip II Concerning Amphipolis and Pydna," *CQ²* 13 (1963), pp. 110–119; cf. Ellis, *Philip II*, pp. 63–67, Hammond and Griffith, *History of Macedonia* 2, pp. 236–243, Carlier, *Démosthène*, pp. 95–96, Worthington, *Philip II*, p. 41.

[95] Demosthenes 1.5. On the siege, see Worthington, *Philip II*, pp. 41–42.

e the walls had been breached, some Macedonians poured through the openings while others climbed the ladders to drop down on the enemy. Philip did not punish the city although he did oversee the exile of some Amphipolitans, who were no doubt anti-Macedonians.[96] As soon as he had made his arrangements in Amphipolis he unexpectedly besieged Pydna, which quickly fell to him.[97]

The Athenians finally realized they had been deceived and declared war on Philip, calling it "the war for Amphipolis."[98] Their reaction was merely a face-saving gesture—as has been rightly said, "the professed Athenian desire to recover Amphipolis can easily be dismissed as a mere quest for empty prestige."[99] On the other hand, they would have been concerned about their access to the timber they needed for their fleet. To protect their interests, they now formed alliances with Grabus of Illyria, Cetriporis of Western Thrace, and the Paeonian king Lyppeius, and appealed for help from Olynthus.[100] This combination of forces posed no small threat to Philip, causing him to move quickly to neutralize it.

For once the king combined diplomacy with military action. To deter the Olynthians from making an alliance with Athens, Philip offered to wrest Potidaea (an Athenian cleruchy on the neck of the Pallene peninsula, only a mile from Olynthus) from Athenian control and give it to them, together with Anthemus (a Macedonian possession in the west Chalcidice).[101] The Olynthians had long resented Athens' presence at Potidaea and they welcomed Philip's offer. They agreed to a treaty with him in the winter of 357/6, after which he besieged Potidaea.[102] True to his word (for a change), when Potidaea capitulated he handed it over to the Olynthians, but he allowed the Athenians living in the city to depart

---

[96] Diodorus 16.8.2 (Philip "exiled those who were disaffected toward him, but treated the rest considerately"), Rhodes and Osborne, *Greek Historical Inscriptions*, no. 49 (exile of Stratocles and Philon).

[97] Theopompus, *FGrH* 115 F 30a–b, Diodorus 16.8.3.

[98] Aeschines 2.70 and 3.54, Demosthenes 5.14, Isocrates 5.2, Diodorus 16.8.2–3. Sealey, *Demosthenes*, p. 110, suggests that because this name appears in speeches of Demosthenes and Aeschines over a decade later, they might have been trying to minimize the extent of the clash between Philip and Athens.

[99] Sealey, *Demosthenes*, p. 110.

[100] Or possibly in 356: Rhodes and Osborne, *Greek Historical Inscriptions*, no. 53.

[101] Demosthenes 1.12, Demosthenes 6.20.

[102] Rhodes and Osborne, *Greek Historical Inscriptions*, no. 50; cf. Diodorus 16.8.5, Demosthenes 2.14, 4.20, 23.108.

unharmed.[103] Then in three short campaigns, of which the details are vague, his general Parmenion defeated Grabus while Philip did the same against Cetriporis and Lyppeus.[104] According to Plutarch, at the same time he received news that Olympias had borne him a son, Alexander.[105]

The Athenians were unable to assist either Amphipolis or Potidaea because of crises that suddenly presented themselves. The first involved the strategically important island of Euboea, off Attica's eastern coastline, which provided some of the city's grain.[106] In 357 the Thebans were seeking to extend their influence on the island and were negotiating with a number of its cities, forcing the Athenians to send troops there. Demosthenes served on this expedition as a volunteer trierarch.[107] Thirty days later the Athenian commander Timotheus reported that the island was again pro-Athenian.[108] However, the Athenians' success on Euboea was offset a year later by the Social War, a major revolt of their allies.[109]

THE SOCIAL WAR AND ATHENIAN DISTRESS

For some years the allies in the Second Athenian Confederacy had resented the Athenians' heavy-handed treatment of them (see above). In 356 Chios, Rhodes, and Cos, with the support of Byzantium (which had probably seceded in 364), accused the Athenians of "plotting against them" and revolted, thereby instigating the Social War.[110] They also received military assistance from Mausolus, the satrap of Caria, in

---

[103] "He was particularly solicitous toward the people of Athens on account of their importance and repute of their city": Diodorus 16.8.5.

[104] Diodorus 16.22.3, Plutarch, *Alexander* 3.8–9, Demosthenes 1.23, 23.189.

[105] Plutarch, *Alexander* 3.8.

[106] Thucydides 8.96.2, cf. 7.28.1 (of 411, but there is no reason to assume the situation had changed by the time in question).

[107] Demosthenes 18.99, 21.161, with E. Ruschenbusch, "Demosthenes' erste freiwillige Trierarchie und die Datierung des Euböaunternehmens vom Jahre 357," *ZPE* 67 (1987), pp. 158–159, Badian, "Road to Prominence," p. 40 n. 24.

[108] Demosthenes 8.74, Diodorus 16.7.2, Rhodes and Osborne, *Greek Historical Inscriptions*, no. 48; cf. Demosthenes 16.14, Aeschines 3.85.

[109] Diodorus 16.7.3–4, 16.21.1, 16.22.2; see G. L. Cawkwell, "Notes on the Social War," *Class. & Med.* 23 (1962), pp. 34–49, Sealey, *Demosthenes*, pp. 103–108, Lehmann, *Demosthenes*, pp. 66–67.

[110] E. Badian, "The Ghost of Empire: Reflections on Athenian Foreign Policy in the Fourth Century," in W. Eder (ed.), *Die athenische Demokratie im 4. Jahrhundert v. Chr.* (Stuttgart: 1995), pp. 94–95, following Cawkwell, "Notes on the Failure of the Second Athenian Confederacy," pp. 51–52.

southwestern Asia Minor, who was then in a dispute over the status of islands off his coastline with the King of Persia.[111] Demosthenes falsely accused Mausolus of starting the Social War, but the root cause was the Athenians' treatment of their allies.[112] Given its timing, Philip may also have privately encouraged the ringleaders to revolt so as to distract Athenian attention from his siege of Potidaea.

The Athenians sent a fleet of sixty triremes under their generals Chares and Chabrias against the rebel fleet, which was stationed at Chios. In the fighting, Chabrias was killed and Chares was forced to retreat.[113] Other allies, including the islands of Lemnos and Samos, now deserted Athens, forcing the people the following year to send sixty triremes under the generals Iphicrates, Menestheus (his son), and Timotheus to reinforce Chares' fleet. As they prepared to engage the rebels at Embata (perhaps off Erythrae), bad weather struck, making it hard for them to maneuver their heavy triremes. The new commanders decided to wait out the weather, but Chares recklessly disregarded their decision and attacked the enemy. He was soundly defeated, losing a number of ships in battle while storms and heavy seas claimed more.[114]

The Athenians had no other choice but to admit defeat in the Social War. Their naval confederacy continued to exist, but Chios, Cos, and Rhodes formally defected from it, and other allies followed suit. In an effort to escape blame for his defeat, Chares indicted his co-commanders for refusing to do battle, alleging they took bribes from the enemy. A politician named Aristophon of Azenia, eager to claim some political limelight, prosecuted them.[115] Iphicrates and Menestheus were acquitted, but Timotheus was fined 100 talents, forcing him into exile. No charges were ever brought against Chares, the person most responsible for the Athenian defeat.

Athens after the Social War was a very different city.[116] Its costs financially exhausted the Athenians, who spent one thousand talents on

---

[111] Demosthenes 15.3, Diodorus 16.7.3. On Mausolus in detail, see S. Hornblower, *Mausolus* (Oxford: 1982).

[112] Demosthenes 15.3, 11, 14, 27, Diodorus 16.7.3.

[113] Diodorus 16.7, Demosthenes 20.81.

[114] Nepos, *Timotheus* 3.

[115] J. K. Davies, *Athenian Propertied Families* (Oxford: 1971), pp. 64–66, D. Whitehead, "The Political Career of Aristophon," *CP* 81 (1986), pp. 313–319.

[116] See, for example, R. Sealey, "Athens after the Social War," *JHS* 75 (1955), pp. 74–81 and *Demosthenes*, passim, Hunt, *War, Peace, and Alliance in Demosthenes' Athens*, pp. 259–264.

mercenaries alone,[117] and its immediate aftermath may be the period when Demosthenes stated the city's annual revenues were only 137 talents in contrast to the thousand at the outbreak of the Peloponnesian War in 431.[118] Several works addressed Athens' financial plight at this point. For example, in the closing stages of the war the orator Isocrates wrote *On the Peace*, urging the Athenians to come to terms with Chios, Rhodes, Byzantium, and "all mankind," to abandon their thoughts of empire, and to focus only on economic matters to improve the city's well-being. In 354, Xenophon, a soldier turned historian and philosopher, produced his *Poroi* (*Ways and Means*), which also implored the people to forget about their former imperial days and fix the city's economic problems. Among other things, he recommended building up trade with other states, encouraging metics (resident aliens) to return to Athens to help stimulate trade and commerce, settling commercial and similar disputes more speedily and equitably in the courts, and boosting the output of the silver mines at Laurium (in southern Attica). He also tried to persuade the Athenians to buy the slaves needed to work the mines rather than "outsourcing" them from individual slave owners, who grew rich at the city's expense.[119] Also in the same year, 354, Demosthenes delivered his first political speech, *On the Symmories*, which advocated a reform of the trierarchy to improve the city's finances (Chapter 4 pp. 85–89). The arguments of all three men, however, were unsuccessful.

RETURN TO PHILIP

Before his siege of Potidaea in 356, Philip had responded to an appeal for assistance from the people of Crenides, forty miles east of Amphipolis and eight miles north of the Athenian ally Neapolis (Kavala), who were being threatened by Cetriporis of Thrace. The rich gold and silver mines at Crenides lured Philip back after Potidaea fell to him. He took Crenides over and renamed it Philippi after himself, making it Macedonia's first colony.[120] The annual income from its mines eventually rose to 1,000 talents, which was a stark contrast to the financially

---

[117] Isocrates 7.9.

[118] Demosthenes 10.37, with Sealey, *Demosthenes*, p. 113.

[119] See further, on these works, Sealey, *Demosthenes* pp. 113–116, Jaeger, *Demosthenes*, pp. 50–55, Hunt, *War, Peace, and Alliance in Demosthenes' Athens*, pp. 259–264.

[120] Diodorus 16.8.6–7. Cf. Hammond and Griffith, *History of Macedonia* 2, pp. 358–361, Borza, *Shadow of Olympus*, pp. 214–216.

crippled Athenian state.[121] Philip followed up his action at Crenides by removing the Athenian presence in the cities along his coastline on the Thermaic Gulf. By 355 only Methone, where the Athenians had landed Argaeus in 359, was left.

Philip marched to Methone in late 355. He ordered the people to surrender, but they refused, so he called for his siege engines and battering rams and began attacking the city's walls.[122] Their thickness and the valiant stand on the part of the defenders impeded his progress substantially. Every time the Macedonians scaled the walls the defenders beat them back and the battering rams initially made little progress. A further hindrance was that the Athenians deployed troops to the city as a decree of December 355 attests.[123] However, the principal reason why the siege stalled was that Philip was shot in the eye while inspecting his line by a defender on the ramparts.[124] His doctor Critobulus saved his life but could not save the sight in his eye, and the siege was perhaps scaled back or even temporarily suspended while he recovered.[125]

The story of Philip's eye wound is of immense importance in helping to identify his tomb at Vergina, discovered in 1977. The artifacts in the tomb included several small ivory heads. One of them is a bearded adult male, with a disfigurement around an apparently sightless right eye (Figure 7). The tomb also held a gold box (*larnax*) in which were found broken skeletal remains of an adult male in his mid forties, with scraps of purple cloth on them. The sources tell us that when Philip was killed in 336, his body was burned on a funeral pyre. Then his bones were washed in wine, wrapped in purple cloth, and put into a gold *larnax*. A team of forensic anthropologists assembled the skull fragments and reconstructed the face, which shows trauma around the right eye (Figure 2, p. 4). The reconstruction, together with the

---

[121] Diodorus 16.8.6.

[122] Siege: Diodorus 16.31.4, 35.5–6, Justin 7.6.13–14, and see Worthington, *Philip II*, pp. 48–49. Chronology: J. Buckler, *Philip II and the Sacred War* (Leiden: 1989), pp. 181–185.

[123] *IG* ii² 1, 130, honoring a man named Lachares of Apollonia for entering Methone.

[124] Duris, *FGrH* 76 F 36 (javelin), Theopompus, *FGrH* 115 F 52, Demosthenes 18.67, Justin 7.6.14–15. On the eye injury and the role it plays in later variant traditions of Philip, see A. S. Riginos, "The Wounding of Philip II of Macedon: Fact and Fabrication," *JHS* 114 (1994), pp. 106–114.

[125] This may have permitted Lachares and his men the opportunity to enter Methone and reinforce the defenders.

FIGURE 7. Ivory head of Philip II found in what is probably his tomb at Vergina.

ivory head, identifies the tomb as that of Philip and suggests his wounded eye was the right one.[126]

In the spring of 354 the Athenians voted to send a fleet to Methone's assistance, but it arrived too late.[127] Philip ordered Methone's walls and buildings destroyed, but allowed the survivors to leave unharmed, although they could take with them only one item of clothing. He then gave Methone's land to his people.[128]

RETURN TO DEMOSTHENES

By the mid-350s Demosthenes had begun to create a name for himself in public life, helped also by spending some of the money he had earned from speechwriting on liturgies, which ambitious men used as

---

[126] Further on the identification and controversy surrounding this tomb, see Worthington, *Philip II*, pp. 234–241.

[127] Demosthenes 4.35.

[128] Diodorus 16.34.5.

a stepping-stone to a political career.[129] His first liturgy was a trierarchy (equipping a trireme for one year), probably in 364/3, and his
second was another trierarchy in 360/59. For the latter he received a
trierarchic crown, an award the Athenians gave to the trierarch who
got his ship ready first and best equipped it. For some reason the other
trierarchs challenged him, forcing him to justify his award in his speech
On the Trierarchic Crown to the Boule.[130] His trireme was part of a fleet
deployed under the command of Cephisodotus (who sailed on Demosthenes' ship) to the Thracian Chersonese.[131] Cephisodotus' mission
was unsuccessful and he was put on trial when he returned and fined
five talents.[132] Demosthenes was possibly called as a witness at his trial,
but the story that he prosecuted him is probably untrue.[133]

The Athenians' financial plight called for a change in fiscal policy
and Philip's encroachment on their power in the north arguably
demanded a change in foreign policy as well. Philip's unification of
Macedonia and his securing of its borders and coastline, as well as the
creation of a professional army and his exploitation of natural resources,
demonstrated that he was an opponent with which to be reckoned.
Against this background, Demosthenes delivered his first major speeches
in the courts and Assembly. Yet they ignored the threat from Philip and
dealt with financial issues, as the following chapter discusses.

---

[129] On the political usage of liturgies, see J. K. Davies, "Demosthenes on Liturgies: A
   Note," *JHS* 87 (1967), pp. 33–40, P. J. Rhodes, "Political Activity in Classical Athens,"
   JHS 106 (1986), p. 137.

[130] Speech 51, *On the Trierarchic Crown*: see Blass, *attische Beredsamkeit*² 3.1, pp. 214–219,
   MacDowell, *Demosthenes*, pp. 133–136. Translation of the speech with notes:
   V. Bers, *Demosthenes, Speeches 50–59* (Austin: 2003), pp. 39–45.

[131] He sailed on Demosthenes' ship perhaps because he had been a friend of his father
   (Aeschines 3.51–52).

[132] See Demosthenes 23.163–168, Androtion, *FGrH* 324 F 19.

[133] See Sealey, *Demosthenes*, p. 100, Badian, "Road to Prominence," p. 18, Davies, *Athenian Propertied Families*, p. 136, and Schaefer, *Demosthenes*² 1, pp. 453–454 n. 5 against
   Demosthenes being the prosecutor.

4

Into the Public Eye

DEMOSTHENES HAD PROVED himself to be a successful forensic speechwriter, but his ambition would take him beyond the realm of the law courts to the Assembly. In 355 and 354 he was hired to write prosecution speeches in two important and politically charged cases. The first was against the career politician Androtion and the second against a controversial tax law introduced by a man named Leptines. Despite the developing threat to Athens from Philip, Demosthenes' first political speech that survives, *On the Symmories* (*Navy Boards*), of 354, ignored the king and addressed the dire financial straits that Athens was facing after the Social War and its relations with Persia. These three speeches marked Demosthenes' move from private to public speaker.[1]

THE INDICTMENT OF ANDROTION

Androtion, born in about 410, was the son of Andron, one of the oligarchs who had briefly ruled Athens in 411.[2] Androtion studied under Isocrates and began a highly influential political career in the

---

[1] There are chronological problems with several of Demosthenes' early political speeches, which are noted in the book where relevant. See further, R. Sealey, "Dionysius of Halicarnassus and Some Demosthenic Dates," pp. 77–120 and R. Lane Fox, "Demosthenes, Dionysius, and the Dating of Six Early Speeches," *Class. & Med.* 48 (1997), pp. 167–203.

[2] J. K. Davies, *Athenian Propertied Families* (Oxford: 1971), p. 34.

mid-380s.[3] In the early to mid-350s, he was governor of Arcesine, on the island of Amorgos, and received a crown "on account of his goodness and justice and goodwill toward the city."[4] In 356/5, he served a second term on the Boule,[5] where he discovered that trierarchs from previous years owed the state fourteen talents. The law of Periander had spread the huge cost of the trierarchy among the 1,200 richest men in the city (see Chapter 2 p. 20). However, some of them defaulted on their payments or tried to avoid the liturgy entirely.[6] The people were critical of these delinquents, probably because of their sufferings in the Social War, and authorized a man named Euctemon to collect the debts. Evidently he did not do a good job, as Androtion's discovery attested. Androtion persuaded the Assembly to sack Euctemon and establish a commission of inquiry, on which he and his friend Timocrates served.[7] The people gave him carte blanche to act as he saw fit to recoup the money, and he showed little mercy. Among other things, he forced his way into private homes and chased anyone who fled from him. Men were so afraid of him that apparently they hid under their beds. Even with these methods, he had collected only seven talents by the time the commission ended.[8]

Androtion's attack on Euctemon embarrassed and angered him considerably. In the summer of 355, with the backing of his friend Diodorus, he sought revenge. Androtion earlier had proposed a decree to award the customary crowns to the members of the Boule for his year.[9] He was required by law to put the recommendation to the Boule, which then brought it before the Assembly for formal approval. Androtion, however, put the matter directly to the Assembly, affording Euctemon

---

[3] Demosthenes 22.66, 24.173. On Androtion, see P. E. Harding, "Androtion's Political Career," *Historia* 25 (1976), pp. 186–200 and *Androtion and the Atthis* (Oxford: 2001), pp. 13–25, 53–59; cf. R. Sealey, "Athens after the Social War," *JHS* 75 (1955), pp. 79–80, E. Badian, "The Road to Prominence," in Ian Worthington (ed.), *Demosthenes: Statesman and Orator* (London: 2000), pp. 20–22

[4] P. J. Rhodes and R. Osborne (eds.), *Greek Historical Inscriptions, 404–323 BC* (Oxford: 2003), no. 51 (the quotation is from their translation on p. 251).

[5] His first time was in 378/7. Members were selected by lot, and could serve on the Boule twice in their lifetime, but not in successive years: P. J. Rhodes, *The Athenian Boule* (Oxford: 1972), pp. 242–243.

[6] Cf. Demosthenes 14.16.

[7] Demosthenes 22.47–58, Harding, "Androtion's Political Career," pp. 192–194.

[8] Demosthenes 22.44; contra 24.162, where it is only five talents.

[9] Demosthenes 22.36–37.

the means to indict him for proposing an illegal decree (a procedure called *graphe paranomon*).[10] His indictment included three other charges against Androtion: the Boule had not completed the construction of new triremes, as it was required to do, and therefore was not entitled to crowns; Androtion was a state debtor; and Androtion was said to have been a male prostitute.[11]

Why Androtion went straight to the Assembly is unknown. During his tenure on the Boule, the treasurer appointed to supervise ship-building absconded with over two talents, so no triremes were built.[12] At this difficult time it is hardly a surprise that the Athenians would condemn such actions,[13] and the members of the Boule may have decided not to ask for crowns because the law clearly stated that they would be ineligible to receive them if too few triremes were built.[14] Evidently Androtion thought differently.

The case against Androtion was high-profile and like many forensic cases was politically charged.[15] It was held in the first half of the archon year 355/4.[16] Both Euctemon and Diodorus prosecuted Androtion, for

---

[10] On the procedure in detail, see H. Yunis, "Law, Politics, and the *Graphe Paranomon* in Fourth-Century Athens," *GRBS* 29 (1988), pp. 361–382; cf. MacDowell, *Demosthenes*, pp. 152–155. See also M. J. Sundahl, "The Rule of Law and the Nature of the Fourth-century Athenian Democracy," *Class. & Med.* 54 (2003), pp. 127–156.

[11] Demosthenes 22.5–8, 21–24, 33–34.

[12] Demosthenes 22.17.

[13] Cf. Badian, "Road to Prominence," p. 21: "That all this happened in the midst of a serious war, in which Athens suffered from a shortage of ships, illustrates the moral decline of the Athenian democracy at this time."

[14] [Aristotle], *Athenian Constitution* 46.1; cf. Demosthenes 22.8, with Rhodes, *Athenian Boule*, pp. 115–116, V. Gabrielsen, *Financing the Athenian Fleet: Public Taxation and Social Relations* (Baltimore: 1994), pp. 134–135.

[15] See, for example, E. Hall, "Lawcourt Dramas: The Power of Performance in Greek Forensic Oratory," *BICS* 40 (1995), pp. 39–58, P. E. Easterling, "Actors and Voices: Reading Between the Lines in Aeschines and Demosthenes," in S. Goldhill and R. Osborne (eds.), *Performance Culture and Athenian Democracy* (Cambridge: 1999), pp. 154–165, Ober, "Public Speech and the Power of the People" and "Power and Oratory in Democratic Athens: Demosthenes 21, *Against Meidias*" in J. Ober (ed.), *The Athenian Revolution: Essays on Ancient Greek Democracy and Political Theory* (Princeton: 1996), pp. 86–106, and C. Cooper, "Demosthenes: Actor on the Political and Forensic Stage," in C. J. Mackie (ed.), *Oral Performance and its Context* (Leiden: 2004), pp. 145–161.

[16] Date: Dionysius of Halicarnassus, *To Ammaeus* 1.4: Sealey, "Dionysius of Halicarnassus and Some Demosthenic Dates," pp. 89–92, G. L. Cawkwell, "Notes on the Social War," *Class. & Med.* 23 (1962), pp. 40–45.

the Athenian judicial system admitted multiple prosecutors. Euctemon spoke first at the trial, followed by Diodorus. Euctemon's prosecution speech is not extant but that of Diodorus, who hired Demosthenes to write it, survives.

Against Androtion[17]

Demosthenes not only had to prove that Androtion had broken the letter of the law but also needed to dash any esteem in which the people held him, especially as the Assembly had authorized him to act as he saw fit. He knew that he did not need to detail the circumstances of the charge against Androtion because Euctemon would have dealt with that in his speech. Therefore he had Diodorus begin by simply stating that Androtion had unsuccessfully indicted his uncle for impiety (1–3). Prosecutors routinely admitted that they were motivated by personal reasons as long as they had a genuine legal fault on the part of the accused.[18] After the brief opening, Demosthenes intended the rest of Diodorus' speech to rebut Androtion's defense (4–78). He knew some aspects of it from the preliminary hearing (*anakrisis*), where disputants outlined their cases and produced their evidence, but anything else he had to anticipate.

Androtion's crime was that he had bypassed the Boule when he took his proposal to the Assembly. The speech emphasized that the law on crowns unequivocally stated that the Boule must discuss the matter before it went to the Assembly. Diodorus thus warned the jurors that Androtion would be lying if he told them there were occasions when the Boule was not involved (5–8), urging them to trust him (6):

> Well now, he contends that all the Councils that have ever received an award from you have received it in this way and there was never a preliminary motion passed for even one of them. I believe, no I am certain, that he is not speaking the truth.

---

[17] On the speech, see Schaefer, *Demosthenes*[2] 1, pp. 354–361, Blass, *attische Beredsamkeit*[2] 3.1, pp. 226–231, Pickard-Cambridge, *Demosthenes*, pp. 112–119, Jaeger, *Demosthenes*, pp. 58–62, Sealey, "Dionysius of Halicarnassus and Some Demosthenic Dates," pp. 89–92, S. Usher, *Greek Oratory: Tradition and Originality* (Oxford 1999), pp. 198–201, Lehmann, *Demosthenes*, pp. 71–72, MacDowell, *Demosthenes*, pp. 167–181; cf. Badian, "Road to Prominence," pp. 20–22. See also G. Rowe, "Anti-Isocratean Sentiment in Demosthenes' *Against Androtion*," *Historia* 49 (2000), pp. 278–302. Translation with notes: E. M. Harris, *Demosthenes, Speeches 20–22* (Austin: 2008), pp. 167–196.

[18] On this aspect, see A. Kurihara, "Personal Enmity as a Motivation in Forensic Speeches," *CQ*[2] 53 (2003), pp. 464–477.

Diodorus next turned to the building of the triremes (9–20). He implored the jury to ignore any claims Androtion might make that the Boule should not be held accountable for the treasurer absconding with the money to build the ships. To reinforce his case, he discussed the pivotal role triremes had played in Athens' military victories from the time of the Persian War in the early fifth century and their importance for securing and maintaining Athenian control of Greece (13–16). Historical passages are a common rhetorical feature in oratory, but in Demosthenes' hands they were "suffused with patriotism [to become] one of the special features of his deliberative oratory":[19]

> There are the men who built the Propylaea and the Parthenon and decorated the rest of the temples with the spoils taken from the barbarians, achievements that rightly give us all a sense of pride. You certainly know this from hearing about it that after leaving the city and being shut off on Salamis, they saved all their own possessions and the city by winning the victory at sea because they had triremes. . . . Yet why do I need to discuss ancient history? During the last war against the Spartans, you know what state the city was in when you thought you would not be able to send the fleet out. You remember that even vetches [plants to improve soil] were for sale. But when you did send the fleet out, you obtained the kind of peace you wanted. Because triremes had such a great impact in both cases, you were therefore right, men of Athens, to impose this requirement on the Council as a way of determining whether it should receive an award or not.[20]

Demosthenes was concerned that the jury might favor Androtion because the Boule had discharged its other duties well and therefore he peppered the earlier part of his speech with appeals that the Boule's good works must not outweigh the legal issues of the case.[21]

So far Diodorus was on incontrovertible legal ground: by law, if no ships were built, regardless of the reason, the Boule members could not be crowned. Juries in Athens, however, did not always vote according to the law, so to reinforce his arguments Demosthenes turned to attack Androtion's character. What today would be ruled as irrelevant, inadmissible, or prejudicial to a case was fair game in an Athenian court—little that Diodorus now said in the rest of the speech had any formal bearing on the charge against Androtion.

[19] Usher, *Greek Oratory: Tradition and Originality*, p. 199.

[20] Demosthenes 22.13, 15–16.

[21] Demosthenes 22.12, 16, 35.

Diodorus claimed that Androtion was a male prostitute, calling him the equivalent of a "bottom" in a homosexual relationship (21–32). Male prostitutes were debarred from participating in civic life, including speaking at an Assembly.[22] Androtion therefore could not legally make proposals and therefore was in breach of the law. Diodorus warned the jury that Androtion would accuse him of slander, and further, would question why Euctemon had brought a *graphe paranomon* against him rather than a *graphe hetaireseos* (indictment for prostitution). Against that argument, Diodorus stated that the subject of a *graphe paranomon* could be indicted for his personal life. The veracity of his claim cannot be determined, although if it were slander Androtion could easily have rebutted it in his defense speech. Perhaps, then, there was something about Androtion's character or the public's perception of him that allowed Demosthenes to denigrate him in this way and get away with it.[23] Demosthenes, after all, never brought a similar accusation against his bitter personal enemies Aphobus, Meidias, and Aeschines.[24]

Even more questionable is Demosthenes' accusation that Androtion spoke in the Assembly although he had inherited his deceased father's debt—a state debtor lost his citizenship rights until he discharged the debt. Diodorus merely challenged Androtion to refute his claim and passed over it so quickly that it may well be untrue (33–34)—"Show then that your father did not owe money or that he got out of prison not by running away but by paying the debt" (34). Nevertheless, Demosthenes knew that he had only to convince some of the jurors that Androtion was corrupt, for in an Athenian court there was no time for jury deliberation. When the defense had delivered its case, the jury voted, and a majority (not unanimous) vote decided the case.

Diodorus was now over the halfway point in his speech. In the remainder of it he attacked Androtion for not conducting himself as a citizen in how he recovered some of the money owed to the state (42–78). Forcing his way into people's homes and causing men to flee over the roofs of their houses or hide under their beds in fear of being taken to jail was not how a democrat treated his fellow citizens. Diodorus compared Androtion's behavior to the violent methods of the Thirty

[22] Cf. Aeschines 1.19–20, with D. M. MacDowell, "Athenian Laws about Homosexuality," *RIDA* 47 (2000), pp. 20–24.

[23] Cf. MacDowell, *Demosthenes*, pp. 173–174—he uses the word "catamite" of Androtion (explained on p. 171 n. 62).

[24] MacDowell, *Demosthenes*, p. 174.

Tyrants, the oligarchy set up by the Spartans at the end of the Peloponnesian War in 404. The oligarchy lasted only one year, but it was one
of the bloodiest periods in Athenian history (52):

> But when in the past did the worst atrocities ever occur in our city? Under
> the Thirty you would all say. But at that time, as one can hear, there was
> no one who lost hope of survival as long as he kept himself hidden inside
> his house. Instead, we criticize the Thirty for arresting men unjustly in
> the Agora. Yet this man's brutality so far surpassed theirs that he made
> each man's own home his prison by bringing the Eleven into private
> houses—even though he was conducting public business in a democracy!

His portrayal of Androtion's alleged shameful action was so masterful that the jury forgot that the men he had abused were the actual
criminals. To Diodorus, Androtion was a "disgusting person" (66), and
he wanted the jury to feel the same way. As a final attack on Androtion's character, the speech ended by accusing him of impiety for
melting down gold votive crowns on the Acropolis (69–78).

The prosecution rested, and Androtion spoke in his defense. Euctemon and Diodorus had proved he had broken the law, so he threw
himself on the jurors' mercy by admitting his guilt. At the same time
he defiantly argued that because of a corrupt treasurer the Boule should
not be held accountable for its failure to build triremes. Whether he
refuted the claims that he was a male prostitute or a state debtor or
even justified his behavior in recouping some of the taxes is unknown.
Most likely he did, for despite the compelling legal evidence against
him he continued to speak in the Assembly and play a role in public
affairs, indicating that the jury acquitted him.[25]

Demosthenes' speech against Androtion had failed, but he still circulated copies of it among the Athenians. In doing so, he wanted people
to recognize his rhetorical skills and even associate the views expressed
by Diodorus in it with him. Some scholars have suggested that he was
motivated to take the case by his moral revulsion at Androtion's behavior or his wish to do something about the city's financial plight.[26] While

---

[25] See, for example, Badian, "Road to Prominence," p. 21.

[26] Outraged morality: Pickard-Cambridge, *Demosthenes*, pp. 114–115; cf. Schaefer,
Demosthenes² 1, p. 449, that Demosthenes had a message to push in this speech, that
of public morality. Blass, *attische Beredsamkeit²* 3.1, p. 231, suggests a moral under-
tone but ultimately Demosthenes wrote the speech simply for a client. Economics:
E. M. Burke, "The Early Political Speeches of Demosthenes: Elite Bias in the
Response to Economic Crisis," *Class. Antiquity* 21 (2002), pp. 176–177.

morality and economics may have been factors, they were no doubt secondary to the publicity Demosthenes knew he would earn from this politically charged trial.[27] Androtion was "an ideal opponent for an orator trying to make his way in the wider political sphere, and he could exploit his role as speechwriter to make his client his mouthpiece."[28] Demosthenes' self-serving motive is evident because Euctemon was a friend and political ally of his enemy Meidias, against whom he had earlier brought charges for abusing his mother and sister. He would write for Diodorus again in 354 when he and Euctemon brought charges against Androtion's colleague Timocrates (Chapter 5 pp. 103–105). Then, in 348, Euctemon indicted Demosthenes on a trumped-up charge of desertion—at Meidias' bidding, claimed Demosthenes[29]— during a military campaign to Euboea (Chapter 6 p. 146). Such was the interpersonal nature and conflict of Athenian politics.[30]

In 354 Demosthenes accepted an equally high-profile public case, against the law of Leptines, for the first time personally delivering his own speech.[31]

THE INDICTMENT OF LEPTINES

In 355 (the same year as Androtion's trial), a man named Leptines, about whom nothing is known other than he was an orator,[32] introduced a law designed to boost state revenue. In the past, men who had performed illustrious deeds on behalf of the city were exempted from paying taxes and performing liturgies, excluding the all-important, expensive trierarchy.[33] The award was called *ateleia* and in certain cases was hereditary. Leptines' law ended that immunity for everyone except the descendants of the "tyrannicides" Harmodius and Aristogeiton, who in 514 had murdered an Athenian tyrant named Hipparchus, and

[27] Badian, "Road to Prominence," pp. 22 and 24.

[28] Usher, *Greek Oratory: Tradition and Originality*, p. 199.

[29] Demosthenes 21.103, Aeschines 2.148; cf. Carlier, *Démosthène*, p. 132.

[30] On this, see the works cited in Chapter 2 note 134.

[31] The archon year is given as 355/4 by Dionysius of Halicarnassus, *To Ammaeus* 1.4; cf. Plutarch, *Demosthenes* 15.3. The case had to go to court a year after the law was passed; cf. Schaefer, *Demosthenes*² 1, pp. 415–447.

[32] Aristotle, *Rhetoric* 1411a5; see also Davies, *Athenian Propertied Families*, p. 340.

[33] Demosthenes 20.2, 26, 28, 97, 129, 160; on exemptions, see D. M. MacDowell, "Epikerdes of Kyrene and the Athenian Privilege of *Ateleia*," ZPE 150 (2004), pp. 127–133.

it also gave the people the means to pursue rich men who had not paid taxes.[34] Only a small number of individuals must have been affected, however, which Demosthenes used to suggest that Leptines was biased against those that held this privilege.[35] Exemptions were now illegal, and any man trying to secure one lost his citizenship and had his property confiscated.[36]

In Athenian law, any citizen who believed that a new law violated an existing one or harmed the city was free to indict its proposer for up to one year after it came into effect. After that time, the law (but not its originator) could still be challenged. When that happened, the actual law was put on trial and the state appointed a commission to defend it. Leptines' law was unpopular among the wealthy for obvious reasons and at least three men indicted him for it. However, when one of his accusers, Bathippus, died, the others for reasons unknown withdrew their indictments, and Leptines' law came into effect.[37] Then in 354 Bathippus' son Apsephion challenged the law.[38] He wanted it repealed, *ateleia* reinstated, and an inquiry panel set up to ensure that no one again obtained the exemption illegally.[39] Demosthenes' reputation was growing by now, so Apsephion tapped him and another man named Phormion (about whom nothing is known) to lend weight to his indictment.[40] The state duly appointed a commission of five men including Leptines, the powerful Aristophon (who currently enjoyed *ateleia*), and Cephisodotus.[41]

Apsephion spoke first at the law's trial, followed by Phormion and then Demosthenes.[42] Only Demosthenes' lengthy speech survives,[43] which he gave on behalf of Ctesippus, the son of the general Chabrias,

---

[34] Demosthenes 20.29, 127, 160.

[35] Demosthenes 20.142.

[36] Demosthenes 20.55, 156, 160.

[37] Cf. Demosthenes 20.145 claiming that Leptines bribed them to do so, but this cannot be corroborated.

[38] Under the *graphe nomon me epitedeion theinai* procedure, which was used to attack laws, whereas the *graphe paranomon* questioned laws and decrees: see MacDowell, *Demosthenes*, pp. 152–155. Date of 355/4: Dionysius of Halicarnassus, *To Ammaeus* 1.4

[39] Demosthenes 20.89–101.

[40] Demosthenes 20.1, 51, 97, 100, 159.

[41] The same man who had sailed on Demosthenes' ship on a mission to the Chersonese in 360/59 (Chapter 3 p. 70).

[42] Demosthenes 20.1, 51, 100, 144, 159.

[43] Demosthenes 20.51 and 159 suggests that Pasion named those rewarded with *ateleia* and that Leptines' law conflicted with a current law that allowed *ateleia* for anyone killing someone trying to overthrow the democracy.

who had died during the Social War. Chabrias' defeat of a Spartan fleet off Naxos in 376 had allowed Athens to regain its naval ascendancy of the Aegean, and he was awarded an expensive public statue and hereditary *ateleia*.[44] Under Leptines' law Ctesippus lost that exemption. Since Leptines' law was ultimately intended to generate more income in the grim financial aftermath of the Social War, Demosthenes had to base his case on its injustice.

Although the Athenians had been at war with Philip for three years, it is in this speech that Demosthenes first mentioned him. Even then, he merely alluded to the betrayal of Pydna and the favors people expected Philip to bestow on them.[45]

Against the Law of Leptines[46]

The speech is more than twice the length of *Against Androtion* on account of its treatment of many individuals who had previously received *ateleia* (29–86).[47] Because Demosthenes followed Apsephion and Phormion, he did not need to gain the jury's goodwill, so he immediately launched into an attack on Leptines' law as harmful to the democracy, since it would discourage citizens from doing their best for the city (1–6):

> Judges, it is mainly because I think that the city will benefit by annulling the law and then also for the sake of Chabrias' young child that I have agreed to speak to the best of my ability. . . . Certainly [Leptines] cannot argue that his contention that the men who have received exemptions

[44] Demosthenes 13.22–23, 20.84–86, Aeschines 3.243, Aristotle, *Rhetoric* 3.1411b9–11, Diodorus 15.33.4.

[45] Demosthenes 20.16: "What encouraged the men who betrayed Pydna and the rest of these places to wrong us? Is it not obvious to everyone that they were counting on the rewards that they expected to receive from Philip?"

[46] On the speech, see Schaefer, *Demosthenes*² 1, pp. 398–401, Blass, *attische Beredsamkeit*² 3.1, pp. 231–240, Pickard-Cambridge, *Demosthenes*, pp. 116–119, Jaeger, *Demosthenes*, pp. 64–67, Carlier, *Démosthène*, pp. 76–78, Usher, *Greek Oratory: Tradition and Originality*, pp. 192–198, Lehmann, *Demosthenes*, pp. 73–74, MacDowell, *Demosthenes*, pp. 156–167; cf. Badian, "Road to Prominence," pp. 26–28. Translation and notes: Harris, *Demosthenes, Speeches 20–22*, pp. 15–74; text, translation, and commentary: C. Kremmydas, *Commentary on Demosthenes against Leptines* (Oxford: 2012) (which I was not able to consult for this book).

[47] Because of time constraints, Demosthenes may have merely selected from this part in the oral speech and retained the full account for the revised version.

do not deserve them rests on the same grounds as his view that the people do not deserve to have the power to grant them to whomever they wish. No, by Zeus, but he might perhaps reply to this point by arguing that the people are easily misled and that this is the reason why he framed the law in this way. But according to this line of reasoning, what then prevents him from taking everything away from you, even your entire form of government?[48]

To counter the state's argument that the law generated extra revenue and spread liturgies more equitably among the wealthy, Demosthenes deliberately minimized the number of annual liturgies to show the income was too small to benefit Athens (7–28).[49] Then he threw a more practical scare into the jurors. Athenians were always concerned about the grain route from the Black Sea, and to this end they maintained good relations with the Spartocid rulers of the Bosporus area.[50] They had granted citizenship and *ateleia* to one of its kings, Leucon (who ruled 393–353). Demosthenes now warned the jury that the law threatened their relationship with Leucon, which in turn could disrupt the grain supply (29–40). A long list of individuals who received the exemption for their exemplary loyalist and military deeds followed, which Demosthenes arranged in an order of importance rather than chronologically (41–87).[51] Demosthenes' point here was to show how unfairly the Athenians treated these men and their sons who inherited their *ateleia*.[52] In return for their deeds and sacrifices, Demosthenes argued, the people owed them a debt: *ateleia* was a just and moral way

---

[48] Demosthenes 20.1, 2–3.

[49] See J. K. Davies, "Demosthenes on Liturgies: A Note," *JHS* 87 (1967), pp. 33–40.

[50] S. M. Burstien, "*IG* II² 653, Demosthenes and Athenian Relations with Bosporus in the Fourth Century B.C.," *Historia* 27 (1978), pp. 428–436.

[51] Cf. W. C. West, "The Decrees of Demosthenes' *Against Leptines*," *ZPE* 107 (1995), pp. 237–247, who notes the value of the list Demosthenes supplies for the wording and formulae of these honorary decrees.

[52] Prominent among them were the generals Conon (68–74) and Chabrias (75–86). Chabrias, as noted above, performed great deeds for the city and was held in high esteem. In 394, Conon defeated a Peloponnesian fleet at the Battle of Cnidus, crippling the Spartans' hegemony of Greece: Demosthenes 20.68, 70, Xenophon, *Hellenica* 4.3.10–14, 8.1, Diodorus 14.83.4–7. On his activities, see R. Seager, "Thrasybulus, Conon and Athenian Imperialism, 396–386 B.C.," *JHS* 87 (1967), pp. 95–115, B. S. Strauss, "Thrasybulus and Conon: A Rivalry in Athenian Politics in the 390s B.C.," *AJP* 105 (1984), pp. 37–48.

to repay it, and was in keeping with Athens' national character.[53] More than that, even, *ateleia* encouraged citizens to fight and so helped to maintain Athens as a military power in Greece.[54]

Demosthenes next turned to the legislative procedure that Leptines' law had breached (88–104). After the restoration of democracy in 403 the Athenians required all new laws to be considered and ratified by a permanent group of officials termed *nomothetai* (lawgivers).[55] Any existing law that contradicted a proposed new one had first to be annulled, something Leptines had not done (94–97). On the other hand, Apsephion followed the correct procedure by indicting Leptines' law before submitting his own (98–101).[56] In the final third of his speech, Demosthenes attempted to rebut arguments that he expected the state to put forward, criticizing men who supported a law that worked against the city's best interests and its democracy, and contrasting Leptines' law with Apsephion' far better one (105–167), while making it clear that he favored a scrutiny procedure that weeded out men who did not deserve exemptions (97–108).

The state defenders then presented their case followed by the jury's vote. Apsephion and his fellow prosecutors must have won, even though only one (much later) writer stated they did,[57] because in 346 the Athenians granted the same privileges to Spartocus and Berisades, the sons of Leucon of Bosporus, as they had to their father.[58] These

---

[53] Cf. West, "Decrees of Demosthenes' *Against Leptines*," p. 245: "the theme of Athens' national character, so characteristic of all of Demosthenes' public speeches, is here developed extensively for the first time and is directly related to the decrees which Demosthenes makes his principal argument against the law."

[54] In his section on "militarism," the comment of P. Hunt, *War, Peace, and Alliance in Demosthenes' Athens* (New York: 2010), p. 55, is very apt here: "I am not sure what would have happened to a Greek city-state that did not reward military service, prowess, and sacrifice. I do not think it would have won many battles. In fact, the Greeks were quite aware that those states that rewarded military prowess and best harnessed their citizens' ambitions would prosper not only materially but also in prestige and in power; those that did not would not."

[55] D. M. MacDowell, "Law-Making at Athens in the Fourth Century B.C.," *JHS* 95 (1975), pp. 62–74.

[56] Demosthenes here may have intentionally misled the jurors, because there is scholarly disagreement as to whether in fact Leptines needed to follow the "new" rules of 403 or whether an even older set were still on the books but not enforced: MacDowell, *Demosthenes*, pp. 160–161, citing others on this matter.

[57] Dio Chrysostom 31.128.

[58] Rhodes and Osborne, *Greek Historical Inscriptions*, no. 64.

included *ateleia*, thereby attesting that the Athenians repealed Leptines' law.[59]

Plutarch related that Demosthenes wrote this speech in "the conviction that honor ought to be pursued for its own sake."[60] Elsewhere,
however, Plutarch claimed that the orator wanted to marry Ctesippus'
mother, which cannot be corroborated.[61] While Demosthenes' themes
of justice and even morality in his speech were doubtless sincere,
self-promotion was again his real reason for taking the case. Chabrias'
exploits had made him a household name, and the opportunity for
Demosthenes to piggyback off his reputation by championing his son
was too good an opportunity to miss. Moreover, Ctesippus' guardian
was the stalwart general Phocion, a friend and ally of Eubulus (see
below).[62] There was no question that, win or lose, Phocion would be
favorably disposed to Demosthenes for championing the rights of his
ward (75):

> But, by Zeus, there is also Chabrias' son: should we allow him to lose
> the exemption that his father justly received from you and passed on to
> him? I think that no person in his right mind would say this is fair.

Demosthenes' speech, however, ultimately advocated a tax break for
the wealthy. Those in the lower and middle strata of society would
have seen no justice in that—no different from today. That was why in
his next speech of 354/3, also his first political one, *On the Symmories*
(*Navy Boards*), he attempted to appeal to everyone.[63]

---

[59] Contra, for example, Sealey, *Demosthenes*, p. 127, that the trial's result was unknown;
cf. Badian, "Road to Prominence," p. 28. In the 320s, Ctesippus paid for a *choregia*
(providing a chorus for a play), although that liturgy could have been voluntary: *IG*
ii² 3040, with Davies, *Athenian Propertied Families*, p. 561.

[60] Plutarch, *Demosthenes* 13.5. Cf. (surprisingly) Harris, *Demosthenes, Speeches 20–22*, p.
18, that Demosthenes had only the city's best interests at heart.

[61] Plutarch, *Demosthenes* 15.3. Demosthenes' wife was from Samos: see Chapter 2
pp. 30–31.

[62] Plutarch, *Phocion* 7.3–4. On Phocion, see L. Tritle, *Phocion the Good* (London:
1988).

[63] Date: Dionysius of Halicarnassus, *To Ammaeus* 1.4, with Sealey, "Dionysius of Hali-
carnassus and Some Demosthenic Dates," p. 117, Sealey, *Demosthenes*, pp. 128–129,
G. L. Cawkwell, "Notes on the Social War," *Class. & Med.* 23 (1962), pp. 46–47, Lane
Fox, "Demosthenes, Dionysius, and the Dating of Six Early Speeches," pp. 177–181,
C. Karvounis, *Demosthenes: Studien zu den Demegorien orr. XIV, XVI, XV, IV, I, II, III*
(Tübingen: 2002), pp. 71–75, MacDowell, *Demosthenes*, p. 143.

THE SPECTER OF PERSIA

In 354 news reached the Athenians that the Persian king Artaxerxes III Ochus had raised an army and fleet as part of his campaign against rebellious satraps (governors) in his empire and against the Egyptians.[64] A group of men in Athens, however, sensationally warned the people that Artaxerxes intended to use his fleet against the Athenians as a precursor to waging war on all Greece and urged the people to unite the Greeks and strike first.[65] They further claimed that if the people did this, then Athens would become an imperial power again and generate enough money from the war to solve their financial problems.[66]

Athenians of the fourth century were generally informed about foreign affairs and despite being swayed by the rhetoric of speakers were able to evaluate issues and make sensible decisions.[67] However, the idea of attacking the Persian Empire at this time was ludicrous. The Athenians were far from recovered from the Social War and were embroiled not only in the war with Philip (who was now busily reducing Athenian influence on his seaboard) but also in a sacred war in Greece (see below). The identities of the men calling for war against Persia are unknown, but they were clearly neither seasoned nor savvy politicians.[68] Nevertheless, their call led to a debate in the Assembly about war with Persia. Although over 120 years had passed since the Persian Wars (480–479), the Athenians had never forgotten that in 480 Xerxes' troops had looted and burned Athens. In fact, in 337 Philip, then in control of Greece, cunningly put forward revenge on Athens' behalf as one of his reasons for invading Asia.

---

[64] On the background, cf. Sealey, *Demosthenes*, pp. 104–105.

[65] Demosthenes 14.7.

[66] Demosthenes 14.8, 12, 35, 38, for example.

[67] P. E. Harding, "Athenian Foreign Policy in the Fourth Century," *Klio* 77 (1995), pp. 105–125; cf. E. Badian, "The Ghost of Empire: Reflections on Athenian Foreign Policy in the Fourth Century," in W. Eder (ed.), *Die athenische Demokratie im 4. Jahrhundert v. Chr.* (Stuttgart: 1995), pp. 79–106, and see in detail H. Montgomery, *The Way to Chaeronea* (Oslo: 1983), passim and Hunt, *War, Peace, and Alliance in Demosthenes' Athens*, passim.

[68] They were hardly the adherents of the powerful Chares and Aristophon: Jaeger, *Demosthenes*, p. 72. Badian, "Road to Prominence," p. 29, gives good reasons why they would not be influential speakers.

There was, then, plenty of ill feeling toward the Persians, even though they had not showed any interest in subduing Greece since the Persian Wars.

Demosthenes by now was a successful speechwriter in the law courts but he was also politically ambitious. However, before he formally spoke in the Assembly he needed an issue that was gripping the city, for then the people were more likely to listen to him, and he would attract the attention of more seasoned politicians. The Persian threat gave Demosthenes the opportunity he was waiting for, and he seized it. He realized the absurdity of contemplating war against Persia, but given anti-Persian sentiment in Athens he was anxious that his arguments to deter the people would be badly received or even considered unpatriotic.[69] Therefore, his speech subtly urged the people to wait for a better time to attack Persia when the other Greeks would throw in their lot with Athens.[70]

An ancient critic commented that a better title for *On the Symmories* (*Navy Boards*) was "On a Policy with Respect to the Persian King," and Demosthenes later mentions it was "about things to do with the King."[71] (King with a capital "K" is commonly used to denote the Persian king.) It got its title, however, from the reforms Demosthenes proposed for the *symmories*, the boards of people that funded Athens' navy.[72] Stylistically, the speech has been described as a "landmark in the development of Demosthenes' oratory" for its use of imagery, word-play, and construction,[73] and its didactic tone set a trend for his future speeches.[74] Demosthenes was thus on his way to political power.

---

[69] See the comments of Hunt, *War, Peace, and Alliance in Demosthenes' Athens*, p. 80, on this aspect of the speech as well as its (and so Demosthenes') panhellenic sentiments.

[70] Demosthenes 14.3, 5, 38.

[71] Demosthenes 15.6; cf. 14.10–11, 41.

[72] Demosthenes 14.16–28.

[73] MacDowell, *Demosthenes*, pp. 146–147, with examples.

[74] On this aspect, see the chapter on Demosthenes in H. Yunis, *Taming Democracy: Models of Political Rhetoric in Classical Athens* (Ithaca: 1996), pp. 237–277. On Demosthenes' rhetoric of war in this and other speeches, see also J. Roisman, *The Rhetoric of Manhood: Masculinity in the Attic Orators* (Berkeley and Los Angeles: 2005), pp. 113–116.

On the Symmories (Navy Boards)[75]

In his short opening (*prooimion*), Demosthenes warned the people not to attack Persia despite the previous speakers' nationalistic appeals to Athens' history. He contrasted their message to his (1–2):

> Those who praise your ancestors, men of Athens, seem to me to have chosen to deliver speeches that will find favor with you but no benefit to those whom they praise. For in seeking to speak about achievements to which no one could do justice, they win for themselves the reputation of being able speakers but leave their audience with a lesser opinion of those men's excellence. . . . I, by contrast, will seek to explain how you can best prepare yourselves. The situation is as follows: Even if all of us who wish to address you were to show ourselves to be skilled speakers, I am certain that this would not lead to any improvement in your affairs. But if every one, whoever he is, who comes up to speak can tell you convincingly what kind of preparation will benefit our city, and on what scale it should be and how it should be paid for, the current panic would be wholly defused. That is what I shall try do, if I can, after I have briefly told you what I think about our relations with the King.

Demosthenes' didactic tone continued in his survey of relations between the Greeks and the Persians, although he took care to echo the popular belief that the Great King was an enemy and should be treated with suspicion (3–13). Since an attack on Persia was futile, he sought to rebut what previous speakers had evidently urged: a declaration of war on the King (8) and sending embassies to the Greek states calling them to war (12). He told the people "your ambassadors travelling around will be doing nothing but rhapsodize" (12),[76] meaning they would be like poets who entertained an audience but did not achieve anything practical. If the Athenians declared preemptive war on Persia, they would technically be the aggressors, and the King might then

---

[75] On the speech, see Schaefer, *Demosthenes²* 1, pp. 459–465, Blass, *attische Beredsamkeit²* 3.1, pp. 240–244, Pickard-Cambridge, *Demosthenes*, pp. 119–122, Jaeger, *Demosthenes*, pp. 70–82, L. Pearson, *The Art of Demosthenes* (Meisenheim am Glan: 1976), pp. 112–116, Carlier, *Démosthène*, pp. 78–81, Usher, *Greek Oratory: Tradition and Originality*, pp. 209–211, Lehmann, *Demosthenes*, pp. 75–78, MacDowell, *Demosthenes*, pp. 142–147; cf. Badian, "Road to Prominence," pp. 28–30. Translation with notes: J. Trevett, *Demosthenes, Speeches 1–17* (Austin: 2011), pp. 241–256; detailed discussion and commentary: Karvounis, *Demosthenes*, pp. 71–116.

[76] Translation: MacDowell, *Demosthenes*, p. 144.

bribe other Greeks to join him in attacking Athens. Demosthenes later named the Thebans as potential enemies of Athens (33–40). It would be a different matter, Demosthenes stressed, if the King invaded Attica, for then the Athenians would be able to rally other Greeks to their cause. They should therefore wait to see what the Persians did (4–5, 12–13).

Demosthenes was concerned with the strength of the Athenian fleet, which he warned needed to be increased before the people thought seriously about attacking Persia. In the middle of his speech he proposed a series of reforms to enhance naval funding to build more ships (16–28). Principal among these was to expand the number of people eligible for the *symmories* from the 1,200 called for under the law of Periander to 2,000. Demosthenes claimed that Periander's law was not working in practice because trierarchs, as well as heiresses, orphans, cleruchs, associations, and invalids (who were responsible for paying maintenance costs) were avoiding their financial responsibilities (16). The system needed 1,200 actual contributors to work,[77] but since it was impossible to prevent some of them from evading their payments Demosthenes wanted to add a further 800 so that "if you designate this number, once heiresses, orphans, the property of cleruchs and associations, and invalids have been removed, you will have twelve hundred remaining" (16).

Demosthenes' financial provisions were detailed and practical. He concluded his speech by returning to his theme of the first part, recommending that the people avoid antagonizing the King, given his resources (31–41). As he had in his earlier law court speeches, Demosthenes appealed to a sense of justice to persuade the people to maintain peace, especially given the mood of the Greeks:

> I think that justice is on our side and that those who are on it will be stronger than the traitors and the foreigners in any situation. And so I say that we should not be afraid without good reason nor be induced to start a war. . . . But let us not act unjustly, both for our own sake and because

[77] D. M. MacDowell, "The Law of Periandros about Symmories," *CQ*² 36 (1986), pp. 438–449, E. Ruschenbusch, "Die athenischen Symmorien des 4. Jh. v. Chr.," *ZPE* 31 (1978), pp. 275–284 and "Die Zahl der athenischen Trierarchen in der Zeit nach 340 v. Chr.," *Class. & Med.* 41 (1990), pp. 79–88, Karvounis, *Demosthenes*, pp. 91–106, 117–123, but see Gabrielsen, *Financing the Athenian Fleet*, pp. 182–199; cf. his "The Number of Athenian Trierarchs after ca. 340 B.C.," *Class. & Med.* 40 (1989), pp. 145–159 and "Trierarchic Symmories," *Class. & Med.* 41 (1990), pp. 89–118.

of the disturbed condition and unreliability of the rest of Greece. If we unanimously agreed to attack him, I would not consider it wrong for us to wrong him. But since that is not the case, I say that we should be on our guard not to offer the King any excuse to seek justice on behalf of the other Greeks. For if you remain at peace, such an action would make him suspect; but if you go to war, he could reasonably represent himself, because of their hatred for you, as a friend of the others. Do not then put the evils of Greece to the test, by summoning the Greeks when they will refuse to come and by fighting a war that you will be unable to win.[78]

Demosthenes did not persuade the people to reform the symmories. He later said that hardly anyone agreed with him,[79] so perhaps he was naive to think more people would voluntarily spend money to cover shortfalls from tax dodgers.[80] Moreover, his listeners may have found it difficult to follow the dense argumentation that characterizes this and all his early speeches.[81] They may also have thought him to be patronizing because the speech is peppered with the first person pronoun *ego* ("I"), which probably became wearing after a while.[82] The Athenians did, however, abandon any thoughts of war with Persia, so perhaps this aspect of his speech was persuasive.[83]

Demosthenes' failure ultimately did not matter because he got what he wanted: he attracted the attention of prominent Athenians, who were likewise in favor of financial reform and against war.[84] One of

[78] Demosthenes 14.35, 36–38.
[79] Demosthenes 15.6.
[80] Badian, "Road to Prominence," p. 30: "In view of the widespread tax evasion, adding further taxes to a new segment of the population was rather naive. The proposal had no chance of passing, and Demosthenes no doubt knew it."
[81] L. Pearson, "The Development of Demosthenes as a Political Orator," *Phoenix* 29 (1975), p. 97, calls it "bewildering"; cf. R. D. Milns, "The Public Speeches," in Ian Worthington (ed.), *Demosthenes: Statesman and Orator* (London: 2000), pp. 210–211. Demosthenes learned his lesson and switched to a simpler style better suited to a listening audience by the time of *On the Freedom of the Rhodians in* 351.
[82] Pearson, *Art of Demosthenes*, p. 114; cf. MacDowell, *Demosthenes*, p. 142.
[83] The view of Pickard-Cambridge, *Demosthenes*, pp. 122–123.
[84] Lehmann, *Demosthenes*, pp. 77–78. Jaeger, *Demosthenes*, pp. 76–78, argues that Demosthenes' proposal has affinities with that of *Against Leptines* to increase the number of men eligible for the *choregia*, so both proposals are evidence of a "policy of systematic disburdenment of the wealthy class." That is going too far, for Demosthenes could not afford to alienate the mass of the ordinary people, as his patriotic criticisms of Persia in *On the Symmories* show.

them was Eubulus, who from the mid- to late 350s was the most important politician in Athens, and under whose wing Demosthenes would
become the consummate politician.[85]

EUBULUS AND DEMOSTHENES

Eubulus had been an archon in 370 and oversaw a number of public
works, including the water supply.[86] Afterward he gained notoriety
by prosecuting various venal and inept officials.[87] Eventually he
turned to financial and economic reform, and his success in this area
accounted for his rise to greater political prominence.[88] Military
campaigns were the largest drain on any city's finances, as they are
today, so Eubulus strove to persuade the Athenians not to get
involved in costly wars or overseas ventures, which they could not
afford, or even to conclude alliances that might draw them into war.
He knew, like most Athenians, that peace brought prosperity, so he
advocated a noninterventionist foreign policy, curtailing military
expenditure by decreasing the amount of money from the annual
budget that was paid into the city's Military Fund.[89] Thanks to him,
for much of the 350s Athens stood aloof from foreign involvement,
and benefited economically. Eubulus was not a strict isolationist in
the sense that he wanted Athens to have a policy of "splendid isola-
tion" like that of Great Britain in the nineteenth century. When the
city's safety was directly threatened, he knew the people needed to
secure strategic alliances and take military action. To this end, he
enacted a series of military reforms to strengthen the city's naval
reserves and cavalry.

---

[85] G. L. Cawkwell, "Eubulus," *JHS* 83 (1963), pp. 47–67, Carlier, *Démosthène*, pp.
67–75, Karvounis, *Demosthenes*, pp. 106–111; see also Schaefer, *Demosthenes²* 1, pp.
186–214, Sealey, *Demosthenes*, pp. 116–118.

[86] Demosthenes 3.29.

[87] Demosthenes 19.290–294.

[88] Cawkwell, "Eubulus," pp. 48, 54–61, Hunt, *War, Peace, and Alliance in Demosthenes'
Athens*, pp. 32, 49–50, 258.

[89] It is unknown exactly when this fund (referred to as *ta stratiotika* in the sources) was
created and by whom, but the Athenians must have had such a fund given their military endeavors in the fourth century: see further, G. L. Cawkwell, "Demosthenes
and the Stratiotic Fund," *Mnemosyne* 15 (1962), pp. 377–383 (exploding the theory
that Demosthenes created it in 349/8).

Eubulus arranged for the remainder of the city's annual surplus to be paid into a newly created repository, the Theoric Fund. Its name came from the Greek word *theoria*, which meant looking or observing, and the fund initially provided money to the people to attend religious festivals and the theatre.[90] The Theoric Fund was not just a type of dole, for eventually it was used to maintain various public buildings and roads.[91] It became so important to city life that the people nicknamed it "the glue of democracy."[92] Because of its religious nature, the fund was inviolable: those who suggested using its money for other purposes faced indictment and possibly execution.[93] The amount of money it held was enormous and those who controlled it played a dominant role in the city's administration.[94] At first probably only one man—the treasurer—administered the fund, but at some point in the mid- to late-fourth century a board of ten men took on the role. The treasurers were appointed for a four-year term. As the sole treasurer of the fund that he created Eubulus dictated financial policy from 354 to 350.[95]

From an annual income of 137 talents after the Social War, Eubulus boosted state revenues to 400 talents.[96] He may well have put into practice some of Xenophon's recommendations in his *Ways and Means*,

---

[90] Plutarch, *Pericles* 9, says that Pericles created the fund in the 450s, but that is unlikely: Cawkwell, "Eubulus," pp. 53–58, Sealey, *Demosthenes*, pp. 256–258. However, D. K. Roselli, "Theorika in Fifth-Century Athens," *GRBS* 49 (2009), pp. 5–30, argues that the Theoric Fund was not created until the middle of the fourth century and that in the fifth century there was a system of ad hoc payments of money to the people.

[91] Aeschines 3.25.

[92] [Plutarch], *Moralia* 1011b. On the fund, see J. J. Buchanan, *Theorika* (New York: 1962); cf. Cawkwell, "Demosthenes and the Stratiotic Fund," pp. 377–383, Cawkwell, "Eubulus," pp. 53–58, M. H. Hansen, "The Theoric Fund and the *Graphe Paranomon* against Apollodorus," *GRBS* 17 (1976), pp. 235–246, Carlier, *Démosthène*, pp. 73–74, Rhodes, *Athenian Boule*, pp. 235–240, Sealey, *Demosthenes*, pp. 256–258, Lehmann, *Demosthenes*, pp. 68–69.

[93] For an alternative view on the penalty, see E. M. Harris, "Demosthenes and the Theoric Fund," in W. R. Wallace and E. M. Harris (eds.), *Transitions to Empire: Essays in Honor of E. Badian* (Norman: 1996), pp. 57–76, citing bibliography.

[94] Cf. Aeschines 3.25.

[95] Cawkwell, "Eubulus," pp. 54–61. On the term of office, see R. Develin, "From Panathenaia to Panathenaia," *ZPE* 57 (1985), pp. 133–138, citing bibliography.

[96] Theopompus, *FGrH* 115 F 166.

specifically those encouraging metics to return to Athens, stimulating trade, and speeding up the legal process.[97] Crucial to his success, however, was his passive foreign policy, which he adopted for purely fiscal reasons.

Eubulus' achievements were remembered for many years after he died. Thus in 323, when Demosthenes was put on trial for his involvement in a bribery scandal (Chapter 15), his prosecutor contrasted his alleged lack of good works with Eubulus' civic achievements:[98]

> What triremes are there which have been built by this man [Demosthenes] for the city, as in the time of Eubulus? What dockyards have been constructed under his administration? When has this man either by decree or law increased the cavalry? When such opportunities presented themselves after the battle of Chaeronea, what force did he levy, either by land or by sea? What ornament to the goddess has this man carried up to the Acropolis? What building did Demosthenes construct in your Exchange, or in the city, or anywhere else in the country? No one could show one anywhere!

In the mid-350s Demosthenes deliberately echoed Eubulus' program of financial reform and the need for peace. Though his name was becoming better known in Athens, he still lacked political connections, and clearly his oratorical ability was not enough to sway an assembly. He needed support, and Eubulus was the man to court. However, as the threat to Greece from Philip accelerated in the next years, Demosthenes realized that the Athenians needed a more aggressive policy to deal with him than the one that the fiscally conservative Eubulus advocated.

PHILIP, THRACE, AND THESSALY

In 354 the fall of Methone gave Philip control of his entire Macedonian coastline. In the same year, he invaded Thrace again, seizing the towns of Pagae, Abdera, Maroneia, and Neapolis.[99] His moves alarmed

---

[97] Cawkwell, "Eubulus," pp. 63–64, Sealey, *Demosthenes*, p. 116. See also J. Engels, "Anmerkungen zum 'Ökonomischen Denken' im 4. Jahrh. v. Chr. und zur wirtschaftlichen Entwicklung des Lykurgischen Athen," *MBAH* 7 (1988), pp. 90–132.

[98] Dinarchus 1.96. The passage is important for the information it gives on Eubulus' military reforms, although note the caution of Cawkwell, "Eubulus," pp. 65–66.

[99] Demosthenes 23.183, Diodorus 16.34.1, Polyaenus 4.2.22.

the Athenians, who were at the time concerned about their relations with Cersebleptes, the king of eastern Thrace. His kingdom bordered directly on the Hellespont, which was a vital point on the grain route, and Athenian influence here rested on Cersebleptes' benevolence. He was, however, a fickle ally, who had his own ambitions to unify all Thrace. The two other Thracian kings, his brothers Berisades and Amadocus, viewed his activities suspiciously, and they courted Athenian favor in case he moved against them. Eventually it would be Philip, not them, who would cripple Cersebleptes' power and in the late 340s add Thrace to his empire.[100]

Then in 353 Philip again went to the aid of the Aleuadae of Larissa against Lycophron, the ruler of Pherae, who was bent on winning control of all Thessaly. By now the Thessalians were involved in a sacred war against the state of Phocis, whose troops had earlier seized Delphi, home to the Oracle of Apollo (see below). During the war, however, Lycophron had made an alliance with Phocis, so when Philip entered Thessaly Lycophron turned to Phocis for help. Onomarchus, the Phocian commander at Delphi, sent him troops commanded by his brother Phayllus, but Philip easily repelled them. His action prompted Onomarchus to march personally to Thessaly with 20,000 infantry and 500 cavalry, and in the late summer he unexpectedly defeated Philip in two battles.[101] Some of Philip's men immediately fled northwards, forcing him to return to Pella. As the king left, he proclaimed he would return "like a ram, which next time would butt harder."[102]

Philip's defeat spawned serious repercussions. Sensing weakness, the Illyrians, the Paeonians, and perhaps even the king of Epirus prepared to invade Macedonia. The Olynthians ended their alliance with Philip and solicited one with Athens. The Athenians also seized the chance to undermine Philip's authority in Thrace and, with Eubulus' consent, dispatched Chares and twenty Athenian ships to Neapolis to apply pressure to Cersebleptes. In the spring or summer of 353, Chares captured Sestos, an important port on the grain route, and killed all

---

[100] On relations between Macedonia and Thrace, including Philip's reign, see Z. Archibald, "Macedonia and Thrace," in J. Roisman and Ian Worthington (eds.), *Blackwell Companion to Ancient Macedonia* (Malden: 2010), pp. 326–341.

[101] Diodorus 16.35.2, Polyaenus 2.38.2; see further, Worthington, *Philip II*, pp. 58–59, and especially R. A. Gabriel, *Philip II of Macedon: Greater than Alexander* (Washington: 2010), pp. 127–132.

[102] Diodorus 16.35.2–3, Polyaenus 2.38.2.

of its male citizens and sold its women and children as slaves. The following year cleruchs settled there to increase Athenian prominence in this area.[103]

Chares' action at Sestos was not lost on Cersebleptes, now also aware of Philip's defeat at Onomarchus' hands. On the urging of Cersebleptes' mercenary general Charidemus (who hailed from Oreus on Euboea), he recognized the Athenians' control of the entire Chersonese (apart from Cardia on the isthmus) and promised to help them recover Amphipolis. The Athenians were so delighted with Charidemus' intervention on their behalf that they bestowed citizenship on him.[104] A politician named Aristocrates even proposed a decree in the Boule to protect Charidemus' person at all times: if anyone killed him, the murderer was to be arrested and executed, and any state that offered him protection would be an enemy of Athens.[105] Before his decree came before the Assembly, however, Euthycles of Thria (a town west of Athens on the route to Eleusis) brought a *graphe paranomon* against Aristocrates. His trial, in which Demosthenes delivered the prosecution speech, took place in 352 (Chapter 5, pp. 110–114).

By the end of 353 the Athenians' fortunes were on the rise and those of Philip were on the decline. That would soon change. In 352 Philip returned to Thessaly, defeated and killed Onomarchus, and involved himself in the sacred war to increase his personal influence in Greece. The origins and early events of this war may now be traced in order to understand how seizing control of Apollo's oracle dictated the politics of central Greece for a decade.

THE THIRD SACRED WAR

As the home of the oracle of the god Apollo, Delphi was one of the most important sacred places in Greece (Figure 8).[106] The Greeks felt that cities with oracles in them needed special protection because of their sacred nature. Accordingly, states bordering on oracular sites, known as

[103] *IG* ii² 1613, 297–298, Diodorus 16.34.3–4; cf. Demosthenes 23.103, 181.

[104] Davies, *Athenian Propertied Families*, p. 571, dates the citizenship to 375.

[105] Demosthenes 23.16, 34–35, 91.

[106] Cf. H. W. Parke, *A History of the Delphic Oracle* (Oxford: 1939), J. E. Fontenrose, *The Delphic Oracle, Its Responses and Operations, with a Catalogue of Responses* (Berkeley and Los Angeles: 1978).

FIGURE 8. The Temple of Apollo at Delphi, home of the oracle of the god.

amphictyonies ("people who dwell around or near"), established amphictyonic leagues and came together in an amphictyonic council to administer the oracle. Over time, other states joined a particular amphictyony even if they were geographically distant from the actual oracle. The amphictyonic council had the authority to punish any state that committed a sacrilegious act, even combining religion and politics to declare a sacred war against it, and so demand troops for it from its members.[107]

Greece had already been the scene of two sacred wars, the first in 595–586 and the second in the mid-fifth century. Exactly what happened in them is unknown, but at the conclusion of the first one the Delphic Amphictyonic Council took over actual control of Delphi.[108] By the fourth century, Delphi's Amphictyonic League consisted of twenty-four states, including Athens, Thebes, and Thessaly. Exactly how many votes each state had is unknown, although perhaps because of its size and location Thessaly had approximately half, and a Thessalian was almost always the president of the council.

---

[107] Hunt, *War, Peace, and Alliance in Demosthenes' Athens*, pp. 86–89, with comments on the sacred war.

[108] It is even possible that the first war did not take place but was a later invention. See further, J. K. Davies, "The Tradition about the First Sacred War," in S. Hornblower (ed.), *Greek Historiography* (Oxford: 1994), pp. 193–212.

At the Amphictyonic Council's meeting at Delphi in 356, the Thebans brought up the fact that the small state of Phocis, comprising twenty-two cities on the border of northwest Boeotia, had an outstanding fine. The Phocians at some point had been fined for sacrilegiously cultivating part of the plain below Delphi, home to the god's sacrificial animals.[109] The Thebans also reminded the council that the Spartans had not yet paid the fine imposed on them for attacking Thebes in 382 and seizing the Cadmea. The Thebans' motive in raising these issues now had nothing to do with justice but was that of revenge. In 362, Epaminondas of Thebes had requested troops from Phocis for a campaign in the Peloponnese. The Phocians refused him because of their friendship with Sparta and their favorable stance toward Athens. The Thebans were also concerned that their influence in the Peloponnese was declining while that of Sparta was rising.

If the Thebans expected to see Phocis and Sparta suffer, they were mistaken. Although they asked for Sparta's fine to be doubled, the city refused to pay.[110] So too did the Phocians, who argued that they had an ancient claim to the plain in question based on some lines in Homer's *Iliad*.[111] To protest the Thebans' agenda, the Phocian general Philomelus boldly decided to seize Delphi and successfully petitioned the Spartans for money, which he used to hire 5,000 mercenaries and capture Delphi. He fought off amphictyonic troops sent to displace them and during the winter of 356–355 dispatched diplomatic embassies to the Greek states to explain his action and solicit help.

Sparta and later Athens supported Phocis—more to counter Thebes' influence than anything else—but elsewhere Philomelus' call was unsuccessful. In the spring of 355 the Amphictyonic Council declared a sacred war against Phocis, and this Third Sacred War lasted from 355

[109] Diodorus 16.23.

[110] Cf. Justin 8.1.4–6. For a different view on the outbreak of the war, see J. Buckler, "Thebes, Delphi, and the Outbreak of the Sacred War," in J. Buckler and H. Beck (eds.), *Central Greece and the Politics of Power in the Fourth Century BC* (Cambridge: 2008), pp. 213–223, that the Phocians and Spartans were guilty of the charges brought against them, which were brought up by the council, not by the Thebans who were operating for any political reasons.

[111] Homer, *Iliad* 2.517–519: "And the Phocians were ruled by Schedius and Epistrophus, sons of big-hearted Iphitus, son of Naubolus; these were they who lived in Cyparissus and in rocky Pytho, and sacred Crisa."

to 346.[112] Despite its religious nature, it was as political as any other war. The Spartans hoped that it would force Thebes to reduce its presence in the Peloponnese, thereby allowing them to reassert their authority there.[113] The first sign of their aspirations came in 353 when they threatened independent Arcadia in the north. The Athenians viewed the war as a means of muzzling Theban interference in central Greece, and in the same year as it broke out the orator Hegesippus tried to persuade the Athenians to send troops to Phocis. However, the people were still reeling from their defeat in the Social War.[114] Finally, Philip saw in the war the opportunity to involve himself in central Greek politics.

Philomelus immediately went on the offensive. There were at Delphi a number of sacred treasuries that different Greek cities had built, containing money and valuable artifacts, dedicated as thank offerings to the god for his advice or to commemorate military victories. They were sacrosanct, but nonetheless Philomelus stole money and precious items from them to hire another 5,000 mercenaries, giving him 10,000 "of the worst knaves, and those who despised the gods, because of their own greed."[115] He invaded Locris, where he defeated a Locrian and Theban army, and then at Argolas in eastern Locris defeated a Thessalian and allied army of 6,000 men. His successes were short-lived, however, for in 354 the Theban general Pammenes at the head of an amphictyonic army defeated him at Neon. Rather than suffer capture, Philomelus committed suicide by jumping off Mount Parnassus.[116]

The Phocians at once elected Onomarchus their commander in chief and his brother Phayllus as general.[117] The following year he too plundered from the Delphic treasuries to hire more mercenaries and bribe the powerful Thessalians to stay out of the war.[118] He also

---

[112] In detail on the war, see J. Buckler, *Philip II and the Sacred War* (Leiden: 1989); cf. his *Aegean Greece in the Fourth Century BC* (Leiden: 2003), pp. 397–429 and 442–452. More detailed treatment of the politics behind its outbreak: Buckler, *Philip II and the Sacred War*, pp. 9–19.

[113] On Sparta in the war, see C. D. Hamilton, "Philip II and Archidamus," in W. L. Adams and E. N. Borza (eds.), *Philip II, Alexander the Great, and the Macedonian Heritage* (Lanham: 1982), pp. 61–77.

[114] Aeschines 3.118; cf. Demosthenes 18.18.

[115] Diodorus 16.30.1–2.

[116] Justin 8.1.13; see also Diodorus 16.30.3–31.4, Pausanias 10.2.4.

[117] Diodorus 16.21.1–3, Pausanias 10.2.5, Justin 8.1.14.

[118] Diodorus 16.33.3.

made an alliance with Lycophron of Pherae and even invaded Boeotia, seizing the town of Orchomenus, to try to cripple the Theban
war effort. At this point, Onomarchus, learning of the defeat of
Phayllus by Philip in Thessaly, broke off his campaign in Boeotia and
marched north to Thessaly, where he defeated the Macedonian king
(see above).

The Athenians were now involved in two wars, the Third Sacred
War and their own war against Philip. Yet Demosthenes' next speeches,
all dealing with foreign policy, ignored him. Instead, Demosthenes
focused on affairs in the Peloponnese, the balance of power in Greece
between Thebes and Sparta, and Athenian involvement in Thrace. It
was only in 351 that he finally turned to deal with the threat from
Philip in his first *Philippic*, but by then the king was an unstoppable
force. In hindsight, Demosthenes would have been better off worrying
less about Athenian interests in Greece in the mid- to late-350s and
more about Philip.

5

The Aspiring Politician

DESPITE THE REBUFF Demosthenes had suffered over *On the Symmories*, however, he did not forsake his political ambitions. He know that it was still crucial to speak in an informed manner on pressing issues, and at the present time Athenian interests in key areas from the Peloponnese to as far afield as Thrace were of immediate public concern. Thus, he turned from speaking on financial matters to these foreign policy issues. His next speeches contained themes of morality and justice, but he was not motivated by idealism. Nor did his unhappy youth and upbringing enable him to empathize with those badly treated to the extent that he wanted to champion their cause. Again, his motivation in speaking lay in his single-minded ambition.

His next speeches were, however, unsuccessful, not because he failed to display an incisive grasp of international affairs or put forward flawed policies but because more influential speakers like Eubulus got the better of him. This was also the period when Demosthenes began to show more independence and criticize current leadership because he thought that Eubulus' fiscal conservatism was detrimental to Athenian security in light of Philip's inroads into Greece. He also moved from speaking on behalf of a wealthy elite to evoking populist sentiments, whereby he appealed directly to the people and their needs, and especially called on their patriotism to act in the city's best interests.

Yet even though Demosthenes still failed to carry the day, he achieved what he sought the most: public attention. If alive today, he might well be a partisan pundit debating the pros and cons of foreign policy on cable news programs who was out to make a name for himself.

BALANCE OF POWER: SPARTA AND THEBES

After the Thebans ended the Spartan hegemony of Greece in 371 at the Battle of Leuctra and then in the following year invaded the Peloponnese, the Spartans had harbored hopes of returning to their former influence in the Peloponnese. However, the Theban liberation of the helots (serfs) of Messenia and of the Arcadians in the northern Peloponnese, who formed an independent Arcadian League, were major blows to Spartan ambition.

In 360 the Spartan king Agesilaus died and was succeeded by his son Archidamus. Sparta was unique among the Greek states in having a constitution that was a mixture of monarchic, oligarchic, and democratic elements. There were two kings, but as members of a thirty-person governing council called the Gerousia their authority was not absolute. Still, they wielded considerable influence, and in 360 Archidamus put into action a plan to return Sparta to the time when it had headed a Peloponnesian League and defeated Athens in the Peloponnesian War. Among other things, he cunningly suggested that the Greek cities of the mainland take back the towns and areas they had previously controlled but lost as a result of war or diplomatic arrangement. Athens, for example, would expect to regain control of the border town of Oropus, which Thebes had seized in 366.[1] The Spartans would gain the most, because in reasserting their control over Arcadia and Messenia they would again come to dominate the Peloponnese. Archidamus' plan was, however, unsuccessful because the Greeks did not support it. For one thing, the Thebans, who were also intent on extending their authority in Peloponnesian affairs, had no desire to witness a resurgence of Spartan power.

For some years little happened as both Thebes and Sparta monitored each other's activities. When in 353 Onomarchus' actions forced the Thebans to switch their attention from the Peloponnese to the Third Sacred War, the Spartans prepared to invade Arcadia and then Messenia. At this time, or perhaps even earlier, when the Spartans' intentions were becoming clearer, the Messenians pleaded for an alliance with Athens.[2] The Athenians had been allies of the Messenians' former enemies the Spartans since 370 because of a mutual distrust of Thebes,

---

[1] When Callistratus was indicted for the loss of Oropus, and Demosthenes was said to have heard his defense and decided on a career in oratory: see Chapter 2 pp. 17–18.

[2] Pausanias 4.28.1, 2.

but still they responded favorably to the Messenians' overtures since they felt an alliance would distract Thebes and so help them reassert their claim to Oropus. The philosophy "the enemy of my enemy is my friend" has drawn previously opposing states and countries together against common enemies throughout history. News of this alliance emboldened the people of Megalopolis, the capital city of the Arcadian League, to dispatch an urgent embassy to the Athenians for help. With Thebes now preoccupied in the Third Sacred War and unable to protect them, the only option for the Megalopolitans was to approach Athens. The Spartans also sent an embassy to the Athenians urging them to remain true to their alliance with Sparta.

Against this background of escalating tensions in the Peloponnese Demosthenes delivered his speech *On Behalf of the Megalopolitans* in an assembly held shortly after Philip's defeat in Thessaly in 353.[3] He may even have done so because of Onomarchus' victory over Philip.[4] In looking to the long-term interests of Athens, Demosthenes pointed out that Sparta's ascendancy in the Peloponnese at Theban expense affected the balance of power in Greece between Sparta and Thebes. Demosthenes' claim was a precursor of the modern balance of power argument,[5] first expounded by the British politician Lord Brougham in the nineteenth century.[6] Demosthenes' message was simple: the Athenians needed to make an immediate alliance with Megalopolis despite their treaty with Sparta but not send troops.[7] In return for Athenian assistance, the Megalopolitans had to end their treaty with Thebes.[8]

---

[3] Date: Dionysius of Halicarnassus, *To Ammaeus* 1.4; cf. R. Sealey, "Dionysius of Halicarnassus and Some Demosthenic Dates," *REG* 68 (1955), p. 118, R. Lane Fox, "Demosthenes, Dionysius, and the Dating of Six Early Speeches," *Class. & Med.* 48 (1997), pp. 181–183, C. Karvounis, *Demosthenes: Studien zu den Demegorien orr. XIV, XVI, XV, IV, I, II, III* (Tübingen: 2002), pp. 141–142.

[4] T. T. B. Ryder, "Demosthenes and Philip II," in Ian Worthington (ed.), *Demosthenes: Statesman and Orator* (London: 2000), p. 48.

[5] Jaeger, *Demosthenes*, p. 229 n. 37, Lehmann, *Demosthenes*, p. 81, and especially P. Hunt, *War, Peace, and Alliance in Demosthenes' Athens* (New York: 2010), pp. 169–180.

[6] "Dissertation on the Eloquence of the Ancients," in Lord Brougham, *Works* 7 (Edinburgh: 1856), p. 54.

[7] Demosthenes 16.4–5, 12, 14–15, 20–22, 25.

[8] Demosthenes 16.28; see also H. G. Ingenkamp, "Die Stellung des Demosthenes zu Theben in der Megalopolitenrede," *Hermes* 100 (1972), pp. 195–205, Karvounis, *Demosthenes*, pp. 151–154.

Dovetailing into his practical issues, Demosthenes struck a moral stance in his speech, urging the Athenians to act honorably and help victims of injustice as they always had in the past and so side with Megalopolis.

On Behalf of the Megalopolitans[9]

Demosthenes' speech revealed there had been previous speakers in the debate about Megalopolis' appeal, but in what was becoming his signature opening he dismissed and castigated them to capture the people's attention (1–2):

> Both groups—those speaking in support of the Arcadians and those speaking in support of the Spartans—seem to me to be wrong, men of Athens. For they accuse and slander each other, as if they had come here from one or other of these cities, rather than being your fellow-citizens and the recipients of these embassies. Their behavior would be appropriate if they were foreigners; but those who propose to offer you advice should be discussing the situation impartially and considering in an amicable spirit what is best for you. As it is, if I did not know these men and if they were not speaking Attic, I think that many people would suppose some of them to be Arcadian and the others, Spartan.[10]

He emphasized the point that of Thebes and Sparta the Spartans posed the greater threat to Athens' interests in southern Greece (4–10). The Athenians therefore needed to form an alliance with Megalopolis for reasons of justice as well as expediency (9–10):

---

[9] On the speech, see Schaefer, *Demosthenes*[2] 1, pp. 513–519, Blass, *attische Beredsamkeit*[2] 3.1, pp. 251–254, Pickard-Cambridge, *Demosthenes*, pp. 131–137, Jaeger, *Demosthenes*, pp. 82–90, L. Pearson, *The Art of Demosthenes* (Meisenheim am Glan: 1976), pp. 116–117, Carlier, *Démosthène*, pp. 81–83, S. Usher, *Greek Oratory: Tradition and Originality* (Oxford 1999), pp. 211–213, E. Badian, "The Road to Prominence," in Ian Worthington (ed.), *Demosthenes: Statesman and Orator* (London: 2000), pp. 30–31, Lehmann, *Demosthenes*, pp. 79–82, MacDowell, Demosthenes, pp. 207–210. Translation with notes: J. Trevett, *Demosthenes, Speeches 1–17* (Austin: 2011), pp. 275–285; detailed discussion and commentary: Karvounis, *Demosthenes*, pp. 124–173.

[10] The reference to Attic is to the Attic dialect; the Arcadians and Spartans would have spoken in the Doric dialect.

Ask yourselves, is it better and more honorable for us to begin our resistance to Spartan wrongdoing by supporting Megalopolis or by supporting Messene? In the former case, you will be seen both to be helping the Arcadians and to be intent on maintaining the peace, for which you risked battle. But in the latter case, everybody will see that you desire the survival of Messene not from a sense of justice but out of fear of Sparta. You should always determine what is right and do it—but at the same time you should ensure that this coincides with your own interests!

He argued that an alliance with Sparta would combat Thebes and present the people with the chance to regain Oropus (11–18). But then he unexpectedly urged the people to give up their claim to Oropus rather than sanction Spartan domination of the Peloponnese (18):

But if it were to become clear to you that we cannot take Oropus unless we allow the Spartans to conquer the Peloponnese, I think that it would be preferable, if I may say so, to leave Oropus alone than to abandon the Messenians and the Peloponnese to the Spartans.

Demosthenes knew his argument here would be provocative and unpopular, but he wanted to startle his audience into seeing the danger he believed Sparta posed. He even went so far as to declare that if Sparta became too strong and turned on Thebes, the Athenians might have to rescue Thebes or they could be Sparta's next victim (20).

In addition to allying with Megalopolis to defy Sparta in the Peloponnese, Demosthenes recommended a course of action to weaken Theban strength in Boeotia by assisting the three cities of Orchomenus, Plataea, and Thespiae, which were not part of the Boeotian League headed by Thebes (25–26).[11] He finished his speech with the moral invocation that the Assembly cannot "abandon any weaker state to a stronger one" (32).

Demosthenes did not endorse a troop deployment to the Peloponnese, but that was not enough—Eubulus spoke against him and carried the Assembly. Demosthenes later claimed Eubulus did not wish to anger the Thebans, but more likely is that he wanted to avoid any action that might cost the city unnecessary expenditure.[12] While Demosthenes was

---

[11] Ingenkamp, "Stellung des Demosthenes zu Theben," pp. 195–205, Lehmann, *Demosthenes*, pp. 79–81.

[12] Demosthenes 18.162.

correct to perceive that an alliance with Megalopolis (hence all Arcadia) would strengthen Athens' influence while curbing that of Thebes in the Peloponnese, his arguments and reasons were flawed. He did not take into account, for example, that the Thebans would come to Megalopolis' defense, as indeed they did—thus in 353, when the Spartans attacked Megalopolis, Thebes and other Peloponnesian states sent it troops.[13] Nor could he be certain that the Spartans would be able to conquer all of Arcadia or Messenia. In fact, he overplayed the power of Sparta, which was seriously crippled from a manpower shortage and weak, for in 350 the Spartans were defeated and forced to recognize the independence of Arcadia. A further factor in the Assembly's decision was that of Megalopolitan loyalty to Athens. Soliciting Athenian backing was logical, but Eubulus' non-interventionist policy did not guarantee the Athenians would march to their rescue, despite the alliance. To preserve their independence, the Arcadians would act as they saw fit if they did not receive Athenian help, even if that meant reneging on their alliance.[14]

THE CASE AGAINST TIMOCRATES

Not long after his speech about Megalopolis, Demosthenes returned to the law courts with a prosecution speech against Timocrates, who had been Androtion's colleague on the commission to collect tax arrears in 354 (Chapter 4 p. 72).[15] Timocrates' connection to Androtion made the case another high-profile one and so served Demosthenes' political aspirations.[16]

After Androtion's acquittal for illegally recommending crowns for the Boule, he and two other men, Melanopus and Glaucetes, had served on a diplomatic mission to Mausolus of Caria. The ship on which the three ambassadors were traveling encountered a merchant vessel from Naucratis in Egypt and they seized its cargo, which was worth nine and a half talents (or 57,000 drachmas).[17] The state rejected a plea by the

---

[13] Diodorus 16.39, Pausanias 8.27.9–10.

[14] A further possible reason for the speech's failure was its convoluted and highly rhetorical arguments, which a listening audience would have had difficulty following: R. D. Milns, "The Public Speeches of Demosthenes," in Ian Worthington (ed.), *Demosthenes: Statesman and Orator* (London: 2000), pp. 210–211.

[15] Date: Dionysius of Halicarnassus, *To Ammaeus* 1.4.

[16] Cf. Badian, "Road to Prominence," pp. 23–24.

[17] Demosthenes 24.11.

shipowner to return the cargo and instead ordered the three men to hand the money over to it. They refused (which technically made them state debtors, for which they lost their civic rights), were fined, and faced imprisonment until they discharged their debts. Their fine may even have been doubled because they did not pay it immediately so that in the end they might have owed as much as twenty-four talents.[18] Eventually, Timocrates, on Androtion's urging, passed a law delaying payment for any state debtor until the end of the year, which saved the three men from prison.[19] His measure was considered illegal, and the same men who had prosecuted Androtion a year earlier, Euctemon and Diodorus, indicted him for it.[20] Demosthenes again wrote for Diodorus, whose speech survives.

Against Timocrates[21]

Demosthenes built a careful case to show that Timocrates' law was unconstitutional, undemocratic, and unjust, and, to resonate especially with the present jurors, that it overturned the honest vote of any jury (1–40). In exaggerated fashion, he stressed that the law would bring economic ruin to the city, and that if the men did not pay what they owed the state the various democratic organs and even the armed forces would be severely impaired (96–99). His masterful argument exploited the financial problems facing the city by attacking the venal characters of both Timocrates and Androtion. As in his earlier speech against Androtion, Demosthenes lambasted the venal practices of tax collectors, who he said introduced new laws only for their own well-being not the good of the city (142).[22] He even repeated a section of his speech against Androtion to

---

[18] See MacDowell, *Demosthenes*, p. 183 for details.

[19] Demosthenes 24.24–27, 79–83; contra J. Roisman, *The Rhetoric of Conspiracy in Ancient Athens* (Berkeley and Los Angeles: 2006), pp. 103–114 (Timocrates' reason was unknown).

[20] Demosthenes 24.17–67, 70–107.

[21] On the speech, see Schaefer, *Demosthenes*² 1, pp. 372–387, Blass, *attische Beredsamkeit*² 3.1, pp. 244–251, Pickard-Cambridge, *Demosthenes*, pp. 137–141, Jaeger, *Demosthenes*, pp. 58–64, Usher, *Greek Oratory: Tradition and Originality*, pp. 201–204, Badian, "Road to Prominence," pp. 22–24, Lehmann, *Demosthenes*, pp. 71–75, MacDowell, *Demosthenes*, pp. 181–196; see also Roisman, *Rhetoric of Conspiracy*, pp. 103–114. Translation: J. H. Vince, *Demosthenes*, Loeb Classical Library 3 (Cambridge and London: 1986).

[22] On the complex financial and legal arguments, see MacDowell, *Demosthenes*, pp. 181–196, citing bibliography.

denigrate Timocrates further.[23] Demosthenes was clearly speaking here
to the poorer stratum of society, who principally suffered at the hands
of unscrupulous wealthy individuals. A lengthy conclusion to the speech
repeated that Timocrates' law was damaging and illegal and called
upon the jurors to find him guilty out of respect for their own laws
(187–218).

Demosthenes presented Timocrates and Androtion as the worst
types of citizens and as conspirators to undermine the democracy, yet
in truth they had worked, however high-handedly, to improve Athens'
finances.[24] Likewise flawed was Demosthenes' argument that the
Athenian democracy and military could not function effectively, for
only a year earlier, in his speech against the law of Leptines, he had
stated that reintroducing *ateleia* would have had little effect on state
coffers—yet the money Androtion and his two friends owed was less
than the latter. The jury probably acquitted Timocrates, for in 347 a
man of that name and his son supported Meidias (an associate of
Eubulus) against Demosthenes.[25] Androtion and his colleagues probably had to pay the state the value of the ship's cargo and perhaps also
the original fine.

Demosthenes would clearly have earned the enmity of Androtion
and Timocrates, who happened to be friends of Eubulus, whom Demosthenes was courting politically. Yet Demosthenes' prosecution of
them did not necessarily jeopardize his relations with Eubulus, for
Athenian political life, unlike today, was not arranged around a particular ideology or party[26]—as Demosthenes strove to establish himself
he took on any case that would realize his ambition.[27]

THE RAM RETURNS

If in 353 the Greeks thought that Philip was a spent force after his defeat
at Onomarchus' hands they were sadly mistaken. In the late spring or
summer of the following year, 352, he returned to Thessaly with a

[23] Sections 160–186 are taken from 22.47–56 and 65–78.

[24] Criticisms of his presentation: Roisman, *Rhetoric of Conspiracy*, pp. 104–114.

[25] Demosthenes 21.139.

[26] On this, see the works cited in Chapter 2 note 134.

[27] Against Schaefer, *Demosthenes*² 1, pp. 179–180, 361–363, 415–416, that the trial showed
collusion between politicians; contra Sealey *Demosthenes*, p. 113. Compare Demosthenes taking the case against the law of Leptines, who was a supporter of Eubulus.

substantial army of 20,000 infantry and 3,000 cavalry, bent on revenge. Onomarchus, with the same number of infantry but only 500 cavalry, marched to engage him at the Krokion Plain, or Crocus Field, near the coast of Magnesia. The Phocians had earlier enlisted Athenian aid for their cause, and the Assembly now dispatched Chares, newly returned from Thrace, and a fleet to Pagasae (Volos), Thessaly's principal harbor, to prevent it from falling to Philip and to land troops there who would march to reinforce Onomarchus. Philip, however, moved very quickly to take Pagasae before Onomarchus had even arrived at the Crocus Field, thereby preventing Chares from putting into the harbor. All he could do was sail up and down the western coast of the gulf.

Not many details of the battle of the Crocus Field are known, but Philip was victorious.[28] His cavalry first routed that of the Phocians and then attacked the enemy flanks while the massed battalions of the Macedonian phalanx wreaked havoc with their sarissas on the opposing center, forcing it to turn into the gulf waters. Some of the soldiers tried to swim to Chares' ships but drowned under the weight of their armor. 6,000 Phocians and their mercenaries were killed, including Onomarchus, and 3,000 were captured. As punishment for stealing from the sacred treasuries at Delphi, they were drowned as temple robbers.[29] Yet the Phocians, who lost almost half their army at the Crocus Field, refused to admit defeat and immediately elected Onomarchus' brother Phayllus commander. For the next several years the sacred war deteriorated into skirmishes between Phocian and Boeotian troops.[30]

Philip's return marked a new era in his relations with the Greeks. Instead of merely seeking revenge on Onomarchus, he proclaimed his involvement in the sacred war by commanding his men wear crowns of laurel—"as though the god were going before"[31]—and symbolically drowning the captives from the battle. Macedonia was not a member of the Amphictyonic Council and had no formal involvement in the

---

[28] Diodorus 16.35.4–5, 38.1, Justin 8.2.1–4; on the background and battle, see Worthington, *Philip II*, pp. 62–63, 64, R. A. Gabriel, *Philip II of Macedon: Greater than Alexander* (Washington: 2010), pp. 132–138.

[29] Diodorus 16.35.5.

[30] See further, J. Buckler, *Philip II and the Sacred War* (Leiden: 1989), pp. 86–114; cf. his *Aegean Greece in the Fourth Century BC* (Leiden: 2003), pp. 421–429.

[31] Diodorus 16.35.5, Justin 8.2.3. Griffith in N. G. L. Hammond and G. T. Griffith, *A History of Macedonia* 2 (Oxford: 1979), pp. 274–275, sees the wreaths as merely a ruse to restore army morale, but this is unlikely.

sacred war. However, Pherae's alliance with Phocis potentially disrupted Macedonian relations with Thessaly, and Phocis' reliance on Athens and Sparta also alarmed Philip. At all costs he had to safeguard his southern border with Thessaly and repair the damage that Onomarchus had inflicted on his military reputation in 353. Bringing a rebellious Pherae to heel simply by his military presence was one thing—quite another was leading an army into Greece. Philip did not wish to be seen as an invader, thereby giving the Greeks common cause to unite against him. To achieve his objectives he marched into Greece as a defender of Apollo and enemy of the sacrilegious Phocians. He knew his action would cause anxiety in Athens and Thebes, but it also offered him the opportunity to extend Macedonian influence in Greece. Thus, following the dramatic repercussions of his defeat of the previous year, Philip had now turned from border security and economic stimulation to creating a Macedonian empire.[32]

Philip now further consolidated his hold over Thessaly, of vital importance for his southern border. He attacked various cities that had resisted him in the past, and expelled Lycophron and Peitholaus from Pherae, along with 2,000 mercenaries. He then tried to win over the rebellious city by marrying a Pheraean lady, Nicesipolis (his fifth marriage), naming their daughter Thessalonice ("Thessalian Victory").[33] Ultimately, Pherae continued to defy him, but Larissa, as head of the Thessalian League, now elected him lifelong archon of Thessaly.[34] The position was a constitutional one, which permitted Philip to muster Thessalian infantry

---

[32] On the manner of Philip's return and change in his attitude to the Greeks, see Ian Worthington, "Alexander, Philip, and the Macedonian Background," in J. Roisman (ed.), *Brill Companion to Alexander the Great* (Leiden: 2003), pp. 94–96 and *Philip II*, pp. 61–62; see also J. R. Ellis, "The Dynamics of Fourth-Century Macedonian Imperialism," *Ancient Macedonia* 2 (Institute for Balkan Studies, Thessaloniki: 1977), pp. 103–114 and J. Buckler, "Philip II's Designs on Greece," in W. R. Wallace and E. M. Harris (eds.), *Transitions to Empire. Essays in Honor of E. Badian* (Norman: 1996), pp. 77–97.

[33] Athenaeus 13.557c, [Plutarch], *Moralia* 141b–c. J. R. Ellis, *Philip II and Macedonian Imperialism* (London: 1976), p. 212; see also E. Carney, *Women and Monarchy in Macedonia* (Norman: 2000), pp. 60–61. On the order of the wives, see A. D. Tronson, "Satyrus the Peripatetic and the Marriages of Philip II," *JHS* 104 (1984), pp. 121–126.

[34] See Worthington, *Philip II*, pp. 65–66; on the office, cf. S. Sprawski, "Philip II and the Freedom of the Thessalians," *Electrum* 9 (2003), pp. 61–64. Chronology: Griffith in Hammond and Griffith, *History of Macedonia* 2, pp. 220–221.

and cavalry, provided him with income from harbor and market taxes, and—significantly—allowed him representation on Thessaly's behalf on the Amphictyonic Council. Moreover, the people of Larissa voluntarily bestowed the office on him; the "barbarian" Macedonian now held a Greek constitutional office in, of all places, powerful Thessaly.[35]

DEFYING PHILIP

From Thessaly Philip moved southward ninety miles to the strategically important pass of Thermopylae, the "Gates of Greece." In modern times, the silting up of the Malian Gulf has turned the pass into a wide flat plain, but in antiquity the pass, with the sea to its north and mountains to its south, afforded the most direct access from northern to central Greece. That meant that whoever controlled it could check movement in and out of central Greece at the pass.

Philip now had the option of marching through Thermopylae to Phocis and ending the sacred war.[36] Phayllus, the Phocian commander, fully expected Philip to do this, and so hired more mercenaries and was joined by 2,000 troops from Achaea, 1,000 from Sparta, the 2,000 men Philip had expelled from Pherae with Lycophron, and the Athenians. They threw their weight behind Phocis not out of sympathy for its plight but to protect themselves. The Spartans and Achaeans feared that Philip might join Thebes in invading the Peloponnese whereas the Athenians feared he might march through Boeotia into Attica to besiege their city, with which he was still at war. The threat of a Macedonian invasion of Attica, especially through a friendly Boeotia that might even join Philip, persuaded the frugal Eubulus to dig into his pockets. To be on the safe side, he acted on the motion of Diophantus of Sphettus to block Philip at Thermopylae by sending there a force of 5,000 men and 400 cavalry, transported by 50 triremes, all of which cost the huge sum of 200 talents.[37] Thus, when Philip reached the northwest entrance to Thermopylae in August 352, he found the Athenian commander, Nausicles, and his men standing fast against him.

---

[35] See Sprawski, "Philip II and the Freedom of the Thessalians," pp. 55–66. Philip may already have been a citizen of Larissa, perhaps after his marriage to Philinna: E. Badian, "Philip II and the Last of the Thessalians," *Ancient Macedonia* 6 (Institute for Balkan Studies, Thessaloniki: 2000), p. 115.

[36] Diodorus 16.38.1.

[37] Diodorus 16.73.3, 38.1, Demosthenes 19.84, 319.

Philip faced several unenviable options. He could try to force his way through Thermopylae from its southern end. However, the narrow pass prevented a deployment of cavalry and an infantry charge—the Persians in 480 had discovered the downside of being the invader at Thermopylae. For two days the Greeks had withstood the Persian advance. Only when a path behind the pass was betrayed to King Xerxes on the third day were his troops able to cut the Greeks off from behind. There then followed the famous Battle of Thermopylae, in which 300 Spartans refused to yield and were annihilated.[38] Alternatively, he could call on the Thebans to attack Nausicles, but their preoccupation with the sacred war prevented them from sending troops. A third alternative was for him to circumvent Thermopylae, but that meant marching through hostile Doris, where he would be vulnerable to Phocian attack. He chose his last resort, which was simply to go home.[39] As it was, he still faced problems from the places that had shown their disloyalty to him after his defeat in 353. He needed to deal with them decisively before he could focus exclusively on affairs in Greece.

When Philip retreated from Thermopylae, Nausicles led his troops back to Athens, where Eubulus stood them down. The Athenians were so relieved that Philip had been prevented from marching through Thermopylae that a politician named Demophantus successfully proposed that they hold a sacrifice of thanks to the gods.[40] Nausicles' success had a profound influence on Demosthenes, who realized that with the right troop deployments Philip could be stopped. Demosthenes had largely ignored Philip until now, making only a passing mention of him in his *Against the Law of Leptines* of 354. In his *Against Aristocrates* of 352 (see below), he raised the specter of Philip more openly, albeit underestimating him as "an enemy, but a distant enemy; he is not a threat impinging directly on the needs or the security of the Athenians."[41] It was not until his first *Philippic* of the following year (351)— almost *five* years after the Athenians had declared war on Philip—that Demosthenes finally took the threat from Philip seriously (see below).[42] In doing so, he shaped his own political career.

---

[38] Herodotus 7.201–228. On the Persian Wars, see, for example, A. R. Burn, *Persia and the Greeks*[2] (London: 1984) and P. Green, *The Greco-Persian Wars* (Berkeley: 1996).

[39] Worthington, *Philip II*, p. 67; contra Buckler, "Philip II's Designs on Greece," p. 83.

[40] Demosthenes 19.86.

[41] Sealey, *Demosthenes*, p. 125.

[42] The title of the speech is a modern one.

ARISTOCRATES AND THRACE

In the meantime public attention turned to events in Thrace, prompting Demosthenes to write his next speech against Aristocrates. This was the man who had been indicted by Euthycles under the *graphe paranomon* procedure the previous year for proposing inviolability for Cersebleptes' general Charidemus (Chapter 4 p. 93). Now, in 352, Aristocrates was put on trial,[43] and Demosthenes wrote his speech for the prosecution.[44]

The Athenians were dependent on Cersebleptes' goodwill to preserve their presence in the Chersonese and so ensure the security of their grain route. Cersebleptes, however, was intent on unifying Thrace under his rule, and if he was successful no one in Athens knew how that would affect his relationship with the city. Men such as Eubulus, who supported the king, anticipated that he would continue to protect the Athenians' authority in the Chersonese, hence they did not need to maintain a strong and, especially, costly military presence there. Others, including Demosthenes, distrusted Cersebleptes, arguing that it was in Athens' better economic interests to back the other two Thracian kings, his brothers Berisades and Amadocus, against him.

Demosthenes insisted that Aristocrates' decree was undemocratic because of the Athenians' unwavering belief in the rule of law, which guaranteed that even murderers stood trial. Aristocrates' decree circumvented the law because it subjected anyone who harmed Charidemus (by now an Athenian citizen) to summary arrest.[45] Demosthenes had a sound legal argument that the decree robbed both the criminal of his right to seek justice and the courts of performing their

---

[43] Date: Dionysius of Halicarnassus, *To Ammaeus* 1.4. The date is certain, helped also by reference at Demosthenes 23.124 to Phayllus being the Phocian leader. Lane Fox, "Demosthenes, Dionysius, and the Dating of Six Early Speeches," pp. 183–187 and Roisman, *Rhetoric of Conspiracy*, pp. 165–167, argue that the speech should be dated to 356, and that it was revised in 352.

[44] MacDowell, *Demosthenes*, p. 196, Badian, "Road to Prominence," p. 42 n. 44. Sealey, *Demosthenes*, p. 131, believes Demosthenes himself may have delivered the speech. Euthycles was a former trierarch (Demosthenes 23.5), but whether he was from the upper stratum of society as Jaeger, *Demosthenes*, p. 99 says, is unknown—Demosthenes 23.4 suggests he was untrustworthy.

[45] Demosthenes 23.22–99.

constitutional role.[46] However, he widened his speech's legal arguments to include Athenian policy in Thrace, thereby turning it into a foreign policy debate.[47] In arguing that the Athenians should support Cersebleptes' brothers Demosthenes opposed Eubulus' policy, which was further evidence that he was becoming more critical of nonintervention in international affairs. Demosthenes first mentioned Philip in any sort of detail in this speech, although he still considered Thrace, not Philip, to be of more pressing concern for Athens.[48]

Against Aristocrates[49]

After a short introduction to gain the jurors' favor (1–3),[50] Demosthenes warned the people that Cersebleptes' advocates in Athens were mistaken to think he would permit Athens any presence in the Chersonese if he united Thrace under himself (8–17). Demosthenes intended his opening sally to be the foundation of a lengthy, three-pronged attack on Aristocrates' decree. To begin with, he emphasized that executing Charidemus' assassin without trial ran counter to the spirit of the law and, further, that his decree breached democratic equality—if one citizen was inviolable like Charidemus, then all citizens should be (24–99).

---

[46] On weakness in Demosthenes' legal arguments, see MacDowell, *Demosthenes*, pp. 198–202; cf. Sealey, *Demosthenes*, p. 131.

[47] Note the view of Jaeger, *Demosthenes*, p. 100, that Demosthenes brought the indictment so he could set out his views on foreign policy in the north, hence "a trial and a decision were more effective weapons for such agitation than another speech in the Assembly would have been."

[48] Demosthenes 23.107–109, 111–113.

[49] On the speech, see Schaefer, *Demosthenes*² 1, pp. 424–437, Blass, *attische Beredsamkeit*² 3.1, pp. 254–261, Pickard-Cambridge, *Demosthenes*, pp. 164–168, Jaeger, *Demosthenes*, pp. 98–109, Carlier, *Démosthène*, pp. 104–106, Usher, *Greek Oratory: Tradition and Originality*, pp. 204–209, Lehmann, *Demosthenes*, pp. 82–84, MacDowell, *Demosthenes*, pp. 196–206; cf. Badian, "Road to Prominence," pp. 24–25. See also T. L. Papillon, *Rhetorical Studies in the Aristocratea of Demosthenes* (New York: 1998) and Roisman, *Rhetoric of Conspiracy*, pp. 96–103. Translation: J. H. Vince, *Demosthenes*, Loeb Classical Library 3 (Cambridge and London: 1986).

[50] Unusually, Euthycles stated that his suit had nothing to do with personal animosity directed at Aristocrates (1), which was a common feature of forensic oratory: A. Kurihara, "Personal Enmity as a Motivation in Forensic Speeches," *CQ*² 53 (2003), pp. 464–477.

Second, in a move from legal issues to foreign affairs, Demosthenes argued that the decree damaged Athens' relations with Thrace (100–122). Here, he resorted to a similar balance of power argument as in his speech for the Megalopolitans: if the Athenians supported the other two Thracian kings against Cersebleptes' attempt to unite Thrace, then their internal power plays would divert their attention from the Athenian presence in the Chersonese. Demosthenes further claimed that a threefold division of Thrace would better thwart Philip's expansionist plans because he would be dealing with three enemy kings and not one. Moreover, the two other kings, interpreting Aristocrates' decree as the Athenians throwing their weight behind Cersebleptes, would feel alienated. If ever Cersebleptes proved disloyal to Athens, they would feel no obligation to go to the city's aid against their brother. To Demosthenes, Cersebleptes was unpredictable and untrustworthy, like Philip (111–116). Demosthenes combined history with psychology in this part of the speech to show the unreliability of greedy and ambitious rulers (114):

> But why is there need to name Philip, or any one else? Cersebleptes' own father, Cotys, whenever he was quarrelling with anyone, used to send his ambassadors, and was ready to do anything, realizing that being at war with Athens was an unprofitable exercise. But, as soon as [Cersebleptes] had all Thrace in his power, he would seize cities, do mischief, go on a drunken rampage, damaging first himself and then us in his desire to possess the whole country—it was impossible to do business with him. For everyone bent on wrongful gain tends to calculate, not the extreme difficulties he may encounter, but the gain he will achieve if he is successful.[51]

Third, Demosthenes argued that Charidemus' venality and immorality made him unworthy of the privilege Aristocrates wanted to bestow on him (123–195).[52] To this end he gave an in-depth treatment of Charidemus' unsavory, immoral, and treacherous career, using his examples to show also that he was actually an enemy of the city. He contrasted Charidemus with previous distinguished men of Athens who had fully deserved their honors (185):

---

[51] Translation: Usher, *Greek Oratory: Tradition and Originality*, pp. 206–207.

[52] Note, however, the stylistic criticisms of Pearson, *Art of Demosthenes*, pp. 69–74, on this narrative.

All others who have received any favour from you have been honoured for the benefits they have bestowed on you; Charidemus is unique in receiving honours for the incompetence of his attempts to injure you.[53]

To conclude his speech Demosthenes warned the people about the dangers of excessive awards and beseeched them to take action against corrupt speakers, who grew rich and powerful while the city suffered (196–220). Great generals of the past, like Themistocles and Miltiades (heroes of the Persian Wars), believed that simply serving the city as best they could was sufficient honor (196–197). Now, bestowing awards had become a matter of course, as had the ostentation of political leaders, whose visible wealth no longer lay in the public buildings they funded but in their own private homes (207–208)—"back then the people were the masters, but now they are the servants, of politicians" (209).

In attacking the anonymous politicians courting Cersebleptes, Demosthenes must have had Eubulus and his ilk in mind.[54] Eubulus resorted to every means possible to save money, so he must have welcomed Cersebleptes' apparent willingness to recognize an Athenian presence in the Chersonese and return Amphipolis to them for free with open arms.[55] On the other hand, it seems unlikely that Eubulus was venal and growing rich at the city's expense, as Demosthenes insinuated all politicians were doing (146–147, 201, 207–208). Demosthenes was clearly criticizing Eubulus' passive foreign policy and his favoring Cersebleptes, which he judged did not serve the city's interests; the time was ripe for a more aggressive stance.

Demosthenes also discussed Philip in more detail in this speech than in any of his previous ones. Among other things, he detailed Philip's activities in Thrace, including the towns he had seized (183), yet naively did not consider Philip a threat to all Thrace. In naming Philip, Demosthenes' principal intention was to show that he was as untrustworthy as Cersebleptes. For example, Philip had broken his promise and kept Amphipolis instead of returning it to the Athenians (116), despite his offer of friendship when they sent troops with Argaeus to

---

[53] Translation: Usher, *Greek Oratory: Tradition and Originality*, p. 208.

[54] A passage in this speech (206–210) is repeated three years later in Demosthenes' third *Olynthiac*, where Eubulus was the target of attack (3.25–31); cf. Pickard-Cambridge, *Demosthenes*, pp. 165–167, Papillon, *Rhetorical Studies in the Aristocratea of Demosthenes*, pp. 105–111, Roisman, *Rhetoric of Conspiracy*, pp. 98–99.

[55] Jaeger, *Demosthenes*, p. 103.

Macedonia in 359 (212). Unlike previous Macedonian kings who trusted only the Athenians, Philip had made a number of costly and wrong alliances for his kingdom (111–112), and he was Athens' bitterest enemy (121). For that reason, urged Demosthenes, the Athenians must ally with Berisades and Amadocus to keep Philip away from the Chersonese (123–137).

The outcome of the trial is unknown, but Charidemus served the Athenians as a general for many years and was the first person to send them news of Philip's death in 336. It cannot be said whether the views expressed in the speech about Thrace were those of either Demosthenes and Euthycles or even both of them, although Demosthenes' employment of a balance of power argument lends some weight to Euthycles being more of his mouthpiece.[56] Certainly Demosthenes chose to circulate his speech so that his own political views came to the attention of a wider public, especially as Philip's activities in 352 and 351 demonstrated the very real threat he posed to Athens and the balance of power in the entire Greek peninsula.

PHILIP, THRACE, AND OLYNTHUS: REGAINING THE STATUS QUO

Philip had returned to Pella after being blocked from entering the pass at Thermopylae. He was intent on reasserting control over the places that had defied him the previous year, and he turned to deal first with the treacherous Cersebleptes. He joined the coalition of Byzantium, Perinthus, and Amadocus that was then besieging Cersebleptes at Heraion Teichos ("Hera's Wall"), one of his eastern fortresses on the coast of the Sea of Marmara, close to Perinthus (Marmara Ereğlisi). Philip arrived by November 352.[57] Perhaps still buoyed by their recent success at Thermopylae[58] and moved by Demosthenes' warnings in *Against Aristocrates*, the Athenians decided to send forty triremes, manned by citizens between the ages of twenty and forty-five, to Cersebleptes' assistance. They levied an *eisphora* (military tax) from the

---

[56] Papillon, *Rhetorical Studies in the Aristocratea of Demosthenes*, pp. 92–93, uses the balance of power argument to suggest that Demosthenes expressed his own views in the speech; MacDowell, *Demosthenes*, p. 203, is cautious.

[57] Demosthenes 3.4–5.

[58] Ryder, "Demosthenes and Philip II," pp. 49–50 ("the euphoria . . . was still stirring their adrenaline").

wealthy citizens to fund the expedition, but the fleet never set sail, perhaps because the people had second thoughts about the size of Byzantium's opposing fleet or Cersebleptes' loyalty.[59]

Several months elapsed when news reached Athens that Philip was
either dead or ill.[60] Not wanting to miss this apparent golden opportunity,
in late 351 the Athenians sent out a smaller mercenary force of ten ships
commanded by Charidemus, by then in Athens. It was a case of too little
too late. Philip recovered from whatever sickness had afflicted him and
forced Heraion Teichos into capitulation.[61] To ensure Cersebleptes' loyalty, he took his son to Pella as a hostage,[62] most likely handing control of
the fortress to Perinthus. He may also have replaced Amadocus with his
son Teres, who would thus owe loyalty to the Macedonian king. Philip's
sudden and renewed influence in Thracian affairs alarmed the Athenians
intensely: it now appeared that Demosthenes' call to side with the other
Thracian kings had been the correct one after all. Whether he was right
to claim, three years later, that if the Athenians had initially sent troops to
Heraion Teichos Philip would no longer be a threat is doubtful.[63]

On his way home from Thrace Philip detoured to Olynthus, which
had reneged on its treaty of 357 by soliciting an alliance with Athens.
He did not attack Olynthus, although Demosthenes later stated he
"made an attempt on the city,"[64] but issued a stern warning to its
rulers.[65] As a result, the Olynthians broke off negotiations with Athens,
expelled a prominent anti-Macedonian, Apollonides, and elected two
pro-Macedonians, Lasthenes and Euthycrates, as commanders of their
cavalry (hipparchy).[66] Philip's warning was clearly effective only in the
short term because in 349 he embarked on a full-scale invasion of the
Chalcidice to end Olynthus' hegemony of the Chalcidian League and
absorb the promontory into his kingdom.

---

[59] Background: Worthington, *Philip II*, pp. 68–69.

[60] Demosthenes 3.5; cf. 1.13, 4.10–11.

[61] Here I follow the view of Ellis, *Philip II*, p. 88 over Griffith, in Hammond and Griffith,
History of Macedonia 2, p. 284, that Philip returned home to Pella when he fell ill and
never took Heraion Teichos (cf. Ryder, "Demosthenes and Philip II," p. 50).

[62] Theopompus, *FGrH* 115 F 101.

[63] Demosthenes 3.5; cf. Ryder, "Demosthenes and Philip II," p. 50.

[64] Demosthenes 1.12–13.

[65] Telling them an apocryphal story about war and arrogance (*hybris*): Theopompus,
FGrH 115 F 127. Background: Worthington, *Philip II*, p. 69.

[66] Apollonides: [Demosthenes] 59.91; Lasthenes and Euthycrates: Demosthenes 9.56–
66, 19.265.

DEMOSTHENES AND PHILIP

Philip had not forgotten his war with Athens. During his recent campaigns he had given orders to attack Athenian grain vessels at Geraestus, on the southern tip of Euboea, and to seize the state galley *Paralos* at Marathon, on Attica's east coast, as it prepared to sail to a religious gathering at Delos.[67] It is no surprise that the Athenians feared that Philip might use his involvement in the Third Sacred War to ally with their enemy Thebes. Demosthenes had merely touched on the danger from Philip in his *Against Aristocrates*, but his next political speech, the first *Philippic*, dealt exclusively with him. From then on, all but two of his surviving political speeches presented Philip as plotting not only to crush Athens but also take over Greece.[68] His most famous speeches were the four *Philippics*, delivered between 351 and 341, in which he repeatedly called on the Athenians to do battle with Philip personally and so save Greece.

Throughout history, Demosthenes has been best remembered for his opposition to Philip. Because of this, a great deal of importance has been attached to the first *Philippic*, which has been called "a prelude to that decade of struggle."[69] It has even been baldly stated that Demosthenes "became a one-issue politician in 351 with the *First Philippic*,"[70] and that it must have "propelled [him] immediately into the front rank of Athenian politicians."[71] These sorts of viewpoints explain why scholars all too often interrupt the chronological order of Demosthenes' earliest speeches to discuss the first *Philippic* as if it did set a trend for his later speeches. As a result, a misleading impression not only of the speech's importance but also of when and why Demosthenes focused exclusively on Philip is generated.

[67] Demosthenes 4.34, *Prooimion* 21.2, [Demosthenes] 59.3; cf. Aeschines 2.72.

[68] Ryder, "Demosthenes and Philip II," pp. 45–89. Elaboration of this conspiracy argument: Roisman, *Rhetoric of Conspiracy*, pp. 118–132.

[69] Badian, "Road to Prominence," p. 33. In discussing these early speeches, Badian also abandons chronological order, putting the first *Philippic* last, although well aware he does so—"we shall leave high politics and even strict chronological order" (p. 20). He then thematically treats Demosthenes' court speeches before his political ones. Others who also abandon chronological order include H. Montgomery, *The Way to Chaeronea* (Oslo: 1983), Carlier, *Démosthène*, Lehmann, *Demosthenes*, and Usher, *Greek Oratory: Tradition and Originality*.

[70] P. E. Harding, *Didymos, On Demosthenes* (Oxford: 2006), p. 244.

[71] MacDowell, *Demosthenes*, p. 218.

The first *Philippic* was not the last of Demosthenes' earliest speeches nor did it represent a turning point that saw him emerge as a "one-issue politician." Shortly after he gave the speech, he spoke for the cause of exiled democrats from Rhodes, mentioning Philip only in passing (see below), and a year later, in 350, he addressed the Athenians on financial affairs that had nothing to do with Philip. Another year later, in 349, he turned again to Philip in his first two *Olynthiac* speeches, and it was only from then on that he concerned himself solely with the king. The first *Philippic* was one of several speeches against Philip, but Demosthenes could not have *planned* it to be the first of that many. At this juncture, it was simply one of a number of speeches, political and forensic, on different aspects of foreign policy that were intended to win Demosthenes political support.[72] There is no question that it was an important speech, but whether it elevated him to the "front rank" of Athenian politicians is questionable—not least because it failed.

The date of the speech is controversial, but the consensus view places it toward the tail end of the archon year 352/1.[73] Furthermore, references in the speech to Philip's campaigns at Thermopylae, in the Chersonese, and at Olynthus and to his death or illness in Thrace help to date it to the late summer of 351, before he took Heraion Teichos from Cersebleptes (see above).[74]

---

[72] Cf. Badian, "Road to Prominence," pp. 35–36.

[73] Date: Dionysius of Halicarnassus, *To Ammaeus* 1.4. The mention of Olynthus could date it to 349, when Philip invaded the Chalcidice: E. Schwarz, "Demosthenes' erste Philippika," in P. Jors, E. Schwartz, and R. Reitzenstein (eds.), *Festschrift Theodor Mommsen zum fünfzigjährigen Doctorjubiläum* (Marburg: 1893), pp. 1–56. However, this "attack" may have been nothing more than the verbal warning he gave to the Olynthians in 351 (see above). J. R. Ellis, "The Date of Demosthenes' First *Philippic*," *REG* 79 (1966), pp. 636–639, argues for a date in the next archon year 351/50, specifically 350 (echoed in J. R. Ellis and R. D. Milns, *The Spectre of Philip* (Sydney: 1970), pp. 13–14); cf. Lane Fox, "Demosthenes, Dionysius, and the Dating of Six Early Speeches," pp. 195–199. In favor of Dionysius' dating, see especially Sealey, "Dionysius of Halicarnassus and Some Demosthenic Dates," pp. 81–89, G. L. Cawkwell, "The Defence of Olynthus," *CQ*² 12 (1962), pp. 122–127, Carlier, *Démosthène*, p. 110, Karvounis, *Demosthenes*, pp 223–232, Lehmann, *Demosthenes*, p. 88, C. Wooten, *A Commentary on Demosthenes' Philippic 1* (Oxford: 2008), p. 11, MacDowell, *Demosthenes*, pp. 211–213; cf. Badian, "Road to Prominence," pp. 33–34. Dionysius at 1.10 divided the speech into two separate ones at the end of section 29. Arguments have been made that the first part (1–29) was given in 352/1 and the second (30–51) in 347/6, but these have been refuted (see Cawkwell, Karvounis, and Sealey above, for example).

[74] Demosthenes 4.11, 17.

The First *Philippic*[75]

Philip had proved himself capable of moving quickly, unpredictably, and decisively. Against someone like that, Eubulus' rigid fiscal conservatism and policy of mobilizing troops only when Athens was threatened—prudent though they may be—left Athens dangerously vulnerable. Demosthenes therefore proposed a more aggressive opposition policy in this speech, thereby making a formal break with Eubulus. In the first and final parts of the speech (or about half of it) he attempted to stir the people from their despair as well as criticizing them for running the war poorly and being swayed by the flattery of previous speakers.[76] The central part of the speech contained specific military measures and urged the citizens to serve in the army.[77]

A law permitting men over the age of fifty to speak first at Assembly meetings had probably by now fallen into abeyance, but it was still polite for younger men to defer to the elder speakers.[78] Demosthenes, now in his early thirties, ignored etiquette, and ascended the rostrum to address his fellow citizens first. He explained why (1):

---

[75] On the speech, see Schaefer, *Demosthenes*[2] 2, pp. 58–70, Blass, *attische Beredsamkeit*[2] 3.1, pp. 261–265, Pickard-Cambridge, *Demosthenes*, pp. 185–189, Jaeger, *Demosthenes*, pp. 115–124, Pearson, *Art of Demosthenes*, pp. 123–127, Carlier, *Démosthène*, pp. 109–117, Usher, *Greek Oratory: Tradition and Originality*, pp. 217–220, Badian, "Road to Prominence," pp. 33–37, Lehmann, *Demosthenes*, pp. 88–94, MacDowell, *Demosthenes*, pp. 210–218; cf. Milns, "Public Speeches of Demosthenes," pp. 210–212, 214, 216. See also G. O. Rowe, "Demosthenes' First Philippic: the Satiric Mode," *TAPA* 99 (1968), pp. 361–374, A. M. Prestianni Gialombardo, "*Philippika* I: Sul 'Culto' di Filippo II di Macedonia," *Siculorum Gymnasium* 28 (1975), pp. 1–57, J. W. Leopold, "Demosthenes' Strategy in the First Philippic, 'An Away Match with Macedonian Cavalry'?," *Anc. World* 16 (1987), pp. 59–69, and G. Mader, "*Quantum mutati ab illis* . . .: Satire and Displaced Identity in Demothenes' *First Philippic*," *Philologus* 147 (2003), pp. 56–69. Translation with notes: Trevett, *Demosthenes, Speeches 1–17*, pp. 69–87; translation and commentary: Ellis and Milns, *Spectre of Philip*, pp. 11–33; text and commentary: J. E. Sandys, *The First Philippic and the Olynthiacs of Demosthenes* (Cambridge: 1910) and especially Wooten, *Commentary on Demosthenes' Philippic 1* (with analysis of its rhetorical style); detailed discussion and commentary: Karvounis, *Demosthenes*, pp. 223–260. C. Wooten, *Cicero's Philippics and their Demosthenic Model* (Chapel Hill: 1983), discusses the style and content of all four *Philippics* extensively.

[76] Demosthenes 4.1–12, 34–51.

[77] Demosthenes 4.13–33.

[78] K. A. Kapparis, "The Law on the Age of Speakers in the Athenian Assembly," *RhM* 141 (1998), pp. 255–259.

If some new matter were the topic of discussion, men of Athens, I would have waited until most of the regular speakers had given their opinion, and if anything they said pleased me, I would have kept quiet; only if it did not would I have ventured to state my own opinion. But since we are dealing with matters that these men have often addressed on previous occasions, I think that I can reasonably be forgiven for standing up to speak first. For if they have given the necessary advice in the past, there would be no need for you to be deliberating now.

Demosthenes thus criticized past speakers who had allowed Philip to increase his power, yet were not going to change their policies, so the people would continue getting nowhere. Demosthenes felt justified to speak first as he expected other speakers would repeat the same things.[79]

Demosthenes needed the people to embrace his plan to oppose Philip for it to work. He moved to a stinging rebuke of them for allowing Philip to become all-powerful while encouraging them to be neither depressed nor apathetic (2–12).[80] If they rallied, and especially if they followed his advice, they would overcome him (4–7):

And if any of you, men of Athens, thinks that Philip is hard to wage war against, considering the size of the forces at his disposal and our city's loss of all its possessions, he is quite correct. But let him consider this. Once, men of Athens, Pydna and Potidaea and Methone and the whole surrounding region were on good terms with us, and many of the peoples that are now on his side were autonomous and free and preferred to be on good terms with us more than with him. But if Philip at that time had decided that it would be difficult for him to wage war on the Athenians, since they had such strong outposts in his own territory, whereas he was without allies, he would not have achieved any of the things that he has, nor would he have acquired so much power. But he knew very well, men of Athens, that all these places lie in the open as prizes of war, and that it is natural for those who are present to take the possessions of those who are absent, and for those who are willing to toil and face danger to get the possessions of those who are negligent.

---

[79] Cf. Badian, "Road to Prominence," pp. 36–37, also pointing out that Philip's recent actions at sea "injected a new element in the situation" that Demosthenes wanted to seize before any other speaker did.

[80] Demosthenes' willingness to chastise his audience: J. Ober, *Mass and Elite in Democratic Athens: Rhetoric, Ideology and the Power of the People* (Princeton: 1989), pp. 318–324 and H. Yunis, *Taming Democracy: Models of Political Rhetoric in Classical Athens* (Ithaca: 1996), pp. 257–268.

In consequence, and with this resolve, he has conquered and now possesses places everywhere, some as one would possess them after taking them in war, others after making them his allies and well disposed toward him; for they are all willing to ally themselves to and obey anyone whom they see to be well prepared and willing to do what is needed. If, men of Athens, you too are prepared to adopt such a resolve now, since indeed you were not previously, and each of you is willing to drop all pretence and take action wherever it is needed and wherever he may be able to benefit the city, those with money by paying taxes, those in the prime of life by going on campaign, in short if you are simply willing to get a grip on yourselves, and stop each hoping that you can get away with doing nothing, while your neighbor does everything on your behalf, you will recover what is yours, god willing, and will regain what has been negligently lost, and will punish that man.

The speech's dramatic and emotional style lent an immediacy to it that must have captivated the listeners even while he was abusing them! For example, in a memorable passage of imaginary dialogue he was scathing about Athenian apathy (11):

"Is Philip dead?" "No, by Zeus, but he is sick." What difference does it make to you? Even if something were to happen to him, you would soon create another Philip, if this is how you apply yourselves to the situation, since even he has not prospered by reason of his own strength as much as because of our neglect.

He later compared the people's confusion and "too little too late" reaction to a "barbarian" boxer, who covers where he has been hit rather than going on the attack (40–41), an unexpected reversal of roles as the Athenians are likened to the sorts of "barbarians" Demosthenes implored them to resist:[81]

You wage war on Philip in the same way that a foreigner boxes. For when one of them is struck, he always moves his hands to that spot, and if he is struck on the other side, his hands go to that place: he has neither the knowledge nor the will to put up his guard or watch for the next blow. It is the same with you. If you hear that Philip is in the Chersonese, you vote to send a relief force there, and likewise if you hear that he is at Thermopylae. And if you hear that he is somewhere else, you run up and down at his heels and are at his command; you have no

---

[81] See the comments of M. Golden, "Demosthenes and the Social Historian," in Ian Worthington (ed.), *Demosthenes: Statesman and Orator* (London: 2000), pp. 160–161.

plan to turn the war to your advantage, and fail to anticipate any eventuality until you learn that it has happened or is happening.

He wanted the people to plan and execute military operations as they did the Dionysia and Panathenaea festivals—because money was properly budgeted for them and everyone knew what they had to do they were never celebrated late (35–37). Instead, complained Demosthenes, "we spend the time for action on preparation, but the opportunities offered by circumstance do not wait on our slowness and dissimulation."

Demosthenes believed that the only way to stop Philip was by taking the war to him. To this end, the heart of his speech was a series of military recommendations, which were clearly influenced by Nausicles' success at Thermopylae in 352 (13–33). Demosthenes demanded a standing army of citizen soldiers and 500 cavalry (half of the Athenians' total complement), to be transported on a fleet of 50 triremes, together with the necessary horse-carrying triremes and support vessels, to wherever Philip was to be found—"These, in my view, are needed to counter his sudden campaigns from his own land to Thermopylae and the Chersonese and Olynthus and anywhere else he wishes" (17). He also required a strike force of 2,000 infantry (500 citizens and the rest mercenaries) and 200 cavalry (50 citizens and the rest mercenary) to campaign "for as long as you think appropriate" (21). Speed being of the essence, these troops were to sail north on 10 "fast" (that is, first-class) triremes (21). This force was intended to block Philip from threatening Athenian interests until the main army arrived. In wintertime the fleet would be based at Lemnos, Thasos, and Sciathos, allowing it to operate against Philip when weather conditions made it virtually impossible to sail from Athens.

Then Demosthenes turned to the issue that, like today, would have most captured the listeners' attention—"what you most wish to hear is how much money is needed and where it will come from" (28–30). He proposed that the city pay entirely for the standing army and provide half pay for the strike force, which would make up the remainder however it could when it was on campaign. He brought with him into the Assembly a detailed financial statement of how the money would be raised (29), but that document was unfortunately not preserved with the speech. The number of men Demosthenes wanted to recruit was enormous—the rowers of the triremes (170 per trireme) alone numbered over 9,000. Equally enormous was the cost: Demosthenes estimated the smaller strike force at 92 talents (excluding pay) and the standing army would have cost considerably more. He ended the speech by repeating that his policy was the right one for the Athenians to follow: "I choose to speak in the firm conviction that that you will benefit from agreeing to this policy— so long as you put it into practice. May what will benefit all win out" (51).

Demosthenes was correct to insist that a standing army be levied that could be deployed immediately. He was also correct to insist on citizen soldiers serving in it because they would fight harder for their native city and, unlike mercenaries, would not defect to the enemy side if promised more pay. As well conceived as his measures were, however, they failed, principally because of funding.[82] Athens was simply not in a position to pay for so many troops and vessels nor did the people want to commit so many of their fleet of 300 triremes to fighting in the north.[83] Unlike countries in recent history, the classical Athenians could neither print money nor borrow it to finance their military operations.

Furthermore, Demosthenes might well have exhorted the people to put the running of the war in the hands of generals (27), but he—like so many speakers in the Assembly—was a citizen-soldier with no military expertise. He had not given any time frame for the campaigns against Philip or made it clear what the Athenian forces would do when they confronted the king: keep him at bay? Engage him in battle? Bluff him into retreating? At least today policy makers reveal some aspects of their strategy to justify a country's involvement in another war, allow people to monitor its effectiveness, and even provide the means of exit, and military professionals are responsible for planning and conducting operations.

What would become one of Demosthenes' most famous speeches thus failed, but he was not completely to blame. Despite his impassioned rhetoric and Philip's steady encroachment in the Greek peninsula, the people simply did not want to fight in the army. Their indifference proved costly.

---

[82] Cf. Sealey, *Demosthenes*, pp. 132–133; cf. Hunt, *War, Peace, and Alliance in Demosthenes' Athens*, p. 31.

[83] Demosthenes 14.13; see G. L. Cawkwell, "Athenian Naval Power in the Fourth Century," *CQ*² 34 (1984), p. 344, on the inability to have a standing force of fifty ships at this time. On costs in general, see M. L. Cook, "Timokrates' 50 Talents and the Cost of Ancient Warfare," *Eranos* 88 (1990), pp. 69–97.

APPEAL FROM RHODES

The island of Rhodes had declared its independence from Athens at the end of the Social War of 356–355, but soon after it was the scene of internecine war between oligarchs and democrats. With the backing of Mausolus, satrap of Caria, the oligarchs established a brutal regime and many democrats fled into exile, some to Athens. When Mausolus died in 353 or early 352, he was succeeded by his widow (and sister) Artemisia.[84] In 351, probably not long after the Assembly in which Demosthenes delivered his first *Philippic*, the democrats in Athens beseeched the people to help overthrow the oligarchy so they might return home.

Their request was heard at an Assembly, at which Demosthenes spoke in their favor with his *On the Freedom of the Rhodians*.[85] At first sight his stance seemed like political suicide, for as far as the Athenians were concerned the Rhodians were the enemy because of their role in the Social War. Thanks to them the Athenians were still financially exhausted and the city had lost many men in battle against rebel fleets, which included Rhodian contingents. Yet, despite his recent failures in the Assembly, Demosthenes risked unpopularity.

An explanation for his controversial stand is that he did not merely wish to remain in the public spotlight by giving yet another speech but wanted to be seen as something of a maverick rather than pandering to popular favor. In choosing this course, he probably expected to fail. His intent, however, was to challenge the people to live up to their ideals as democrats and what their duties ought to be, regardless of the types of people with whom they had to deal. In doing so, Demosthenes' name would become synonymous with moral considerations and "doing the right thing." The plight of the Rhodians was thus the backdrop against which Demosthenes discussed, once again,

[84] Diodorus 16.36.2, 45.7.

[85] Date: Dionysius of Halicarnassus, *To Ammaeus* 1.4, Sealey, "Dionysius of Halicarnassus and Some Demosthenic Dates," p. 118, J. Radicke, *Die Rede des Demosthenes für die Freiheit der Rhodier* (Stuttgart: 1995), pp. 33–43, Karvounis, *Demosthenes*, pp. 175–192; see also Badian, "Road to Prominence," pp. 31–32, Lehmann, *Demosthenes*, pp. 93–94, MacDowell, *Demosthenes*, p. 219. However, Carlier, *Démosthène*, p. 87 and Lane Fox, "Demosthenes, Dionysius, and the Dating of Six Early Speeches," pp. 187–191, date it to 352 because of the reference to Philip at 15.24 as being inconsequential, whereas the first *Philippic* (of 351) made him out to be a serious threat to Greece. On the issue of 15.24, see below.

philosophical and practical issues. He based his argument on justice and especially the need to champion democracy over oligarchy, something that often motivated the people to make alliances or declare war.[86] However, he also had to allay the people's fears that by throwing their weight behind the democrats and bringing an end to the Rhodian oligarchy they would incur the enmity of Artemisia or even the Great King of Persia, who considered Rhodes part of his realm.[87] Demosthenes' attitude to Persia was, therefore, quite different from that in his *On the Symmories* of only a few years ago, and so he took care to explain the change.[88]

On the Freedom of the Rhodians[89]

Demosthenes began his speech by acknowledging that Rhodes was one of several states that had gone to war against Athens. However, he put the blame for its defection on Mausolus rather than on the Athenians' heavy-handed treatment (1–4). He argued that the Athenians had to put Rhodes' defection behind them and seize the opportunity now to help the exiles because of the goodwill and trust they would generate in every Greek city (4):

> You, however, whom they used to fear, will now be single-handedly responsible for rescuing them. If you make this clear to everybody, you will cause the majority in every city to regard friendship with you as a guarantee of their own freedom. There is no greater benefit you could secure than the willing and trusting goodwill of all.

He reminded the Athenians that he had previously spoken against waging war on the Great King, though now he was advising a course

---

[86] Demosthenes 15.4, 17–21, 28; on championing democracy over oligarchy as a motive, see too Hunt, *War, Peace, and Alliance in Demosthenes' Athens*, pp. 90–92.

[87] Demosthenes 15.3–4, 6, 9–13, 40–51.

[88] Demosthenes 15.9–10.

[89] On the speech, see Schaefer, *Demosthenes*² 1, pp. 475–480, Blass, *attische Beredsamkeit*² 3.1, pp. 265–268, Pickard-Cambridge, *Demosthenes*, pp. 135–137, Jaeger, *Demosthenes*, pp. 90–97, Pearson, *Art of Demosthenes*, pp. 117–119, Carlier, *Démosthène*, pp. 83–86, Usher, *Greek Oratory: Tradition and Originality*, pp. 213–215, Badian, "Road to Prominence," pp. 31–33, Lehmann, *Demosthenes*, pp. 94–98, MacDowell, *Demosthenes*, pp. 218–223. Translation with notes: Trevett, *Demosthenes, Speeches 1–17*, pp. 257–273; detailed discussions and commentaries: Karvounis, *Demosthenes*, pp. 175–221, Radicke, *Rede des Demosthenes für die Freiheit der Rhodier*.

of action that could cause war with Persia (5–9). To explain his inconsistency, he drew the subtle distinction that earlier the Athenians had been debating war against Persia itself but now, because Rhodes was independent of Persia under the terms of the King's Peace, any Athenian involvement would not be a direct attack on the King (9–10). He reinforced his argument by citing the example of the Athenian general Timotheus, who had expelled a Persian garrison from Samos in 365, after which the Athenians had suffered no reprisals at the hands of the Persian king. In any case, Demosthenes pointed out, the King was too busy fighting to restore his rule in Egypt and did not have the time to bother Athens. Likewise, the people should not expect any retaliation from Artemisia (11–13):

> I do not believe that even Artemisia would be opposed to our taking this action, if the city is fully committed to it . . . And so in my view she would rather that you have it, as long as she does not surrender it to you publicly, than that [the King] take it.[90]

Demosthenes next dealt with affairs on Rhodes, criticizing both oligarchs and democrats for their dealings with one another and their disloyalty to Athens (14–16). He asserted that the Athenians had a tradition of supporting democracies against oligarchies, and so presented Rhodes as an instance that called for their immediate action (17–29). In exaggerated fashion, he insisted that oligarchy was everywhere and that even Athenian democracy faced danger (19):

> I am surprised if none of you sees that, with Chios and Mytilene ruled by oligarchies, and now Rhodes and almost the whole world reduced to this form of slavery, our own constitution is also at some risk; or that if oligarchies are set up everywhere else, they will surely not allow us to retain our democracy.

After all, he continued, anyone who founded an oligarchy is "the common enemy of all who desire freedom" (20). This ideal motivates democratic governments to intervene against totalitarian regimes in repressed countries even now. Demosthenes then argued the need to overthrow oligarchies in order to protect Athens and its trade routes in the eastern Aegean, on which some cautious speakers—he must have had Eubulus in mind—were not focusing their attention (21–29). His argument here dovetailed into the conclusion of his speech, which

---

[90] Demosthenes 15.11, 14.

warned the people to beware of politicians who did not have their interests at heart (31–34).

Demosthenes mentioned Philip only once in the speech (24):

> I see that some of you frequently despise Philip as being of no consequence but are afraid of the King on the ground that he is a formidable enemy to whomever he chooses. But if we are to take no measures against the former on the ground that he is insignificant, and are to yield in every respect to the latter on the ground that he is formidable, against whom, men of Athens, are we to take the field?

His question possibly indicated that he viewed Philip as less of a danger than the Persian King.[91] However, he spoke of only "some" men, not the entire citizenry. Ever more critical of Eubulus' passive policy toward Philip, his pointed rhetorical question here underscores his mood. Eubulus was the man who had stood down Nausicles' force in 352 because he no longer saw Philip as a threat—he was "of no consequence." Demosthenes thought the opposite, as his first *Philippic* showed. The present speech built on the first *Philippic* and so afforded him an excellent opportunity to liken Philip to the Great King and emphasize the threat that both posed.

Demosthenes' arguments ultimately achieved little, for the Athenians rejected the exiles' plea.[92] They were probably afraid that the Great King or even Artemisia would retaliate and so did not take Demosthenes at his word. Then again, the people's animosity toward the Rhodians must also have been a factor. Later the democrats possibly petitioned the Athenians to change their minds, but the oligarchs countered by sending their own embassy to Athens.[93] Arguably, the Athenians' decision not to help the exiles was to their disadvantage since the Rhodians and Chians later concluded alliances with Philip.[94] On the other hand, the Athenians were better off directing their efforts on the ever-encroaching Philip.[95]

---

[91] Cf. Badian, "Road to Prominence," p. 35: "Demosthenes himself no longer depicted [Philip] as a menace: he was advocating new adventures in the eastern Aegean"; cf. Lehmann, *Demosthenes*, pp. 93–94.

[92] Demosthenes 5.25, 13.8.

[93] Two of the Demosthenic *prooimia* (24 and 46) indicate these embassies in connection with the Rhodian issue: see MacDowell, *Demosthenes*, pp. 222–223, citing bibliography.

[94] Theopompus, *FGrH* 115 F 164.

[95] Radicke, *Rede des Demosthenes für die Freiheit der Rhodier*, pp. 53–54.

PHILIP IN ILLYRIA, PAEONIA, AND EPIRUS:
THE STATUS QUO REGAINED

After he had dealt with the Olynthians in 351, Philip returned to Pella, and from there embarked on a campaign against the Paeonians and Illyrians, the details of which are obscure.[96] More is known of his invasion of Epirus in 350, in which he quickly overcame Arybbas.[97] He allowed Arybbas to retain his throne, probably reducing him to vassal status, and took his twelve-year-old nephew and heir to the throne, Alexander, to Pella, intending to install him as king when he came of age.[98]

Within three years of his defeat in 353, then, Philip had overwhelmed his enemies and extended his power southward into central Greece. Little wonder that Demosthenes spoke enviously of his speed and decisiveness, which were in contrast to the slowness and indifference of the Assembly and indeed of the Greeks:[99]

> Does any of you observe or reflect on the means by which Philip, who was weak, has become strong? First he took Amphipolis, then Pydna, and then Potidaea, next Methone, then he attacked Thessaly, and after that, Pherae, Pagasae and Magnesia. After winning over the whole country in the way he wanted, he invaded Thrace. Then, after expelling some of the kings there and installing others, he fell sick. When he recovered his health, he did not sink into idleness but immediately made an attempt on the Olynthians. And I pass over his campaigns against the Illyrians and Paeonians and Arybbas and wherever else one might mention.

Given the threat that Demosthenes alleged Philip posed to the Greeks in the later 350s, why did they not unite against him as they had done a century and a half earlier against Xerxes? To begin with, Philip had not expressed any desire to conquer Greece, as had the Persians, and was technically at war only with the Athenians. His involvement in the Third Sacred War actually made him an ally of the Amphictyonic

---

[96] Demosthenes 1.13, Isocrates 5.21.
[97] Justin 8.6.4–8. Background and discussion of Philip's relations with Alexander of Epirus: Worthington, *Philip II*, p. 70.
[98] Alexander of Epirus was Olympias' younger brother, and so Philip's brother-in-law. The story that Philip had a pederastic relationship with him (Justin 8.6.6–8) is based on a hostile tradition and probably untrue: Worthington, *Philip II*, p. 70.
[99] Demosthenes 1.12–13.

League and hence of the two dozen states that were its members. Further, the scenario was fast emerging that he would again intervene in the sacred war, meaning less fighting (and losses) for the Greeks. Another explanation is that many of the smaller states welcomed his presence in Greece because they were discontented by the self-serving actions of Athens, Thebes, and Sparta, which had caused only instability in Greece since the days of the Peloponnesian War. After Philip ended the sacred war and made peace with Athens in 346, for example, some Greeks regretted his return at that time to Pella. Even though Sparta's power was now spent, the Athenians and Thebans continued to be unpopular—few states rallied to their call to arms against Philip in 338 when Greece's very freedom was at stake at Chaeronea.

All of this was some time in the future of course. In 350 Demosthenes was still far from a successful politician, and his string of recent failures boded ill for his political aspirations. It is a tribute to his tenacity—and his single-minded ambition—that over the next years he worked to reverse the Athenians' attitude toward Philip, believing that it was the only way to save Greece from the king. It was not until the next year that he finally tasted victory in the Assembly.

6

Swaying the Assembly

Demosthenes' career was to all intents and purposes stalled. He had spoken sincerely and sensibly on financial and foreign policy matters, ultimately to no avail. A passage in his next speech, *On Organization*, indicated he knew his political career was at a crossroads (see below). Perhaps his lack of success explained his retreat from the public limelight after his *On the Freedom of the Rhodians* in late 351 until the middle of 349, for only *On Organization* survives from that period. Then again, in those years little was happening in Athens to attract his attention, and Philip was busy elsewhere.

In 349 Philip led his army into the Chalcidice, intent on bringing an end to the power of the Chalcidian League. The Olynthians called on Athens for assistance, offering Demosthenes the opportunity to rekindle his fading career. In the course of 349 to 348, he gave what would be the game changer of his career, three *Olynthiac* speeches urging military help and calling on the people to fight Philip in the north – otherwise, he sensationally warned, they would face him in Attica. His intention here (and generally in his speeches against Philip) was to represent Macedonia as the "new Persia, an intrinsically hostile, barbarian state threatening Greece."[1] In this depiction he was not alone, for Aeschines, Eubulus, Hegesippus, and Hyperides, none of whom had any wish to

---

[1] P. Hunt, *War, Peace, and Alliance in Demosthenes' Athens* (New York: 2010), p. 81, and see pp. 80–84 on Demosthenes' general exploitation of ethnic differences for rhetorical effect.

see Greece fall to Philip, talked of him in the same way.[2] Demosthenes, then, was simply echoing common rhetoric.[3]

The speech *On Organization* may be dated 350,[4] and its subject was "financial matters."[5] An earlier conjecture, based on stylistic arguments, that Demosthenes did not write it has rightly been rejected.[6] In this speech, Demosthenes proposed that theoric money be given only to those who performed services for the city rather than distributed as a dole to everyone. He had in mind military services, so he evidently wanted to supplement what money was available in the Military Fund. Since Eubulus' law protected theoric money, Demosthenes needed to avoid actually naming the fund because the people were quick to censure their leaders.[7] Two years later, in 348, an orator named Apollodorus recommended diverting money from the fund for the same purposes and was fined one talent.[8]

---

[2] Demosthenes 19.303–304, [Demosthenes] 7.7, Hyperides 6.12, and fragments 4 and 6 of the recently discovered Hyperides, *Against Diondas*: C. Carey, M. Edwards, and Z. Farkas, "Fragments of Hyperides' *Against Diondas* from the Archimedes Palimpsest," *ZPE* 165 (2008), pp. 1–19.

[3] Hunt, *War, Peace, and Alliance in Demosthenes' Athens*, pp. 81–82.

[4] Date (omitted by Dionysius of Halicarnassus): R. Sealey, "Dionysius of Halicarnassus and Some Demosthenic Dates," *REG* 68 (1955), pp. 251–253, Carlier, *Démosthène*, p. 120, R. Lane Fox, "Demosthenes, Dionysius, and the Dating of Six Early Speeches," *Class. & Med.* 48 (1997), pp. 191–195, MacDowell, *Demosthenes*, pp. 227–229.

[5] Demosthenes 13.1–2.

[6] See, for example, Blass, *attische Beredsamkeit*[2] 3.1, pp. 352–356, G. L. Cawkwell, "Eubulus," *JHS* 83 (1963), p. 48, R. Sealey, "Pseudodemosthenes xiii and xxv," *REG* 80 (1967), pp. 250–255; cf. R. D. Milns, "The Public Speeches of Demosthenes," in Ian Worthington (ed.), *Demosthenes: Statesman and Orator* (London: 2000), p. 205: "I find it hard, however, to believe that . . . [*On Organization*] could have emanated from the same pen that wrote the third *Olynthiac* or third *Philippic*. . . . [It] is so feeble and full of platitudes and empty rhetoric . . ." On authenticity, see J. Trevett, "Demosthenes' Speech *On Organization* (Dem. 13)," *GRBS* 35 (1994), pp. 179–193; cf. MacDowell, *Demosthenes*, pp. 226–227.

[7] See, for example, W. K. Pritchett, *The Greek State at War* (Berkeley and Los Angeles: 1974), pp. 4–33 and 126–132, R. A. Knox, "'So Mischievous a Beaste'? The Athenian *Demos* and its Treatment of Politicians," *G&R*[2] 32 (1985), pp. 132–161.

[8] [Demosthenes] 59.3–8. Apollodorus' prosecutor Stephanus originally asked the jury to impose a fine of fifteen talents. On the incident and its implications for the law governing the fund, see M. H. Hansen, "The Theoric Fund and the *Graphe Paranomon* against Apollodorus," *GRBS* 17 (1976), pp. 235–246, K. A. Kapparis, *Apollodoros: Against*

On Organization[9]

Demosthenes insisted that military affairs should take precedence over everything else, and he returned to his call for a citizen army to serve the city, admonishing the people for their conduct (3–5):

> In my opinion—and do not heckle me for what I am going to say, but listen and then make up your minds—just as we are devoting an assembly to the receipt of public money, so we should devote one to organization and military preparation, and each of us should be prepared not only to listen willingly but also to take action, men of Athens, in order that you may hold your hopes of success in your own hands, rather than inquiring what this or that man is doing. Of all the city's income, both what you now squander to no purpose from your own funds and all that comes from the allies, I say that you should each take an equal share—those in the prime of life as military pay, those who are too old for military service as auditors' pay or whatever else one might call it—and should campaign in person and not leave this task to someone else.

There is none of the intensity in this speech that Demosthenes displayed in his other orations, and he merely demanded another meeting to discuss the distribution of public money. Why he even bothered to give such a lackluster speech is revealed by the tirade in it against the city's leaders. He criticized their venality and undemocratic attitudes, contrasting them with honorable leaders of earlier days. This type of rhetorical abuse is found in his other speeches, but a major difference

Neaira [D. 59] (Berlin: 1991), pp. 174–178, J. Trevett, *Apollodorus the Son of Pasion* (Oxford: 1992), pp. 144–145; cf. Cawkwell, "Eubulus," pp. 53–58, Carlier, *Démosthène*, pp. 128–129 (Apollodorus inspired by Demosthenes, p. 129), Sealey, *Demosthenes*, pp. 256–258. On the implications of this case for the legal penalty, see E. M. Harris, "Demosthenes and the Theoric Fund," in W. R. Wallace and E. M. Harris (eds.), *Transitions to Empire. Essays in Honor of E. Badian* (Norman: 1996), pp. 65–70.

[9] On the speech, see Blass, *attische Beredsamkeit*[2] 3.1, pp. 352–356, L. Pearson, *The Art of Demosthenes* (Meisenheim am Glan: 1976), pp. 135–136, Carlier, *Démosthène*, pp. 120–121, S. Usher, *Greek Oratory: Tradition and Originality* (Oxford 1999), pp. 215–217, MacDowell, *Demosthenes*, pp. 223–229, citing bibliography. See also Sealey, "Pseudodemosthenes xiii and xxv," pp. 250–255. Translation with notes: J. Trevett, *Demosthenes, Speeches 1–17* (Austin: 2011), pp. 224–239.

is that he criticized their attacks on him and his policies (12–17, 19–20, 30–33). He thus took advantage of the issue of dividing up public money to exonerate his past failures and attempt to turn his career around (12–13):

> But perhaps someone has already spoken like this, men of Athens—not one of you the majority, but one of those who burst with anger at the prospect of these plans being put into effect: "What good have the speeches of Demosthenes done us? He comes forward whenever he likes, fills our ears with words, disparages the present situation and praises our ancestors, and after inflating your hopes and puffing you up, steps down from the platform." As for me, if I could persuade you of any of my arguments, I would think that I was doing the city such great services that if I were to try to describe them, many people would reject them as being exaggerated.

On Organization was unsuccessful. With another failed speech to his discredit, Demosthenes' career now appeared all but over. Then Philip unwittingly came to its rescue.

PHILIP INVADES THE CHALCIDICE

The Olynthians had offered asylum to Philip's surviving two half-brothers, the sons of his father's marriage to Gygaea.[10] Philip interpreted the Olynthian move as a sign of hostility to him because his half-brothers were potential claimants to the throne. He declared that the Olynthians had broken their treaty of 357 with him and bade them surrender these men. When they refused, he marched into the Chalcidice in the late summer or perhaps autumn of 349.[11]

Philip's strategy was psychological. He wanted to strike fear in the Chalcidic cities so they would yield to him, in the process isolating powerful Olynthus. To this end, he first besieged the northeastern city of Stageira (the birth-place of Aristotle), and when it capitulated he razed it to the ground. His message was not lost on the people. The towns of Stratonicia, Acanthus, Apollonia, and Arethusa immediately

---

[10] Demosthenes 23.107–109. They were most likely Menelaus and Arrhidaeus, since Philip had Archelaus killed in 359: Diodorus 16.2.6, Justin 8.3.10. See in detail J. R. Ellis, "The Stepbrothers of Philip II," *Historia* 22 (1973), pp. 350–354.

[11] Justin 8.3.10. On Philip's Chalcidian campaign in detail, see Worthington, *Philip II*, pp. 74–82, citing bibliography.

surrendered to him rather than risk the same fate (Map 2). The grim situation caused the Olynthians to send an embassy to Athens (logically the only place to which they could turn) in September or October appealing for help.[12]

Demosthenes supported the Olynthian request in three *Olynthiac* speeches of 349/8—the first two at this time and the third in 348 (when Philip actually besieged Olynthus).[13] He spread four principal themes over all three speeches: (1) the situation at Olynthus, (2) Philip's character and the Athenians' ability to defeat him, (3) funding for military assistance, and (4) the need for the Athenians to pull themselves together and fight.[14] In all of them, Demosthenes grossly distorted Philip's weaknesses and aims in order to persuade the people to adopt his proposals.[15] They are thus excellent examples of the dangers of rhetoric and misinformation for a political agenda.

In his first *Olynthiac*, Demosthenes spoke of Olynthus' situation and the need to send immediate military assistance as a heaven-sent opportunity for the Athenians. In a slight variation from the first *Philippic*, he

[12] Philochorus, *FGrH* 328 FF 49–61, [Plutarch], *Moralia* 845d–e.
[13] Date: Dionysius of Halicarnassus, *To Ammaeus* 1.4, assigning all three to 349/8, with Sealey, "Dionysius of Halicarnassus and Some Demosthenic Dates," pp. 92–96, C. Karvounis, *Demosthenes: Studien zu den Demegorien orr. XIV, XVI, XV, IV, I, II, III* (Tübingen: 2002), pp. 287–316. Lehmann, *Demosthenes*, p. 111, suggested all three were delivered in spring 348. Their order is disputed. Dionysius ordered them 2-3-1. However, the third speech is commonly believed to be the last, because in the first speech there is a guarded mention of the Theoric Fund, no mention of it in the second, but then a startling call to change its distribution of money in the third. That suggests a rising boldness on Demosthenes' part as affairs worsened. It has been argued based on the lack of mention of the Theoric Fund in the second speech and the discussion of affairs in Thessaly in the first and second that the order should be 2-1-3: J. R. Ellis, "The Order of the *Olynthiacs*," *Historia* 16 (1967), pp. 108–111. Absolute certainty is impossible. In favor of the traditional order, see especially C. Eucken, "Reihenfolge und Zweck der olynthischen Reden," *Museum Helveticum* 41 (1984), pp. 193–208 and C. Tuplin, "Demosthenes' *Olynthiacs* and the Character of the Demegoric Corpus," *Historia* 47 (1998), pp. 276–291, Karvounis, *Demosthenes*, pp. 304–305. MacDowell, *Demosthenes*, p. 238 (who also favors the traditional order), suggests that all three speeches were prepared for the Assembly but Demosthenes may have been unable to deliver them all because of time restraints.
[14] MacDowell, *Demosthenes*, p. 230.
[15] Tuplin, "Demosthenes' *Olynthiacs* and the Character of the Demegoric Corpus," pp. 276–320; see also T. T. B. Ryder, "Demosthenes and Philip II," in Ian Worthington (ed.), *Demosthenes: Statesman and Orator* (London: 2000), pp. 49–50, 54–57.

asked for two forces, one to go to Olynthus and the other to defeat Philip in the north rather than have him invade Attica.[16] He also demanded that the city better fund military operations by spending theoric fund money and levy an *eisphora* tax.[17]

When the Athenians did nothing, Demosthenes delivered his second *Olynthiac*, in which he repeated the need to send help. He was especially concerned with firing up the people to be as active as Philip, deliberately downplaying his successes and resources in the process.[18] Demosthenes cleverly besought the people to send an embassy to Thessaly to divert Philip's attention from Olynthus and urged political leaders to put aside their differences.[19]

The First and Second *Olynthiacs*[20]

Demosthenes presented the Olynthian petition as a golden opportunity (*kairos*) furnished by fate (the gods) and fortune (*tyche*) for the Athenians to combat Philip (1–4).[21] However, they had to move quickly in seizing it (2):

[16] Demosthenes 1.4, 12–15, 17–18, 24–28.

[17] Demosthenes 1.18–20.

[18] Demosthenes 2.3–13, 14–23, 31.

[19] Demosthenes 2.11, 29–31.

[20] The three *Olynthiacs* are usually discussed together and treated thematically: see Schaefer, *Demosthenes*² 2, pp. 126–152, Blass, *attische Beredsamkeit*² 3.1, pp. 268–281, Pickard-Cambridge, *Demosthenes*, pp. 193–227, Jaeger, *Demosthenes*, pp. 127–144, Pearson, *Art of Demosthenes*, pp. 120–121, 127–135, Carlier, *Démosthène*, pp 121–126, Sealey, *Demosthenes*, pp. 137–143, Usher, *Greek Oratory: Tradition and Originality*, pp. 220–226, Lehmann, *Demosthenes*, pp. 111–119, MacDowell, *Demosthenes*, pp. 229–239. See also Tuplin, "Demosthenes' *Olynthiacs* and the Character of the Demegoric Corpus," pp. 276–320, H. Yunis, *Taming Democracy: Models of Political Rhetoric in Classical Athens* (Ithaca: 1996), pp. 257–268. The *Olynthiacs* are also treated extensively in C. Wooten, *Cicero's Philippics and their Demosthenic Model* (Chapel Hill: 1983). Translation with notes: Trevett, *Demosthenes, Speeches 1–17*, pp. 27–67; translation with commentary: J. R. Ellis and R. D. Milns, *The Spectre of Philip* (Sydney: 1970), pp. 44–76 (given in the order 2, 1, 3), E. I. McQueen, *Demosthenes: Olynthiacs* (London: 1986); text and commentary: J. E. Sandys, *The First Philippic and the Olynthiacs of Demosthenes* (Cambridge: 1910); detailed discussion and commentary: Karvounis, *Demosthenes*, pp. 287–352.

[21] On *tyche*, see Jaeger, *Demosthenes*, pp. 132–133.

The present situation, men of Athens, all but takes voice and says that you must take control of the Olynthians' affairs, if indeed you are concerned about their preservation—though I find it difficult to describe our attitude toward them. In my opinion, you should vote for an immediate relief force, and make preparations as quickly as possible to send help from here, to avoid suffering a recurrence of what happened previously, and should send an embassy to announce these decisions and observe what is happening.

He contrasted the need for speed now with the people's slowness in the past, which had lost them valuable possessions to Philip (8–9):

You must not pass up such an opportunity, men of Athens, when it has fallen into your lap, nor suffer the same fate as you have suffered many times already. For if, when we had returned from helping the Euboeans, and the Amphipolitans Hierax and Stratocles were here on this very platform urging us to sail, and take possession of their city, we had shown the same concern for our own interests as we had for the security of the Euboeans, we would have held on to Amphipolis then and would have avoided all our subsequent troubles. Again, when it was announced that Pydna, Potidaea, Methone, Pagasae, and the other places—I do not wish to waste time talking about them individually—were being besieged, if we had energetically dispatched an appropriate relief force to the first of these, we would now be dealing with a more tractable and weaker Philip.[22]

Demosthenes was right to try to rouse the Athenians to action and to claim that an independent Chalcidian League had to be preserved at all costs, given the extent of Philip's conquests in the north (7–8) and his potential to attack Athens (15). Demosthenes' rhetorical prowess is chillingly shown in one of the features of his style, a dramatic series of hypothetical questions (25–27):[23]

If Olynthus holds out, you will be waging war there and ravaging his territory while enjoying your own land without fear. But if Philip takes Olynthus, who will prevent him from marching here? The Thebans? I fear it may be rather harsh to say so, but they will readily join in attacking us. The Phocians then? But they are unable to defend their own territory without your help. Or some other city? But, my dear sir, no one will be willing. . . . Nothing more, I think, needs to be said about the great difference between fighting here and fighting there.

[22] See also Demosthenes 1.12–13, quoted in Chapter 5 p. 127.
[23] Cf. Milns, "Public Speeches of Demosthenes," pp. 212–213.

Between his opening and closing arguments, Demosthenes put forward practical measures to defeat Philip. As in his first *Philippic*, he insisted on two forces, one to go to the Chalcidice to protect its towns and the other to inflict damage on the Macedonian coastline (6, 16–18)—otherwise, "I fear that the campaign may be in vain" (17). To meet its costs, Demosthenes hinted at tapping the Theoric Fund (19–20).[24] He did not specifically name the fund otherwise he would have left himself open to a *graphe paranomon* because of its inviolability (19):

> As for the provision of money, you have money, men of Athens, you have more than anyone else: this money you receive in the form you wish. If we hand it over to those who are on campaign, you will need no further source of money. But if you do not, you will need a further source, or rather you will be in need òf the whole amount. "What is this?" someone may say, "Do you propose that this money be transferred to the military fund?" No, by God, I do not propose that.

The speech failed, and no troops were sent to help the Olynthians. Perhaps the people reacted against Demosthenes' suggestion of redirecting public money, but then he may have simply been unable to better speakers like the cautious Eubulus. That the second *Olynthiac* followed the first by only a few days suggests that Demosthenes may have contributed to public hesitation about what to do. If he had, that would explain why his speech ended with an attack on current political leaders to sway the people to his viewpoint (see below).[25]

The second *Olynthiac* speech repeated many of the arguments from the first one, such as the heaven-sent opportunity to help the Olynthians and to wage war on Philip and the need for the people themselves to serve on campaign and not employ mercenaries. Philip, however, takes more of the center stage in this speech. Demosthenes strove to convince the people that Philip was rapidly becoming a spent force

---

[24] On the suggestion of using theoric monies, cf. Sealey, *Demosthenes*, pp. 137–143, 256–258; cf. MacDowell, *Demosthenes*, pp. 233–234. By contrast, Harris, "Demosthenes and the Theoric Fund," especially pp. 60–65, reinterprets Demosthenes' statements in the first and third *Olynthiacs* to argue that the orator was criticizing the misuse of the Military Fund, not the Theoric. The belief that the discussion of money in this speech and the third *Olynthiac* indicated that Demosthenes created a new military fund at this time is erroneous: see G. L. Cawkwell, "Demosthenes and the Stratiotic Fund," *Mnemosyne* 15 (1962), pp. 377–383.

[25] Ryder, "Demosthenes and Philip II," p. 55.

thanks to the way he conducted himself, and he claimed that Philip was reviled by his own people. To this end, Demosthenes deliberately downplayed the king's power and abilities, claiming that Philip's successes had nothing to do with diplomatic or military skills but were rather owing to treachery and deceit—"in short, there is no associate of his whom he has not cheated, since it is by deceiving and winning over all of those who are ignorant of him, one after another, that he has grown in power" (7).

Demosthenes' assertions that Philip was actually feeble and, further, that his own people disliked him for always going to war, that his army was incompetent, and that his power would collapse at any moment, were completely unrealistic (5–21)![26] If the Athenians mobilized, then "not only will Philip's alliances be shown to be weak and unreliable but his very kingdom and power will be proved to be in a parlous state" (13). Even the Macedonian army's track record of success did not stop Demosthenes belittling it (17):

> The attitude of most Macedonians to Philip can easily be gathered from these facts: the mercenaries and Foot Companions in his entourage have the reputation of being wonderful and disciplined fighters but I have heard from someone who has been in that country, and who is incapable of lying, that they are no better than anyone else.

To round off his character denigration, Demosthenes portrayed Philip's court as debauched and the king as surrounded only by "brigands and flatterers and men whose drunken dancing is so vile that I shrink from describing it to you."[27] Demosthenes had not yet visited Pella, so his account at best was based only on hearsay. In reality, Philip was in no danger of losing his kingship, and his army was far from debilitated. The identity of Demosthenes' informant who was "incapable of lying" was unknown, but he may have been a fiction otherwise the orator would have produced him in the Assembly. Demosthenes deliberately beguiled the people with erroneous information about the ruler's position, resources, threat, and even morality—little has changed in the modern world.

---

[26] He repeated this argument in his last extant political speech, *To Philip's Letter* (11) of 340: the passage is quoted in Chapter 9 p. 232.

[27] Demosthenes 2.19: the passage is quoted in Chapter 3 p. 52. Note Pickard-Cambridge, *Demosthenes*, p. 196, that the argument does more credit to Demosthenes' moral principles than to his insight into the situation of the moment!

On the other hand, Demosthenes was right to draw attention to the problems emerging in Thessaly, thanks to a rebellious Pherae, which would divert Philip's attention (11). In a bid to counter opposition from Eubulus, especially if the people were wavering in their feelings for Olynthus, Demosthenes in his conclusion called for the enmity among the leaders to end (29–31). Everyone had to "join together in deliberating, speaking, and taking action for the common good" (30).[28]

Finally, Demosthenes was successful in the Assembly: the Athenians voted to make an alliance with Olynthus and deploy troops to its assistance.[29]

THE ATHENIANS MOBILIZE

Despite Demosthenes' repeated calls for citizen soldiers, the Athenians sent Chares as commander of a force of 2,000 Thracian mercenary peltasts, or javelin throwers (named for the *pelta* or wicker shield they carried), and thirty triremes to Olynthus.[30] Philip, however, was no longer in the Chalcidice but had left for Thessaly, so Chares' troops had little choice but to go back to Athens.[31] Philip had broken off his Chalcidian campaign because Peitholaus, one of the tyrants he had expelled from Pherae, had returned and was demanding the return of Pagasae.[32] Philip could not permit Peitholaus to recoup his power and therefore he marched immediately to Pherae. The details of the campaign are not known, but Peitholaus offered little resistance. The king deposed him and returned to Pella, where he spent the remainder of 349.

In March of 348 Philip resumed his Chalcidian campaign. The Olynthians appealed again for help to the Athenians, who commanded their general Charidemus (then based at the Chersonese) to assist them

---

[28] On the passage, cf. MacDowell, *Demosthenes*, pp. 236–237.

[29] See further: G. L. Cawkwell, "The Defence of Olynthus," *CQ*² 12 (1962), pp. 122–140 and J. M. Carter, "Athens, Euboea and Olynthus," *Historia* 20 (1971), pp. 418–429.

[30] Philochorus, *FGrH* 328 F 49, Diodorus 16.52.9. The peltasts were mercenaries, so Demosthenes failed to have citizen soldiers serve on campaign.

[31] See further: Worthington, *Philip II*, pp. 76–77.

[32] Demosthenes 1.22, 2.11; cf. Diodorus 16.52.9. See also E. Badian, "Philip II and the Last of the Thessalians," *Ancient Macedonia* 6 (Institute for Balkan Studies, Thessaloniki: 1999), pp. 117–120.

with 18 triremes, 4,000 peltasts, and 150 cavalry (withdrawn from Euboea—see below).[33] Charidemus joined an Olynthian army of 1,000 cavalry and 10,000 infantry, and together they recaptured some cities in the Pallene promontory, which Philip had taken the previous year. They also went on the offensive by devastating parts of Bottiaea, a district of Macedonia south of the river Lydias.

None of their operations stopped Philip. He systematically subjugated more Chalcidic towns and in the late spring or early summer seized Mecyberna, the port of Olynthus, less than three miles from the city.[34] His victory sounded the death knell for the Olynthians, who were now denied access to their port. Five miles from their city, Philip issued them an ultimatum: "there were two alternatives—either they should stop living in Olynthus or he should stop living in Macedonia."[35] In despair they called on Athens again for help, urging the city for citizen soldiers rather than mercenaries.

At the Assembly that met to consider this latest appeal, Demosthenes presented his third and final *Olynthiac*. The same warning that Philip would invade Attica and criticism of the Athenians' minimal effort to block him run through this speech. Although Demosthenes' dramatic claim that "our situation has deteriorated so badly that we are reduced to examining how to prevent [Philip] from harming us first"[36] was overstated, the situation was in fact grim. That is why he solicited a special committee to repeal the laws governing the Theoric Fund so as to increase funding for military operations.[37]

The Third *Olynthiac*[38]

Demosthenes scolded the people for not taking advantage of Philip's illness to attack him but said they could still redress the situation if they mobilized immediately (1–9). He attempted to shame them into action by a series of striking rhetorical questions (16–17):

[33] Philochorus, *FGrH* 328 F 50, Diodorus 16.52.9.

[34] Diodorus 16.53.2 says that Mecyberna and Torone (the main town of the Sithonian peninsula) were betrayed to him.

[35] Demosthenes 9.11.

[36] Demosthenes 3.1.

[37] Demosthenes 3.1–2, 8, 10–13, 19, 27–28. On Demosthenes and the Theoric Fund, see note 24 above.

[38] On this speech, see above, note 20.

What occasion or opportunity, men of Athens, do you seek that will be better than the present one? When will you do your duty, if not now? Has this man not taken all our territories? If he becomes master of this land [Olynthus], shall we now suffer the utmost ignominy? Are those people, whom we promised to support if they were to go to war, not now at war with him? Is he not our enemy? Does he not possess what is ours? Is he not a foreigner? Can anyone find words to describe him? But, by the gods, after we have neglected everything and all but helped him in his preparations, are we now to inquire who was responsible for this state of affairs?

What was different about this speech from the previous *Olynthiacs* was Demosthenes' explicit call to amend the laws governing the Theoric Fund (10–13):

Do not be amazed, men of Athens, if I say something that most of you will find unexpected. You should appoint lawmakers. Use these lawmakers not to pass a law—you have enough of them—but to repeal those laws that are presently harming your interests. I am referring directly to the laws relating to the theoric fund and to certain of the laws relating to those who go on campaign. Some of these laws distribute military funds as theoric payments to those who stay at home; others let those who shirk military service get off scot-free and make even those who wish to do their duty more despondent. When you have repealed these laws and made it safe to offer the best advice, only then should you look for someone to propose the measures that you all know to be beneficial.

His point echoed his *On Organization* in that public money should not be a mere dole but should be paid to people for their military services to the city.[39] As he said, there were no other funds in Athens that could be mined (19):

But if someone is able to leave the theoric fund to one side and identify other sources of money for military spending, is this not preferable, it might be asked. I agree, men of Athens, if this is really possible. But I would be amazed if it has ever happened to anybody, or ever will happen, that after spending what he has on things that he does not need, he should be able to afford the things that he does need from the money he no longer has.

---

[39] Demosthenes 13.25–31.

There is no question that his recommendation was a courageous one and he must have known it would be unpopular.[40] He did, however, cleverly protect himself from prosecution because he did not propose that the Theoric Fund should be drained for military operations. Instead, he requested the *nomothetai* (a committee of legislators whose job it was to evaluate the laws) evaluate Eubulus' law governing the disbursement of theoric money. If the lawmakers decided there were grounds for changing it, then the Assembly would have the final say.

The rest of the speech attacked political leaders for their venality and failure to grasp opportunities (21–36).[41] He accused them of being self-serving and pandering to the people (21–22). He contrasted them with the preeminent leaders of the fifth century, such as Pericles, Aristides, and Miltiades, under whom Athens prospered and became an imperial power. They lived modestly, unlike leaders now, who live in splendid palaces while the city is in economic decline (23–32):

> In private they were so restrained and so true to the nature of their constitution that if any of you knows which is the house of Aristides or of Miltiades or of the distinguished men of that time he sees that it is no grander than that of its neighbor. For they did not conduct the affairs of the city with a view to their own profit, but each of them thought it right to make the commonwealth more prosperous. . . . How do we fare nowadays, under the leadership of these men who are now deemed admirable? Do we fare the same, or nearly so? . . . "But, my dear sir, even if these things are unsatisfactory, the city itself is now in a better state." Why, what improvement can you name? The battlements we plaster, the roads we repair, the fountains, and similar rubbish? Look at the politicians who are responsible for these things. Some of them were beggars and are now rich; others were obscure and are now prominent. Some have built private houses that are grander than our public buildings. The more our city has declined, the more these men have flourished.

The Athenians were not sufficiently moved to alter the Theoric Fund, but Demosthenes did persuade them to deploy another contingent of troops to Olynthus.

---

[40] As Pickard-Cambridge, *Demosthenes*, pp. 203–204, says, despite the idealism, it took considerable courage on Demosthenes' part to say what he did, given who he was opposing and that the whole people would find his suggestion unpopular.

[41] Some material is repeated from Demosthenes 13.25–31.

THE FALL OF OLYNTHUS

The Athenians appointed Chares to command a force of 2,000 citizen infantry and 300 cavalry (one-third of Athens' cavalry force) and 17 triremes.[42] The fleet could not put to sea for forty days, however, because of the northerly Etesian winds (modern *meltemi*), which blow intermittently between May and September.[43] Philip took advantage of the Athenian delay to attack Olynthus frontally. The sling bullets and bolt-heads with his name (*Philippou*) on them from his siege machinery testify to the determination of the defenders to resist him.[44] Demosthenes later stated that Philip bribed two pro-Macedonian cavalry commanders, Euthycrates and Lasthenes, to betray the city to him.[45] His assertion has been rejected as an attempt to downplay Philip's victory,[46] but it is consistent with the king's use of bribes. Philip may well have resorted to bribery when the siege grew protracted, especially as he needed to end it before Athenian help arrived.

Chares and his troops finally set sail when the Etesian winds abated but arrived too late to save Olynthus. The city must have capitulated by the end of August or possibly early September, for later in that month Philip celebrated the festival of Zeus of Olympus at Dium, Macedonia's religious centre. The Macedonians massacred many of the Olynthians and razed the city to the ground. The survivors either fled or were captured and taken back to Macedonia as slaves to work in the mines and fields.[47] Included among those killed were Philip's two half-brothers.[48] Demosthenes in a speech of 341 claimed that Philip destroyed all the cities of the Chalcidian League—"I say nothing about

---

[42] Philochorus, *FGrH* 328 F 51, Diodorus 16.52.9; cf. Aristotle, *Rhetoric* 3.1411a.

[43] Philochorus, *FGrH* 328 F 49, Dem. 21.161; cf. Cawkwell, "Defence of Olynthus," p. 131.

[44] Diodorus 16.53.2. On these, see E.W. Marsden, "Macedonian Military Machinery and its Designers under Philip and Alexander," *Ancient Macedonia* 2 (Institute for Balkan Studies, Thessaloniki: 1977), pp. 213–215.

[45] Demosthenes 8.40, 19.265, 342, 18.48; cf. Diodorus 16.53.2.

[46] T. T. B. Ryder, "The Diplomatic Skills of Philip II," in Ian Worthington (ed.), *Ventures into Greek History. Essays in Honour of N. G. L. Hammond* (Oxford: 1994), pp. 231–232, drawing attention to Demosthenes' similar disparaging remark about the fall of Amphipolis in 357.

[47] Philochorus, *FGrH* 328 FF 50–51 and 156, Diodorus 16.53.2–3, 55.1; cf. Demosthenes 9.26.

[48] Justin 8.3.11.

Olynthus and Methone and Apollonia and thirty-two cities on the coast of Thrace (i.e., the Chalcidice), all of which he destroyed with such cruelty that it would be hard for a visitor to tell whether they had ever been inhabited."[49] That is exaggeration. The Chacidice's timber and mineral resources (especially the gold and silver mines at Strato-nici) were another boost to the rapidly expanding Macedonian economy, hence devastating the area would have made little economic sense.[50] The Chalcidian League was, however, brought to an end and Philip incorporated the Chalcidice into his kingdom.

Among the prisoners taken at Olynthus were some Athenians, who played a role in the peace negotiations between Philip and Athens two years later. To express their anger at his actions, the Athenians passed a decree condemning Philip and offered Olynthian escapees refuge in the city, where they lived as metics (resident aliens).[51]

Philip's attack on Olynthus was later characterized as a "blood-red meteor, which fell to earth."[52] The punishment he meted out to the city was also likened to Alexander the Great's destruction of Thebes in 335 (Chapter 12 p. 280), and ancient writers cobbled these two lamentable events together as a literary topos:[53]

> Olynthus and Thebes . . . were plundered by Alexander and Philip and razed to the ground, and the horror of the destruction caused great alarm to many of the Greeks for their all and gave many orators an opportunity to explain in due manner the details of the calamity by their oratory.

The Athenian reaction to Philip's treatment of Olynthus was moti-vated by guilt for their not doing more or deploying troops faster.[54]

---

[49] Demosthenes 9.26; cf. Diodorus 16.53.3.

[50] Diodorus 16.53.3 and Justin 8.3.11 say nothing about wholesale destruction, which is a surprising omission if Philip did devastate the area, though cf. Griffith in N. G. L. Hammond and G. T. Griffith, *A History of Macedonia* 2 (Oxford: 1979), pp. 365–366. In the second century AD, Appian stated that only the foundations of the temples could be seen (*Bell. Civ.* 4.102).

[51] Demosthenes 19.267.

[52] Pliny, *NH* 2.27.

[53] Hegesias, *FGrH* 142 T 3; translation: C. A. Robinson, *The History of Alexander the Great* 1 (Providence: 1953), p. 249; cf. "What need is there to speak of Olynthians and Thebans and with what sufferings they died in his own city?" (Hegesias, *FGrH* 142 F 11; translation Robinson, *History of Alexander the Great* 1, p. 255).

[54] Cf. [Demosthenes] 59.3.

Then again, despite their financial straits they had sent three expeditions to help Olynthus, in all committing some 65 triremes and 13,000 citizen troops, as well as cavalry and mercenaries.[55] They were also faced with other concerns that affected their support of Olynthus including Philip's speed from a slow build-up to a fast strike that the Assembly could not mirror, his exploitation of the Etesian winds, and their uncertainty of ever properly knowing what his strategy was or indeed where he was. There was no guarantee, for example, that he would not take advantage of a major Athenian troop movement to the Chalcidice to march quickly into Greece, penetrate Thermopylae, and invade Attica.[56] After all, when Chares first sailed to help Olynthus in 349 the Athenians were completely unaware that Philip was then in Thessaly. The major reason for the people's caution, however, was the worrying events taking place on their very doorstep, the island of Euboea, which required their immediate attention.

THE EUBOEAN FACTOR

Relations between Athens and Euboea had been amicable for some time, but they underwent a dramatic decline in 348 when Callias, the tyrant ruler of the city of Chalcis, attempted to create a league of Euboean cities. The potential for Callias allying with Philip, whose influence would then extend almost to Attica's eastern coastline, alarmed the Athenians. Indeed, Philip may even have been backing Callias to divert Athenian attention from his siege of Olynthus.[57] Therefore they decided to respond to a call from Plutarchus, the tyrant of another Euboean city, Eretria,[58] who was under attack from a man named Cleitarchus.[59] Plutarchus had several influential contacts in

---

[55] Cawkwell, "Defence of Olynthus," pp. 130–134, Sealey, *Demosthenes*, pp. 142–143, Karvounis, *Demosthenes*, pp. 292–301, 343–352. Justification for what the Athenians did and did not do, and why: Cawkwell, "Defence of Olynthus," especially pp. 130–140; cf. Worthington, *Philip II*, pp. 80–82.

[56] See Ryder, "Diplomatic Skills of Philip II," pp. 235–238.

[57] Aeschines 3.87 says that Callias "summoned additional forces from Philip," and Demosthenes 4.37 refers to a letter Philip sent to the Euboeans; cf. Ryder, "Demosthenes and Philip II," p. 56.

[58] No writer states that Plutarchus was a tyrant, but the way Demosthenes' refers to him at 9.57 indicates he was one: Ryder, "Diplomatic Skills of Philip II," p. 236.

[59] Philochorus, *FGrH* 328 F 160.

Athens, including Meidias, a friend of Eubulus. This was the same Meidias Demosthenes had prosecuted in 364 for breaking into his house (Chapter 2 pp. 21–22). Eubulus himself initiated the dispatch of military support to Plutarchus, indicating the importance of Euboea to Athens. Eubulus' friend Phocion was the troop commander and his second-in-command was Eubulus' cousin Hegesileus, while Meidias commanded the cavalry of his tribe.[60] Demosthenes served on this campaign but returned early from it (see below).

Phocion crossed to Euboea, but Plutarchus never sent him troops. Worse, Callias and his brother Taurosthenes besieged Phocion and his troops at the inland city of Tamynae.[61] Phocion's position was grim, especially as he had earlier dismissed his cavalry, thinking it was not needed.[62] Nevertheless, he spurred his men to charge the enemy line and managed to fight his way through it. The Euboeans fell away, allowing Phocion to march swiftly to Eretria and expel the untrustworthy Plutarchus. Then the Athenians committed a strategic error by recalling Phocion (who was sent to Lesbos), replacing him with a general named Molossus. Plutarchus took advantage of the new commander's unfamiliarity with the island to attack him, capturing all the Athenian troops in the process. The city had to pay a ransom of fifty talents for their return, and to add insult to injury all of Euboea (apart from Carystus at its southern tip) declared its independence of Athens.[63]

The fallout from the Euboean debacle must have affected Eubulus' political reputation in Athens. Demosthenes later claimed that he had tried to persuade the people to avoid intervention in Euboea and focus only on Philip in the north:[64]

> I was the first, indeed the only one to come forward and oppose it, and
> I was virtually torn apart by those who were trying to persuade you, for
> the sake of small profits, to commit many great errors.

[60] Demosthenes later ridiculed Meidias' military service: Demosthenes 21.133. On Athenian involvement in Euboea, see P. A. Brunt, "Euboea in the Time of Philip II," *CQ*[2] 19 (1969), pp. 245–265, Carter, "Athens, Euboea and Olynthus," pp. 418–429, Cawkwell, "Defence of Olynthus," pp. 127–130, E. M. Burke, "Eubulus, Olynthus, and Euboea," *TAPA* 114 (1984), pp. 111–120, Worthington, *Philip II*, pp. 81–82.

[61] Plutarch, *Phocion* 12–13.

[62] Demosthenes 21.132; cf. 197.

[63] Demosthenes 21.161–164.

[64] Demosthenes 5.5.

His assertion may well be true because prior to the Euboean expedition Meidias apparently criticized Demosthenes for not championing Plutarchus, who was a friend of Athens.[65] The enmity between Demosthenes and Meidias, which went back almost two decades, now exploded.

DEMOSTHENES AND MEIDIAS

Before Athens involved itself in Euboea Demosthenes had volunteered to provide a chorus for his tribe (Pandionis) at the spring festival of the Dionysia.[66] For this liturgy (the *choregia*), he would have been excused military service, yet he still served on the Euboean campaign. He was not legally bound to be in the city for his liturgy and could have appointed someone to oversee all the arrangements for the chorus.[67] Nevertheless, he left Euboea in the middle of the campaign to return home. He may well have wanted to bask in the glory he would receive from the people for undertaking a tribal *choregia*.[68] Yet that understandably human reason would not explain why he went to Euboea in the first place. A more plausible explanation lies in his political aspirations, which also led to a clash with Meidias.

Demosthenes' recent successes with his second and third *Olynthiacs* were a turning point in his career, but he had no way of knowing whether his winning streak would continue. He had put forward intelligent and patriotic proposals in his previous speeches, only to see them undermined by Eubulus. Plutarchus' unexpected treachery, which had endangered Phocion and his men on Euboea, must have affected Eubulus' credibility with the people, and Demosthenes wanted to capitalize on that discredit. His liturgy gave him a reason to return to the city and thus be able to address his fellow citizens in the Assembly, and he seized it. Later a man named Euctemon—at Meidias' behest, according to Demosthenes—charged him with desertion (*graphe lipotaxiou*).[69] He either was not brought to trial or was acquitted, for under Athenian law he would have lost his citizenship if found guilty.

---

[65] Demosthenes 21.110.

[66] Demosthenes 21.13.

[67] Cf. Antiphon 6 (*On the Chorister*), where the *choregos* was not present, and had arranged for another man to ensure everything was arranged for the chorus.

[68] My thanks to Professor Christopher Pelling for an e-exchange on this point.

[69] Demosthenes 21.103, Aeschines 2.148; cf. Carlier, *Démosthène*, p. 132.

Meidias had decided to make Demosthenes' life miserable, possibly motivated not so much by the animosity between the two men that went back to when Demosthenes indicted him but by the blow his political ally Eubulus had suffered, which Demosthenes was exploiting for his own political gain.[70] Instead of opposing Demosthenes in the Assembly, Meidias targeted his *choregia*.[71] Demosthenes had hired the best flute player in Athens, Telephanes, and was determined that his chorus would win first prize at the festival. Thanks to Meidias, Demosthenes alleged, it lost. One night, for example, he broke into the house of the goldsmith who was making the chorus' gold crowns and Demosthenes' festival robes and destroyed them. He bribed the leader of the chorus to neglect its training and even tried to bribe the judges at the Dionysia. Worse still, at the actual festival he went up to Demosthenes in the theater and in full view of everyone punched him in the face.[72]

Assaulting anyone at a religious festival was a serious crime, given Athenian respect of the gods. The following day the Assembly convened as was customary, and Demosthenes brought a formal complaint against Meidias under a procedure called *probole*.[73] Eubulus did not speak for Meidias at the meeting, suggesting he did not wish to be associated with a man who had so disrupted a religious event. The Assembly considered Demosthenes' case and delivered its verdict (officially called the *probole*) condemning Meidias. There was no punishment, and the matter was not automatically referred to a law court, presumably because of the public humiliation an individual suffered. Meidias had thick skin, however. He continued to badger Demosthenes for two years until the orator finally silenced him in court (Chapter 7 pp. 156–162).[74]

---

[70] D.M. MacDowell, *Demosthenes: Against Meidias (Oration 21)* (Oxford: 1990), pp. 1–13, argues that the clash between the two men that led to the assault was due to personal rather than political reasons.

[71] Demosthenes 21.13–18.

[72] Demosthenes 21.16, 18, 78, 156, Aeschines 3.52; on the assault, see MacDowell, *Demosthenes: Against Meidias*, p. 8, P. Wilson, *The Athenian Institution of the Khoregia: The Chorus, The City and the Stage* (Cambridge: 2000), pp. 156–162.

[73] Demosthenes 21.1 (law on *probole* quoted at 47). On the procedure, see D. M. MacDowell, *The Law in Classical Athens* (London: 1978), pp. 194–197, MacDowell, *Demosthenes: Against Meidias*, pp. 13–16; cf. 263–265 on the law.

[74] On the interval of time, see Demosthenes 21.13, 112.

PHILIP SOLICITS PEACE

In the summer of 348, Macedonian pirates captured an Athenian man named Phrynon from the deme of Rhamnus. He was rich enough to buy his freedom and go home to Athens. He petitioned the people to send an embassy to Philip demanding reimbursement because he had been captured during the Olympic truce when everyone traveling to and from the Olympic Games was protected. The Athenians sent an ambassador named Ctesiphon to Philip to discuss the matter, and the king agreed that Phrynon had a case.[75] Ctesiphon returned to the Athenians with a surprising message: Philip wanted to end the war with them. Moreover, he was not only soliciting peace but also an alliance (*symmachia*), meaning both parties would refrain from hostilities against each other and each would support the other if attacked.[76]

Philip's motives for peace will never be properly known.[77] The most plausible explanation is that events in the Third Sacred War were attracting his attention and he was becoming increasingly alarmed about a possible union of Athens and Thebes against him. He decided therefore to curb Thebes' presence in Greece, to which end he needed to win over the Athenians and arrange a settlement of Greece that would isolate Thebes.[78] He probably targeted Thebes because of its ambitions, which upset stability in Greece, and as a form of revenge for the years he spent in the city as a young hostage. Certainly Philip dealt with the Thebans differently from the other Greeks, especially the

---

[75] Ambassadors were not, like today, senior diplomatic representatives living in a foreign country but men selected by the people merely to serve on an embassy to another state: cf. the comments of D. M. MacDowell, *Demosthenes: On the False Embassy (Oration 19)* (Oxford: 2000), pp. 14–15.

[76] Aeschines 2.12–17.

[77] See the analyses of J. R. Ellis, *Philip II and Macedonian Imperialism* (London: 1976), pp. 101–103 and "Philip and the Peace of Philokrates," in W. L. Adams and E. N. Borza (eds.), *Philip II, Alexander the Great, and the Macedonian Heritage* (Lanham: 1982), pp. 43–59, G. L. Cawkwell, "The Peace of Philocrates Again," *CQ²* 28 (1978), pp. 93–104, Griffith in Hammond and Griffith, *History of Macedonia* 2, pp. 329–347, MacDowell, *Demosthenes: On the False Embassy*, p. 2, Worthington, *Philip II*, pp. 82–85.

[78] Ellis, "Philip and the Peace of Philokrates," pp. 43–59. See also Carlier, *Démosthène*, pp. 157–160 (Philip's plans in 346, but relevant to the situation in 348), N. Sawada, "A Reconsideration of the Peace of Philocrates," *Kodai* 4 (1993), pp. 21–50; contra, for example, Ryder, "Diplomatic Skills of Philip II," p. 244.

Athenians, throughout his reign.[79] Needless to say, he had to keep the Thebans in the dark, so over the next two years he maintained his pattern of trickery and deceit by pretending he was their ally.

Ctesiphon related Philip's message to the Assembly. Philocrates of Hagnus proposed that Philip send an embassy to the people with his terms and the people enthusiastically rallied around him.[80] Then it was discovered his motion was illegal, perhaps because it breached a clause in the Athenian alliance with Olynthus that neither party should receive envoys from Philip without the other's agreement.[81] If so, then the Athenians at this juncture were not aware that Olynthus had fallen to Philip.

Philocrates was indicted for *graphe paranomon*, but because of his apparent illness Demosthenes defended him. He won his case so convincingly that less than one-fifth of the jury voted for his accuser, Lycinus, who was fined 1,000 drachmas and lost the right to bring similar suits in future.[82] Demosthenes' backing for Philocrates did not mean he had suddenly turned into an advocate for peace with Philip. His motive was likely self-serving: to position himself for a role in forthcoming negotiations with Philip over peace. Like many Athenians, Demosthenes must have realized in 348 that peace with Philip was inevitable and necessary for the city to recover fully from the Social War—the suspension of the jury system in the same year for lack of money evinced that. Regardless of how well peace negotiations with Philip went, Demosthenes the junior politician was thirsty for involvement in them, which would advance his political career considerably.

Philip did not send the requested embassy to Athens because he was still campaigning against Olynthus. The news of the city's capitulation brought about a radical reversal of opinion about peace with Philip. Eubulus and an up-and-coming orator named Aeschines (see below) went so far as to bring into the Assembly a man named Ischander who had recently returned from Arcadia claiming that Philip was gathering support against Athens from everywhere including the

---

[79] See further, Worthington, *Philip II*, pp. 84–85, 86, 88, 90, 95, 98–99, 100–101, 142; see also G. L. Cawkwell, "Philip and Athens," in M. B. Hatzopoulos and L. D. Loukopoulos (eds.), *Philip of Macedon* (Athens: 1980), pp. 100–110 and Ryder, "Diplomatic Skills of Philip II," pp. 251–257.

[80] Aeschines 2.13.

[81] Worthington, *Philip II*, pp. 82–83.

[82] Aeschines 2.14, 109; cf. 3.62. This was the penalty when a litigant received less than one-fifth of the votes at a trial: MacDowell, *Law in Classical Athens*, p. 64.

Peloponnese.[83] In some panic the people sent an embassy to all Greek states and "almost to the Red Sea," at Eubulus' instigation, calling for them to join Athens in war against Philip.[84] Philocrates' earlier call to hear Philip's peace terms was set aside.

Demosthenes did not serve on this embassy to the Greek states, and he remained on the sidelines of public life for the rest of 348. He may have deliberately chosen to do so. If he backed the embassy in any way and it failed, the people would not want an advocate of war discussing peace with Philip. If he criticized the embassy and its mission succeeded, he would seem less credible when encouraging the people to fight Philip. Demosthenes involved himself in some important cases at this time, so he may have returned to his speechwriting career.[85] He did not, however, abandon political life as he submitted his candidature to serve on the Boule in 347/6.[86]

The embassy to the Greek states convinced only the Arcadians to support the Athenian cause.[87] Its failure was hardly a surprise because many Greeks still saw no threat to them from Philip, and they had little desire to side with Athens, whose unpopularity as a leader had been illustrated by the revolt of its allies in the Social War.[88] Eubulus might even have expected this embassy to fail, thereby giving him the chance to convince the people to make peace with Philip.[89]

THE RISE OF AESCHINES

In 348 a man made his debut in the Assembly speaking in favor of peace negotiations with Philip. His name was Aeschines, and for the next fifteen years he was Demosthenes' most vocal political opponent

---

[83] Demosthenes 19.10–11, 303, Aeschines 2.79. On Aeschines' activities in this period, see G. L. Cawkwell, "Aeschines and the Peace of Philocrates," *REG* 73 (1960), pp. 416–438.

[84] Demosthenes 19.304.

[85] For example, the two speeches *Against Boeotus* (39 and 40) *and Against Pantainetus* (37), on which see MacDowell, *Demosthenes*, pp. 66–79 and 266–271, respectively.

[86] Aeschines 3.62 accused Demosthenes of using bribes to become a member of the Boule, which is a falsehood, as its members were selected by lot.

[87] Demosthenes 19.10–11, 303–306, Aeschines 2.79, 164, 3.58, 64.

[88] Diodorus 16.64.3; cf. J. Buckler, "Demosthenes and Aeschines," in Ian Worthington (ed.), *Demosthenes: Statesman and Orator* (London: 2000), pp. 117–119, Sealey, *Demosthenes*, pp. 151–153.

[89] Pickard-Cambridge, *Demosthenes*, p. 234.

FIGURE 9. Bust of the orator Aeschines, Demosthenes' most vocal political opponent.

and his personal enemy (Figure 9).[90] He was born in the 390s (the exact year is unknown).[91] Information on his background and early career comes from Demosthenes, and so may well be distorted. According to Demosthenes, Aeschines began a career as a teacher's aide, in which he "rubbed the ink, wiped the benches, and swept the schoolroom."[92] He then became a third-rate bit actor, who, if we can trust Demosthenes, was hissed off the stage.[93] Demosthenes also claimed that his father was

[90] On his career and politics, see E. M. Harris, *Aeschines and Athenian Politics* (Oxford: 1995) and R. Lane Fox, "Aeschines and Athenian Politics," in R. Osborne and S. Hornblower (eds.), *Ritual, Finance Politics. Athenian Democratic Accounts Presented to David Lewis* (Oxford: 1994), pp. 135–155; cf. Schaefer, *Demosthenes²* 1, pp. 215–259. On the private and political rivalry with Demosthenes, see in detail Buckler, "Demosthenes and Aeschines," pp. 114–158.

[91] E. M. Harris, "The Date of Aeschines' Birth," *CP* 83 (1988), pp. 211–214.

[92] Demosthenes 18.258.

[93] Demosthenes 18.261–262, 19.246, 337.

a teacher and his mother had several different occupations, from prostitute to priestess of a secret orgiastic cult.[94] There is no question that Aeschines came from lower social circles than Demosthenes, but he married well. He and Demosthenes may even have been related by marriage,[95] making them political allies for a time.[96]

Aeschines became an assistant to various public officials in the city's administration and eventually a secretary to the Assembly.[97] These were not highly paid or influential positions, and wealthier citizens mocked him. However, he learned much about public records and state administration, which served him well in his political career. His knowledge of state affairs and perhaps also his fine speaking voice, thanks to his acting career,[98] brought him to the attention of either the powerful Aristophon[99] or the general Phocion,[100] who introduced him to Eubulus. His views on peace endeared him to the like-minded Eubulus, and the two men quickly became political allies.

After his debut in the Assembly, Aeschines served on the embassy to the Greek states, visiting Arcadia,[101] as well as on embassies to Philip to discuss peace in 346. Soon he and Demosthenes would bitterly oppose each other over Athenian policy toward Macedonia. Aeschines was also an orator, although not a speechwriter. Only three of his speeches have survived, which may well be all he wrote. They show his rhetorical style was even on a par with that of Demosthenes,[102] and because of his skills as an actor his delivery was probably exceptional.[103]

---

[94] Demosthenes 18.129–130, 257–266, 19.199–200, 249, 281; for Aeschines' family background and early career, see J. K. Davies, *Athenian Propertied Families* (Oxford: 1971), pp. 543–545 and especially Harris, *Aeschines and Athenian Politics*, pp. 17–40.

[95] E. Badian, "The Road to Prominence," in Ian Worthington (ed.), *Demosthenes: Statesman and Orator* (London: 2000), pp. 14–15; note the cautious remarks of Lane Fox, "Aeschines and Athenian Democracy," pp. 138–139.

[96] Demosthenes 19.302–303; cf. 19.16, Aeschines 2.58–62; cf. Cawkwell, "Aeschines and the Peace of Philocrates," pp. 424–425.

[97] Demosthenes 18.261, 19.70, 200, 237, 314.

[98] Demosthenes 18.127, 259, 19.126, 199, 206, 337.

[99] Demosthenes 19.291, 18.162.

[100] Harris, *Aeschines and Athenian Politics*, pp. 37–39.

[101] Demosthenes 19.303–306, Aeschines 2.79.

[102] Blass, *attische Beredsamkeit²* 3.2, pp. 129–236, G. Kennedy, *The Art of Persuasion in Greece* (Princeton: 1963), pp. 236–246, and Usher, *Greek Oratory: Tradition and Originality*, pp. 279–295; cf. J. F. Kindstrand, *The Stylistic Evaluation of Aeschines in Antiquity* (Upsala: 1982).

[103] C. Carey, *Aeschines* (Austin: 2000), p. 10.

THE DEATH THROES OF THE THIRD
SACRED WAR

The sacred war by now had turned into a stalemate between Boeotia and Phocis. Phayllus had died in late 352, "of a wasting disease, after a long illness, suffering great pain as befitted his impious life."[104] His successor Phalaecus (Onomarchus' son) had successfully invaded Boeotia and captured the towns of Coronea, Corsiae, and Orchomenus.[105] In the summer of 347, however, Phalaecus was unexpectedly deprived of his command. The official explanation was stealing from the temple treasuries although Aeschines' reason of "internal fighting" in Phocis was closer to the mark.[106] After all, previous generals were just as guilty of temple robbery but the Phocians had not deprived them of their posts. Phalecus was replaced by three generals, Deinocrates, Callias, and Sophanes, who immediately reinvaded Boeotia. In desperation the Thebans beseeched Philip for assistance, thereby providing him with a legitimate excuse to lead his army into Greece.

The problem for Philip was that if he went to Thebes' assistance he risked further alienating the Athenians, who would expect Philip and Thebes to end the sacred war, thereby affording Thebes the opportunity to regain authority in central Greece and even the Peloponnese. The Athenians would also be concerned lest Philip and the Thebans invade Attica and attack Athens. Yet if Philip refused the Theban plea, he risked their joining with Athens against him. He had no wish to see the Thebans return to power, and indeed he was "pleased to see their discomfiture and disposed to humble the Boeotians' pride after Leuctra."[107] Therefore he responded cautiously by sending his general Parmenion at the head of only a small contingent of troops to Thebes.

Needless to say, the Thebans were unimpressed by Philip's commitment. Still, they managed to defeat a Phocian force at Abae in Boeotia,[108] prompting the Phocians to turn to Athens and Sparta for help. They sweetened their offer with the promise of handing over to them the three key towns that controlled Thermopylae—Alponus, Thronium, and Nicaea. Both states naturally scrambled to send troops. Sparta dispatched 1,000 soldiers under King Archidamus and the Athenians

---

[104] Diodorus 16.38.4.
[105] Diodorus 16.56.1–2.
[106] Aeschines 2.132.
[107] Diodorus 16.58.3.
[108] Diodorus 16.58; cf. 16.33.4, 16.35.3, 16.56.1–2.

Proxenus with 50 ships, manned by men up to the age of 40. If Philip tried to breach Thermopylae, he would find the pass blocked as in 352.

THE GAME CHANGER

Demosthenes' success with his second and third *Olynthiacs*—far more so than the arguably more famous first *Philippic*—showed him that stand-alone speeches on aspects of foreign and fiscal policy were not going to advance his political career. *On Organization* was a defiant justification of his policies, but it was not enough. The threat of Philip finally presented the ambitious Demosthenes with the means to turn his career around, and he seized it. His fixation on Philip, self-serving but understandable, was part of a pattern to elevate himself in public life by any means available. In encouraging the Athenians to adopt his measures against Philip in the *Olynthiacs*, he had resorted to scare tactic rhetoric, embellishment of the truth, and even outright lies in his portrayal of Philip and his aims and activities. None of that would change in the future. The downside was whether Demosthenes' personal ambition would ultimately cost Athens and Greece dearly.

7

An Uneasy Peace

THE ATHENIANS IN 348 were well aware of the acute need to make peace with Philip. Two years would elapse, however, before a peace was negotiated in 346. The Third Sacred War had likewise degenerated into lackluster fighting between the Phocians and only the Boeotians, so in the best interests of Greece it also needed to be resolved. Because of Philip's military strength and influence in Greek affairs, the expectation was that he, not the Amphictyonic Council, would settle the war. The events of the sacred war's final year in 346, and especially the question of Phocis' fate, meshed closely with the negotiations leading to peace between Philip and Athens, so much so that the dividing line between the two separate wars was often blurred.[1]

The principal contemporary sources for the peace negotiations and the end of the Third Sacred War are the two speeches *On the False Embassy*, which Demosthenes and Aeschines gave at Aeschines' trial in 343 (see below), and their speeches in the Crown trial of Demosthenes in 330 (Chapter 13).[2] The narrative writers for this period are sparse

---

[1] Cf. T. T. B. Ryder, "The Diplomatic Skills of Philip II," in Ian Worthington (ed.), *Ventures into Greek History: Essays in Honour of N. G. L. Hammond* (Oxford: 1994), pp. 244–248 and J. Buckler, "Demosthenes and Aeschines," in Ian Worthington (ed.), *Demosthenes: Statesman and Orator* (London: 2000), pp. 119–123.

[2] For example, Aeschines 3.58–78, Demosthenes 18.17–52, 79–94, 160–187, 211–226.

on detail.[3] The information the two orators impart is often distorted, and it has to be treated with caution. In 343, Aeschines was defending himself against Demosthenes' prosecution for misconduct on the second embassy to Philip. In 330 the tables were turned because Demosthenes had to justify his entire political career against Aeschines' attack. In addition to their personal enmity, by 343 Demosthenes was distancing himself from his role in effecting the peace and blaming Aeschines for how it detrimentally affected Athens. In turn, Aeschines was arguing that his policy toward Macedonia, not that of Demosthenes, was in the best interests of Greece.[4] A definitive account of the events of 346 is impossible, although later in the chapter a plausible version of them will be given.

THE TRIAL OF MEIDIAS

Despite the Assembly's *probole* of 348, Meidias continued to bother Demosthenes. Even in the same year, when Demosthenes put forward his name to serve on the Boule for the following year, Meidias challenged his candidature, forcing Demosthenes to rebut his claims.[5] Enough was enough, and in 347/6 Demosthenes formally indicted Meidias for assaulting him at the Dionysia.[6] Whether Demosthenes actually prosecuted him in court is controversial because several

---

[3] Diodorus describes the end of the sacred war but omits the diplomatic negotiations that led to the Peace of Philocrates. Justin is more concerned with events in Macedonia.

[4] On their veracity, see Buckler, "Demosthenes and Aeschines," pp. 121–132 and 148–154; on Demosthenes' ability to switch policy around the Peace of Philocrates and its aftermath, cf. T. T. B. Ryder, "Demosthenes and Philip II," in Ian Worthington (ed.), *Demosthenes: Statesman and Orator* (London: 2000), pp. 58–72. See also the discussion of E. M. Harris, *Aeschines and Athenian Politics* (Oxford: 1995), pp. 52–62.

[5] Demosthenes 21.111.

[6] Plutarch, *Demosthenes* 12.3; cf. Demosthenes 21.13. Date: R. Sealey, "Dionysius of Halicarnassus and Some Demosthenic Dates," *REG* 68 (1955), pp. 96–101, E. M. Harris, "Demosthenes' Speech against Meidias," *HSCP* 92 (1989), pp. 121–123, D. M. MacDowell, *Demosthenes: Against Meidias (Oration* 21), (Oxford: 1990), pp. 10–11. Quarrel between Demosthenes and Meidias: Lehmann, *Demosthenes*, pp. 120–123, MacDowell, *Demosthenes: Against Meidias*, pp. 1–13. The indictment was a *probole*, so G. O. Rowe, "The Charge against Meidias," *Hermes* 122 (1994), pp. 55–63, MacDowell, *Demosthenes: Against Meidias*, pp. 13–16, not a *graphe hubreos*, so Harris, "Demosthenes' Speech against Meidias," p. 130.

ancient writers say that he either accepted a bribe to drop the case or that Meidias paid Demosthenes 3,000 drachmas.[7] The latter amount was substantially less than the standard payment in lieu of the death penalty for a sacrilegious crime, suggesting it was an out-of-court settlement.[8] However, a very lengthy prosecution speech by Demosthenes survives. It is difficult to imagine that he would have spent time writing it if he was not going to deliver it in court, especially when he was preoccupied with the debates in Athens about peace with Philip and the sacred war. Moreover, Meidias' actions had contributed to Demosthenes' failure as *choregos* at the Dionysia, and he was not the sort of man to forgive and forget.[9]

The controversy can be resolved because of Plutarch's revelation that Demosthenes was preparing to prosecute Meidias but, because of his junior standing and Meidias' rich and powerful friends, he "gave in to the men who appealed on his behalf."[10] It may well be that Meidias' friend and ally Eubulus personally called upon Demosthenes. Eubulus' reputation may have suffered because of the Athenians' abortive campaign in Euboea in 348, but it was rising again even in the same year as his successful proposal to send an embassy to the Greek states proved. If Demosthenes was positioning himself to take part in peace negotiations, Eubulus would be influential in the Assembly's selection of the negotiators. Since the strained relations between the two men would not be to Demosthenes' advantage, he may well have bowed to Eubulus' entreaty. Yet a passage in the surviving speech indicated that Eubulus spoke on behalf of Meidias in court.[11] Demosthenes and Eubulus therefore decided on a settlement to appease both of them. The jury would have found Meidias guilty given the Assembly's *probole* against him, but a condemned man could suggest an alternative penalty. Since Demosthenes had demanded the death penalty in his speech,[12] Meidias may well have put forward the alternate penalty of a 3,000-drachma fine,

---

[7] Aeschines 3.52, Plutarch, *Demosthenes* 12.3–6, [Plutarch], *Moralia* 844d.

[8] Plutarch, *Demosthenes* 12.3–6. Jaeger, *Demosthenes*, p. 147: Demosthenes never delivered the speech but accepted a settlement for political reasons; cf. S. Usher, *Greek Oratory: Tradition and Originality*, (Oxford: 1999), p. 226 n.193.

[9] On composition and delivery, see further, MacDowell, *Demosthenes: Against Meidias*, pp. 23–28; cf. MacDowell, *Demosthenes*, p. 246.

[10] Plutarch, *Demosthenes* 12.3–6.

[11] Demosthenes 21.205–207, with MacDowell, *Demosthenes: Against Meidias*, ad loc. (pp. 409–412).

[12] Demosthenes 21.21, 70, 118, 201.

which Demosthenes graciously accepted.[13] Demosthenes therefore had his day in court—and a face-saving victory over Meidias—but did not incur the enmity of Eubulus, who in turn did not lose a political ally.

In his speech against Meidias Demosthenes intended to establish that Meidias had not merely assaulted him but had intended to humiliate him (*hybris*). The word *hybris* has various translations, "outrage," "abuse," "dishonor," and "insult" being the most common. Today, *hybris* is most commonly thought of as being simple pride or arrogance in a person. To the Greeks, however, *hybris* took on a legal meaning when a criminal intended to dishonor the victim, which the Athenians considered especially heinous.[14] Demosthenes therefore outlined the enmity between the two men that began in his youth, followed by an acidic character assassination that cast Meidias as venal, immoral, and undemocratic.[15]

Against Meidias[16]

Demosthenes' first words were strongly condemnatory—"The bullying, judges, and the insolence with which Meidias always treats everyone, I think is well known to all of you and to the other citizens" (1).

---

[13] MacDowell, *Demosthenes: Against Meidias*, pp. 23–28; cf. MacDowell, *Demosthenes*, p. 246, A. Lintott, *Plutarch: Demosthenes and Cicero: Oratory and Political Failure* (Oxford: 2012), ad Plutarch, *Demosthenes* 12.4–6.

[14] See D. M. MacDowell, "Hybris in Athens," *G&R*[2] 23 (1976), pp. 14–31, N. R. E. Fisher, "*Hybris* and Dishonour," *G&R*[2] 23 (1976), pp. 177–193 and 26 (1979), pp. 32–47 and *Hybris: A Study in the Values of Honour and Shame in Ancient Greece* (Warminster: 1992); see also MacDowell, *Demosthenes: Against Meidias*, pp. 18–23. It is sometimes thought that Demosthenes charged Meidias with *hybris*, but that is not so; see above, note 6.

[15] Demosthenes 21.77–174.

[16] On the speech, see Schaefer, *Demosthenes*[2] 2, pp. 97–108, Blass, *attische Beredsamkeit*[2] 3.1, pp. 287–299, Pickard-Cambridge, *Demosthenes*, pp. 219–220, Carlier, *Démosthène*, pp. 131–138, Usher, *Greek Oratory: Tradition and Originality*, pp. 226–230, Lehmann, *Demosthenes*, pp. 120–125, MacDowell, *Demosthenes*, pp. 245–256. See also H. Erbse, "Über die Midiana des Demosthenes," *Hermes* 84 (1956), pp. 135–152, Harris, "Demosthenes' Speech against Meidias," pp. 117–136, P. Wilson, "Demosthenes 21 (*Against Meidias*): Democratic Abuse," *PCPS* 37 (1991), pp. 164–195, Rowe, "The Charge against Meidias," pp. 55–63, and J. Ober, "Power and Oratory in Democratic Athens: Demosthenes 21, *Against Meidias*," in J. Ober (ed.), *The Athenian Revolution: Essays on Ancient Greek Democracy and Political Theory* (Princeton: 1996), pp. 86–106. Translation with notes: E. M. Harris, *Demosthenes, Speeches 20–22* (Austin: 2008), pp. 75–166; text and commentary: W. W. Goodwin, *Demosthenes, Against Meidias* (Cambridge 1906; repr. New York 1979); text, translation, and commentary: MacDowell, *Demosthenes: Against Meidias*.

"Insolence" here is *hybris*, instances of which pepper the speech, so from the outset the jury was left in no doubt about the sort of despicable man Meidias was. Demosthenes next reminded the jurors that Meidias had attacked him at the Dionysia in 348 in front of witnesses, and by issuing a *probole* against him the "entire Assembly acted honorably and did what was right" (1–12). In a fast-paced narrative, he went on to describe Meidias' attempt to wreck his *choregia* (13–18), for which he "committed outrage against my person and was primarily responsible from preventing the winning tribe from gaining the prize!" (18).

Demosthenes next turned to a discussion of the *probole*, expecting his opponent to critique his use of it (25–41). Bad enough, he argued, that Meidias' crime intended to humiliate him (42–50), but it was made even worse because it took place at a festival in honor of a god (51–61). Moreover, Demosthenes was not a mere private individual but was performing a liturgy on the city's behalf. It was a tribute to his personal self-control that he did not defend himself with force against Meidias' outrage (62–76). Instead, he relied on the laws for justice (76):

> I have acted so cautiously to prevent any irreparable damage from being done that I did not even strike back; from whom should I receive revenge for the wrongs that I have suffered? From you and the laws, I think. This case indeed should serve as an example that one should not strike back in the heat of anger at all men who commit outage and are abusive, but bring them before you because you are the men who maintain and preserve the protections for victims provided by the laws.

Demosthenes had to prove that Meidias intended his attack to humiliate him (*hybris*). To this end, a long section of the speech detailed his personal history with Meidias that went back to when Demosthenes sued his guardians in 364.[17] Meidias and his brother Thrasylochus forced their way into Demosthenes' house when his mother and sister were home and Demosthenes indicted him (77–82).[18] When Meidias did not appear before the arbitrator, a man named Straton—"a poor man, inexperienced, but otherwise not a scoundrel and actually quite honest" (83)—, awarded Demosthenes 1,000 drachmas in damages (83–92). Meidias never paid but successfully brought an accusation of bias against Straton, who lost his citizenship (83–101). Demosthenes

---

[17] On the contacts and clashes between Demosthenes and Meidias, see MacDowell, *Demosthenes: Against Meidias*, pp. 1–13.

[18] See the quotation in Chapter 2 p. 21.

led Straton before the jury at this point. Although he could not testify because he was no longer a citizen,[19] Demosthenes simply stood him before the jury. In a brilliant passage full of pathos, he praised the man's decency and lamented his pitiable situation, contrasting him in a series of rhetorical questions with Meidias, who subverted the law and deserved no pity (95–99):

> This man, men of Athens, is perhaps poor, but he is certainly not a bad person. Yet although he was a citizen, had served on all the campaigns when he was eligible, and had never done anything terrible, this man stands now in silence, deprived not only of other common privileges but even of the right to speak or express his grief. He is not even allowed to tell you whether what happened to him was just or unjust. This is what he suffered at the hands of Meidias and Meidias' wealth and arrogance because of his poverty and isolation, one man in a crowd. If he had broken the law and accepted the fifty drachmas from Meidias, then reported the judgment entered against him as one decided in his favor, he would have kept his rights and shared without any disadvantages equal privileges as the rest of you. But, because he paid more attention to justice than to Meidias and feared the laws more than this man's threats, he has fallen into such a deep and serious misfortune thanks to this man. If this man is so brutal and insensitive and inflicts such an enormous punishment for injustices that he only claims to have suffered (in fact, he has suffered no wrong), will you acquit him after catching him committing abuse against a citizen? Will you not convict him when he shows no concern for the festival, the sacred rites, the law, or anything else? Won't you make an example out of him?

Demosthenes next rebutted Meidias' accusation that he persuaded an impressionable youth named Aristarchus to murder one of his opponents named Nicodemus in 348. Aristarchus was found guilty and exiled. Demosthenes pointed out to the jury that Meidias socialized with Aristarchus after the murder until he went into exile, thereby implicating him in Nicodemus' murder (104, 116–122).[20] Demosthenes also claimed that Meidias had committed *hybris* against

---

[19] [Demosthenes] 59.26–27.

[20] The allegations that Demosthenes used Aristarchus as a pawn to kill Nicodemus and that he had a sexual relationship with him occur in later prosecution speeches against him: Aeschines 1.170–173, 2.148, 166, Dinarchus 1.30, 47; see further, Ian Worthington, *A Historical Commentary on Dinarchus* (Ann Arbor: 1992), pp. 179–180 and MacDowell, *Demosthenes: Against Meidias*, pp. 328–330.

the laws and his tribe, "a tenth part of you" (126). From the time of Cleisthenes in 508, the Athenians had been divided into ten tribes, so Demosthenes neatly accused Meidias of dishonoring one-tenth of the entire population.

A lengthy list of Meidias' public services and liturgies followed, which Demosthenes contrasted to his own (143–174). He belittled all of them, including his military services, describing them as failures undertaken only for self-serving purposes. He took great pains to criticize Meidias' ostentatious lifestyle so as to provoke the poorer jurymen's hostility (158–174). For example (158–159):

> What distinction, then, has this man achieved, what are his liturgies or his grand expenditures? I do not see anything one could consider aside from these: he has built a house at Eleusis, which is so large that it casts a shadow over all his neighbors; he drives his wife to the Mysteries and anywhere she wishes in a carriage drawn by white horses from Sicyon;[21] he swaggers around the marketplace, taking three or four attendants with him and calling out the names of chalices, drinking horns, and fine plates so that bystanders hear him. I do not know what benefit most of you derive from all these items that Meidias purchased for his personal luxury and extravagance. Yet I do see the abusive treatment that these items encourage him to dole out on many of us ordinary people.[22] You should not show any respect or admiration for things like this nor consider it a mark of his desire for honor if someone builds conspicuously or acquires many maidservants or beautiful furnishings, but only if a man shows his distinction and pursuit of honor in those things in which all of you have a share. You will not find any of these traits in this man.

In a notable section, Demosthenes contrasted Meidias to the fifth-century turncoat Alcibiades (143–150). Alcibiades performed more illustrious deeds than Meidias but nevertheless was exiled (143):

> Think about the number and extent of his services to the city, then how your ancestors treated him when he decided to become offensive and insolent. Of course, I have not mentioned this story because I want to compare Meidias to Alcibiades—I am not that foolish or deranged—but so that you know, men of Athens, and understand that there is not, nor will there be anything, not family, not wealth, not power, that you, the majority, ought to tolerate if insolence is added to it.

[21] Sicyon was famous for the pedigree of its horses.
[22] Demosthenes was pandering to the jury here, as he had just detailed all his liturgies, which proved that he was rich and far from ordinary!

Demosthenes ended his speech with a call to the jury to find Meidias guilty, given that other men who suffered *probole* were punished severely (175–183). He concluded by arguing, among other things, that Meidias treated the people with contempt and exhorted the jury not to be beguiled by his rich and powerful friends but to vote according to the law (184–227).[23]

On a number of occasions Demosthenes begged the jurors not to be swayed by any rich men that supported Meidias and to accept the *probole* of the popular Assembly against him (205–218). He also alluded to wealthy men flouting the law, extorting the people, and being inactive when danger threatened (123–127, 202–204). It has been argued that the speech was deliberately ideological, with Demosthenes, like today's "class warfare" of the 1 percent versus the 99 percent in the United States, championing the ordinary citizens against the venal wealthy.[24] Meidias and his rich friends were, therefore, enemies of the people and so of the democracy. That is reading too much into the speech. Demosthenes wanted to secure Meidias' conviction by any means he could, whether legal, rhetorical, or ideological, because at the end of the day he wanted to win as he and Meidias "really hated each other."[25]

Demosthenes had little time to bask in the glory of his victory over Meidias, as his attention was abruptly switched to Philip's activities in Greece and possibly Thrace. It was time to leave the law courts for the Assembly again.

PHILIP'S WEAK LINK

A wrinkle in Philip's plan to arrange a settlement of central Greece developed in 346 when he sent a token force of men under Parmenion to assist the Thebans, who inflicted a minor defeat over Phocian troops at Abae. The Athenians and Spartans had responded to a Phocian appeal for help, for which they were given control of Thermopylae.

---

[23] On Meidias' supporters, see the comments of MacDowell, *Demosthenes: Against Meidias*, p. 12; cf. MacDowell, *Demosthenes*, pp. 253–254.

[24] See, for example, Wilson, "Demosthenes 21 (*Against Meidias*): Democratic Abuse," pp. 164–195 and Ober, "Power and Oratory in Democratic Athens: Demosthenes 21, *Against Meidias*," pp. 86–106; contra MacDowell, *Demosthenes: Against Meidias*, pp. 11–13 and MacDowell, *Demosthenes*, pp. 252, 253–256.

[25] MacDowell, *Demosthenes: Against Meidias*, p. 13.

Alarmed that Philip had actively sided with Thebes, albeit with fewer troops than the Thebans had expected, Demosthenes proposed an expedition to Thrace and the Hellespont in case Philip next tried to negate Athenian influence there. The Athenians mobilized Chares and a contingent of troops and established several garrisons along the coastline of the Propontis and north Aegean. The Athenians, perhaps at Demosthenes' behest, also sent troops to help save Halus in Thessaly (on the Gulf of Pagasae), which was under siege from the people of Pharsalus (about thirty miles to its northwest) with Philip's support. Halus was strategically located on the main route south from Larissa, Pherae, and Pagasae. The Athenians knew that Philip could not allow them to erode his authority in Thessaly so their rationale was to distract him from central Greek affairs.

Even more aggressive on the Athenians' part was the dispatch of a second embassy to the Greek states at the instigation of Eubulus and Aeschines.[26] The second embassy was subtly different from the failed first one of 348 because it called on the Greeks to decide whether there should be peace with Philip or war against him under Athenian leadership. Also, the Athenians decided to petition Philip for the release of the Athenian prisoners taken at Olynthus in 348, and sent Aristodemus, an actor and friend of the king, to Pella.[27]

The Athenian request was problematic for Philip and very much the weak link in his chain. He correctly anticipated that the Athenian prisoners would be a valuable bargaining chip in peace negotiations and did not intend to release them until he had concluded peace on terms that suited him. By holding onto them, however, he gave Demosthenes the grounds to accuse him of untrustworthiness and pursuing a personal agenda.

Aristodemus returned to Athens but did not immediately present his report to the Boule, as he was required to do, excusing himself on the grounds of attending to private business. Finally he was ordered to give his report.[28] Surprisingly, he said nothing about the prisoners, even though his mission to Pella was specifically about them, but reiterated Philip's hope for a peace and alliance (*symmachia*) with Athens. The

[26] Demosthenes 19.15, 18.23–24, Aeschines 2.89, 3.64–70, with G. L. Cawkwell, "Aeschines and the Peace of Philocrates," *REG* 73 (1960), pp. 416–438.

[27] Demosthenes 19.15 ff. He probably went with Neoptolemus, another actor: Demosthenes 19.12, 315. Since Demosthenes later cautioned the Athenians against him (5.6, 7), he may have taken a bribe from Philip against Athenian interests.

[28] Aeschines 2.16–17.

mood of the Assembly was euphoric, and Demosthenes nominated him for a crown.[29] Philocrates successfully recommended that the Athenians send an embassy of ten men (a large number) to the king to discuss "peace and the common interests of Athens and Philip," and that he should send envoys to Athens to conclude peace.[30] Thus the first of what would be four Athenian embassies to Philip was constituted— they should not be confused with the two embassies to the Greek states, the first in 348 and the second which was still on its business.

The members of the first embassy to Philip were Aeschines, Aristodemus,[31] Cimon, Ctesiphon, Dercylus, Iatrocles (a prisoner from Olynthus, also released by Philip to convey his wish for peace), Nausicles, Philocrates, Phrynon, and Demosthenes, whom Philocrates nominated.[32] A man named Aglaocreon, whom Demosthenes never mentioned, from the island of Tenedos accompanied them as the representative of the Athenians' allies in their confederacy.[33] Surprisingly, Eubulus was not selected, perhaps because of Aeschines' inclusion and their close political ties. Demosthenes, now not quite forty, was the youngest man (Aeschines the second youngest), but despite his junior status his selection shows his political prominence. Thus, not knowing what to expect, he prepared to meet his nemesis for the first time.

THE FIRST EMBASSY TO PHILIP

The ambassadors left Athens in probably February of 346. At Larissa in Thessaly, Philip's herald met them to escort them formally to Pella.[34] They appeared as a group before the king and each one recited a prepared speech about the peace and alliance. They also discussed matters that lay outside the peace negotiations including Athenian interests in Thrace, relations with Cersebleptes, the sacred war, and the siege of Halus. The ambassadors may well have intended to include

---

[29] Aeschines 2.15–17.

[30] Aeschines 2.18–20.

[31] Demosthenes successfully moved a resolution in the Boule to have him excused from his professional acting engagements in various towns so he could serve on the embassy: Aeschines 2.17–19, 3.63.

[32] Aeschines 2.18.

[33] Aeschines 2.20, 97, 126.

[34] Demosthenes 19.163.

Cersebleptes, Phocis, and Halus as their allies in the peace, but Philip could not permit that. Aeschines later stated that he tried to persuade Philip to return Amphipolis to Athens, but the king would not have entertained that idea.[35]

As in the Athenian Assembly, the eldest man spoke first, and then the others in descending age. As the youngest Demosthenes spoke last, after Aeschines, by which point he probably had little to add to the previous speeches.[36] However, from the moment he talked he apparently ran into trouble:[37]

> With all listening so intently, this creature offered an obscene prologue in a voice dead with fright, and after a brief narration of earlier events, suddenly fell silent and was at a loss for words, and finally abandoned his speech. Seeing the state he was in, Philip encouraged him to take heart and supposed that he had suffered a complete catastrophe . . . But Demosthenes . . . was now unable to recover; he tried once more to speak, and the same thing happened. In the ensuing silence the herald asked us to withdraw.

Aeschines reported Demosthenes' lapse in his speech *On the False Embassy* of 343, by which time he and Demosthenes were bitter enemies. His account needs to be treated skeptically. Embellishment of the truth was common in oratory, and Plutarch in his life of Demosthenes stated that Philip "was the most careful to answer his speech."[38] Plutarch, however, may have confused Philip's reaction with the second embassy to him some months later when Demosthenes spoke more eloquently (see below). Demosthenes himself never mentioned this audience with Philip again, despite criticizing Aeschines for his role in the peace negotiations.[39] Aeschines' claim may have its origins in his comment that on the journey to Pella Demosthenes boasted of his superlative speech.[40] As the youngest ambassador, his self-satisfaction was likely to have

---

[35] Aeschines 2.25–33. Good discussion of the first embassy to Philip: Harris, *Aeschines and Athenian Politics*, pp. 57–62.

[36] Carlier, *Démosthène*, p. 150, Sealey, *Demosthenes*, p. 145; contra Harris, *Aeschines and Athenian Politics*, p. 57, that Aeschines spoke earlier: see the comment of D. M. MacDowell, *Demosthenes: On the False Embassy (Oration 19)* (Oxford: 2000), p. 4 n. 10.

[37] Aeschines 2.34–35; cf. 38.

[38] Plutarch, *Demosthenes* 16.2. Schaefer, *Demosthenes²* 2, pp. 197–205, doubts the account completely, Lehmann, *Demosthenes*, p. 132, suggests it is exaggerated.

[39] MacDowell, *Demosthenes: On the False Embassy*, p. 5 n. 12. On the later speeches, see Chapter 8 (False Embassy) and 13 (Crown).

[40] Aeschines 2.21.

angered the others. Therefore, Demosthenes may have nervously stuttered before the king,[41] which Aeschines seized upon to discredit his opponent.

In his defense speech against Demosthenes in 343, Aeschines also accused Demosthenes of attacking him for his speech when the embassy left the king's presence: "You have irritated Philip to such an extent by what you said that the result of our embassy is not likely to be peace but an interminable war."[42] The exchange cannot be corroborated, but Aeschines may have fabricated it to alert the jury to Demosthenes' eagerness for peace in 346.[43]

Philip met the embassy later the same day with his formal response. Exactly what he said is unknown, but evidently he repeated his desire for peace and alliance and encouraged the Athenians to agree to a bilateral treaty between himself and his allies and the Athenians and their allies in the confederacy.[44] To this he added the significant stipulation that each party was to recognize only the other's current allies. The qualification neatly excluded Phocis, Cersebleptes, and Halus, who were Athenian allies but not members of their confederacy from the peace treaty. Since Philip was preparing to campaign against Cersebleptes, to the alarm of the Athenians, he indicated his willingness to avoid the Chersonese while they were debating peace.[45] Finally, Philip insisted that the Athenians withdraw from Halus immediately and join him in a campaign to curtail piracy in the Aegean. As a show of good faith, he promised to return Oropus to Athens and help restore Athenian interests in Euboea. Demosthenes was said to have acted badly at a state banquet that evening.[46] Aeschines, who related the anecdote, gave no details, but Demosthenes may have attempted to discuss the status of those excluded from the peace.[47]

The Athenian embassy stayed at Pella for at least a week before leaving on Anthesterion 20 (about March 18). On the same day Philip left for Thrace.[48] The ambassadors took with them a goodwill letter

---

[41] He "started to stammer" ("s'est mis à bafouiller"): Carlier, *Démosthène*, p. 151.

[42] Aeschines 2.36–37.

[43] Cf. Pickard-Cambridge, *Demosthenes*, pp. 244–245.

[44] Ryder, "Demosthenes and Philip II," pp. 62–63.

[45] Aeschines 2.82.

[46] Aeschines 2.38, 39.

[47] The implication of Aeschines 2.40–43 is that Demosthenes on the way home said he agreed with Aeschines' views on Amphipolis. Demosthenes' attendance at this event led to his criticism of Philip's court as rough and lewd and of Macedonians as heavy drinkers, which is quoted in Chapter 2 p. 52.

[48] Aeschines 2.82.

from the king, which they delivered to the Boule. Demosthenes requested that each of the envoys receive a customary olive crown and be guests at a state banquet in the Prytaneum (city hall) the next day.[49] Shortly after, a Macedonian embassy led by Philip's generals Antipater, Parmenion, and Eurylochus arrived to reconfirm his terms and receive the Athenians' oaths to the peace.[50] The Athenians would then send an embassy to Philip to receive his oath and the peace would come into effect. At an Assembly held on Elaphebolion 8 (about April 3), the Athenian ambassadors spoke favorably of Philip, Aeschines even calling him "the purest Greek, the most skillful speaker, Athens' greatest friend" and criticizing men for "labeling him a barbarian."[51] When it was Demosthenes' turn to talk, however, he accused Aeschines of taking a bribe from Philip:[52]

> But when I addressed the Assembly, I said that [Aeschines] had left me none of the points he wished to make to Philip, for he would sooner lend a man his blood than his words. Rather, having accepted Philip's money, he could not, I take it, offer any protest, because Philip gave him the money precisely to retain Amphipolis.

He advised the people to debate Philip's terms carefully and pressed for a two-day Assembly meeting.[53] The first day would be given over to discussion and the second day, with Philip's envoys present, a vote.[54] The allied *synedrion* (of the Athenian confederacy) urged the people not to hold a debate until the second embassy to the Greek states (over a possible war with Philip) returned. However, the *synedrion* agreed to back any Athenian decisions.[55] Since the week-long festival of the Dionysia was due to begin on Elaphebolion 9, during which period assemblies and the courts were suspended, the Athenians set a date of Elaphebolion 18 and 19 (April 15 and 16) for the special Assembly.[56]

---

[49] Aeschines 2.45–46, Demosthenes 19.40–41, 3.16, [Demosthenes] 7.33.

[50] Demosthenes 18.28, 19.235, Aeschines 2.111, 3.76; cf. Dinarchus 1.28.

[51] Demosthenes 19.308.

[52] Demosthenes 19.254.

[53] Further on Demosthenes' activities in connection with the eventual peace with Philip: Sealey, *Demosthenes*, pp. 143–157.

[54] Aeschines 2.61–62, 65, 109. Aeschines 2.65 says the second day was simply for the vote, but he is distorting the truth, as debate did take place: see below.

[55] Aeschines 2.60.

[56] Aeschines 3.67 says that Demosthenes at first proposed Elaphebolion 8 for the Assembly meeting. However, the ceremony of the Proagon, a prelude to the Dionysia, was held on that day, and so the date had to be changed.

Demosthenes also made a motion that in the interim the Macedonian ambassadors be granted *proedria* (a front seat in the theatre) at the festival's theatrical performances. When they eventually left Athens he personally escorted them as far as Thebes.[57] Aeschines later accused him of sycophancy, but Demosthenes was simply being diplomatic.[58]

PEACE DELIBERATIONS

On Elaphebolion 18 the Assembly conducted some minor business before turning to the issue of Philip's terms.[59] Philocrates proposed that the people should agree to all of them, thereby including only the Athenian allies in the confederacy.[60] Philocrates was opposed by speakers who were concerned about the well-being of the Phocians and about retaining Cersebleptes' goodwill in Thrace. Philip had insisted that only the Greek city of Cardia (on the isthmus linking the Chersonese to the mainland) should be his ally, and its people concurred.[61] There was no guarantee, however, that he would abide by his assurance. Coupled to these concerns were the problems they faced elsewhere, as a surviving fragment allegedly from Philocrates' speech illustrated:[62]

> Bear in mind then that this is not the time to engage in contentious rivalry, that the affairs of the state are not in a good situation, that many grave dangers surround us. For we know that the Boeotians and the

---

[57] Demosthenes 19.234–235, 18.28.

[58] Demosthenes 19.234–235, 18.28, Aeschines 2.55, 110–111, 3.76. Normal diplomacy: F. E. Adcock and D. J. Mosley, *Diplomacy in Ancient Greece* (London: 1975), p. 164.

[59] On the lead-up to the Assembly and the meeting, see Carlier, *Démosthène*, pp. 141–156, Harris, *Aeschines and Athenian Politics*, pp. 63–77, Ryder, "Demosthenes and Philip II," pp. 62–66, Buckler, "Demosthenes and Aeschines," pp. 120–123, and especially A. Efstathiou, "The 'Peace of Philocrates': The Assemblies of 18th and 19th Elaphebolion," *Historia* 53 (2004), pp. 385–407; cf. Cawkwell, "Aeschines and the Peace of Philocrates," pp. 433–438, Sealey, *Demosthenes*, pp. 145–148.

[60] Demosthenes 19.159.

[61] [Demosthenes] 12.11, Demosthenes 19.74, with G. L. Cawkwell, "Demosthenes' Policy after the Peace of Philocrates II," *CQ²* 13 (1963), p. 200.

[62] Theopompus, *FGrH* 115 F 164: translation: N. G. L. Hammond, *Philip of Macedon* (London: 1994), p. 99. Philocrates' speech is doubted by P. E. Harding, *Didymos, On Demosthenes* (Oxford: 2006), p. 255.

Megarians are at enmity with us, the Peloponnesians are courting some of the Thebans and others the Spartans, the Chians and the Rhodians, and their allies are hostile to our state, and they are negotiating with Philip for his friendship.

The allied *synedrion* submitted its own proposal, which called on the Athenians to make a common peace (*koine eirene*) with Philip. A common peace was an agreement of all Greek states, each one individually allied to the others and ready to come to the defense of any member that was attacked. The *synedrion* added a proviso admitting any state into this peace within three months.[63] Philip would have dismissed this plan immediately, given that it permitted Cersebleptes, the Halians, and the Phocians to join the peace, thereby debarring him from acting against them. Aeschines and Demosthenes, allies through marriage as well as by politics in this regard,[64] accepted the allied recommendation.[65] Despite Philocrates' warnings, the Assembly decided that Demosthenes would recommend a common peace to the Macedonian ambassadors the following day.[66] At the end of the first day, then, the people expected to agree to peace with Philip but not alliance.

The second day of the Assembly produced a surprising change. Instead of continuing his support of a common peace, Demosthenes drafted a resolution of peace and alliance with Philip, thereby rejecting the *synedrion*'s motion, which he showed to a man named Amyntor.[67] Demosthenes' change of heart was perhaps because overnight the Macedonian ambassadors Antipater, Parmenion, and Eurylochus made it clear to him that a common peace was out of the question if the Athenians wanted to end their war with Philip. Demosthenes' therefore threw his weight behind Philocrates' proposal, which meant abandoning Cersebleptes, Phocis, and Halus, as well as thwarting any plans Aeschines had formed to keep Greece united against Philip.[68]

[63] Aeschines 3.69–70. Discussion of Common Peace in Greece: T. T. B. Ryder, *Koine Eirene* (Oxford: 1965).
[64] For example, cf. E. Badian, "The Road to Prominence," in Ian Worthington (ed.), *Demosthenes: Statesman and Orator* (London: 2000), pp. 14–15.
[65] Aeschines' role at the debate: Cawkwell, "Aeschines and the Peace of Philocrates," pp. 433–438.
[66] Demosthenes 19.14–15, 16, 144, 311, Aeschines 3.71.
[67] Aeschines 2.64–68; cf. Demosthenes 18.71, 72. Aeschines' veracity cannot be proved.
[68] Cawkwell, "Aeschines and the Peace of Philocrates," pp. 437–438.

When Antipater ascended the speakers' platform at the Assembly, Demosthenes asked him whether Philip would agree to a common peace. He replied no: Philip would only accept Athens and its allies in the confederacy in his peace.[69] Demosthenes accordingly brought out the resolution he had shown to Amyntor and advised the people to adopt Philocrates' original motion of peace and alliance.[70] Eubulus added his support by bluntly warning the people that without peace they would have to divert theoric money to the Military Fund to meet the war's high costs.[71] There was opposition from politicians such as Hegesippus and Aristophon, who, Theopompus tells us, unrealistically argued that the Athenians should not renounce their claim to Amphipolis:[72]

> Bear in mind that the most cowardly thing of all that we could do would be to accept the peace while conceding Amphipolis, we who live in the greatest of the Greek states, have most allies, possess 300 triremes and receive almost 400 talents in revenue; which being so, who would not condemn us for making concessions contrary to our just rights because we are scared of the power of Macedonians?

The Athenians, however, voted for peace and alliance, but in a modification of Philocrates' proposal they insisted that peace should be between Philip and simply (and ambiguously) "the Athenians and their allies," thereby leaving room for others like Cersebleptes and the Phocians to join it.[73]

The Athenians swore their oaths on behalf of themselves and their league allies to the Macedonian envoys. The latter left Athens, but before returning to Pella they went to Thebes, in keeping with Philip's instructions. Their object was to lull the Thebans into thinking Philip was still keen to ally with them and recognize their hegemony of the Boeotian League, although they must also have informed the Thebans of events in Athens.[74] Philip's diplomatic deceit would allow him to negotiate with Athens and Phocis without the Thebans breathing down his neck.

---

[69] Aeschines 3.71–72, Demosthenes 19.174, 278.

[70] Demosthenes 19.14–16, 144, 159, 32, Aeschines 3.71–72.

[71] Demosthenes 19.291.

[72] Theopompus, *FGrH* 115 F 166: translation: Hammond, *Philip of Macedon*, p. 99.

[73] Demosthenes 19.159.

[74] Buckler, "Demosthenes and Aeschines," p. 124.

Since only the king could swear on behalf of Macedonia, the Assembly arranged for a second embassy (comprising the same ten men as the first) to go to Philip for his oath and to arrange the release of the Athenian prisoners from Olynthus.[75] That would not prove to be as straightforward as they predicted.

THE SECOND EMBASSY TO PHILIP

The second embassy did not immediately leave Athens.[76] After a week of delays, Demosthenes persuaded the Boule to command it to leave on Mounychion 3 (about April 29).[77] Then it took twenty-three days to reach Pella, by which stage Philip had been campaigning in Thrace for several weeks because on Elaphebolion 23 (April 20) he defeated Cersebleptes at his stronghold at Heraion Oros ("Holy Mountain").[78] Philip designated Cersebleptes his vassal, and took more of his sons as hostages to ensure their father's good behavior—Aeschines reported that he personally saw them at Pella.[79] Philip spent almost another two months subjugating independent coastal Thracian forts, which the Athenians would have known about and which Demosthenes later discussed in detail to denigrate Philip.[80] Finally, on Thargelion 23 (about June 18), Philip returned to Pella.

Demosthenes pestered his colleagues to follow Philip into Thrace before he took more towns, which would become his allies when he swore his oath to the peace, but they refused.[81] Demosthenes was right to be worried about Philip's actions in Thrace, but the embassy faced the problem of actually finding Philip, therefore remaining at Pella

---

[75] Demosthenes 19.278, Aeschines 2.103–104.

[76] Demosthenes 19.278, 18.25–31. Information on the second embassy is mostly found in Demosthenes 19.150–178, who was hostile to his colleagues on the embassy. Discussion of this embassy: Harris, *Aeschines and Athenian Politics*, pp. 78–94.

[77] Aeschines 2.91–92, Demosthenes 18.25, 19.154.

[78] The chronology is that of J. R. Ellis, *Philip II and Macedonian Imperialism* (London: 1976), pp. 110–111. Aeschines 2.89–92 says that Philip captured Cersebleptes the day before the Athenians themselves swore the oath, which was about April 16. The timing is roughly right, since modern equivalents of ancient dates are not exact.

[79] Aeschines 2.81.

[80] See, for example, Cawkwell, "Demosthenes' Policy after the Peace of Philocrates II," pp. 200–201.

[81] Demosthenes 19.155–157.

was sensible in the circumstances. Also waiting in Pella for Philip were embassies from Sparta, Thebes, Thessaly, Chalcis, and Phocis—"from virtually the whole of Greece," as Aeschines asserted.[82] This was the time when "Demosthenes began to distrust the efficacy of the peace and Philip's designs for it," and split from Aeschines because he suspected the king would use the peace against Athens.[83] The embassies wanted to know what Philip had in mind for Greece, and so for them.[84] The Thebans, for example, were alarmed at the prospect of Philip actively encouraging Sparta in the Peloponnese, where they had alliances with Messenia, Megalopolis, Argos, and Arcadia.[85]

Twenty-seven days after the Athenian embassy arrived in Pella Philip returned home. He received the other embassies first. The Thebans and the Thessalians petitioned him to end the sacred war and punish the Phocians en masse for their sacrilegious acts. The Phocians, knowing that punishment was unavoidable, nevertheless implored him to protect their state.[86] When the Athenian embassy came before the king Demosthenes apparently spoke first because he did not want to be last again and have nothing new to say. He pressed Philip for his oath and the freeing of the Athenian prisoners, dramatically producing a talent of his own money to help meet the ransom costs.[87] Later, he claimed he challenged Philip to pay the outstanding amount by using money he normally gave to diplomats as gifts. Since the Athenian ambassadors had already taken their money, all sides were embarrassed.[88]

Aeschines then called for Philip to champion the Amphictyonic Council's duty to punish any member that acted in a harmful way to another, reciting the oath of the league for support. He reminded Philip that the Thebans had broken the oath when they destroyed Boeotian cities and beseeched him not to champion Thebes over

---

[82] Aeschines 2.112.

[83] Buckler, "Demosthenes and Aeschines," p. 124.

[84] Aeschines 2.112, 120, 136, Demosthenes 19.139–140, Justin 8.4, with Worthington, *Philip II*, pp. 96–97.

[85] Aeschines 2.136. Cf. C. D. Hamilton, "Philip II and Archidamus," in W. L. Adams and E. N. Borza (eds.), *Philip II, Alexander the Great, and the Macedonian Heritage* (Lanham: 1982), pp. 75–76.

[86] Harris, *Aeschines and Athenian Politics*, pp. 96–97.

[87] Demosthenes 19.166–173, Aeschines 2.97–100, 106–112, 139–142.

[88] Demosthenes 19.166–170, with MacDowell, *Demosthenes: On the False Embassy*, pp. 272–273.

Athens or recognize Thebes' domination of Boeotia.[89] Finally, he advised Philip to punish those who despoiled Apollo's shrine at Delphi. Aeschines therefore did not call for the punishment of all of Phocis but only those Phocians who had seized Delphi, thereby saving the majority of Phocians from execution.[90] Aeschines' suggestion, contrary to how Demosthenes later interpreted it, was a means for Athens not to be party to the annihilation of one of its allies and for Phocis to continue to act with Athens against Thebes.[91]

It is possible that Philip was behind the implication of Aeschines' wording. The king met with all the embassies in private, promising "the one not to open hostilities and binding the ambassadors with an oath not to divulge his response to anyone, and assuring the other that he would join them and bring them assistance."[92] Certainly, after the return of the second embassy to Athens, Aeschines became an advocate of Philip's peace terms in contrast to his adversarial stance at the Assembly of Elaphebolion 18 and 19. His change was not necessarily the result of being bribed, as Demosthenes later charged in 343.[93] Perhaps swayed by the appeals of the Phocians and his need to settle Greece to his satisfaction, Philip needed a supporter in Athens. He may well have identified Aeschines as the most gullible of the Athenian ambassadors and flattered him sufficiently to endorse his intentions.[94]

Demosthenes' call for the release of the prisoners placed Philip in a quandary. He had agreed to peace and was ready to swear his oath to it, and therefore, as Demosthenes must have said, there was no need for him to hold onto the prisoners. However, Philip was reluctant to release them until he and his army were in Greece and he was assured of the settlement he sought. Therefore he promised the Athenians he would liberate the prisoners before the festival of the Panathenaea (in honor of Athens' patron deity Athena), which began in two months' time. Demosthenes exploited Philip's decision

---

[89] Aeschines 2.101–117, 113–119.

[90] Demosthenes 19.31–50; cf. 55, 310; see also J. Buckler, *Aegean Greece in the Fourth Century BC* (Leiden: 2003), pp. 446–447.

[91] G. L. Cawkwell, "Aeschines and the Ruin of Phocis in 346," *REG* 75 (1962), pp. 453–459; cf. Buckler, *Aegean Greece*, pp. 446–447 and "Demosthenes and Aeschines," p. 126—"Aeschines had a far clearer, more realistic, and intelligent view of the situation than had Demosthenes."

[92] Justin 8.4.11.

[93] Demosthenes 19.167–169.

[94] Cf. Ryder, "Demosthenes and Philip II," pp. 67–68.

as another example of his untrustworthy nature, and he had reasonable grounds to do so.

Interestingly, Aeschines accused Demosthenes of being pro-Theban at this time.[95] In 339 Demosthenes persuaded the Athenians to ally with Thebes against Philip, the culmination of a policy that Philip had worked to prevent for the latter half of the 340s.[96] Plausibly, the origins of Demosthenes' policy may be traced to 346. Philip might have told the Athenian envoys that he would protect Athens and curtail the influence of Thebes, but his track record affirmed that he did not live up to his word. Demosthenes was concerned that once Philip led an army through Thermopylae against Phocis he could march wherever he wanted. If he were to march against the Athenians, Demosthenes knew they would need allies, and the Thebans could field a substantial army. It was abundantly clear that Eubulus' passive policy served only to weaken the city, and therefore Demosthenes took care at Pella not to antagonize the Thebans. In the years after the peace he slowly worked to effect an alliance with them that would have the capability of resisting Macedonia.

Philip swore to the peace at Pella, although his allies did not— many of them, after all, would not have been at the Macedonian capital.[97] After further delays while Philip assembled an army to fight the Phocians,[98] the Athenian ambassadors left Pella with him. Demosthenes was apparently so disgusted with his fellow ambassadors' conduct that he rented a ship to sail home and denounce them to the people before they returned. They prevented him. They also refused to let him send a letter with his own version of events in advance of their return. Clearly, he had not endeared himself to his colleagues, though whether they would not eat with him or even stay at the same hostel, as Aeschines claimed, is unknown.[99] At Pherae (only two or three days' march from Thermopylae), Philip's allies finally swore

---

[95] Aeschines 2.106.

[96] Contra Cawkwell, "Demosthenes' Policy after the Peace of Philocrates II," pp. 206–209.

[97] Demosthenes 18.32. In his third *Philippic* (of 341), Demosthenes lied that Philip swore his oath before moving against Doriscus and Serrhium on the north coast of the Aegean, and Myrtenum, Ergiske, and Ganos on the coast of the Propontis (9.15).

[98] Demosthenes accused his colleagues of taking bribes to delay departure: 19.167, 18.31–32.

[99] Aeschines 2.97.

their oaths—in an inn according to Demosthenes.[100] There the ambassadors parted ways with the king, who did not immediately march against Phocis but ended the siege of Halus.[101]

THE PEACE OF PHILOCRATES

The second embassy arrived in Athens on Skirophorion 13 (about July 8) and two days later (Skirophorion 15) reported to the Boule. Demosthenes immediately denounced his colleagues for loitering on their way to Pella and waiting there until Philip returned from Thrace, and accused them of taking bribes from Philip.[102] He also urged the people not to abandon Thermopylae or Phocis, naively believing that Athens would be safe.[103] The Boule must have sided with him because it did not pass the customary vote of thanks and host a dinner for the ambassadors in the Prytaneum.[104]

An Assembly was held on Skirophorion 16 (about July 11), at which representatives from Phocis begged protection.[105] Aeschines, together with Philocrates, declared that in two or three days the people would learn, among other things, that Philip would settle the sacred war, besiege Thebes, restore Thespiae and Plataea, and give them back Oropus.[106] The impression he gave the people was that Philip was their friend and would be a curse to the Thebans. Then Demosthenes spoke. He cautioned the people—correctly as events bore out—that Philip was untrustworthy and that they should treat anything Aeschines said skeptically. He again entreated them not to abandon Phocis and called for a fleet to be deployed to the north coast of Euboea to prevent Philip taking control of Thermopylae. At all costs Philip had to be blocked from entering Greece. His pleas fell on deaf ears. Aeschines and Philocrates apparently stood either side of him and heckled him, and

---

[100] Demosthenes 19.158. Sealey, *Demosthenes*, p. 148, suggests this was reasonable because "the Thessalians were the most formidable of his allies." See also D. J. Mosley, "Oaths at Pherae, 346 B.C.," *Philologus* 116 (1972), pp. 145–148.

[101] When Philip later ended the siege, he returned Halus to Pharsalus. In a grim show of revenge Pharsalus deported the population of Halus: Demosthenes 19.36–39.

[102] Demosthenes 19.167–169.

[103] Demosthenes 19.18.

[104] Demosthenes 19.31–32.

[105] Demosthenes 19.59.

[106] Demosthenes 19.18–22, 34–35, 58, with Carlier, *Démosthène*, pp. 163–165.

when Philocrates remarked "no wonder that Demosthenes and I cannot agree, for he drinks water and I drink wine" the people convulsed with laughter.[107]

Thus the Peace of Philocrates ended the war between Athens and Philip over Amphipolis. The Athenians were discontented that the terms included only their allies in their confederacy and that Amphipolis was lost to them for good, but they still naively supposed Philip would crush Thebes and the state of Phocis would escape unscathed. When a letter from Philip was read out at an Assembly, in which he expressed his friendship, Philocrates successfully moved a motion to extend the peace to Philip's descendants and to liberate Delphi if Phocians—not *the* Phocians (in other words, not the entire Phocian state)—did not surrender it.[108] The same Assembly decided to send a third embassy to Philip with news of its latest resolution.

Soon after the conclusion of the peace the Athenian orator Isocrates wrote his *To Philip*. He encouraged the king to reconcile Argos (the traditional home of the Argeads, Philip's dynasty), Sparta, Thebes, and Athens and lead a panhellenic (all-Greek) invasion of Persia, in the process liberating the Greek cities in Asia Minor from Persian rule.[109] His treatise expanded his call for a voluntary union of the Greek states to invade Asia which he had expressed in his *Panegyricus* of 380.[110] Isocrates' vision of this panhellenic venture was completely unrealistic, not least because of Philip's actions in Greece. The Thebans, incensed at Philip's brusque treatment of their appeals to him, decided to march to Thermopylae to confront him. The Athenians, devastated that he took no action against Thebes and did not protect Phocis, reacted adversely against those associated with the peace.[111]

---

[107] Demosthenes 19.23–24, 44–46; cf. 6.29–30.

[108] Demosthenes 19.48, Aeschines 2.119–123.

[109] On the *To Philip*, see Jaeger, *Demosthenes* pp. 152–155, Usher, *Greek Oratory, Tradition and Originality*, pp. 305–306; cf. S. Perlman, "Isocrates 'Philippus'—A Reinterpretation," *Historia* 6 (1957), pp. 306–317. Translation with notes: T. Papillon, *Isocrates II* (Austin: 2004), pp. 74–108. On panhellenism, see, for example J. M. Hall, *Hellenicity: Between Ethnicity and Culture* (Chicago: 2002), pp. 205–220.

[110] Isocrates 4.16–17, 99, 173, and see Usher, *Greek Oratory: Tradition and Originality*, pp. 298–301.

[111] Cf. Sealey, *Demosthenes*, pp. 156–157.

THE FINAL EMBASSIES TO PHILIP AND THE
END OF THE THIRD SACRED WAR

The third embassy was to meet Philip at the meeting of the Amphicty-onic Council that would officially call an end to the sacred war.[112] Dem-osthenes entered a sworn excuse not to serve on it.[113] Aeschines, possibly suspecting Demosthenes might attempt to persuade the people to prop up Phocis, remained behind to thwart his opponent, using illness as an excuse.[114] The ambassadors on the third embassy set out on Skiropho-rion 17 (about July 12). They never reached Philip because of events at Thermopylae.

As Philip marched into Greece the Phocian government deposed the three Phocian commanders at Thermopylae, Deinocrates, Callias, and Sophanes, and reinstated Phalaecus.[115] He immediately dismissed the Athenian and Spartan troops that had been sent to the pass earlier and surrendered Thermopylae to Philip. Phaelaecus and his army of 8,000 mercenaries departed unharmed,[116] and the state of Phocis for-mally surrendered to Philip.[117] The Phocian action was so striking that Philip may have had a hand in it. Clearly, the Phocians had to suffer some punishment for their crimes and the Athenians were in no posi-tion to go to their rescue.[118] Since the Athenian and Spartan troops at Thermopylae were able to block Philip's passage into Greece, the sce-nario emerges for an agreement between Philip and the Phocians, per-haps decided with the Phocian embassy in Pella, whereby they would restore Phalaecus and he would hand over Thermopylae to Philip. Support for this may be evidenced from Justin's comment that as "vic-tims of necessity [the Phocians] struck a bargain for their lives and ca-pitulated."[119] Thus Philip came into possession of Thermopylae without

---

[112] Demosthenes 19.47–49, 121.

[113] Demosthenes 19.122.

[114] Demosthenes 19.121–124, 129–130, Aeschines 2.94–95, 140.

[115] Diodorus 16.59.2; cf. Aeschines 2.135.

[116] Demosthenes 19.53–66, Diodorus 16.59.3, Justin 8.5.1–3. They first went to the Peloponnese, then to Italy, and eventually to Crete, where Phalaecus was killed in fighting: Diodorus 16.61.3–63.

[117] Demosthenes 19.61, Aeschines 2.130, Justin 8.6.1.

[118] Cf. Cawkwell, "Aeschines and the Peace of Philocrates," pp. 454–455, Harris, *Aeschines and Athenian Politics*, pp. 96–97.

[119] Justin 8.5.3.

a fight, "a disaster of the first magnitude for Greek freedom,"[120] and ended the sacred war.[121]

The Athenians were completely ignorant of these events otherwise, at the Assembly of Skirophorion 16, Demosthenes would not have presumed they could still defend Thermopylae. When news of Philip's actions broke in the city some citizens feared he might take action against the people for trying to resist him at Thermopylae.[122] Instead, he asked for troops to join him against the Phocians at Delphi.[123] Taken by surprise, the Athenians were "still up in the air and the future unclear, all kinds of views were being expressed by people gathering in the Agora."[124] Then all of a sudden, because of the Thebans' outrage at Philip's peace with Athens, which marginalized them, he "found himself caught between the Thessalian cavalry and the infantry of Thebes, and was therefore led to make concessions."[125] Demosthenes took advantage of this unexpected situation to argue that Philip intended to capture the Athenian troops—after all, he had not yet released the prisoners from Olynthus—and the alarmed people refused Philip's request.[126]

The third embassy heard of the dramatic events at Thermopylae when it reached Chalcis in Euboea on Skirophorion 23 (about July 18). The ambassadors were concerned about their safety and one of them, Dercylus, returned to Athens for instructions.[127] At an Assembly held on Skirophorion 27 (about July 23), a politician named Callisthenes carried an emergency decree evacuating the country population to the city, repairing forts on the Attic borders, strengthening the Piraeus defenses, and holding the rural festival of Heracles in Athens itself.[128] The third embassy most likely returned to the city at this time.

Philip may well have been aggrieved at the Athenians' actions, but he maintained diplomatic courtesy, sending them a letter to express

---

[120] G. L. Cawkwell, "Demosthenes' Policy after the Peace of Philocrates I," *CQ²* 13 (1963), p. 120.

[121] Diodorus 16.59.2; cf. Aeschines 2.132–135, Demosthenes 19.322.

[122] Demosthenes 5.14–15, 25–26; cf. Ryder, "Demosthenes and Philip II," pp. 56–69.

[123] Demosthenes 19.36, Aeschines 2.137.

[124] Demosthenes 19.122.

[125] Demosthenes 6.14.

[126] Demosthenes 19.121–124, Aeschines 2.94–95, 137–138.

[127] Demosthenes 19.58–60, 125, Aeschines 2.95.

[128] Demosthenes 19.86, 125, 18.37, Aeschines 2.139, 3.80.

his surprise.[129] He also released their prisoners from Olynthus in time for the Panathenaea (mid-August), as he had earlier promised. The relieved Athenians voted to send a fourth embassy to him,[130] on which Aeschines served.[131] The embassy was to attend a special meeting of the Amphictyonic Council at Thermopylae (on Philip's orders) to decide the Phocian punishment.[132] Philip treated the ambassadors hospitably, inviting them to celebrate the end of the sacred war with him, for which Demosthenes criticized them on their return.[133]

THE PHOCIAN PUNISHMENT

Two hundred envoys from all over Greece attended the Amphictyonic Council meeting.[134] The large number had less to do with the matter of the Phocians' punishment and more with finding out what Philip was going to do—as well as curiosity about what he actually looked like. Philip's activities so far had been largely confined to northern Greece and Thessaly. All Greeks knew of him by now, but few would have seen him in person. His attendance at this council meeting was really his first public meeting in Greece so the chance to put face to name finally for many Greeks was not to be missed.

Thessaly and Thebes dominated the meeting.[135] Some states insisted on the maximum legal penalty, which was executing all of the Phocian men by throwing them from the top of the towering Phaedriades cliffs. Philip, however, persuaded the council to be more lenient.[136] He may

---

[129] Cf. Demosthenes 18.39.

[130] It is possible that the third embassy did not return to Athens but was told to go from Chalcis to the Amphictyonic Council meeting: Aeschines 2.143, with Sealey, *Demosthenes*, p. 150. However, since Aeschines served on it, it is difficult to accept that he would rush from Athens to catch up to it before it met Philip.

[131] Demosthenes 19.51, 126–127, 172, Aeschines 2.95–96, 139.

[132] Aeschines 2.139.

[133] Demosthenes 19.128–130.

[134] Aeschines 2.162, with Worthington, *Philip II*, pp. 101–102.

[135] Diodorus 16.59.2, Aeschines 2.140–141, Demosthenes 19.315–328, 18.35–36, 42–43.

[136] Diodorus 16.60.1–3, Pausanias 10.3.1–3, and in detail see J. Buckler, *Philip II and the Sacred War* (Leiden, 1989), pp. 138–142.

well have been assisted by Aeschines, who later claimed that his role at the meeting saved the Phocians from a worse fate.[137]

Phocis lost its membership of the Amphictyonic Council. Its two votes on the council were transferred to Philip and it was no longer authorized to consult the Delphic oracle. The Phocians were to repay the amount of money stolen from the sacred treasuries in annual installments of sixty talents, beginning in 343, and could not own horses and arms again until they had done so.[138] The amount must have been several thousand talents. The cost of hiring mercenaries alone has been calculated from 1,622 to 3,244 talents,[139] to which can be added the jewelry and other precious items that some of the commanders gave to their wives or favorite whores—Philomelus, for example, gave a gold crown to a Thessalian dancing girl named Pharsalia.[140] All of the Phocian towns except Abae in eastern Phocis (which had not condoned the seizure of Delphi) were razed and their populations relocated to new villages comprising no more than fifty houses. The small size was to prohibit villages combining together in the future to form opposition strongholds. Demosthenes painted a pitiful picture of a devastated Phocis:[141]

> When we recently made our way to Delphi, we could not help but see everything—houses razed, fortifications demolished, countryside empty of adult men, a handful of women and children, miserable old people. No one could find words to describe the troubles [the Phocians] now have.

Those who had seized Delphi and fled in the wake of the Phocians' surrender to Philip were cursed, liable to arrest and forcible return, and their property was confiscated. They were not, however, to be killed. Phocian supporters were also punished. The Athenians, for example, lost their entitlement to *promanteia* (priority rights in consulting the oracle), which was given to Philip. However, they were not expelled from the council, although the Spartans may have been.[142]

---

[137] Aeschines 2.142–143, Cawkwell, "Aeschines and the Ruin of Phocis in 346," pp. 453–459.

[138] In 341, the annual payment was reduced to thirty talents, and after 337 it was only ten talents: P. J. Rhodes and R. Osborne (eds.), *Greek Historical Inscriptions, 404–323 BC* (Oxford: 2003), no. 67.

[139] M. Trundle, *Greek Mercenaries from the Late Archaic Period to Alexander* (London: 2004), pp. 95–96.

[140] Theopompus, *FGrH* 115 F 248.

[141] Demosthenes 19.65.

[142] Pausanias 10.8.2.

The Amphictyonic Council was responsible for enforcing the punishment, but some of its members—Thebes in particular—intended to victimize the Phocians as they carried out the council's mandate. To combat any brutal treatment of the Phocians Philip stationed troops in various towns, thereby permitting him to keep his own men under arms in Greece.[143] The Phocians' punishment, while severe, could have been far worse, but the Athenians were aggrieved that Philip had not done more to protect them.[144] The internal breakup of Phocis robbed them of an important ally against Thebes. What incensed the Athenians even more was Philip's treatment of the Thebans. Far from decreasing the city's influence in Greece, as Aeschines had confidently asserted, or even punishing them as he had the Phocian state, Philip celebrated the end of the sacred war with the Thebans. To make matters worse, Aeschines was with Philip in Thebes, where, according to Demosthenes, he joined in the celebrations.[145]

Philip gained the most from the Third Sacred War. His settlement of Greece was not what he had originally anticipated, but the "barbarian" Macedonian was now a member of the Amphictyonic Council, one of the most venerable of Greek institutions. Further, in recognition of his services to Apollo, the council elected him president of the Pythian Games at Delphi.[146] Part of the four-year Olympic cycle, the games not been held for the dozen years that the Phocians had occupied Delphi.[147]

The Athenians and the Spartans already begrudged Philip receiving the two Phocian votes on the Amphictyonic Council but making him president of the panhellenic games proved too much. Although Philip had treated the Athenians considerately at the conclusion of their war against him, they refused to send their official deputations to the games.[148] Philip had overlooked Athenian defiance before but could not allow it now. He dispatched an embassy to

---

[143] Victimization: Justin 8.5. Philip's moves: J. Buckler, "Philip II's Designs on Greece," in R. W. Wallace and E. M. Harris (eds.), *Transitions to Empire: Essays in Honor of E. Badian* (Norman: 1996), pp. 84–85.

[144] Buckler, "Demosthenes and Aeschines," p. 132, exaggeratedly talks of the punishment as "draconian," which would be the case if all the adult males had been killed and the women and children sold into slavery.

[145] Demosthenes 19.126–128, Aeschines 2.162–163.

[146] Demosthenes 5.19–23.

[147] Diodorus 16.59.4–60, Justin 8.5.4–6.

[148] Demosthenes 19.128, 132, 5.22; cf. 9.32.

Athens comprised of Macedonians and Thessalians to insist that the people acquiesce in the council's decision and so attend the games.[149] The Thessalian contingent represented the Amphictyonic Council, thus the Athenians would be defying not only Philip but also the council. There was abundant potential for the council declaring a sacred war against them, as Demosthenes acknowledged in his next speech *On the Peace*, which addressed the situation. The very existence of the Peace of Philocrates was under threat mere weeks after it had been concluded.

---

[149] Demosthenes 19.111–113.

8

Resisting Philip

DEMOSTHENES BLAMED AESCHINES and Philocrates for the situation in which the Athenians now found themselves. Because of their false promises at the Assembly of Skirophorion 16 the Athenians had lost a valuable ally in the Phocians, Thebes was unchecked in Greece, the Athenians had agreed to a peace that they already resented, and now Athens had been instructed to accept Philip's membership of the Amphictyonic Council and presidency of the Pythian Games. The people convened an Assembly, at which Aeschines urged the people to adhere to Philip's wishes.[1] Aeschines was the only man in Athens to speak in this way, so Demosthenes claimed—if this is true, then the people's mood was clearly belligerent.[2]

Defiance of Philip, however, was not in Athens' best interests, as Demosthenes argued in his short speech *On the Peace*.[3] The circumstances of the speech explain why it is "somewhat less fiery and assertive and more defensive."[4] The danger of Philip raising an amphictyonic army against Athens was too great, especially as the other Greeks would be quick to join him in marching on the city.[5] To combat Aeschines' advice, Demosthenes stressed that he was not only the

---

[1] Demosthenes 19.111–113.

[2] MacDowell, *Demosthenes*, p. 327, does not believe Demosthenes delivered the speech at this debate.

[3] Date: Dionysius of Halicarnassus, *To Ammaeus* 1.10.

[4] R. D. Milns, "The Public Speeches of Demosthenes," in Ian Worthington (ed.), *Demosthenes: Statesman and Orator* (London: 2000), p. 211.

[5] Demosthenes 5.13–14, 17–19, 24–25.

better speaker but also luckier than his opponent on every issue on which he had ever addressed the city.[6] Knowing that the message of his speech would be unpopular, Demosthenes stated that the people should view the peace as nothing more than a breathing space in hostilities with Philip. They should use the interval before they again went to war against him to rebuild their military resources.[7]

The speech therefore was Demosthenes' first overt statement that he expected the peace to be ephemeral.[8] Aeschines, however, wanted to keep the peace in existence, imagining that as allies of Philip the Athenians would suffer no harm if the king again intervened in Greece. Thus, their attitudes to Philip led to vehement clashes in the Assembly and law courts over the next several years.

On the Peace[9]

Demosthenes devoted the first half of his speech to a lengthy preamble about his earlier policies and warnings that had worked out to Athens' advantage since his aim was to persuade the Athenians to attend the Pythian Games (1–12). He acknowledged that the Athenians were in a predicament, but criticized them because of their penchant for deliberating after the fact, when it was too late, which made it hard for speakers to suggest action—"all other people are in the habit of deliberating before they act, but you do so afterwards!" (2). Nevertheless, he entreated them to focus less on whether the peace should have been enacted and more on the future. He also claimed that Aeschines and Philocrates had taken bribes from Philip during the second embassy to hoodwink the people (10):

---

[6] Demosthenes 5.4–12.

[7] Demosthenes 5.17.

[8] Cf. Carlier, *Démosthène*, p. 169: "Démosthène aurait saboté la paix," with pp. 169–177.

[9] On the speech, see Schaefer, *Demosthenes*[2] 2, pp. 297–303, Blass, *attische Beredsamkeit*[2] 3.1, pp. 299–303, Jaeger, *Demosthenes*, pp. 157–162, L. Pearson, *The Art of Demosthenes* (Meisenheim am Glan: 1976), pp. 138–141, Carlier, *Démosthène*, pp. 167–168, S. Usher, *Greek Oratory: Tradition and Originality* (Oxford 1999), pp. 230–232, MacDowell, *Demosthenes*, pp. 327–328. Pickard-Cambridge, *Demosthenes*, pp. 289–290, simply glosses over it. Translation with notes: J. Trevett, *Demosthenes, Speeches 1–17* (Austin: 2011), pp. 88–99; translation with commentary: J. R. Ellis and R. D. Milns, *The Spectre of Philip* (Sydney: 1970), pp. 77–90; text and commentary: J. E. Sandys, *Demosthenes, On the Peace, Second Philippic, On the Chersonesus and Third Philippic* (Cambridge: 1900).

At that time [Aeschines and Philocrates] were promising that Thespi-
aea and Plataea would be restored, and that Philip would preserve the
Phocians, if he got control of them, and would disperse the city of
Thebes into villages, and that Oropus would be given to us and that
Euboea would be surrendered in return for Amphipolis, and were offering such hopes and deceiving you with promises, by which you
were induced, either to your advantage nor perhaps to your credit, to
abandon the Phocians. But I shall show that I did not deceive you and
was not silent about any of these matters but declared to you, as I am
sure you remember, that I neither knew nor expected that any of
these things would happen, and that I thought the speaker was talking
nonsense.

In the second part of his speech (13–25), Demosthenes warned the
Athenians that if they defied Philip they risked a sacred war, in which
other states hostile to Athens would participate (13–14, 17):

Now then, I say that one condition should hold, that if anyone wishes to
provide allies or financial contributions or anything else for our city, he
should do so without breaking the existing peace—not because the
peace is wonderful or worthy of you but because, whatever its character,
it would be better for us that it had never been made than that we should
break it now that it has been made. For we have squandered many
things, the possession of which would have made war easier and safer for
us then that it is now. Second, men of Athens, we must see that we do not
provide these people who have come together and now claim to be
Amphictyons with the need or excuse for a common war against us. For
if war should break out between Philip and us over Amphipolis or some
smaller private grievance in which the Thessalians and Argives and Thebans are not involved, I do not imagine that any of these would go to war
with us . . . What then do I find a frightening prospect, and what is it that
you must guard against? It is that the coming war may offer everybody
a common pretext and a shared ground of complaint against us.

Demosthenes followed with a list of people who resented Athens,
such as the Thessalians, because Athens gave refuge to Phocians, the
Argives because of Athenian relations with Sparta, the Thebans because
of Oropus, and Philip, whom the Athenians were slighting (18–25). He
ended his speech by discouraging the Athenians from going to war
"over that shadow at Delphi"—in other words, events at Delphi were
insufficient cause to risk everything (25).

Demosthenes was successful. The Athenians approved Philip's
membership of the Amphictyonic Council and sent a delegation to the

games. After their conclusion, Philip returned home to Pella, although he first arranged for a Thessalian garrison to occupy Nicaea, east of Thermopylae, to ensure his gateway into Greece.[10] Diodorus stated that Philip was now anxious to invade Persia, perhaps influenced by Isocrates' *To Philip*.[11] He may possibly have started to look outside Greece for future campaigns, but an expedition to Persia was not yet possible.

DEMOSTHENES AND THEBES

The Athenians breathed a sigh of relief when Philip left Greece but not every Greek state shared their opinion of him. A number of the smaller ones was pleased to see his intervention in Greek affairs because, as Aeschines stated, they were tired of the "secrets of more powerful states" like Athens and Thebes.[12] Philip's Peloponnesian allies—Messene and Argos for two—likewise welcomed his intervention, which kept Sparta at bay, rather than their having to rely on Athens or Thebes.[13] When Philip was assassinated in 336, having by then imposed hegemony over Greece, not every Greek city revolted from Macedonia. Thus the Athenian reaction to Philip does not translate to all cities, and even in Athens Philip had support from leading intellectuals, including Speusippus, Plato's successor as head of the Academy.[14]

Demosthenes' *On the Peace* has been described as "the most important document as to [Demosthenes'] political position at this difficult time."[15] There is no question that Demosthenes' advice was correct, but in giving it he also revealed that he was intent on securing a union with Thebes against Philip. The Thebans were renowned for their land army, which would complement Athenian naval strength, and they were enraged at Philip's recent treatment of them. Their anger

---

[10] Demosthenes 6.22; see further, T. T. B. Ryder, "The Diplomatic Skills of Philip II," in Ian Worthington (ed.), *Ventures into Greek History. Essays in Honour of N. G. L. Hammond* (Oxford: 1994), pp. 248–249.

[11] Diodorus 16.60.5.

[12] Aeschines 2.120. Note the caution of R. M. Errington, *A History of Macedonia*, trans. C. Errington (Berkeley and Los Angeles: 1990), pp. 72–73, on the dangers of viewing Philip's actions and unpopularity only from the Athenian viewpoint.

[13] Philip and the Peloponnese: Ryder, "Diplomatic Skills of Philip II," pp. 238–242.

[14] On support for Philip, see also Worthington, *Philip II*, pp. 104, 121–122.

[15] Jaeger, *Demosthenes*, p. 157.

did not abate over the next few years.[16] Reminiscent of his speech *On Behalf of the Megalopolitans* of 353, Demosthenes encouraged the Athenians to reconcile their differences with the Thebans.[17] He counseled the Athenians not to engage in a war with Thebes, and to this end to give up their claims to the much-contested Oropus:[18]

> We allow the Thebans to keep Oropus: if anyone should ask us why we do so, insisting that we tell the truth, we should reply "in order to avoid war."

In doing so, the Athenians would not be acting any differently from giving up their claims to Chios, Rhodes, and Cos after the social war.[19] Demosthenes' policy flew in the face of Aeschines and Eubulus, who wanted a lasting peace and alliance with Philip.[20] Within two years Demosthenes would vanquish his opponents, but in steering Athens to a collision course with Macedonia his was not necessarily the right policy for his city or Greek freedom.[21] More than just rivals in a policy split, however, Demosthenes came to view those who strove to uphold peace as traitors to Athens' interests.[22] Philip of course was well aware of Demosthenes' hostile attitude. When the Athenians sent a certain Eucleides to him with a request to return Thracian towns to Cersebleptes and allow him to join the peace, he refused.[23] Nevertheless, he apparently offered to cut a channel across the Chersonese to provide Athenian settlers there with a defensive line against any Thracian attacks.[24] It would not be enough. Then the following year the growing animosity between Demosthenes and Aeschines exploded when Demosthenes indicted him for official misconduct (*parapresbeia*) on the second embassy to Philip. The relationship of the two men transcended the political realm of differing attitudes to Philip and became bitterly personal for the next sixteen years.[25]

---

[16] Cf. Ryder, "Diplomatic Skills of Philip II," pp. 244–247.

[17] Demosthenes 5.15–24. On the relationship of the speech to those Demosthenes delivered before it, see Sealey, *Demosthenes*, p. 158; cf. p. 170.

[18] Demosthenes 5.24.

[19] Demosthenes 5.25.

[20] Cf. Pickard-Cambridge, *Demosthenes*, p. 258, Carlier, *Démosthène*, pp. 170–174.

[21] The thrust of G. L. Cawkwell's arguments in "Demosthenes' Policy after the Peace of Philocrates I and II," *CQ*² 13 (1963), pp. 120–138 and 200–213.

[22] Demosthenes 19.288–297.

[23] Demosthenes 19.162.

[24] Aeschines 1.169, Demosthenes 6.30, [Demosthenes] 7.39, 40.

[25] See the treatment of J. Buckler, "Demosthenes and Aeschines," in Ian Worthington (ed.), *Demosthenes: Statesman and Orator* (London: 2000), pp. 114–158.

INDICTING AESCHINES

In Athens all public officials underwent a scrutiny (*euthune*) at the end
of their office to assess their conduct.[26] When the ambassadors who
had served on the second embassy to Philip were audited, Demosthenes, together with a man named Timarchus of Sphettus, indicted
Aeschines for improperly discharging his duties as an ambassador
(*parapresbeia*) and for misleading the people.[27] Timarchus was a hard-
line anti-Macedonian orator, who had once carried a measure that anyone who sent arms or fittings for warships to Philip should be
executed.[28] Specifically, Demosthenes charged that Aeschines:[29]

> Uttered not a single word of truth in his report, that he prevented the
> Assembly from hearing the truth from me, that he recommended pol-
> icies completely opposed to our interests, that he ignored everything
> you [the people] instructed him to do on the embassy, that he wasted
> time while the city's opportunities for great, far-reaching action were
> thrown away, and that together with Philocrates he took gifts and pay-
> ments in return for all these services.

In other words, Aeschines had accepted bribes from Philip and so
was conspiring with him to misrepresent his intentions toward Phocis
and Thebes at the Assembly meeting of Skirophorion 16 and he and
Philocrates had blocked Demosthenes' warnings to the people.
Aeschines was indeed vulnerable because his promises to the people
had evaporated. Demosthenes also accused him of spending an additional night with Philip at Pherae after the second embassy had left
there to return to Athens,[30] thereby affording Philip another opportunity to bribe him. Demosthenes was exploiting the fine line between
receiving gifts as part of normal diplomatic protocol, which therefore
had to be accepted, and taking them as a bribe. The practice permitted
opponents to cast aspersions on ambassadors and even prosecute them

---

[26] See the useful summary of this procedure by D. M. MacDowell, *Demosthenes: On the False Embassy (Oration 19)* (Oxford: 2000), pp. 16–18.

[27] Date and procedure: MacDowell, *Demosthenes: On the False Embassy*, pp. 14–22.

[28] Timarchus moved over a hundred decrees in his life, more than twice the thirty-nine that Demosthenes moved: M. H. Hansen, "The Number of *Rhetores* in the Athenian Ecclesia, 355–322 B.C.," *GRBS* 25 (1984), p. 153.

[29] Demosthenes 19.8; cf. MacDowell, *Demosthenes: On the False Embassy*, pp. 19–20.

[30] Demosthenes 19.175–176.

for official misconduct.[31] That Philip routinely used bribes throughout his reign gave considerable credence to Demosthenes' allegations.[32]

Demosthenes had a personal agenda for indicting Aeschines. He intended to remove Aeschines from public life, so that he could increase his own political authority, and he wanted to demonstrate he was not after all a supporter of the peace he had helped to negotiate the previous year.[33] However, Demosthenes' involvement of Timarchus, who had allegedly been a male prostitute, in his case proved his undoing. Timarchus' private life left much to be desired, furnishing Aeschines with the means to indict him for being an unfit orator (*dokimasia rhetoron*).[34] Aeschines thus exploited the distinction between private and public behavior.[35] He won his case, which meant that Timarchus was disfranchised, forcing Demosthenes to withdrew his charge.

Aeschines' prosecution speech survives, valuable for the insights it gives into Athenian popular morality, law, and especially the current political situation.[36] Among other things, Aeschines made it plain that

---

[31] S. Perlman, "On Bribing Athenian Ambassadors," *GRBS* 17 (1976), pp. 223–233 and F. D. Harvey, "*Dona Ferentes*: Some Aspects of Bribery in Greek Politics," in P. A. Cartledge and F. D. Harvey (eds.), *Crux: Essays in Greek History Presented to G. E. M. de Ste. Croix on his 75th Birthday* (London: 1985), pp. 76–117. A wider-ranging study is L. G. Mitchell, *Greeks Bearing Gifts: The Public Use of Private Relationships in the Greek World, 435–323 BC* (Cambridge: 1997).

[32] Ryder, "Diplomatic Skills of Philip II," pp. 228–257 and G. L. Cawkwell, "The End of Greek Liberty," in R. W. Wallace and E. M. Harris (eds.), *Transitions to Empire: Essays in Honor of E. Badian* (Norman: 1996), pp. 98–121.

[33] See further, on the background and charges: E. M. Harris, *Aeschines and Athenian Politics* (Oxford: 1995), pp. 115–120, T. T. B. Ryder, "Demosthenes and Philip II," in Ian Worthington (ed.), *Demosthenes: Statesman and Orator* (London: 2000), pp. 58–72, Sealey, *Demosthenes*, pp. 175–176, and in detail Buckler, "Demosthenes and Aeschines," pp. 121–132 and 134–140.

[34] Demosthenes 19.257, 284–286. On the odium attached to male prostitutes, see J. Davidson, *Courtesans and Fishcakes* (London: 1997), pp. 113–116, 252–257, 260–263, 265–274.

[35] Blass, *attische Beredsamkeit²* 3.2, p. 192, Usher, *Greek Oratory: Tradition and Originality*, p. 280. Aeschines' case: Harris, *Aeschines and Athenian Politics*, pp. 101–106, who dates it to late 346, but note the comment of MacDowell, *Demosthenes: On the False Embassy*, p. 21 with n. 59.

[36] On the speech, see Blass, *attische Beredsamkeit²* 3.2, pp. 167–176, Carlier, *Démosthène*, pp. 177–180, Usher, *Greek Oratory: Tradition and Originality*, pp. 280–284. Translation with notes: C. Carey, *Aeschines* (Austin: 2000), pp. 18–87; translation and commentary: N. Fisher, *Aeschines, Against Timarchos* (Oxford: 2001). See also R. Lane

he thought the peace was still to Athens' advantage despite Demosthenes' accusation that he had harmed the city, and Aeschines lauded his personal role in helping to bring it about.[37] Since he never offered incontrovertible evidence that Timarchus used to be a male prostitute, his views on maintaining peace and alliance with Philip may well have resonated with the jurors and so persuaded them to find against Timarchus.

Demosthenes took the rebuff to Timarchus stoically. However, in the spring of the same year he had the chance to upset his adversary. The Assembly had appointed Aeschines to lead an embassy to the Amphictyonic Council to argue for Athens' continued control of the temple of Apollo on Delos, Apollo's home before Delphi, which the Delians were protesting. Then the Areopagus, one of the oldest organs of the Athenian constitution,[38] which met on the "Hill of Ares" next to the Acropolis (Figure 10), intervened. It overrode the Assembly's appointment. Calling Aeschines a "traitor and public enemy," according to Demosthenes,[39] the council replaced him by Hyperides, "foremost of the orators in speaking ability and in his hatred of the Macedonians,"[40] and one of Demosthenes' supporters.[41]

There are two explanations for the Areopagus' action.[42] The first is that Aeschines was simply a bad choice because he may have alienated council members who wanted to impose a harsher punishment on the Phocians at the end of the Third Sacred War. They in turn might now rule against Athenian control of the temple out of spite. Second, Demosthenes persuaded the Areopagus, with which he was building a

---

Fox, "Aeschines and Athenian Politics," in R. Osborne and S. Hornblower (eds.), *Ritual, Finance Politics: Athenian Democratic Accounts Presented to David Lewis* (Oxford: 1994), pp. 135–155.

[37] Aeschines 1.169, 173–176.

[38] On which, see in detail R. W. Wallace, *The Areopagos Council, to 307 B.C.* (Baltimore: 1989).

[39] Demosthenes 18.134–135, [Plutarch], *Moralia* 850a.

[40] Diodorus 18.13.5.

[41] Demosthenes 19.209, 18.134, [Plutarch], *Moralia* 850a, with J. K. Davies, *Athenian Propertied Families* (Oxford: 1971) pp. 517–520. Hyperides as an orator: Blass, *attische Beredsamkeit²* 3.2, pp. 1–72, Usher, *Greek Oratory: Tradition and Originality*, pp. 328–338. Hyperides was later one of Demosthenes' prosecutors in the Harpalus affair: see Chapter 14.

[42] Demosthenes 18.132–135 says it was because Aeschines was involved in a plot to burn the Piraeus dockyards, but that is suspect, and in any case this plot did not occur until 343: see Chapter 9 pp. 212–213.

FIGURE 10. View from the Athenian Acropolis to the "Hill of Ares," where the Areopagus met.

working relationship that lasted for most of his political career, to substitute Hyperides for Aeschines. Hyperides was successful, but Aeschines' relationship with Demosthenes further deteriorated.

CHANGING THE PEACE OF PHILOCRATES

Relations between Philip and Athens remained calm for the next two years, mostly because Philip was preoccupied elsewhere. In 345 he was involved in an obscure campaign in Illyria during which he lost 150 cavalry and broke his right collarbone.[43] Later he systematically transferred population groups from different parts of Macedonia to military outposts on his northwestern border with Illyria.[44] Then in the summer

---

[43] Diodorus 16.69.7; cf. Justin 8.6.3. Rhetorical use of the wound by later writers: A. S. Riginos, "The Wounding of Philip II of Macedon: Fact and Fabrication," *JHS* 114 (1994), pp. 115–116.

[44] Justin 8.5.7–6.2; cf. Demosthenes 19.89. See further, J. R. Ellis, "Population-transplants by Philip II," *Makedonika* 9 (1969), pp. 9–17, Worthington, *Philip II*, pp. 108–110. The quotation is from Justin 8.5.7–6.1.

of 344 he was again forced to intervene in Thessaly. Dissension from Pherae was nothing unusual, but in Larissa Simus, a member of the ruling family, had struck coinage in his own name. Philip suspected Simus' action was a precursor to an attempt to seize power in Thessaly and so he marched to Larissa and expelled the entire ruling family. Philip now decided to subjugate Thessaly once and for all to ensure its future stability.[45] He set up a board of ten men (decadarchy) to rule in various Thessalian cities, including Larissa and Pherae, each one reinforced by a Macedonian garrison.[46] Further, he divided all Thessaly into four administrative districts or tetrarchies,[47] each one under the command of a personally appointed governor.[48] Demosthenes accused Philip of enslaving the Thessalians,[49] but his reaction was typically embellished, and Isocrates, by contrast, said he treated the Thessalians fairly.[50]

Philip next offered money and troops to Messene and Argos to use against the Spartans, perhaps as a prelude to more formal Macedonian intervention in the Peloponnese.[51] Demosthenes exploited Philip's intervention in Thessaly to persuade the Assembly to dispatch an embassy to Messene and Argos, on which Demosthenes, Hegesippus, and Polyeuctus served, to dissuade them from accepting the offer.[52] Philip was clearly the preferred choice because Messenian and Argive embassies traveled to Athens to complain about the city's interference in Peloponnesian affairs,[53] and the Arcadians and Argives erected bronze statues of Philip.[54]

---

[45] S. Sprawski, "All the King's Men: Thessalians and Philip II's Designs on Greece," in D. Musial (ed.), *Society and Religions: Studies in Greek and Roman History* (Torun: 2005), pp. 31–49.

[46] [Demosthenes] 7.32, Demosthenes 6.22, 8.59, 9.12, 18.48. Diodorus 16.69.8 has little to say about the Thessalian campaign: Worthington, *Philip II*, pp. 110–111.

[47] Theopompus, *FGrH* 115 FF 208–209, Demosthenes 6.22, 9.26; contra J. Buckler, *Aegean Greece in the Fourth Century BC* (Leiden: 2003), p. 420: Philip divided Thessaly in 352.

[48] Theopompus, *FGrH* 115 F 208.

[49] Demosthenes 18.295; cf. 19.260, 6.22, 9.26.

[50] Isocrates, *Letter* 2.20.

[51] Demosthenes 6.15; cf. Griffith in N. G. L. Hammond and G. T. Griffith, *A History of Macedonia* 2 (Oxford: 1979), pp. 474–479.

[52] Demosthenes 18.79, 9.72.

[53] [Demosthenes] 7.18–23, 12.18, Demosthenes 18.136, with Ryder, "Demosthenes and Philip II," p. 72.

[54] Demosthenes 6.27, 19.261, 262.

Faced by the Athenians' intention to block his every move in Greece, Philip changed tactics. In late 344 (or possibly early 343) he appointed his friend Python of Byzantium to lead an embassy to Athens that sought to modify the Peace of Philocrates.[55] Python informed the people that Philip was aggrieved over their recent actions against him, but he stressed that the king wanted "to win the friendship of Athens more than that of any other state."[56] To this end, he suggested altering the peace to what the allied *synedrion* had wanted in 346: a common peace.[57] Python also stated that Philip would entertain amendments to its terms as the Athenians saw fit.

Why Philip wanted to solicit the change is unknown, but he may have been concerned by an embassy from the Great King of Persia, Artaxerxes III Ochus, which may still have been in Athens when Python arrived. Artaxerxes planed to reconquer Egypt and was actively seeking assistance from the Greeks. Thebes sent him a thousand troops, but the Athenians rejected his appeal while reaffirming their friendship with the Persians.[58] Given the Great King's vast resources it was imperative for Philip to block any potential alliance between Persia and the Greeks.[59] The Athenians' decision has sometimes been considered a defeat for Demosthenes. In 341 he actively sought Persian support against Philip, but there is no evidence he was advocating a similar policy three or so years earlier.[60]

The timing of the Persian embassy may simply have been coincidental. The proposed change from a bilateral peace to a common peace would weaken the Athenians' hegemony of their confederacy. If implemented,

---

[55] [Demosthenes] 7.18–25, Demosthenes 18.136; cf. Demosthenes 12.18. On the date, see below.

[56] [Demosthenes] 7.21.

[57] Sealey, *Demosthenes*, p. 172 with n. 33, dated Python's mission to 343; cf. Carlier, *Démosthène*, pp. 185–186, Lehmann, *Demosthenes*, p. 150. The commonly accepted date of 344 is more likely. Griffith in Hammond and Griffith, *History of Macedonia 2*, p. 490, suggests it was the Athenians, not Philip, who proposed a common peace, but that is unlikely: cf. Cawkwell, "Demosthenes' Policy after the Peace of Philocrates I," p. 132, Sealey, *Demosthenes*, pp. 172–173.

[58] Philochorus, *FGrH* 328 F 157, Diodorus 16.44; on the date and the embassy, see Cawkwell, "Demosthenes' Policy after the Peace of Philocrates I," pp. 121–127.

[59] See further, J. Buckler, "Philip II, the Greeks, and the King 346–336 B.C.," in J. Buckler and H. Beck (eds.), *Central Greece and the Politics of Power in the Fourth Century BC* (Cambridge: 2008), pp. 233–253.

[60] Cawkwell, "Demosthenes' Policy after the Peace of Philocrates I," pp. 127–130.

each state would swear the requisite oath to Philip and each other and would no longer be bound to Athens. In this way, Philip intended to alter the dynamic between himself and the Athenians.

The Assembly met to debate the issue. Aeschines was in favor of Philip's change and invited any Greek state to join the peace and swear oaths to Athens and Philip.[61] Demosthenes spoke against him with his second *Philippic*.[62] He was right to interpret the alteration as a way to separate Athens from its allies while not weakening Philip, but then he accused the king of breaking the terms of the peace and planning to attack Athens.[63] In 346, he had made it plain in his speech *On the Peace* that renewed warfare with Philip was an eventuality, and now in 344 he seemed convinced that the king was making the first move toward that. He seized the opportunity to denigrate the politicians he alleged had deliberately misrepresented Philip's intentions in 346,[64] and promised he would provide a response to Philip's move to amend the peace.[65] What sets this speech apart from Demosthenes' previous ones is his injection of a psychological element into it: instead of merely reiterating Philip's treacherous exploits or anticipating his future aims he imagined Philip's thoughts, as will be seen.[66]

---

[61] Demosthenes 18.136, [Demosthenes] 7.18–25.

[62] Date: Dionysius of Halicarnassus, *To Ammaeus* 1.10. It makes more sense to place this speech after Python's arrival in Athens and as the reason for it, rather than agreeing with Jaeger, *Demosthenes*, p. 164 with p. 251 n. 23, Hammond and Griffith, *History of Macedonia* 2, p. 479 n.1, Sealey, *Demosthenes*, pp. 171–172, and Lehmann, *Demosthenes*, pp. 148–149, who date it after Demosthenes returned from his mission to the Peloponnese in 344 but before Python's arrival in Athens: see especially Cawkwell, "Demosthenes' Policy after the Peace of Philocrates I," pp. 123–126, MacDowell, *Demosthenes*, p. 329. Its presentation of the danger from Philip better suits Python's mission, and at 6.28 Demosthenes talks of reading a response to a foreign embassy present in Athens. That plausibly refers to Python's embassy. However, the embassy from Persia or even that from the Messenians and Argives complaining about Athens' intervention in the Peloponnese cannot be discounted, and Dionysius said the speech was in response to a Peloponnesian one; cf. Harris, *Aeschines and Athenian Politics*, pp. 108–110.

[63] Demosthenes 6.1–2, 6, 15–19. Further on Demosthenes' response to Python: Cawkwell, "Demosthenes' Policy after the Peace of Philocrates I," pp. 131–133.

[64] Demosthenes 6.29–36.

[65] Demosthenes 6.28.

[66] Demosthenes 6.17–19, for example (quoted below). See also G. Mader, "Praise, Blame and Authority: Some Strategies of Persuasion in Demosthenes, *Philippic 2*," *Hermes* 132 (2004), pp. 59–63. Usher, *Greek Oratory: Tradition and Originality*, p. 233: "no speech illustrates his command of [psychological insight] more tellingly than the *Second Philippic*."

The surviving speech ends abruptly and lacks Demosthenes' instructions to the people, suggesting that it is a draft because Demosthenes did not know in advance what Python would actually say to the people.[67] Thus Demosthenes wrote the first part of the speech, which exhorted the Athenians to action, and the second part, which attacked his opponents, before the Assembly because they suited anything Python might say, and would address the specifics of Python's speech extemporaneously. On the other hand, Demosthenes may have merely wanted to rouse the people against Philip and leave Hegesippus, who followed him in the debate, to advance concrete measures (see below).

The Second *Philippic*[68]

Demosthenes began by imploring the Athenians to check Philip's dominance (1–27), criticizing them for always discussing what needs to be done but never acting on it (1–2):

> Whenever, men of Athens, we discuss Philip's actions and his violent breaches of the peace, I always observed that the speeches on our side are manifestly just and considerate, and those who accuse Philip always seem to say what needs to be said, but virtually no necessary action is taken, which would make the speeches worth hearing. But our entire situation has already reached the point that the more fully and clearly Philip is convicted of breaking the peace with you and of plotting against all of Greece, the more difficult it is to advise you what to do.

---

[67] MacDowell, *Demosthenes*, pp. 331–332.

[68] On the speech, see Schaefer, *Demosthenes*[2] 2, pp. 356–361, Blass, *attische Beredsamkeit*[2] 3.1, pp. 303–308, Pickard-Cambridge, *Demosthenes*, pp. 308–309, Jaeger, *Demosthenes*, pp. 163–168, Pearson, *Art of Demosthenes*, pp. 141–144, Carlier, *Démosthène*, pp. 182–185, Usher, *Greek Oratory: Tradition and Originality*, pp. 232–234, MacDowell, *Demosthenes*, pp. 329–333. See also G. M. Calhoun, "Demosthenes' Second Philippic," *TAPA* 64 (1933), pp. 1–17 and Mader, "Praise, Blame and Authority: Some Strategies of Persuasion in Demosthenes, *Philippic* 2," pp. 56–68. Translation with notes: Trevett, *Demosthenes, Speeches 1–17*, pp. 100–112; text and commentary: Sandys, *Demosthenes, On the Peace, Second Philippic, On the Chersonesus and Third Philippic*. Analysis of the speech's rhetorical style: C. Wooten, *A Commentary on Demosthenes' Philippic 1* (Oxford: 2008), pp. 123–136. C. Wooten, *Cicero's Philippics and their Demosthenic Model* (Chapel Hill: 1983), discusses all four *Philippics* extensively.

From the outset, Demosthenes planted the notion in the people's minds that Philip intended to subdue Greece. To rebut his opponents' position that Philip intended to prolong peace and alliance he threw a further scare into the people by claiming that the king would move against Athens (6):

> First, men of Athens, if anyone is confident when he sees how great Philip is and how much he controls, and thinks that this carries no danger to our city, and that these preparations of his are not all directed against us, I am amazed and wish to ask all of you to listen briefly to the reasons why I expect the opposite result and judge Philip to be our enemy, so that you may be persuaded by me, if you think that I show better foresight; but if you think that those who confidently put their trust in him show more foresight, you may side with them.

Demosthenes related Philip's various actions after making peace in 346 that were to Athens' detriment, especially his siding with Thebes and his recent intervention in the Peloponnese on behalf of Messenia and Argos. Embedded in his description is his novel psychological insight into Philip's thoughts (17–19):

> Think about it: he wishes to rule and regards you as his only rivals in this. He has been acting unjustly for a long time now and is himself fully conscious of doing so, since his secure control of everything else depends on his keeping hold of your possessions. He thinks that if he were to abandon Amphipolis and Potidaea, he would not even be safe at home. He is therefore deliberately plotting against you and knows that you are aware of this. He believes that you are intelligent, and that you justifiably hate him, and is spurred on by the expectation that he will suffer some reverse at your hands, if you seize the opportunity to do so, unless he anticipates you by acting first. For these reasons, he is alert; he stands against you; he courts certain people—the Thebans and those of the Peloponnesians who agree with them—who he thinks will be satisfied with the present situation because of their greed, and will foresee none of the consequences because of their stupidity.

Demosthenes also quoted from the speech he had given on his recent embassy to Messenia and Argos, in which he compared any king to a tyrant as an enemy of freedom and an object of distrust (20–25).[69]

---

[69] Use of distrust: J. W. Leopold, "Demosthenes on Distrust of Tyrants," *GRBS* 22 (1981), pp. 227–246.

To lend weight to his contentions, he drew attention to the fate of the people of Olynthus and Thessaly, who realized too late that Philip was hardly their friend and suffered enslavement. The Messenians therefore needed to be all the more fearful of Philip (25):

> "What do you seek?" I said. "Freedom? Then do you not see that Philip's very titles are inimical to this? Every king and tyrant is an enemy of freedom and an opponent of law. You should be on your guard," I said, "lest, in seeing to escape war, you find yourselves saddled with a master."

It is testimony to Demosthenes' rhetorical skill that by reporting what he said to the Messenians his Athenian audience was likewise affected by his analogy of king to tyrant.[70]

Demosthenes interrupted his narrative at this point in his speech to tell the people what they must do—"You may deliberate later by yourselves about what we need to do, if you are sensible; but now I shall tell you what response you should vote for" (28). The remainder of the speech did not contain any specific proposal (28–37), lending weight to the suggestion that Demosthenes extemporized his response to Python's embassy (see below). Instead, Demosthenes turned to attack his opponents, especially Aeschines and Philocrates (whom he does not name). They had repeatedly told the Athenians that Philip was their friend, would curb Theban influence in Greece, and would take care of Phocis. Although one of the architects of the peace, Demosthenes justified distancing himself from it because he had treated Philip's promises skeptically and was not deceived by him. As examples of Philip's untrustworthiness he rehearsed his actions at Thermopylae and against Phocis and reminded the people that he, Demosthenes, had implored the people not to abandon either of them (28–29). His criticisms allowed him to throw back at Philocrates his contemptuous comment in the Assembly of Skirophorion 16 that Demosthenes drank only water and so was churlish (30–31):

> They said that I drank water and so am naturally an intractable and disagreeable fellow, whereas Philip would answer your prayers, if he should pass through Thermopylae, and would rebuild Thespiae and Plataea, and put an end to Thebes' arrogance, and dig through the Chersonese at his own expense, and would give you Euboea and Oropus in return for Amphipolis. I know you recall all these claims being made from the speaker's platform, although you are not good at remembering

[70] MacDowell, *Demosthenes*, p. 331.

those who injure you. And, most shameful of all, you voted on the basis of these hopes that this same peace should apply to his and our descendants too, so completely were you led on.

Demosthenes overly exaggerated the role of his opponents in the present sorry state of affairs (36):

If you had not been deceived then, there would be no danger to our city, since surely Philip would never be able to attack Attica either with a fleet, by defeating you at sea, or with an army, by marching through Thermopylae and Phocis, but either he would be acting justly and keeping quiet, upholding the peace, or he would immediately find himself in a war similar to the one which led him at that time to desire peace.

The equally radical Hegesippus, who spoke after Demosthenes at that debate, put forward two amendments to the original peace that further upset relations with Philip. Hegesippus' speech has not survived, but he mentioned his proposals in a speech of 343/2 that is extant.[71] The first amendment was that the terms of the peace as they affected the city's allies and possessions should be amended to "each party should have what belongs to it." The second was that any state not part of the original peace should be independent and, if attacked, receive assistance from members of the peace. The first amendment meant of course that Athens could reassert its claim to Amphipolis, Pydna, Potidaea, and Methone, as well as the Thracian fortresses that Cersebleptes and Chares had founded in 347. The second signified that Philip could not take any other places if he planned to extend the frontiers of Macedonia.

Python left Athens to return to Pella. Shortly afterwards, the Athenians sent an embassy to Pella headed by Hegesippus, of all people, to report the city's decision formally. When Hegesippus appeared before the king, Philip lost his temper and bade him leave. He also expelled Xenocleides, an Athenian poet who had lost his citizenship and gone to live in Macedonia, because he had entertained Hegesippus.[72] Although Philip offered to submit the status of the Thracian towns and the Athenian claim to Cardia to arbitration, the people refused.[73]

---

[71] [Demosthenes] 7.18–25. On Hegesippus, see Blass, *attische Beredsamkeit*[2] 3.2, pp. 111–121.

[72] Demosthenes 19.331, [Demosthenes] 59.27, with K. A. Kapparis, *Apollodoros: Against Neaira [D. 59]* (Berlin: 1991), pp. 222–224.

[73] [Demosthenes] 7.39–44.

CLOSING THE DOOR

Demosthenes knew that Philip would never agree to Hegesippus' amendments, which compromised his borders and coastline, reestablished Athenian sway in the Thracian Chersonese, and prevented him from overpowering other places.[74] The Athenians had certainly not lived up to the spirit of the peace—their dislike of it manifested itself almost as soon as the signatories swore to it. Demosthenes has been condemned for his role in the breakdown of relations between Athens and Macedonia, but it was Philip, after all, who made the first move to change the terms of the peace. In 346 he had been vehemently opposed to a common peace, and his volte-face now, which was to Athens' detriment, was suspicious. Given his self-serving track record, and especially his recent intervention in the Peloponnese, it is no surprise that Demosthenes would view Philip's actions in 344 suspiciously. His adverse reaction to Philip's suggested change was not a mere knee-jerk one or even a self-serving one as might have been the case earlier in his career. If criticism is to be leveled against him, it is for trying to downplay his role in the peace process while attacking his colleagues for what they had done.

Demosthenes was a very different person from the unsuccessful young politician of the 350s. Now he was able to combat the influence of Eubulus and certainly of Aeschines. His anti-Macedonian policy closed the door to any peaceful resolution of the disputes between Macedonia and Athens, but for that he need not be blamed. Philip had emerged as a blatant imperialist, who two years later intervened decisively in Epirus and conquered Thrace. Both of these campaigns were not sudden ideas but entailed careful planning. In 344, he may have schemed to detach the Athenians from their allies as he prepared to expand into Thrace, knowing the alarm that would cause them. Indeed, in the following year, 343, he may even have orchestrated a plot to burn the Piraeus dockyards so as to cripple the Athenian navy prior to his Thracian campaign of 342 (Chapter 9).

The Athenian attitude to the peace manifested itself in the following year, 343, when Philocrates and Proxenus were indicted and Demosthenes renewed his attack on Aeschines in the courts.

---

[74] Ryder, "Demosthenes and Philip II," pp. 74–75.

THE TRIALS OF PHILOCRATES
AND PHILOXENUS

In 343 Hyperides indicted Philocrates for treason, accusing him of taking bribes from Philip and pressing for a course of action—that the Athenians should adopt Philip's terms for a peace and alliance—that was to the detriment of the city and harmed Phocis and Halus.[75] The charge was intended to remove Philocrates from public life. Philocrates did not stand trial but fled into exile.[76] He was probably right to do so, given the growing anti-Macedonian sentiment in Athens. His former ally Demosthenes, who had defended him in 348, was working to distance himself from his own role in the peace process.[77] He had even accused Philocrates of "openly exchanging (Macedonian) gold in the marketplace"[78] and of receiving land and women captured at Olynthus from Philip.[79] Philocrates was condemned to death in absentia, and the state seized his property and sold it.[80]

The next man to be put on public trial was Proxenus, who had commanded the Athenian troops dismissed by Phalaecus at Thermopylae in 346. He was found guilty but evidently paid his fine as he continued to be politically active.[81] Proxenus was one of the first men to be tried under a new legal procedure by the Areopagus called *apophasis*, which Demosthenes likely introduced in this year.[82] The Areopagus investigated a crime and issued a report (*apophasis*). If the subject of its inquiry was considered guilty, then the matter was referred to a law court.

---

[75] Demosthenes 19.116–119, Aeschines 2.6, Hyperides 4.29–30.

[76] Demosthenes 19.119—the passage is quoted below.

[77] Demosthenes' relations with Philocrates: Aeschines 3.58–75; succinct comments at P. Cloché, *Démosthène et la fin de la démocratie athénienne* (Paris: 1957), pp. 138–139.

[78] Demosthenes 19.114.

[79] Demosthenes 19.145, 309.

[80] Aeschines 2.6, 3.79.

[81] Dinarchus 1.63; activities after 343: Demosthenes 19.280–281.

[82] Antiphon and Proxenus: Demosthenes 18.133, with R. W. Wallace, *The Areopagos Council, to 307 B.C.* (Baltimore: 1989), pp. 113–119. Procedure: Dinarchus 1.50–63, Wallace, *Areopagos Council*, pp. 113–119 and 176–179.

THE FALSE EMBASSY TRIAL: DEMOSTHENES VERSUS AESCHINES

In the autumn of 343 Demosthenes rekindled his earlier charge of *para-presbeia* against Aeschines on the second embassy to Philip (see above).[83] This time the case went to court. The speeches of both Demosthenes and Aeschines survive, each one titled *On the False Embassy*, although the information in them and the presentation of facts and motives are grossly distorted because of the personal agenda of both orators.[84]

Demosthenes as prosecutor spoke first. His speech is his longest that survives (ninety-seven pages of Greek text).[85] After a brief introduction,[86] over half of the speech is given over to a narrative of the events of 346, including the destruction of Phocis, how Aeschines was bribed by the king, and the disastrous advice he, in tandem with Philocrates, gave to the people in recommending peace with the king.[87] It is not until he is almost halfway through his speech that Demosthenes finally turns to Aeschines' conduct on the second embassy to Philip, his reason for indicting him. The crux of Demosthenes' argument was simply that Aeschines could not have proffered the policy he did, given his anti-Macedonian attitude before the second embassy, unless Philip had bribed him. Interspersed into this narrative were attacks on Aeschines' character and morality to raise the ire of the jury. The second part of the speech comprised arguments to sustain the earlier narrative, including criticism of Aeschines' supporting witnesses such as Eubulus.[88] The conclusion to the speech reiterated Aeschines' principal failures and his venality thanks to Philip (302–336) and ended with an invocation to the jurors to do their moral duty and convict him.[89]

---

[83] The season is inferred from the silence of Demosthenes about Philip's advance into Epirus and toward Ambracia in winter 343/2: Sealey, *Demosthenes*, p. 308 n. 47. Reasons why Demosthenes moved against Aeschines now: MacDowell, *Demosthenes: On the False Embassy*, pp. 21–22.

[84] See Harris, *Aeschines and Athenian Politics*, pp. 52–62, Buckler, "Demosthenes and Aeschines," pp. 134–140, 148–154; cf. Ryder, "Demosthenes and Philip II," pp. 58–72.

[85] On the structure of the speech in linear fashion: H. Yunis, *Demosthenes, Speeches 18 and 19* (Austin: 2005), pp. 120–121.

[86] Demosthenes 19.1–8.

[87] Demosthenes 19.9–177.

[88] Demosthenes 19.183–301.

[89] Demosthenes 19.337–343.

Given the length of Demosthenes' speech there is a view that he intended to present only the narrative part, choosing from the second part what he felt could be fitted into his allotted speaking time.[90] On the other hand, Demosthenes could have given only a short speech, which he revised and enlarged after oral delivery.

Demosthenes: *On the False Embassy*[91]

Demosthenes considered Aeschines corrupt and wanting as an ambassador. He outlined the five expected duties of an ambassador, accusing Aeschines of failing in all of them (4–8):

> You must consider and think through, jurors, what are the matters for which the city should hold an envoy responsible. First, the report he delivered; second, his advice; third, the instructions you gave him; next, his use of the time at his disposal; and on top of all this, whether he was corrupt or not in discharging all these duties. Why precisely these points? First, because your deliberations about policy depend on his report: if it is true, you have the necessary information, but if not, you have just the opposite. And since you treat an envoy as an authority on the issues related to his mission, you find his recommendations especially reliable. Indeed, no envoy should ever be convicted of giving you bad or harmful advice. . . . As for the question of integrity, all of you, I know, would say that to profit at the expense of the city is a terrible and infuriating thing; however, the lawgiver did not define the matter that way, but simply said that no gifts of any kind were to be accepted. He believed, I take it, that once a citizen has accepted a gift and been corrupted by money, he can no longer serve the city as a reliable judge of useful policy. So if I prove and

---

[90] MacDowell, *Demosthenes: On the False Embassy*, pp. 23–27 and *Demosthenes*, p. 335; cf. Usher, *Greek Oratory: Tradition and Originality*, p. 236

[91] On the speech, see Schaefer, *Demosthenes*² 2, pp. 388–401, Blass, *attische Beredsamkeit*² 3.1, pp. 308–324, Pickard-Cambridge, *Demosthenes*, pp. 316–321, Pearson, *Art of Demosthenes*, pp. 158–177, Carlier, *Démosthène*, pp. 188–192, Usher, *Greek Oratory: Tradition and Originality*, pp. 234–237, MacDowell, *Demosthenes: On the False Embassy*, pp. 22–30 and *Demosthenes*, pp. 333–342. Translation with notes: Yunis, *Demosthenes, Speeches 18 and 19*, pp. 114–215; text, translation, and commentary: MacDowell, *Demosthenes: On the False Embassy*; discussion and commentary: T. Paulsen, *Die Parapresbeia-Reden des Demosthenes und des Aischines: Kommentar und Interpretationen zu Demosthenes, or. XIX, und Aischines, or. II* (Trier: 1999).

demonstrate clearly that Aeschines here uttered not a single word of truth in his report, that he prevented the Assembly from hearing the truth from me, that he recommended policies completely opposed to our interests, that he ignored everything you instructed him to do on the embassy, that he wasted time while the city's opportunities for great, far-reaching action were thrown away, and that together with Philocrates he took gifts and payments in return for all these services, then convict him and impose a penalty that fits the crimes. If I do not demonstrate these claims, or do not demonstrate all of them, consider me a scoundrel and acquit him.

Demosthenes turned to the main events of 346 leading up to the Peace of Philocrates. He chronicled how Aeschines changed his view of Philip from the period of the first embassy to the second, and how he persuaded the people to accept Philocrates' recommendation of peace and alliance (9–28). When Demosthenes tried to caution the people, Philocrates ridiculed him by accusing him of drinking only water (quoted in Chapter 7 p. 176). Events, however, showed Demosthenes was right (17–46), thereby bearing out his accusation that Aeschines was Philip's agent (37–38, 48–49). Demosthenes continually portrayed Aeschines' motives and actions in a sinister light (28):

> If all the information he conveyed to you turned out to be accurate, and the result was successful, then you may suppose that friendship [with Philip] to have been formed honestly and for the sake of the city. But if the result has been the exact opposite of what he predicted and still causes the city much shame and great danger, then you should realize that he changed his policy because of his own avarice and because he sold the truth for money.

He spent considerable time on the punishment of Phocis, and painted a pitiful picture of the devastation inflicted on the Phocian state and people (quoted on p. 180). His accusation that Aeschines was to blame was a blatant twisting of the truth as Aeschines, together with Philip, had worked to moderate the Phocian punishment. Still, the pathos of the "terrible and piteous sight" that was now Phocis could not have failed to move the jury. Even worse, continued Demosthenes, was that at the end of the Peloponnesian War in 404 the Phocians had voted against the Thebans' wish to enslave the Athenians—Aeschines' action was therefore all the more reprehensible (65–66):

> And still I hear all of you talk about the vote [the Phocians] once cast against the Thebans, when the question of enslaving us was put to the question. How would your forebears vote, Athenians, if they could see

again, how would they judge those who are responsible for destroying this city? Even if they stoned these men with their own hands, they would not, I expect, consider themselves defiled. How is it not disgraceful—or worse than disgraceful, if that's possible—that those who saved us then and cast the saving vote in our favor should, because of these men, meet the opposite fate and be allowed to suffer what no other Greeks have done? Who is responsible? Who used trickery to bring this about? Is it not this man?

By "this man," Demosthenes meant Aeschines. Thanks to him, Demosthenes continued angrily, the Peace of Philocrates benefited Philip and contributed to Athens' undoing (88–97), all because Aeschines and Philocrates accepted bribes—unlike Demosthenes (119–120):

> What is this connection with Philocrates, what is this great regard for him? Even if Philocrates had conducted the embassy in the most exemplary fashion and achieved the most advantageous outcome but yet admitted to taking money while on the embassy, as he did indeed admit, this connection is the very thing that an honest member of the embassy ought to shun, guard against, and solemnly repudiate in his own behavior. Aeschines has not done that. Is the situation not clear, Athenians? Does it not shout out loud and declare that Aeschines took money and is always wicked for the sake of money, not because he is stupid or ignorant or made a simple mistake? "Yet who testifies that I took bribes?" he will ask. A splendid question! The facts, Aeschines, which are the most trustworthy of all witnesses, for the facts cannot be impugned or blamed for being what they are because they've been seduced or are doing a favor for someone; rather, what you have done though betrayal and corruption determines what the facts turn out to be when examined.

Having dealt with various events of 346, Demosthenes finally turned to the context of his charge: Aeschines' conduct on the second embassy (150–178). His reversal of chronological order was deliberate because he had no solid evidence to produce to the jury that Philip did indeed bribe Aeschines. In an attempt to mask this weakness, Demosthenes discussed Aeschines' conduct up to and including the Peace of Philocrates to show that his change of attitude to the peace and Philip's intents between the first and second embassies could only have been the product of bribery. Demosthenes thus cleverly damned Aeschines in the minds of the jurors so that they had no recourse but to accept that Aeschines must have taken a bribe on the second embassy to explain his subsequent actions.[92]

---

[92] Cf. MacDowell, *Demosthenes: On the False Embassy*, pp. 27–28.

The second part of the speech is riddled with slurs on Aeschines' character. In one notable passage Demosthenes told of Aeschines' conduct at a party hosted for the second embassy by Xenophron, an Athenian exile living at Pella (196–198). Xenophron brought in an Olynthian woman, whom Philip had captured in 348. Aeschines and those with him had been drinking heavily, and they began to torment the lady, forcing her to recline and sing. At that point (197–199):

> The woman became distressed, for she didn't want to sing and wasn't able to, whereupon this man and Phryno, declaring her behavior an outrage, said they would not allow her, a loathsome, accursed Olynthian prisoner of war, to put on airs. "Summon a slave," they said, and "bring a whip." A servant produced a strap, and, since the men, I believe, were drunk and easily provoked, when she said something and began crying, the servant ripped off her tunic and flogged her back repeatedly. Beside herself at this dreadful turn of events, the woman jumped up and fell at the knees of Iatrocles, upsetting their table. If he hadn't rescued her, she would have been killed by their drunken rage, for this piece of trash [Aeschines] is fierce when he drinks. . . . This foul specimen knows full well what he's done, yet he will dare to look you in the face, and in a moment he'll be using his glorious voice to talk of the life he's led. It makes me gag.

This piece of descriptive narrative is all the more brilliant because Demosthenes was not present at the gathering.[93] Because Xenophron was the son of Phaedimus, one of the Spartan-backed tyrants who had ruled Athens in 404–403, Demosthenes did not wish to associate himself with anyone connected to oligarchy—unlike his colleagues. Aeschines denied the entire episode in his defense speech (see below).

The rest of the speech was given over to other instances of Aeschines' corruption and lack of patriotism. The allegations are unfair, for Aeschines was as much a democrat and loyal to Athens as was Demosthenes: the two men simply had differing approaches to Philip.[94] To Demosthenes, Aeschines and his supporters were traitors working for Philip, and he accused Philocrates of spending his bribe money on fish and prostitutes.[95] Warning the people to be on their guard against

---

[93] MacDowell, *Demosthenes*, p. 339.

[94] Cf., for example, Lane Fox, "Aeschines and Athenian Politics," pp. 135–155.

[95] Demosthenes 19.229.

treacherous and venal men, and to punish them accordingly (258–299), Demosthenes likened corrupt politicians to a "disease sweeping through Greece" (259–262). He gave examples of men in Thessaly, Elis, Arcadia, and Olynthus, who took bribes from Philip and ruined their states (258–267), as well as traitors in Athens whom the people punished severely (268–280). Building on these examples, Demosthenes evoked Aeschines' appeal in his speech against Timarchus of 345 to condemn him for the severity of his offenses (281–287). In a series of stunningly dramatic, rhetorical questions Demosthenes implored the jury to find Aeschines guilty, just as the Athenians had done before with men who—unlike Aeschines—had performed illustrious deeds but were corrupt (280–282):

> So what will you do, Athenians? You are the offspring of that illustrious generation, and some of you still with us actually belong to it. The facts are before you. Will you permit Epicrates, the democratic benefactor and partisan of Piraeus, to be cast out and punished; will you permit Thrasybulus, son of Thrasybulus the democrat who restored democracy from Phyle, to incur a fine of ten talents as happened the other day; will you permit like treatment for the citizen descended from Harmodius and your greatest benefactors, those whom, to mark their deeds on your behalf, you include by law in the festive libations at all your sanctuaries and sacrifices, whom you exalt in song and venerate on a par with the heroes and gods;—will you permit all these citizens to face the penalties ordained by law and gain no benefit from clemency, from compassion, from the sobbing children who bear your benefactors' names, from anything at all, and yet [Aeschines] whose father, Atrometus, teaches school, whose mother, Glaucothea, heads a wild cult for which her predecessor was put to death, whose family are people of that sort, whose father and every forebear, like himself, have never availed the city in anyway, when you have this man in your power, you will set him free? What command has he held in the cavalry, in the navy, in the field? Which chorus, which public expenditure, which fiscal obligation (*eisphora*) has he provided? What loyalty has he demonstrated, what danger has he braved? Which of these has this man or his relatives ever done for the city? Even if he could lay claim to all these distinctions but not to those other ones— namely, serving honestly as envoy and remaining free of corruption— surely he still deserves to die. But if he can lay claim neither to these distinctions nor to those, will you not punish him?

Demosthenes ended his speech by calling on the jurors to disregard the supporting testimony of Eubulus (290–299) in light of Aeschines' treachery (315–343). If the jurors acquitted Aeschines, they would be sanctioning anyone to break the law in return for personal gain and damaging their standing and reputation in Greece (343):

> Is there any other citizen who will not become corrupt when he sees that those who sold everything gain money, status, resources, and Philip' friendship, but those who proved themselves honest and chose to spend their own money gain trouble, malice, and spite from some people? Do not let that happen. It will not bring you any advantage to acquit this man—not for your reputation or your piety or your security or anything else; so punish him and make him an example for all men, both in Athens and throughout Greece.

Aeschines: *On the False Embassy*[96]

Aeschines' defense speech was less than two-thirds the length of Demosthenes' prosecution speech. After a brief introduction petitioning the jury to treat him fairly (1–10), Aeschines traced relations between Athens and Philip from the first embassy to the king to the present day, paying special attention to the second embassy and its aftermath (11–143). He knew that rebutting Demosthenes' charges would not exculpate him in the present climate of opinion, so he concentrated on undermining Demosthenes' credibility by connecting him to Philocrates as the architects of the unpopular peace (56):

> So you can see that the active cooperation to bring about the peace was not between me and Philocrates but between Demosthenes and Philocrates; and I think I have given you ample proofs of my account. For the reports that we delivered you are my witnesses, and for what was said in Macedonia and events on our journey I have provided our colleagues as witnesses.

Aeschines argued among other things that he was not inconsistent in his advice to the Assembly of Elaphebolion 18 and 19 (57–69) and had never prevented Demosthenes speaking at an Assembly (121–123).

---

[96] On the speech, see Schaefer, *Demosthenes*² 2, pp. 401–413, Blass, *attische Beredsamkeit*² 3.2, pp. 176–182, Harris, *Aeschines and Athenian Politics*, pp. 116–119, Usher, *Greek Oratory: Tradition and Originality*, pp. 284–287, Paulsen, *Die Parapresbeia-Reden des Demosthenes und des Aischines*. Translation with notes: Carey, *Aeschines*, pp. 88–158.

In his long account of the second embassy, he naturally denied he had bowed to bribery (97–129) and made it plain that he bore no responsibility for the terms of the peace and alliance (118):

> Fortune and Philip were responsible for what was done, but I was responsible for my loyalty to you and for my speech. For my part I said what was just and in your best interests, but the result was not what we prayed for but what Philip brought about.

Likewise, he also refuted Demosthenes' claim that he had helped to destroy Phocis, putting the blame for that on the Phocians' actions in seizing Delphi in the first place, while emphasizing his role in mitigating their punishment (130–143). Throughout, Aeschines portrayed Demosthenes as inept in his dealings with Philip, and he delighted in recounting Demosthenes' embarrassment when he first appeared before the king and could not speak (quoted on p.165). More importantly, by tying him to Philocrates in the peace-making process, Aeschines demonstrated that Demosthenes did not hold true to one policy and switched political associations as and when it suited him. Demosthenes emerged as a hypocrite and deceitful, the worst type of political leader that Athenians who loved their city would desire.

The second part of Aeschines' speech refuted Demosthenes' various character attacks (144–171). For example, he brought forward a man named Aristophanes of Olynthus to explode the story that he abused an Olynthian woman at Xenophron's party as Demosthenes had described (154–158). In particular, Aeschines emphasized the lack of evidence for the allegations of bribery and his work for the city, patriotically pointing out how he had defended it in times of need (167–171). The final part of his speech implored the people to recognize the benefits that peace can bring compared to war and concluded with an adjuration to the jury to find him innocent because of his public service (172–184). At the end of his speech, Aeschines invited his supporting speakers to take the stand— "Eubulus to represent the politicians and men of character, Phocion to represent the generals, a man who had also surpassed everyone in justice, and to represent my friends and contemporaries Nausicles and all the others I have mixed with and whose pursuits I have shared" (184).

The jurors, perhaps numbering 501 or even as many as 1,501, cast their votes.[97] They acquitted Aeschines, but only by thirty votes,[98]

---

[97] [Plutarch], *Moralia* 840c.

[98] Idomeneus, *FGrH* 338 F 10 = Plutarch, *Demosthenes* 15.5, [Plutarch], *Moralia* 840c.

which showed no "significant softening of the people's view of Philip."[99] Demosthenes most likely lost his case because his evidence was merely circumstantial and he never properly proved his suspicions that Aeschines took bribes from Philip. Moreover, Aeschines had proved that Demosthenes and Philocrates had advocated peace with Philip as late as the Assembly of Skirophorion 16, thereby undermining Demosthenes' claim that he had opposed Philip's terms. Aeschines may well have spoken against Philocrates' proposal for peace at the Assembly on Elaphebolion 18 and for it the next day, but that did not mean Philip had bribed him to change his mind. Nor can Aeschines be accused of betraying his city in relating Philip's intentions to the Assembly of Skirophorion 16. If he was guilty of anything, it was a disastrous judgment in taking Philip at his word.

Paradoxically, Demosthenes' failure against his opponent in 343 did not curtail his political career, yet Aeschines was never able to better him again.

---

[99] Ryder, "Demosthenes and Philip II," p. 76; see also Buckler, "Demosthenes and Aeschines," pp. 134–140.

9

"Speeches Like Soldiers"

"Philip used to say that Demosthenes' speeches were like soldiers because of their warlike power, but those of Isocrates were like athletes, because they afforded pleasure like that of a show."[1] Powerful though Demosthenes' second *Philippic* had been, his *On the Chersonese* and the third and fourth *Philippics* of 341 were arguably his fiercest and most rousing. His tone in them was needed because after 343 Philip embarked on a more aggressive expansionist policy that led to the complete collapse of the Peace of Philocrates.

PHILIP AND EPIRUS

In 343 Philip invaded Epirus, expelled Arybbas, and installed his step-son (Philip's brother-in-law) Alexander as king.[2] Philip's move was the culmination of a policy that he initiated in 350 when he took the young Alexander of Epirus to live with him at Pella (Chapter 5 p. 127). Philip's action now consolidated his southwestern border and generated additional income for Macedonia from Epirus' pastureland and timber.

---

[1] [Plutarch], *Moralia* 845d. On the athletic imagery, see M. Golden, "Demosthenes and the Social Historian," in Ian Worthington (ed.), *Demosthenes: Statesman and Orator* (London: 2000), pp. 172–174. On Demosthenes' rhetoric of war in his speeches, see J. Roisman, *The Rhetoric of Manhood: Masculinity in the Attic Orators* (Berkeley and Los Angeles: 2005), pp. 113–116.

[2] Diodorus 16.72.1, Worthington, *Philip II*, pp. 116–117.

Prior to his campaign in Epirus, Philip had sent a letter to the Athenians stressing his willingness to maintain peace with them. He also requested they jointly fulfill a term of the Peace of Philocrates to rid the Aegean of piracy, offering to pay for its entire cost himself.[3] Yet Demosthenes successfully persuaded the people to reject Philip's overtures. Further, when the king marched to free southern Epirus from the control of Ambracia, Demosthenes was instrumental in dispatching troops to assist the people of Ambracia should Philip besiege them, and commissioned embassies (on which he and Hegesippus served) to the Peloponnesian states to rouse them against Philip.[4] The Athenians offered refuge to the deposed Arybbas and even flirted with the idea of restoring him to his throne.[5] Philip did not besiege Ambracia, perhaps because he did not have enough troops or because of the Athenians' unexpected diplomatic successes in forging alliances with at least Argos, Messene, Megalopolis (allies of the king), Mantinea, and Achaea.[6]

GIVE IT BACK: THE HALONNESUS AFFAIR

As a goodwill gesture, Philip had sent the Athenians a letter offering to return the little island of Halonnesus (off the coast of Thrace between Lemnos and Scyros) to them. Halonnesus was an Athenian possession, but in 346 pirates had turned it into a base. Philip had expelled them and installed a Macedonian garrison on the island to prevent the pirates retaking it. The Athenians at that time had shown no interest in his activities, but now Demosthenes cynically seized upon his generosity. He asserted that Philip could not give the island to the Athenians, as it was already their property, but could only give it *back* to them,[7] for which a disgusted Aeschines later accused him of "arguing about syllables."[8] However, Demosthenes' response was more than verbal quibbling. If Philip acknowledged that he was returning a former Athenian possession, then Demosthenes postulated the Athenians had grounds

---

[3] [Demosthenes] 7.14–15.

[4] [Demosthenes] 48.24–26, Demosthenes 9.34, 72, Aeschines 3.97–108.

[5] P. J. Rhodes and R. Osborne, *Greek Historical Inscriptions, 404–323 BC* (Oxford: 2003), no. 70; see also [Demosthenes] 7.32, Diodorus 16.72.1, Justin 8.6.4–7.

[6] Worthington, *Philip II*, p. 118.

[7] Aeschines 3.83, Plutarch, *Demosthenes* 9.6.

[8] Aeschines 3.83; cf. Plutarch, *Demosthenes* 9.5–6, Athenaeus 223d–224b.

to demand the restitution of Amphipolis, Pydna, Potidaea, and Methone. Philip clearly could not agree to the implications of Demosthenes' wording, but he did express his willingness to submit the issue to arbitration.[9] The Athenians continued to maintain an obstructionist attitude over Halonnesus, described as the "final straw" in their relations with Philip.[10]

Demosthenes was not the only politician to react negatively to Philip's gestures. In a speech *On Halonnesus*, which has survived in the Demosthenic corpus but was probably delivered by Hegesippus,[11] the speaker even argued that Philip was using a campaign against piracy as an excuse to seize control of the Aegean.[12] Despite the considerable threat that pirates posed to merchant shipping, the Athenians were swayed by Hegesippus' alarmist rhetoric and rejected Philip's request.

BURNING THE DOCKYARDS

Hegesippus' conjecture that Philip desired naval ascendancy in the Aegean was suspect, not least because of the small size of the Macedonian navy. Yet Philip may have intended to clip Athenian naval power to judge by a conspiracy, in which he was implicated, to destroy the Piraeus dockyards.[13] In his speech against Aeschines of 330, Demosthenes reminded the jury of an Athenian named Antiphon who had been expelled from Athens after losing his citizenship but had returned because Philip bribed him to burn down the dockyards.[14] He was

---

[9] [Demosthenes] 7.7.

[10] N. G. L. Hammond and G. T. Griffith, *A History of Macedonia* 2 (Oxford: 1979), pp. 510–516 (Griffith's section on the Halonnesus affair). On Philip and Greece, see further, J. Buckler, "Philip II's Designs on Greece," in W. R. Wallace and E. M. Harris (eds.), *Transitions to Empire: Essays in Honor of E. Badian* (Norman: 1996), pp. 77–97.

[11] [Demosthenes] 7. On Hegesippus: Blass, *attische Beredsamkeit²* 3.2, pp. 111–121. The speech is more likely to belong to this year than 344, in the context of Python's embassy, as I had originally thought at Worthington, *Philip II*, p. 118.

[12] On the speech, see Pickard-Cambridge, *Demosthenes*, pp. 314–315, MacDowell, *Demosthenes*, pp. 343–346. Translation with notes: J. Trevett, *Demosthenes, Speeches 1–17* (Austin: 2011), pp. 113–128.

[13] On the "conspiracy," see J. Roisman, *The Rhetoric of Conspiracy in Ancient Athens* (Berkeley and Los Angeles: 2006), p. 131.

[14] Demosthenes 18.132–133; cf. Dinarchus 1.63, Plutarch, *Demosthenes* 14.5.

caught red-handed, but when Demosthenes denounced him before the Assembly Aeschines persuaded the people there was no evidence against him, and he was released. Dissatisfied, Demosthenes had the matter investigated by the Areopagus under the *apophasis* procedure.[15] The council determined that Antiphon was guilty of criminal intent, and he was convicted in a regular law court and executed. The Areopagus' report was a slap in the face to Aeschines and underscored how much he was playing second fiddle to Demosthenes in public life.[16]

Antiphon's attempt to set fire to the dockyards may possibly have occurred in 346, 342, or even 341, but 343 is the most likely year.[17] Antiphon and Proxenus were the first men to be tried under the *apophasis* procedure, which was not introduced until 343. Moreover, the silence of Hegesippus in his *On Halonnesus* and especially that of Demosthenes in his *On the False Embassy* speech (of 343) on the affair is significant, as both orators intended to portray Philip's aims and actions in the worst light possible. Assuming the story has credibility, Philip may well have decided to try to neutralize the Athenian navy because of the rebuffs he had suffered at Athenian hands and because he had set in motion plans to conquer Thrace. His intervention there was likely to antagonize the Athenians, therefore stripping them of their navy was to his advantage. His action may have been prompted by his failure to detach the Athenians from their allies the previous year, when he had wanted to change the Peace of Philocrates to a common peace. Thus the stage was set for the final showdown between Athens and Philip.

GATHERING WAR CLOUDS

In the middle of 342, Philip prepared to bring the troublesome Cersebleptes to heel once and for all. Before he departed for Thrace he arranged for Aristotle, the foremost philosopher and intellectual of the

---

[15] R. W. Wallace, *The Areopagos Council, to 307 B.C.* (Baltimore: 1989), pp. 113–115.

[16] J. Buckler, "Demosthenes and Aeschines," in Ian Worthington (ed.), *Demosthenes: Statesman and Orator* (London: 2000), pp. 140–143.

[17] 346: J. R. Ellis, *Philip II and Macedonian Imperialism* (London: 1976), p. 128, Carlier, *Démosthène*, pp. 180–181; 342 or 341: E. M. Harris, *Aeschines and Athenian Politics* (Oxford: 1995) pp. 169–170; cf. MacDowell, *Demosthenes*, p. 359.

day, to tutor his fourteen-year-old son and heir Alexander.[18] For three years Aristotle taught Alexander a number of subjects, including philosophy, rhetoric, geography, zoology, medicine, and geometry at Mieza, part of the Gardens of Midas on the slopes of Mount Bermion. The distinguished philosopher gave him his personal copy of Homer's *Iliad*, which Alexander took with him to Asia, famously keeping it next to a dagger under his pillow when he went to bed.[19]

Philip's official reason for invading Thrace was to protect several cities on the Hellespont that Cersebleptes had attacked. According to Demosthenes, the campaign lasted only eleven months until Philip defeated Cersebleptes and Teres and absorbed Thrace into his rapidly growing empire.[20] The details of Philip's actions are practically unknown because of the brevity of the ancient sources:[21]

> Philip conceived a plan to win over the Greek cities in Thrace to his side, and marched into that region. Cersobleptes (*sic*), who was king of the Thracians, had been following a policy of reducing the Hellespontine cities bordering on his territory and of ravaging their territories. With the aim of putting a stop to the barbarian attacks Philip moved against them with a large force. He overcame the Thracians in several battles and imposed on the conquered barbarians the payment of a tithe to the Macedonians, and by founding strong cities at key places made it impossible for the Thracians to commit any outrages in the future. So the Greek cities were freed from this fear and gladly joined Philip's alliance.

To ensure the passivity of Thrace, Philip installed garrisons and colonists in a number of towns including his own foundations Beroia (Stara Zagora) and Philippopolis (Plovdiv), imposed a tithe tax on the country,[22] and created the administrative position of general (*strategos*) of

[18] Plutarch, *Alexander* 7.2–5; cf. 8.1–2; cf. Worthington, *Philip II*, pp. 120–121. Alexander's boyhood (including education): Ian Worthington, *Alexander the Great, Man and God*, rev. ed. (London: 2004), pp. 30–43.

[19] Plutarch, *Alexander* 8.2.

[20] Demosthenes 8.2, 35, 18.69. Philip and Thrace: E. Badian, "Philip II and Thrace," *Pulpudeva* 4 (1983), pp. 51–71.

[21] Diodorus 16.71.1–2; cf. Demosthenes 12.8–10, with Worthington, *Philip II*, pp. 122–125; the following quotation is from Diodorus 16.71.1–2.

[22] Diodorus 16.71.2.

Thrace.[23] After subjugating Thrace, Philip led his army into the territory of the seminomadic Getae, who lived between Thrace and the Danube basin by the Shipka Pass. He concluded an alliance with their king Cothelas, which included his sixth marriage to his daughter Meda.[24] The Macedonian kingdom was now more than double its size at his accession in 359, extending as far north as the Istrus (Danube) river. The only independent Greek cities to Philip's east now were Perinthus (Marmara Ereğlisi), Selymbria (Silivri), and Byzantium on the Hellespont.

The Athenians were extremely alarmed by Philip's acquisition of Thrace and the fact that his sphere of influence now reached almost to the Hellespont. To retain their presence in that vital area they had recently settled in it more cleruchs, who were protected by the general and politician Diopeithes of Sunium, a friend of Hegesippus.[25] In an effort to distract the Athenians' attention, Philip now intervened in Euboea. In the previous year, Callias, the tyrant of Chalcis, had tried to create a Euboean League under his leadership, but had failed to solicit Philip's support. In the middle of his Thracian campaign the king had a sudden change of heart and ordered his general Hipponicus and a thousand mercenaries to Euboea.[26] Their mission was to assist a rebel force that had overthrown Plutarchus at Eretria and seized neighboring Porthmus. Parmenion and Eurylochus quickly took more troops to Hipponicus, who set up pro-Macedonian tyrants in Eretria, Porthmus, and Oreus, in the process expelling anti-Macedonian groups from these cities. No move was made against Athens' ally Carystus in the south of the island.

Fearing a threat to their coastline, not least because Oreus was on the Euripus straits that narrowly separated the island from Attica, the Athenians may have considered withdrawing Diopeithes from the Chersonese to undo the Macedonian presence on Euboea, as Philip

---

[23] This office is mentioned at Diodorus 17.62.5; cf. Arrian 1.25.2 (implying an already existing office).

[24] Campaign: Worthington, *Philip II*, p. 124; marriage: Athenaeus 13.557d; Meda: E. Carney, *Women and Monarchy in Macedonia* (Norman: 2000), pp. 67–68.

[25] Philochorus, *FGrH* 328 F 158. He had been a syntrierarch and had proposed a naval law in (or shortly before) 323/2: J. K. Davies, *Athenian Propertied Families* (Oxford: 1971), 169

[26] Demosthenes 9.33, 58. On Philip and Euboea, see G. L. Cawkwell, "Demosthenes' Policy after the Peace of Philocrates II," *CQ²* 13 (1963), pp. 202–203, 210–213.

intended. Then Cardia appealed to him for assistance against Diopeithes.[27] The Athenians had given Diopeithes minimal money, forcing
him to forage in Cardian territory and seize merchant ships bound for
Macedonia and various maritime towns for their loot.[28] His piratical
activities broke the terms of the Peace of Philocrates, but they were
not unusual because the Athenians routinely sent out commanders
with insufficient funds, expecting them to acquire what they needed
when on campaign.[29]

Diopeithes, however, had gone too far when he attacked the towns
of Krobyle and Tiristasis, Philip's allies, and took the people hostage. To
secure their release, Philip sent Amphilochus to treat with the Athenian
commander, but he was tortured and held for a ransom of nine talents.
At that point the Cardians approached Philip directly. The king decided
to operate first through diplomatic channels, as was his custom, and in
the spring of 341 he sent a letter to Athens demanding Diopeithes' re-
moval and ominously warned the people that he would protect the
Cardians if the Athenians continued to condone Diopeithes' actions.[30]

The Athenians held an Assembly, at which Demosthenes delivered
his speech *On the Chersonese*.[31] Some of the speakers, Aeschines included, wanted to recall Diopeithes, put him on trial, and replace him
by another general. Demosthenes countered their viewpoint by switching the focus from Diopeithes to Philip's actions against Athens.[32] Far
from bringing the aggressive Diopeithes home, he argued, the people
should send him reinforcements.[33] He stressed that in light of Philip's
past untrustworthy actions the people needed to realize that he had
violated the peace and that after subduing the entire Chersonese he
could destroy Athens.[34] His allegation was without foundation; far from

---

[27] Demosthenes 5.25, 12.11, 19.174.

[28] Demosthenes 8.9, 24–26.

[29] Demosthenes 8.24–26 says this was a normal thing for Athenian commanders to do.
Eubulus in the 350s had decreased the amount of money paid into the Military
Fund, which may account for this practice.

[30] Demosthenes 8.16–17.

[31] Date: Dionysius of Halicarnassus, *To Ammaeus* 1.10, with R. Sealey, "Dionysius of
Halicarnassus and Some Demosthenic Dates," *REG* 68 (1955), pp. 101–110.

[32] Demosthenes 8.14–17.

[33] Demosthenes 8.1–20.

[34] Demosthenes 8.2, 6–8, 9, 16, 31, 39–47, 58, 60. See also J. W. Leopold, "Demosthenes on Distrust of Tyrants," *GRBS* 22 (1981), pp. 227–246.

breaking the peace, Philip's interventions in Greece had been relatively minor and were greatly exaggerated by Demosthenes to create maximum fear of him.[35] Demosthenes defended criticism of his own conduct and rebuked both pacifist politicians and those bribed by Philip, nicknaming them "Philippizers,"[36] and added a dramatic intensity to his speech by putting live dialogue into the mouths of other Greeks to goad the people to action.[37] All Demosthenes had to say about Diopeithes was that he should release the captured merchant ships and return to Athens only if he had committed anything illegal.[38]

On the Chersonese[39]

Demosthenes reprimanded the people from the outset for allowing the accusations leveled against Diopeithes to distract their attention from the pressing issue of Philip (2–3):

> The trouble we face relates to events in the Chersonese and the campaign that Philip has been conducting for more than ten months in Thrace, but most of the speeches that have been made deal with what Diopeithes is doing and is going to do. Yet I think that you already have the power to investigate whatever accusations have been directed against any of these men [Diopeithes and the Athenian cleruchs]— whom you can punish according to the laws whenever you want, either now if you wish or later—and there is absolutely no need for me or anyone else to speak at length about them. But all the places that an

---

[35] Cawkwell, "Demosthenes' Policy after the Peace of Philocrates II," pp. 200–205.

[36] Demosthenes 8.10, 61, 64–67, 69–73.

[37] Demosthenes 8.35–37. On this feature of Demosthenes' style, see L. Pearson, *The Art of Demosthenes* (Meisenheim am Glan: 1976), pp. 148–149, S. Usher, *Greek Oratory: Tradition and Originality* (Oxford 1999), pp. 237–239.

[38] Demosthenes 8.9, 24–29.

[39] On the speech, see Schaefer, *Demosthenes*[2] 2, pp. 455–468, Blass, *attische Beredsamkeit*[2] 3.1, pp. 324–330, Pickard-Cambridge, *Demosthenes*, pp. 332–337, Pearson, *Art of Demosthenes*, pp. 145–150, Carlier, *Démosthène*, pp. 195–196, Usher, *Greek Oratory: Tradition and Originality*, pp. 237–239, Lehmann, *Demosthenes*, pp. 158–161, MacDowell, *Demosthenes*, pp. 346–349. Translation with notes: Trevett, *Demosthenes, Speeches 1–17*, pp. 129–151; text and commentary: J. E. Sandys, *Demosthenes, On the Peace, Second Philippic, On the Chersonesus and Third Philippic* (Cambridge: 1900). The text is probably a revised version of the speech: see MacDowell, *Demosthenes*, pp. 354–355, or may have been only partially used: see note 47 below.

established enemy of our city, who is in the Hellespontine region accompanied by a large military force, is trying to seize before we can
stop him, and which, if we are too late, we will no longer be able to
save—about these I think that it is profitable for us to deliberate and to
make our preparations as soon as possible and not to run away from
them as a result of these irrelevant and rancorous accusations.

A bitter tirade against Philip's actions and those who wanted to recall
Diopeithes followed (4–20), Demosthenes observing (10):

Yet if they are really offering this advice in good faith, I think that just
as they are seeking to disband our city's existing force by slandering the
man who commands it and provides money for it, they should likewise
show how Philip's power will be broken if you follow their advice. Otherwise, observe how they are simply directing the city toward the same
behavior that caused the present disaster.

He warned the people that if they recalled Diopeithes they would have
to dispatch more troops to the Chersonese, which would be costly. To
reinforce his argument, he resorted to a rhetorical dialogue with an
imaginary opponent (17):

If the army that has already been formed remains in existence, it will be
able both to assist [the Chersonese] and to damage some of [Philip's]
interests. But if it is ever disbanded, what will we do if he ever attacks
the Chersonese? "We will put Diopeithes on trial, by Zeus." And how
will that help? "We can provide a relief force ourselves from here."
What if we are prevented by the winds? "By Zeus, he will not attack."
But who will guarantee this?

He rehearsed how quickly and decisively Philip moved, and how de-
ceitfully he acted, calling attention to Philip's campaign in Thrace
when they were swearing their oaths to the Peace of Philocrates in 346.
Philip was now poised to attack Byzantium. In Demosthenes' opinion
Athens would be next. Therefore it was better to fight Philip in the
north than face him in Attica (18). In any case, Demosthenes claimed,
Diopeithes' extortionate activities were due to financial necessity, and
for that should be excused; if he had overstepped the mark, then he
could be tried later (21–29).

Demosthenes widened the context of his speech from a growing
dispute between Athens and Philip in the Chersonese to his intent
to defeat the Athenians and dismantle their democracy (39–43), and
finally to his conquest of all Greece (39–51). In a forceful statement,

Demosthenes presented Philip as the enemy of democracy and the Athenians as having the only constitution able to resist him (39–41):

> First, men of Athens, you must fully acknowledge that Philip is at war with our city and has broken the peace—and please stop accusing each other about this—and is malignantly hostile to the entire city down to its very foundation, and, I should add, to all its inhabitants, including those who most think that they are doing him a favor . . . But it is against our constitution that he is most at war, and toward its overthrow that his plots and policies are above all directed. And in a sense it is reasonable for him to do so. For he is well aware that even if he gets control of everyone else, he will be unable to possess anything securely, so long as you are a democracy; and if ever some slip occurs—and there are many slips that may befall a man—all those places that he has now forced into union will come and seek refuge with you.

Demosthenes then berated his pacifist opponents, who were bribed to preserve the peace (68–72). They hid the danger that Philip presented to the city, and their advice was only a means to an end: to gain popularity. Political criticism was blended with moral considerations here—their venality made them the worst type of politician, in contrast to Demosthenes, who suffered unpopularity to put forward policies in the city's best interests (72):

> Nor do I think that I would be acting as a good citizen if I were to devise policies that will make me the first among you, but you the last among all people. Rather the city must prosper through the policies proposed by its good citizens, and everyone must always advocate what is best, not what is easiest. Nature will move toward the latter of its own accord; toward the former, the good citizen must lead the way, teaching through his words.

After reiterating his call for more money to finance Diopeithes' operations, to send out embassies "in every direction," and to punish those who took bribes (76), Demosthenes concluded (77):

> If you handle matters in this way and stop belittling everything, perhaps, perhaps even now our situation may yet improve. But if you remain in your seats, serious only about heckling or cheering, but shrinking back if anything needs to be done, I do not see how any speech will be able to save the city, if you refuse to do your duty.

Hegesippus echoed Demosthenes in the debate, even telling the people that Philip was guilty not only of acting against Athens but also of illegally campaigning outside Thrace, and that Athens was his next target.[40] The rhetoric of Demosthenes and Hegesippus was successful, and the people voted against recalling Diopeithes.

In May, after Philip had involved himself in Euboea and was preparing to march to the assistance of Cardia (see below), another Assembly was held, at which Demosthenes delivered his third and most aggressive *Philippic*.[41] In similar vein to *On the Chersonese*, Demosthenes addressed the rapidly deteriorating situation in the Hellespont and the fact that Philip had deployed mercenary troops to Cardia.[42] He also called attention to an assault on Byzantium and events in Euboea.[43] The speech's content has the familiar themes of the rise of Macedonian imperialism and the threats Philip's actions presented to Athens.[44] Demosthenes wanted the people to go to war and furnish Diopeithes with even more money and supplies.[45] However, his speech took on a Panhellenic tone, setting it apart from previous ones, when in an effort to win the support of other Greek states against Philip he warned of his intervention in them and how he would treat them.[46]

Some of the criticisms of Philip and Demosthenes' political opponents are found in his fourth *Philippic* delivered later in the same year (see below).[47] Further, two versions of the third *Philippic* exist in the manuscripts of Demosthenes, one shorter than the other. The longer one is regarded as the oration Demosthenes gave in the Assembly. Afterward, he may have shortened it, keeping the salient arguments,

[40] Demosthenes 8.8–9, 14, 28, 43, 9.15.
[41] Dated to 342/1: Dionysius of Halicarnassus, *To Ammaeus* 1.10, with Sealey, "Dionysius of Halicarnassus and Some Demosthenic Dates," pp. 101–110.
[42] Demosthenes 9.16, 27.
[43] Demosthenes 9.19–20, 34, 57–68.
[44] Demosthenes 9.10–14, 21, 26–27, 30–35, 56–68.
[45] Demosthenes 9.71, 73.
[46] Demosthenes 9.22–25, 28, 36–45, 71–74.
[47] Demosthenes 8.38–51 and 52–67 = Demosthenes 10.11–27 and 55–70. Possibly Demosthenes delivered only part of *On the Chersonese* and used the arguments and polemics against his opponents for the fourth *Philippic*: C. D. Adams, "Speeches viii and x of the Demosthenic Corpus," *CP* 33 (1938), pp. 129–144 and S. G. Daitz, "The Relationship of the *De Chersoneso* and the *Philippica quarta* of Demosthenes," *CP* 52 (1957), pp. 145–162, I. Hajdú, *Kommentar zur 4. Philippischen Rede des Demosthenes* (Berlin: 2002), pp. 451–471.

and circulated it as a pamphlet among the Greeks.[48] Alternatively, he may have decided to erase certain passages in it, confusing the person who collected his speeches after his death.[49]

The Third *Philippic*[50]

Demosthenes opened the speech by strongly condemning the people for not taking action against Philip. They, he said scornfully, were just as much to blame as venal leaders for the dire situation in which they now found themselves (1–2):

> I fear it is ill-omened to say, but it is true—if all the regular speakers wished to speak, and you wished to vote, in such a way as to make your situation as bad as possible, I do not think that things could be any worse than they are now. There are no doubt many reasons for this, and matters did not reach their present state from one or two causes only. But most of all, if you examine the matter closely, you will find that it is due not to those men who choose to curry favor rather than to give the best advice— some of whom, men of Athens, cherish the things that give them a good reputation and power, and take no thought for the future, and do not think that you need to do either; others blame and slander those who participate in public life and do nothing other than cause the city to be preoccupied with punishing itself, whereas Philip is able to speak and act as he wishes.

Similar themes to *On the Chersonese* are evident in his speech. Philip was already at war with the Athenians (6–9) and had proved his deceit before, as at Olynthus and Pherae (10–14). Philip's treacherous exploits established that the threat he posed extended beyond the Chersonese

---

[48] P. Treves, "La composition de la Troisième Philippique," *REA* 42 (1940), pp. 354–364, C. Wooten, *A Commentary on Demosthenes' Philippic 1* (Oxford: 2008), 167–173.

[49] MacDowell, *Demosthenes*, p. 353.

[50] On the speech, see Schaefer, *Demosthenes²* 2, pp. 468–479, Blass, *attische Beredsamkeit²* 3.1, pp. 330–337, Pickard-Cambridge, *Demosthenes*, pp. 337–341, Jaeger, *Demosthenes*, pp. 170–175, Pearson, *Art of Demosthenes*, pp. 150–155, Carlier, *Démosthène*, pp. 197–199, Usher, *Greek Oratory: Tradition and Originality*, pp. 239–241, Lehmann, *Demosthenes*, pp. 161–164, MacDowell, *Demosthenes*, pp. 349–354. Translation with notes: Trevett, *Demosthenes, Speeches 1–17*, pp. 152–176; text and commentary: Sandys, *Demosthenes, On the Peace, Second Philippic, On the Chersonesus and Third Philippic*. Analysis of its rhetorical style: Wooten, *Commentary on Demosthenes' Philippic I*, pp. 137–166 (pp. 167–173 on the longer and shorter versions). C. Wooten, *Cicero's Philippics and their Demosthenic Model* (Chapel Hill: 1983), discusses the style and content of all four *Philippics* extensively.

to the freedom of all Greece (15–20). Sensationally, Demosthenes claimed the Athenians had committed fewer misdeeds against the Greeks and their freedom in their history than Philip in a little over a decade since he had assumed the throne (25). He spoke incredulously of the period when Athens, Sparta, and Thebes dominated Greece, and how other Greeks rushed to the aid of any victimized city, unlike the present era, even though Philip was now the aggressor (21–31). For example (25, 29):

> Both we and the Spartans, although at first we had virtually no wrongs to complain of at each other's hands, nevertheless felt driven to go to war because of the injustice that we saw others suffering. And yet all the wrongs that were done by the Spartans in those thirty years, and by our ancestors in seventy, are fewer, men of Athens, that the wrongs that Philip has done to Greece in the fewer than thirteen years since he emerged from obscurity. Or rather, they are scarcely a fraction of them. . . . We overlook his growing power, and though each of us recognizes that Philip profits from the opportunities that others squander, or so it seems to me, none of us deliberates or acts to save Greece. Yet we all know that, like the periodic return of the sudden onset of a fever or some other evil, he visits even those who seem to have kept far away from him.

Worse still, Philip was not even a Greek but a "barbarian" (30–31):[51]

> You also know that all the wrongs the Greeks suffered at the hands of the Spartans or of ourselves were injustices committed by genuine Greeks, and one should treat this in the same way as if a legitimate son, after coming into a great fortune, manages it badly and unjustly: such a person deserves blame and censure for his actions, but it cannot be denied that despite his behavior, he is still a kinsman and heir. But if a slave or a changeling wasted and spoiled what did not belong to him, by Heracles, how much more terrible and deserving of anger would everyone have said this was. And yet they do not take this attitude toward Philip and his actions—he who is not only not Greek and in no way related to the Greeks, nor even a foreigner from a land to which it is honorable to say that one belongs, but a wretched Macedonian,

---

[51] Demosthenes called Philip a barbarian at 3.16. The slur is a racial one, as the Greeks seemed to have believed the Macedonians were not Greeks; on ethnicity, see Chapter 3 pp. 46–47.

from a land from which in the past you could not even have bought a decent slave.

More details about Philip's actions and strengths follow, as Demosthenes encouraged the Athenians to resist him (32–52). Demosthenes' arguments allowed him to spotlight politicians whom Philip had bribed to maintain the peace, but who were merely self-serving and should be punished. He reminded his audience of a certain Arthmius of Zelea (in the Troad), who in the earlier fifth century (the exact date is unknown) took Persian gold to Peloponnesian states to incite them to wage war on Athens. The Athenians at the time declared him and his family *atimos*, and if anyone saw him in Attica he could kill him with impunity (41–45).[52] People now, argued Demosthenes, needed to heed their ancestors' attitudes to corruption and "detest those who speak to you on [Philip's] behalf, keeping in mind that it is not possible to defeat our city's enemies until you punish those in the city itself who are their servants" (53). Demosthenes delivered a lengthy, vitriolic attack against this type of leader in Athens and in other betrayed cities like Olynthus or Eretria on Euboea (54–70). It was time, he stressed, to seek other states' help in resisting Philip (71):

> After making all these preparations in person and in the open, let us then call upon the others, and send out ambassadors to instruct people in every direction—to the Peloponnese, to Rhodes, to Chios, and to the King, since it is in his interests not to allow this man [Philip] to overturn everything[53]—so that if you succeed in persuading them you will have people to share both the risks and the costs, if you need anything; and even if you do not succeed, you may at any rate delay his plans.

With a final appeal for the people to adopt his recommendations and for anyone who "has anything better to say, let him speak and offer his advice. But whatever you decide—all you gods!—may it be to our advantage," Demosthenes ended his speech (76).

---

[52] See also Demosthenes 19.271–272, Aeschines 3.258, Dinarchus 2.24–25, with R. Meiggs, *The Athenian Empire* (Oxford: 1979), pp. 508–512; cf. Ian Worthington, *A Historical Commentary on Dinarchus* (Ann Arbor: 1982), ad loc. Plutarch, *Themistocles* 6.4, says that Themistocles proposed the decree against Arthmius in 480, but a date after 478/7 (when the Athenians founded their Delian League) is more suitable: Meiggs, *Athenian Empire*, pp. 510–511.

[53] The names and places are in the longer version of the speech.

The third *Philippic* won approval, and the Athenians sent Chares with reinforcements and money to Diopeithes as well as embassies to various cities and, significantly, to Persia.[54] Demosthenes himself went to Byzantium, later boasting he had secured its friendship,[55] and also negotiated alliances with Abydos, one of Athens' enemies, and perhaps even with some of the Thracian princes.[56] Hyperides was likewise successful at Chios, Cos, and Rhodes,[57] the former ringleaders of the Social War (356–355)—evidently the threat from Philip called for bygones to be bygones.

The embassy to Persia, led by Ephialtes, was unsuccessful,[58] perhaps because Artaxerxes remembered the Athenian rejection of his petition in 344. However, later writers stated that he gave Ephialtes money to use against Philip, some of which found its way into the pockets of Demosthenes and Hyperides.[59] Artaxerxes also arrested Philip's ally Hermias of Atarneus (in Anatolia) and tortured him for information about a possible invasion of Asia.[60] Hermias could tell him nothing about Philip's plans, for he knew nothing, so he was crucified.[61] Evidently the Persian king was concerned that Philip intended to cross the Hellespont to attack him.

Probably not long after the embassies returned to Athens Demosthenes came out with his fourth and final *Philippic*.[62] Again concerned with the volatile situation in the north, Demosthenes called for embassies to be sent to all Greeks.[63] He employed the same rhetoric from

---

[54] For example, Demosthenes 10.32.

[55] Demosthenes 18.94, 244, 302; cf. Aeschines 3.256.

[56] Demosthenes 18.244, 302.

[57] Diodorus 16.77.2; cf. Demosthenes 9.71, [Plutarch], *Moralia* 847f–850a.

[58] Philochorus, *FGrH* 328 F 157, Aeschines 3.238, Diodorus 16.40.3–53.8.

[59] Dinarchus 1.33, [Plutarch], *Moralia* 847f, 848e.

[60] Demosthenes 10.32, Diodorus 16.52.5–8, Worthington, *Philip II*, p. 127.

[61] Callisthenes, *FGrH* 124 F 2. P. E. Harding, *Didymos, On Demosthenes* (Oxford: 2006), pp. 134–135.

[62] Date: Dionysius of Halicarnassus, *To Ammaeus* 1.10 assigns it to 341/0, but 342/1 is to be preferred: Sealey, "Dionysius of Halicarnassus and Some Demosthenic Dates," pp. 101–110, G. L. Cawkwell, "Demosthenes' Policy after the Peace of Philocrates I," *CQ²* 13 (1963), pp. 134–136, MacDowell, *Demosthenes*, p. 354. Hajdú, *Kommentar zur 4. Philippischen Rede des Demosthenes*, p. 40, believes it was delivered a year earlier in 342.

[63] Demosthenes 10.15–17.

his earlier speeches against Philip as well as against pacifist politicians and those whom Philip had bribed.[64] However, there were two distinguishing features of the fourth *Philippic* that set it apart from his previous speeches. First, in a clear break from his first and third *Olynthiacs*, Demosthenes dissuaded the people from using the Theoric Fund for military purposes. Instead, he wanted the fund to bridge disharmony between the poorer and richer strata of society.[65] Second, he wanted an actual alliance with Persia, which was markedly different from his anti-Persian attitude in *On the Symmories* and *For the Freedom of the Rhodians*.[66] Demosthenes may well have taken heart from the Great King's treatment of Hermias and felt that the Persians might still ally with Athens against Philip.

The authenticity of the fourth *Philippic* has been doubted. Among other things, two sections in it on the dangers of bad politicians occur almost verbatim in *On the Chersonese*.[67] Moreover, a sudden switch in the speech to the Theoric Fund is not only unrelated to its preceding invocation to resist Philip but also contradicted Demosthenes' previous criticisms of the fund.[68] For these reasons, the speech as we have it may perhaps be two different ones from two debates or a complete fabrication. Nevertheless, duplication of material is common in political oratory,[69] and if the people were divided on the issue of Philip's aims Demosthenes may have embraced a different way to unite them against the king. Therefore the common opinion that the speech is Demosthenic should be accepted.[70]

---

[64] Demosthenes 10.15–23, 54–58, 60, 66–74.

[65] Demosthenes 10.34–35. On rich and poor, see P. Hunt, *War, Peace, and Alliance in Demosthenes' Athens* (New York: 2010), pp. 39–48.

[66] Demosthenes 10.31–34.

[67] Chapters 11–27 and 55–70 repeat *On the Chersonese* 38–51 and 52–67: see further, Hajdú, *Kommentar zur 4. Philippischen Rede*, pp. 451–471.

[68] Cf. Demosthenes 3.10–11, 19, but see Hajdú, *Kommentar zur 4. Philippischen Rede*, pp. 279–280.

[69] Cf. on repetition of material J. Trevett, "Did Demosthenes Publish his Deliberative Speeches?," *Hermes* 124 (1996), pp. 438–439, Carlier, *Démosthène*, p. 200, MacDowell, *Demosthenes*, p. 355.

[70] MacDowell, *Demosthenes*, pp. 354–355; in more detail, Adams, "Speeches viii and x of the Demosthenic Corpus," pp. 129–144 and Daitz, "Relationship of the *De Chersoneso* and the *Philippica quarta* of Demosthenes," pp. 145–162, Hajdú, *Kommentar zur 4. Philippischen Rede*, pp. 451–471, Ian Worthington, "The Authenticity of Demosthenes' Fourth *Philippic*," *Mnemosyne* 44 (1991), pp. 425–428.

The Fourth *Philippic*[71]

The fourth *Philippic* continued the themes of *On the Chersonese* and the third *Philippic*. The Athenians needed to act against Philip before he threatened Byzantium and the Hellespont (1–20). Their response to him so far had been sluggish at best, as if they were on drugs—we "are like people who have drunk mandrake juice" (6). Demosthenes also recalled the good old days when Athens dominated Greece before Philip supplanted them with the other Greeks' acquiescence (46–54). Therefore they had to abandon speakers in the pay of Philip or blame themselves for the collapse of Athens (75–76). Given the repetition from previous speeches, quoting similar passages is superfluous, hence we focus on the fourth *Philippic*'s novel arguments.

In the central part of his speech Demosthenes encouraged the Athenians to turn to Persia for alliance (31–45). The Persian king was clearly concerned about Philip because he had given money to Ephialtes and tortured Hermias for information (see above).[72] In light of his actions, Demosthenes was adamant that another Athenian embassy would effect an alliance. To counter the people's previous hatred of Persia, Demosthenes resorted to scare tactic rhetoric (31–33):

> In the first place, the men whom the King trusts and considers his ben-
> efactors hate Philip and are at war with him. Second, the agent who is
> privy to all of Philip's preparations against the King has been arrested,
> and the King will hear everything that has been done not from accusa-
> tions laid by us—whom he would suppose to be speaking with a view to
> our own advantage—but from the agent and manager himself, so that

---

[71] On the speech, see Blass, *attische Beredsamkeit*[2] 3.1, pp. 337–346, Pearson, *Art of Dem-osthenes*, pp. 155–157, Carlier, *Démosthène*, pp. 199–201, Usher, *Greek Oratory: Tradition and Originality*, pp. 241–243, MacDowell, *Demosthenes*, pp. 354–359. Translation with notes: Trevett, *Demosthenes, Speeches 1–17*, pp. 177–200; detailed introduction and commentary: Hajdú, *Kommentar zur 4. Philippischen Rede*. C. Wooten, *Cicero's Philippics and their Demosthenic Model* (Chapel Hill: 1983), discusses the style and content of all four *Philippics* extensively.

[72] Although Demosthenes did not name Hermias in the speech, he could be the man referred to who was seized and interrogated by the king at 10.32. See also R. D. Milns, "Hermias of Atarneus and the Fourth Philippic Speech," *Filologia e forme letterarie: studi offerti a Francesco della Corte* 1 (Urbino: 1987), pp. 287–302. On Hermias, see also P. Green, "Politics, Philosophy, and Propaganda: Hermias of Atarneus and His Friendship with Aristotle," in W. Heckel and L. A. Tritle (eds.), *Crossroads of History: The Age of Alexander the Great* (Claremont: 2003), pp. 29–46.

he will believe them, and our ambassadors will only have to make a speech that the King will be delighted to hear. They should say to him that we ought to join in punishing the man who is harming both of us, and that Philip will be much more frightening to the King if he attacks us first, since if we are abandoned and defeated Philip will move against him with impunity. I think that you should send an embassy to hold discussions with the King about these matters and should abandon that famous slogan, which has often proved damaging to you, "the foreigner, and common enemy of all," and the like.

Next, Demosthenes abandoned his previous stance of diverting theoric money to meet military costs but cast the Theoric Fund as a means to unite society (35–45).[73] It appeared that wealthy citizens resented the extent to which they contributed to public costs while the poor paid nothing but reaped all the benefits. The poorer citizens were also discontented because wealthier and more powerful individuals seemed to make important decisions behind closed doors despite the public forum of the Assembly. Demosthenes considered that the social problems had distracted the people from Philip so he attempted a rapprochement. He argued that rich and poor had an equally important role in the state and needed to cease bickering. Just as there was a law that required sons to look after their parents in old age or suffer prosecution, so the rich had a duty to support the poor (40–42):

Even in private homes I do not see any man in the prime of life who is so ill disposed toward his elders, or so senseless or idiotic, as to refuse to lift a finger because they do not do as much as he does. Indeed, such conduct would make him liable for prosecution under the laws of ill treatment. For in my opinion it is only proper that we take on and willingly discharge for our parents a debt of gratitude, which is doubly required, both by nature and by law. Just as each one of us has a parent, so we should think of all the citizens as the collective parents of the whole city. Far from depriving them of whatever the city gives them, we should consider, if they receive nothing, what other sources we can use to ensure that they have whatever they need. I think that if the

---

[73] On his volte-face, see E. M. Harris, "Demosthenes and the Theoric Fund," in W. R. Wallace and E. M. Harris (eds.), *Transitions to Empire: Essays in Honor of E. Badian* (Norman: 1996), pp. 70–74, who argues that Demosthenes' remarks about the fund in his *Oynthiac* speeches have been misinterpreted, hence there is no inconsistency with what Demosthenes says about it in the fourth *Philippic*.

wealthy take this view, they will be doing what is just and what is to their advantage, since to deprive anyone of the necessities of life will produce in people a common sense of discontent. At the same time, I would advise the needy to get rid of the thing that causes the rich distress and about which they might rightly complain.

One final note is the repetition of the familiar tirade against bad politicians except that Demosthenes singled out a speaker by name: Aristomedes (70–74).[74] Identifying an opponent in a political speech was a breach of social protocol. A speaker normally uttered a vague phrase such as "so and so" or "a certain speaker" when talking of an opponent although the people would know who he meant.[75] Aristomedes, not "a person of note in the city" (71), must have been an especially reprehensible individual to be actually named.

The comment that Demosthenes' "speeches of the 340s raised paranoia to an art form" is not entirely off the mark.[76] However, it is going too far to accept the view that "Demosthenes' hardest task is to make the people see clearly they are no longer called upon to make a final decision of intolerable gravity, but that war is already in full swing."[77] War had not yet broken out, and Demosthenes was wrong to say that Philip was attacking Byzantium.[78] That would come soon enough, however.

THE PEACE OF PHILOCRATES SHATTERED

In the summer of 341 Philip marched to Cardia.[79] The Athenians also expected him to attack Perinthus, Selymbria, and Byzantium, but they did not did not immediately deploy troops to the north to resist him

---

[74] See Hajdú, *Kommentar zur 4. Philippischen Rede des Demosthenes*, pp. 426–428, Harding, *Didymos, On Demosthenes*, pp. 202–204.

[75] In Greek, the phrase is *ho deina*. For example, Demosthenes, *Prooimion* 34.1: "It is clear, gentlemen of Athens, that when you recently thought that you did not need to listen to those who wanted to speak against what so-and-so said"; cf. *Prooimion* 45.1. See further, Ian Worthington, "Oral Performance in the Athenian Assembly and the Demosthenic *Prooemia*," in C. M. Mackie (ed.), *Oral Performance and Its Context* (Leiden: 2004), p. 142.

[76] Harris, *Aeschines and Athenian Politics*, p. 110.

[77] Jaeger, *Demosthenes*, p. 170.

[78] Demosthenes 9.32; cf. 19–20 and 10.68.

[79] Demosthenes 8.58, 64, 12.3, 11.

because of a sudden change in their fortunes on Euboea. Either shortly before Philip left for Cardia or even while he was en route, Callias of Chalcis appealed for Athenian assistance to expel the pro-Macedonian tyrant rulers from his city.

The importance of the island turned Callias' offer into a godsend and Demosthenes successfully (and correctly) persuaded the Athenians to side with him.[80] According to Aeschines, Demosthenes' decree was longer than the *Iliad* and Callias bribed him to bring it before the people, but there is no evidence for his allegation.[81] Under the command of Cephisophon and Phocion, Athenian troops attacked Oreus and Eretria and expelled their Macedonian-backed tyrants. As another blow to Philip, Callias attacked Philip's allies on the Gulf of Pagasae and seized merchant ships sailing to Macedonia, selling their crews as slaves. He also sent embassies to various Peloponnesian cities to solicit help against Philip.[82] His actions earned him Athenian citizenship but the Euboean League he constituted did not formally ally itself with Athens.

Demosthenes, who for a decade had "allowed no act of Philip's to pass uncriticized, and seized upon every occasion to incite and inflame the Athenians against him,"[83] was now the most influential politician in Athens.[84] He may also have been the instigator of various hostile actions at this time.[85] For example, in 341, the Athenians captured a Macedonian herald named Nicias. They read out dispatches he had been carrying in the Assembly and imprisoned him for ten months. They also permitted Byzantine pirate ships to use Thasos as a base, which directly contravened the terms of the Peace of Philocrates. Certainly it was Demosthenes who authorized the arrest, torture, and execution of a man named Anaxinus from Oreus for spying in the city on Philip's behalf. Anaxinus had once entertained Demosthenes in Oreus,[86]

---

[80] For example, Demosthenes 8.36, with Cawkwell, "Demosthenes' Policy after the Peace of Philocrates II," pp. 202–203, 210–213.

[81] Aeschines 3.100.

[82] Diodorus 16.74.1.

[83] Plutarch, *Demosthenes* 16.1.

[84] Although note the comments of Cawkwell, "Demosthenes' Policy after the Peace of Philocrates II," pp. 206–209, who downplays the extent of Demosthenes' influence.

[85] Demosthenes 12.2.

[86] Perhaps during the delay of the Second Embassy at Oreus: Demosthenes 18.82, 137, Aeschines 3.224.

but that previous hospitality mattered little, as did Aeschines' plea that he was in the city shopping for Olympias (Philip's fourth wife). For his services to the people, in the early spring of 340 Demosthenes was crowned in the Theater of Dionysus during the Dionysia (the festival in honor of Dionysus) with a wreath of gold.[87] This was a defining moment in his career.

Events in the Chersonese now took a dramatic turn when Diopeithes died unexpectedly. Chares replaced him as sole commander and the Athenians scrambled to send embassies to Greek cities against Philip.[88] Demosthenes and Callias of Chalcis appeared before the Assembly and exaggeratedly informed the people that the entire Peloponnese, Acarnania, Achaea, Megara, and Euboea were ready to join them in a war against Macedonia. Achaea and Megara would apparently provide 60 talents and the Euboean League 40 talents toward costs.[89]

War between Athens and Philip was now inevitable. Before its formal outbreak in 340, however, Demosthenes delivered his last surviving political speech, *To Philip's Letter*, which responded to a recent letter from the king.[90] In his letter, Philip admonished the Athenians for their actions over the past two to three years, including their verbal quibbling over Halonnesus, interventions in Thrace, embassies to Greek cities and Persia, and the attempts of "speakers" to go to war for their own agendas and even claim that Amphipolis still belonged to Athens.[91] The letter is important because a passage in it may be Philip's declaration of war,[92] which Demosthenes misinterpreted (see below).

The authenticity of Demosthenes' speech and Philip's letter has been questioned, but there are good arguments for accepting both are

---

[87] Demosthenes 18.223–224.

[88] Worthington, *Philip II*, pp. 128–129.

[89] Demosthenes 18.87–92, 240–243, Diodorus 16.77.2–3.

[90] *To Philip's Letter* is numbered eleven in the Demosthenic corpus, but the letter from the king was added to the end of the speech, probably by an Alexandrian scholar, and simply called *Philip's Letter*. It is numbered twelve in the Demosthenic corpus although the letter preceded Demosthenes' speech. See further, Blass, *attische Beredsamkeit²* 3.1, pp. 348–352, Griffith in Hammond and Griffith, *History of Macedonia* 2, pp. 714–716, MacDowell, *Demosthenes*, pp. 363–366. Translation and notes: Trevett, *Demosthenes, Speeches 1–17*, pp. 211–223.

[91] [Demosthenes] 12.5–6, 8, 11, 16.

[92] [Demosthenes] 12.23.

genuine.[93] References in the speech to the siege of Perinthus and the possible fall of Byzantium indicate that it must have been dated to the summer or autumn of 340 after Philip invested Perinthus but before Byzantium (see below).[94] At the outset of his speech, Demosthenes acknowledged that to all intents and purposes Athens was already at war with Philip. He repeated that the king's power was not as formidable as it appeared,[95] that his allies distrusted him, the Persians had taken action against him, and Macedonia was seething with discontent against him.[96] He also returned to his trademark themes of the danger leaders who took bribes from Philip posed to the city and the need for the people to act rather than do nothing.[97]

To Philip's Letter[98]

Demosthenes began in similar fashion to his fourth *Philippic* by strongly asserting that Philip had been at war with Athens for some time (1):

> It is now clear to all of you, men of Athens, that Philip did not make peace with you but merely postponed war. For by handing Halus over to the Thessalians and administering the affairs of the Phocians and overturning all of Thrace, fabricating nonexistent reasons and discovering unjust excuses, he has in reality been waging war against our city for a long time, and now he acknowledges it in the letter he has sent.

He called upon the people to "set out for the war with your persons and money and ships" because they would receive support from other cities in Greece and Persia and even "the supreme gods, since he overlooked his pledges and transgressed his oaths to them when he unjustly broke the peace" (2–6). He returned to a theme of his second *Olynthiac* of 349, that Philip's empire was too large and his people disliked him so intensely that his strength was fast weakening (7–15).[99] For example (9–10):

[93] Dionysius of Halicarnassus, *To Ammaeus* 1.10, with Harding, *Didymos, On Demosthenes*, p. 217 and MacDowell, *Demosthenes*, pp. 361–366.

[94] Demosthenes 11.5.

[95] Compare Demosthenes 11.13–14 with Demosthenes 2.20–21.

[96] For example, Demosthenes 11.3–16.

[97] Demosthenes 11.18, 19–23.

[98] On the speech, see Blass, *attische Beredsamkeit*[2] 3.1, pp. 346–348, MacDowell, *Demosthenes*, pp. 360–363. Translation with notes: Trevett, *Demosthenes, Speeches 1–17*, pp. 201–210.

[99] See Chapter 6 pp. 136–137.

Moreover, his wars and expeditions, and all the things by which one might think him great, have made his kingdom less secure for him. For you should not suppose, men of Athens, that Philip and his subjects take pleasure in the same things. Instead, you should realize that he desires glory, whereas they want security, and that he cannot get glory without risk, whereas they have no wish to leave their children, parents, and wives at home and to be destroyed and to take daily risks on his account. From these considerations it can be seen how the majority of the Macedonians feel about Philip: you will find that both the Companions who accompany him and his mercenary commanders have a reputation for bravery but in fact live in greater fear than those who live in obscurity.

Calling on people to end their apathy, he cautioned them against orators who sold themselves to Philip (18):

He possesses hired men: both soldiers and also—by god!—some of your politicians, who think it right to take home gifts from him, and shamelessly live for Philip, and fail to realize that they are selling both their city and themselves for a small sum.

The people, he declared, must now actually act against Philip and in doing so live up to the example set by their ancestors who fought against Sparta in the Peloponnesian War (20–23). He ended his short speech with a command (23):

Not to speak at length, I say that we must prepare ourselves for war and must summon the Greeks to alliance with us, not by words but by deeds, since all words are pointless if they are not accompanied by action, and this applies most of all to us, since we seem more ready than the other Greeks to use them.

Exactly when war with Philip began or who declared it is controversial. One assumption is that the Athenians declared war after they received his letter, when he was besieging Perinthus and Byzantium (see below).[100] Demosthenes, however, claimed that war broke out later, after Philip seized the Athenian grain convoy.[101] Yet Philip might

---

[100] Demosthenes 18.73 and 139; so also do Dionysius of Halicarnassus, *To Ammaeus* 1.11 (who quotes Philochorus, *FGrH* 328 FF 53–55a) and Diodorus 16.77.2.

[101] Demosthenes 18.73; see also Didymus' commentary on Demosthenes, columns 10.23–11.5, who quoted Philochorus, *FGrH* 328 F 162; cf. Theopompus, *FGrH* 115 F 292.

have been the aggressor, which the Athenians failed to comprehend,[102] because of a passage in his letter to that appeared to indicate he declared war—"having made the gods witnesses, I shall deal with you about these matters."[103] Given the collision course on which Athens and Philip were heading, who declared war ultimately did not matter.

THE SECOND WAR BETWEEN PHILIP AND ATHENS

The second war was short and ended in 338 at the Battle of Chaeronea. In 340 Philip prepared to besiege Perinthus, Selymbria, and Byzantium, which would give him total control of the Hellespont.[104] Prior to his campaign, he directed his son Alexander, now sixteen, to leave Aristotle's tutelage at Mieza and return to Pella as regent of Macedonia. Then, with about 30,000 infantry and his small navy, Philip besieged Perinthus in probably the early summer.[105] He was met with fierce resistance. The city's natural setting on a steep hillside 160 feet high presented him with a difficult logistical problem. The large stones fired from Philip's catapults on top of his siege towers caused considerable damage to the city walls, but its houses were built on terraces that ran up the hillside. Whenever the catapults breached a terrace and the men moved forward to attack, the Perinthians scrambled up to the next terrace, piling rubble behind them as makeshift defenses and to block pathways to thwart the attackers. Moreover, Byzantium and Persia sent supplies and military help to the Perinthians, the Athenian fleet stationed at nearby Elaious kept the Macedonian navy at bay, and Persian troops raided Thrace to distract Philip from the siege.[106]

Philip decided to cut his losses at Perinthus. In August or early September he took half of his infantry and marched the fourteen miles to Selymbria. Whether he besieged Selymbria is unknown, but he soon

---

[102] See G. L. Cawkwell, *Philip of Macedon* (London: 1978), p. 137, and in more detail Buckler, "Philip II's Designs on Greece," pp. 87–89.

[103] [Demosthenes] 12.23. Translation: Buckler, "Philip II's Designs on Greece," p. 88. I believed this was the case at *Philip II*, p. 129, but now I agree with the common opinion that the Athenians declared war.

[104] Theopompus, *FGrH* 115 F 217.

[105] Diodorus 16.74.2–76.4, Justin 9.1.1–7, with Worthington, *Philip II*, pp. 131–132.

[106] Diodorus 16.75.1–2, Arrian 2.14.5, Polybius 1.29.10; cf. Demosthenes 11.5.

left there to invest Byzantium, thirty miles away.[107] Philip's siege of Byzantium was even more difficult than that of Perinthus because of its tall and massively thick defensive walls,[108] and he had with him an inadequate number of men. His new torsion catapults, developed by his engineering corps, were used for the first time at Byzantium,[109] but despite their power they could not breach the walls. One night the Macedonians launched a frontal assault, but barking dogs gave away their position and the defenders were able to stave off the attack. Adding to Philip's duress was that Byzantium received money, manpower, and military supplies from Chios, Cos, Rhodes, and Persia.

Until now, Philip's battle and siege tactics had been meticulously planned and successfully executed. It is therefore unusual that he besieged Perinthus and Byzantium with so few men—and even more surprising that after failing at Perinthus he took only half his troops against the better-defended Byzantium. Philip, however, may never have intended to take Byzantium, but merely to provoke an Athenian military response. If so, his plan succeeded. Demosthenes persuaded the Athenians to smash the *stele* (stone) on which was recorded the Peace of Philocrates,[110] an action that was the "Athenian manner" to show they were at war.[111]

Cephisophon and Phocion immediately sailed north to reinforce Chares at Byzantium against Philip.[112] Demosthenes personally contributed a trireme to their expedition.[113] With both sides formally at war, Philip prepared to seize the huge Athenian grain fleet of 230 vessels, of which 180 were Athenian—the other 50 belonged to

[107] Diodorus 16.76.3–4, Justin 9.1.2–4; see also Worthington, *Philip II*, pp. 132–133.

[108] Cf. Pausanias 4.31.5 (third century AD).

[109] E. W. Marsden, "Macedonian Military Machinery and its Designers under Philip and Alexander," *Ancient Macedonia* 2 (Institute for Balkan Studies, Thessaloniki: 1977), pp. 211–223; see also P. T. Keyser, "The Use of Artillery by Philip II and Alexander the Great," *Anc. World* 15 (1994), pp. 27–49.

[110] Theopompus, *FGrH* 115 F 292, Philochorus, *FGrH* 328 F 55, Demosthenes 18.72, 87–94, 139, 240–243, Diodorus 16.77.2, Justin 9.1.5–8, with Ryder, "Demosthenes and Philip II," p. 79.

[111] Diodorus 16.77.2. "Athenian manner": Carlier, *Démosthène*, p. 204: "C'est la manière athénienne de commencer une guerre."

[112] Demosthenes 8.14, 18.80, 88–92, 244, Diodorus 16.77.2, Plutarch, *Phocion* 14.3–7.

[113] [Plutarch], *Moralia* 851a.

Byzantium, Rhodes, and Chios.[114] The fleet had assembled at Hieron, an island near the Asiatic coast close to the mouth of the Propontis or Sea of Marmara, where Chares and some of Phocion's ships were to escort it on its voyage to Athens. However, when Chares was called away to a meeting of the Persian satraps about supporting Perinthus and Byzantium, Demetrius, the Macedonian commander, captured all the grain vessels as "prizes of war."[115] Philip and his army quickly rounded up the ships' crews, who were ashore at Hieron. He destroyed the 180 Athenian ships, used their timber for his siege engines, and sold the grain for the enormous sum of 700 talents—more than a year's income for the Athenian state.[116]

When he heard of the fate of the Athenian grain fleet Chares immediately returned from his meeting and engaged the Macedonian fleet, which he blockaded in the Propontis. Philip could not return to Pella or conduct operations in Greece with his fleet in harm's way so he resorted to his usual trickery. Fabricating an attack on Macedonian garrisons in Thrace, he sent a letter to his general Antipater informing him he was leaving for Thrace immediately and commanding Antipater to join him there. As planned, Chares intercepted the letter, promptly fell for the ruse, and weighed anchor for Thrace.[117] Demetrius and the fleet were therefore able to sail out of the Propontis and join Philip.

To help meet the war's costs Demosthenes put forward a further reform of the trierarchy since trierarchs were still shirking their duties and ships were not ready in time.[118] In his *On the Symmories* of 354 Demosthenes had proposed sharing the trierarchy among the 1,200 richest men in Athens. Now he decreased the number to only 300 men, whose personal outlay would rise steeply. There was resistance, even to the extent of bribing him to drop his proposal and then prosecuting

---

[114] Theopompus, *FGrH* 115 F 292 (180 ships), Philochorus, *FGrH* 328 F 162 (230 ships); cf. Demosthenes 18.73.

[115] Philochorus, *FGrH* 328 F 162.

[116] Theopompus, *FGrH* 115 F 292.

[117] Justin 9.2.1.

[118] Aeschines 3.222, Demosthenes 18.102–109, Carlier, *Démosthène*, pp. 206–207; see further, D. M. MacDowell, "The Law of Periandros about Symmories," *CQ²* 36 (1986), pp. 445–449, V. Gabrielsen, "Trierarchic Symmories," *Class. & Med.* 41 (1990), pp. 89–118 and *Financing the Athenian Fleet: Public Taxation and Social Relations* (Baltimore: 1994), pp. 207–213.

him under the *graphe paranomon* procedure for putting forward an illegal decree. Still, everyone knew Philip's procurement of the Athenians' grain would cause a food shortage and the people were in no mood to listen to trumped up charges—or to pity the super rich.[119] Demosthenes' prosecutor did not even win one-fifth of the votes cast, and Demosthenes' law came into effect, resulting in a more efficient (albeit less equitable) system as he boasted.[120] Demosthenes probably now carried another recommendation that surplus revenues and the funds budgeted for public buildings be diverted to the war effort.[121]

Before Philip marched home he campaigned briefly in Scythia, where he captured 20,000 horses and the same number of children and women, whom he would sell or employ as slaves.[122] In the Danube area, a collection of fierce and still independent Thracian tribes named the Triballi blocked his passage.[123] When they demanded he pay a toll to pass through their territory he attacked them, but in fierce fighting it appeared that the sarissa of one of his men went through his upper leg or thigh, killing his horse under him. Unconscious and losing much blood, he was rushed from the field, and the Triballi seized most if not all his booty. It took several months for Philip to recover from his serious wound and he limped for the rest of his life.[124]

Philip's physical setback did not stop him returning to Greece to deal with the Athenians the following year. In doing so he permitted Demosthenes to bring about the one thing the king had worked hard to prevent: an alliance with Thebes against Macedonia. That led to the inevitable battle between Philip and Greek coalition troops at Chaeronea in 338: at stake was the freedom of Greece.

---

[119] Cf. Ellis, *Philip II*, pp. 179–180, Sealey, *Demosthenes*, pp. 188–190.

[120] Demosthenes 18.107–108.

[121] Aeschines 3.222, Philochorus, *FGrH* 328 F 56a.

[122] Justin 9.2; cf. Diodorus 16.1.5, and see also Worthington, *Philip II*, pp. 138–140.

[123] Philochorus, *FGrH* 328 F 54, Marsyas, *FGrH* 135/136 F 17, Justin 9.3.1–3; cf. Demosthenes 18.67, Diodorus 16.1.5.

[124] [Plutarch], *Moralia* 331b. On the wound, see A. S. Riginos, "The Wounding of Philip II of Macedon: Fact and Fabrication," *JHS* 114 (1994), pp. 116–118, who among other things argues that Philip's lameness was later embellished by biographers (such as Satyrus) for dramatic effect.

The End of Greek Freedom

THE FOURTH SACRED WAR

When the Athenian envoys arrived at the regular meeting of the Amphictyonic Council in the spring of 339, they were surprised to learn that Amphissa, a city of West Locris and an ally of Thebes in the Third Sacred War, intended to accuse the Athenians of impiety.[1] The Amphissans were angry that the Athenians had recently rededicated gilded Persian and Theban shields seized at the Battle of Plataea in 479 at the new temple of Apollo at Delphi. The previous temple had burned down in 373, but since the new one (completed in about 340) had not yet been consecrated the Athenians were guilty of impiety. Their action might have escaped notice, except that they had added an inscription to the shields: "The Athenians from the Medes and the Thebans, when they fought on the opposite side to the Greeks."[2] Plataea was the battle that expelled the Persian army from Greece, but during the Persian Wars the Thebans had Medized (become pro-Persian) and fought with the Persians against the Greeks at Plataea. They had lived with this disgrace ever since, so the new inscription reopened an old wound.

The Amphissans insisted that the council fine Athens fifty talents and deny the city access to the oracle. The situation for the Athenians was serious, for if they refused to pay the council might well declare a sacred war against them, which would involve Philip. It is unlikely that he conspired with the Amphissans to orchestrate a move into Greece

---

[1] Aeschines 3.115–121, Demosthenes 18.140–155. On the background, see Worthington, *Philip II*, pp. 136–137.

[2] Aeschines 3.115–116.

since he was engaged in Thrace and then Scythia when the council met.[3] Since the Amphissans were unfriendly to Athens, they were likely acting on the request of their Theban allies.[4]

When the issue was debated at the council meeting, all of the Athenian ambassadors apart from Aeschines used illness as an excuse not to speak. His colleagues may well have suspected that the council would uphold the Amphissan charge, and so had no wish to be held accountable back home. Aeschines, however, took the bull by the horns. Instead of arguing that the Amphissans were acting out of personal motives he accused them of impiety. He informed the council they were cultivating part of the sacred Plain of Cirrha (under Delphi) and had even put up buildings on it, dramatically pointing down to the plain below as he spoke.

Cultivating sacred land was a serious offense. The council deployed amphictyonic troops to the plain the following day to discover that Aeschines was correct. Their commander gave orders to burn the buildings, but at that point the Amphissans attacked them and forced them to retreat.[5] The next day the council held another meeting and instructed the Amphissans to destroy the buildings and withdraw from the plain. They refused to comply, no doubt expecting the Thebans to rally to their cause. They were wrong. The council convened a special meeting, at which it declared a sacred war against Amphissa, and on the motion of its president, Cottyphus of Thessaly, elected Philip commander of the amphictyonic army.[6]

The charge of impiety against Athens never surfaced again. Credit therefore must be given to Aeschines, who in turning the tables on the Amphissans at the meeting had "really prevented the declaration of an

---

[3] For example, Jaeger, *Demosthenes*, p. 184, Griffith in N. G. L. Hammond and G. T. Griffith, *A History of Macedonia* 2 (Oxford: 1979), p. 586; cf. T. T. B. Ryder, "Demosthenes and Philip II," in Ian Worthington (ed.), *Demosthenes: Statesman and Orator* (London: 2000), p. 80: "Whether Philip engineered the affair is not known, but the original move of the Locrians came remarkably soon after the Athenians had declared war on him."

[4] P. D. Londey, "The Outbreak of the Fourth Sacred War," *Chiron* 20 (1990), pp. 239–260. The best destruction of the idea of Philip's involvement in any "conspiracy" to start the war is J. Roisman, *The Rhetoric of Conspiracy in Ancient Athens* (Berkeley and Los Angeles: 2006), pp. 133–145.

[5] Aeschines 3.123, Demosthenes 18.151.

[6] Demosthenes 18.151–152.

Amphictyonic war against Athens."[7] It is no surprise that later he spoke highly of his role at the meeting,[8] and equally unsurprising that Demosthenes gave him no credit for his action. In fact, although admitting the Amphissans were cultivating sacred land, he boldly stated that they had never brought a charge against Athens in the first place. Further, he accused Aeschines of accepting a bribe from Philip to engineer a sacred war, thereby allowing Philip to involve himself once more in central Greek affairs.[9] Demosthenes' argument is flawed, not least because no one knew whether Aeschines would be successful in countering the Amphissan charge and Philip was very far away.[10]

The Fourth Sacred War generated little interest among the Greeks, and it spluttered to an end the following year. Some of states were still recovering from the Third Sacred War, but most were resigned to the fact that Philip would decide the war's outcome, as he had the previous one. Against this background Demosthenes struggled to save Greece by winning over Thebes against Philip.[11]

THE ENEMY OF MY ENEMY IS MY FRIEND

Athens and Thebes did not send representatives to the special meeting of the Amphictyonic Council. The Thebans did not want to participate in a vote that declared war against their Locrian allies, nor did they want to plead on their behalf. Thus it suited them better to stay away, despite being partially responsible for the predicament in which the Amphissans found themselves. The Athenians, on the other hand, had no concerns about Amphissan feelings; it was because of Demosthenes that they did not attend the meeting.[12]

---

[7] Pickard-Cambridge, *Demosthenes*, p. 364. On Aeschines at the meeting and his version of it, see E. M. Harris, *Aeschines and Athenian Politics* (Oxford: 1995), pp. 126–130.

[8] Aeschines 3.116.

[9] Demosthenes 18.149–152, 156, 159, 163; cf. Schaefer, *Demosthenes²* 2, p. 533, J. Buckler, "Demosthenes and Aeschines," in Ian Worthington (ed.), *Demosthenes: Statesman and Orator* (London: 2000), p. 144.

[10] See also Harris, *Aeschines and Athenian Politics*, pp. 128–130; cf. Ryder, "Demosthenes and Philip II," pp. 80–81 and Buckler, "Demosthenes and Aeschines," p. 144, Roisman, *Rhetoric of Conspiracy*, pp. 133–145.

[11] See also J. Trevett, "Demosthenes and Thebes," *Historia* 48 (1999), pp. 184–202.

[12] Worthington, *Philip II*, p. 138.

Demosthenes recognized that the new sacred war gave Philip a legitimate excuse for marching an army into Greece, which he could deploy against Athens if he wished. Demosthenes suspected, like most Greeks by now, that Philip intended to effect a lasting settlement of Greece rather than the ephemeral one of 346.[13] Since 346 he had considered that the only way Philip could be stopped was for Athens to ally with Thebes and unite the Greeks against him.[14] Now he was convinced, but the Amphictyonic Council meeting posed a problem. If the Athenians took part in the meeting, and subsequently in the sacred war, they stood to damage their precarious relations with Thebes and would not be treated as deferentially by Philip as in 346. Demosthenes had hopes that he might sway the Thebans to the Athenian side because they had recently defied Philip by seizing Nicaea (in Locris), the fortress town that controlled Thermopylae.[15] They had expelled the Macedonian garrison Philip installed in 344 and set up their own.[16] Their action showed their contempt of Philip, but to capitalize on it Demosthenes needed to persuade the Athenians to absent themselves from the special meeting and to cast aside their past differences with the Thebans.

Aeschines held the opposite view and implored the Athenians to attend the meeting. He was convinced that if Athens fought alongside Philip in the sacred war the king would not only treat the city fairly but also withdraw from Greece.[17] As he pointed out, absence from council meetings was illegal so the Thebans would be held in contempt,[18] thereby providing Philip with grounds for attacking the city and inviting the Athenians to join him. Aeschines' conciliatory policy was pie in the sky: Athenian defiance of Philip over the past half-dozen years meant there could never be a long-term alliance on equal terms between the two of them. Even if Philip did enlist Athenian help against Thebes there was still no guarantee that he would not then turn on Athens.

---

[13] Cf. J. Buckler, "Philip II's Designs on Greece," in W. R. Wallace and E. M. Harris (eds.), *Transitions to Empire: Essays in Honor of E. Badian* (Norman: 1996), pp. 77–97,

[14] Contra G. L. Cawkwell, "Demosthenes' Policy after the Peace of Philocrates II," *CQ*[2] 13 (1963), pp. 206–209.

[15] Philochorus, *FGrH* 328 F 56.

[16] Philochorus, *FGrH* 328 F 56b.

[17] Aeschines 3.128–129.

[18] Aeschines 3.128.

Enough Athenians saw the flaws in Aeschines' argument and sided with Demosthenes. Aeschines later accused Demosthenes of accepting a bribe of 2,000 drachmas from Amphissa for advocating the line he did.[19] That was simply sour grapes because Demosthenes had tempered his diplomatic victory against Amphissa by persuading the Athenians not to involve themselves in the sacred war.

"IN THE VERY MIDST OF THE HORRORS"

Little happened in the sacred war during 339, principally because Philip stayed in Pella to recover from the wound the Triballi had inflicted on him. In early 338, he led his army into Greece, where he was joined by troops from the Thessalians, Aenianians, Dolopians, Phthiotians, and Aetolians. He halted at Cytinium, six miles north of the Gravia Pass, from where he could march south to Amphissa. To all intents and purposes he was fulfilling the charge of the Amphictyonic Council. Then suddenly he turned southeast, down the Cephissus Valley into Phocis. After a brief stop, he moved to the Boeotian border and seized the town of Elatea, which was located a short distance from Nicaea.[20] He could still march on Amphissa if he wished, but now he was only two or three days' march from Thebes and Athens.

Holding his position at Elatea, Philip sent an embassy to the Thebans demanding they surrender Nicaea to the Locrians and, further, that they either join him in attacking Athens or allow his army safe passage through Boeotia to Attica.[21] If they chose the former, Philip promised them whatever booty they could seize when Athens fell to him. To increase pressure, he deliberately placed representatives of the Amphictyonic Council on his embassy so that if the Thebans rejected his impositions they would also be flouting the council.[22]

When the Athenians heard that Philip had seized Elatea and had invited Thebes to join him in attacking Athens they held an emergency Assembly to decide a plan of action. Debate, however, was stifled: "no

---

[19] Aeschines 3.113–114.

[20] Philochorus, *FGrH* 323 F 56, Diodorus 16.84.2–4, Plutarch, *Demosthenes* 18.1.

[21] Theopompus, *FGrH* 115 F 328, Demosthenes 18.152–158, 168, 174–175, 178, 211–215, Diodorus 16.84.3–85.1, Justin 9.3.6.

[22] Plutarch, *Demosthenes* 18.2.

speaker dared to mount the rostrum, nobody knew what advice should be given, the assembly was struck dumb and appeared to be completely at a loss."[23] Eventually one man did stand up—Demosthenes. His speech on this crucial occasion does not survive, but he captured the panic and the thrust of what he said in a brilliant passage of his *On the Crown* of 330:[24]

> It was evening, and a messenger reached the Presiding Officers with news that Elatea had been taken. Immediately they got up from dinner, some to clear the stalls in the marketplace and set the scaffolding alight, others to summon the generals and call out the trumpeter.[25] The city was full of turmoil. At break of dawn the next day, the Presiding Officers called the Council to the Council-house while you proceeded to the Assembly, and before the Council could deliberate and endorse a proposal, the entire citizen body was seated up there. After this, the Council entered and the Presiding Officers announced the news they had received, and they produced the messenger to give his report. Then the herald asked, "Who wishes to speak?" but no one came forward. The herald asked many times but to no avail. No one rose, though all the generals were present and all the politicians too, and the country was calling for a speaker to save it. For the voice of the herald lawfully discharging his task is rightly considered the common voice of the country. If those who desired the city's safety were asked to come forward, all of you and all other Athenians would have risen and advanced to the platform, for all of you, I know, desired the city to be safe . . . But it seems that that moment and that day called for a man who not only was devoted and wealthy but had also followed events from the beginning and figured out correctly what Philip was aiming at and what his intentions were in taking the action he did. Someone who did not know these things and had not studied the situation for a long time, even if he was devoted and even if he was wealthy, would not be better informed about what had to be done or be able to advise you. The one who emerged as the right man on that

---

[23] Plutarch, *Demosthenes* 18.1; cf. Diodorus 16.84.3–5.

[24] Demosthenes 18.169–173. Demosthenes' use of the verb *epiphanein* ("I stepped forward") in this passage is very dramatic: W. J. Slater, "The Epiphany of Demosthenes," *Phoenix* 42 (1988), pp. 126–130. On the rhetoric of this passage, see H. Yunis, *Taming Democracy: Models of Political Rhetoric in Classical Athens* (Ithaca: 1996), pp. 268–277.

[25] These were signals that summoned the people to an emergency Assembly the next day.

day was I. I stepped forward and addressed you . . . I alone of the speakers and politicians did not abandon my post of civic concern at the moment of danger but rather proved to be the one who in the very midst of the horrors both advised and proposed the necessary measures for your sake.

Demosthenes is doubtless exaggerating his response to the crisis. Nevertheless, this was one of the defining moments in his career, and even the critical Theopompus was complimentary.[26] Later authors (inspired by this passage) also recognized that. Diodorus, for example, wrote that "again and again the herald called for someone to come forward to speak for the common safety, but no one came forward with a proposal. In utter perplexity and dismay, the crowd kept their eyes on Demosthenes. Finally he came down from his seat."[27]

The Athenians were indeed in "the very midst of the horrors." Philip's action affirmed the naïveté of Aeschines' policy of supporting Philip against Thebes, and with his credibility lost Demosthenes was the only person left with a plan to rescue Athens. The desperate situation required a radical course of action, prompting Demosthenes to seek authority to travel to Thebes with the people's full authority to negotiate an alliance and develop a strategy to defeat Philip.[28] Since Demosthenes was the Theban *proxenos* in Athens (the official host of Theban envoys to Athens) it made sense for him to head the embassy.[29] He also recommended that all men of military age march immediately to Eleusis (on the road to Thebes) to help induce the Thebans to mobilize. He stressed the need to act quickly before the Thebans, who to their credit had not immediately joined Philip, went over to his side. The Assembly agreed with him.[30] He later said the people's vote "caused the danger then encompassing the city to pass by like a cloud."[31] That was exaggeration: no cloud over either Athens or Greece ever dissipated.

---

[26] Theopompus, *FGrH* 328 F 328.

[27] Diodorus 16.84.4–5; cf. Plutarch, *Demosthenes* 18.1–3 (from Theopompus).

[28] Demothenes 18.160–214, Aeschines 3.137–41.

[29] Demosthenes the Theban *proxenos*: Aeschines 2.141, 143. On *proxenoi*, see F. E. Adcock and D. J. Mosley, *Diplomacy in Ancient Greece* (London: 1975), pp. 160–163.

[30] Diodorus 16.85.1.

[31] Demosthenes 18.188.

A CROWN FOR DEMOSTHENES

Philip's embassy was already in Thebes when the Athenians arrived.[32] The Thebans called an Assembly, at which the Macedonians spoke first. They put Philip's demands to the people, recalled the long-standing enmity between Athens and Thebes, and bluntly told the Thebans that if they defied the king he would invade Boeotia and plunder it mercilessly.[33] Then Demosthenes spoke. Exactly what he said is unknown.[34] He must have assailed the king's ultimatum, especially over Nicaea, and rehearsed how he had treacherously abandoned the Thebans in 346, for Aeschines later stated that these two issues decided the Theban vote.[35] Demosthenes probably also warned the Thebans there was no guarantee that Philip would leave them alone if they did join with him to march on Athens, pointing out that he would not permit them to sustain their influence in Greece, let alone boost it at Athens' expense. Philip's track record of duplicity and deceit worked in Demosthenes' favor. The Thebans voted in favor of an alliance with Athens—and war with Macedonia.[36]

Plutarch reported that "Demosthenes' eloquence, so Theopompus tells us, stirred [the Thebans'] courage, kindled their desire to win glory and threw every other consideration into the shades. As if transported by his words, they cast off all fear, self-interest or thought of obligation towards Macedonia and chose the path of honour."[37] Plutarch is doubtless guilty of excess, but there is no question that the alliance with Thebes, the one thing Philip had worked tirelessly to prevent during the 340s, was one of Demosthenes' greatest diplomatic successes.[38] His cousin Demomeles and the orator Hyperides now

---

[32] Demosthenes 18.211. See further, Carlier, *Démosthène*, pp. 216–219, Sealey, *Demosthenes*, pp. 194–196, Worthington, *Philip II*, pp. 143–145.

[33] Demosthenes 18.213–214.

[34] At his trial in 330, he simply said of his diplomacy in Thebes that "I would give my entire life to relate it in detail" but chose not to do so: Demosthenes 18.214.

[35] Aeschines 3.140.

[36] Aeschines 3.137–151, Demosthenes 18.168–188, 211–217; cf. Diodorus 16.85.1–4, Plutarch, *Demosthenes* 18.1–2, *Phocion* 16.3, Justin 9.3.4–6.

[37] Plutarch, *Demosthenes* 18.2.

[38] P. Cloché, *Démosthène et la fin de la démocratie athénienne* (Paris: 1957), pp. 191–195, Worthington, *Philip II*, p. 144; D. J. Mosley, "Athens' Alliance with Thebes 339 B.C.," *Historia* 20 (1971), pp. 508–510; more critically, J. R. Ellis, *Philip II and Macedonian Imperialism* (London: 1976), pp. 191–193.

requested he be awarded a gold crown for his achievement. Demomeles was indicted under a *graphe paranomon*, but Hyperides defended him so successfully that his prosecutor Diondas failed to win one-fifth of the votes. Demosthenes duly received his crown (his second) at the Dionysia in March of 338.[39]

The alliance with Thebes came at immense cost to Athens, and only the immediate crisis saved Demosthenes from a whiplash of public criticism. Among other things, the Athenians had to pay two-thirds of the cost of the land army and the total cost of any naval engagements. The Thebans were to be in sole charge of the army and co-commanders of the fleet, and would formulate the strategy to defeat Philip. The Athenians also had to recognize Thebes' hegemony of the Boeotian League, cease upholding an independent Thespiae or Plataea, and give up their claim to Oropus. When Aeschines prosecuted Demosthenes in 330, he attacked him mercilessly for agreeing to such humiliating terms.[40] In his defense, Demosthenes lauded only his role in actually effecting the alliance, explaining that the jurors would find other details about it boring:[41]

> As for what we said in response, I would give my entire life to relate it in detail, but since the moment has passed, and you may feel as if a cataclysm has overtaken the political world, I fear that speeches on this subject would seem pointless and tedious.

OPPOSING PHILIP

Philip was thus presented with no other choice than military action. He controlled the mountain road to Cytinium and the Cephissus valley as far as Elatea, but the Thebans had the vital pass of Thermopylae, so they decided on a defensive strategy to bar him from Boeotia and Attica. They sent Theban soldiers and 10,000 Athenian-hired mercenaries under the command of the Athenians Chares and Proxenus to the Gravia Pass.[42] Another Athenian-Theban force was stationed twenty miles away at Parapotamii, on the Boeotian border, close to Phocis. To block Philip attacking from that direction, these troops may

---

[39] Demosthenes 18.222–223, [Plutarch], *Moralia* 848f.
[40] Aeschines 3.142–146.
[41] Demosthenes 18.214.
[42] See further, Worthington, *Philip II*, p. 145, citing sources.

have fortified some Phocian towns destroyed at the end of the Third Sacred War so as to form a defensive line.[43]

Aeschines was unjustly critical of the Theban defensive strategy.[44] The position of the twin forces established a defensive line that controlled the passes from Mount Parnassus to Lake Copais and, because of the terrain, posed a major problem for Philip if he tried to march through them. He was also blocked from invading Boeotia (and beyond that Attica) and cut off from the Gulf of Corinth and his Peloponnesian allies. If, however, Philip managed to break through their line, the Thebans had a Plan B: they would fall back to the plain of Chaeronea (on the border of Phocis, not far from Thebes) and do battle with him there. The Thebans anticipated that the Macedonians would tire of lingering at Elatea and, with winter fast approaching, head for home.

The Greek plan did not win divine favor as Aeschines enjoyed pointing out later. Stories circulated that Apollo prophesied only doom and gloom. A shark ate some of the Athenian initiates into the Eleusinian Mysteries as they purified themselves in the sea. At Thebes, statues dripped with blood.[45] These portents affected the Athenians' resolution to send troops to Boeotia, so Demosthenes immediately accused the Priestess of Apollo of "Philippizing" (becoming pro-Philip). He reminded the Athenians and Thebans that their noteworthy leaders Pericles and Epaminondas scorned such superstition, and so was able to quell the popular fears.[46] Still, Philip was not the sort of king to tire of waiting and go home.

Athens and Thebes alone could not block Philip, so both cities sent embassies to the other Greeks for assistance. Only Megara, Corinth, Achaea, Euboea, Acarnania, and some islands responded. Philip had also beseeched the Greeks for help, but only the Thessalians and Phocians took his side, the latter not so much for his help at the end of the Third Sacred War but because they were caught in between the two armies and expected Philip to be victorious. His Peloponnesian allies (apart from Achaea) stayed neutral.[47] The Greeks may well have declined to support the allied cause because they assumed Philip could not be beaten or because they had no wish to fight for the unpopular Athenians. The real reason ran deeper: they had had enough of fighting.

---

[43] Such as Ambrysus and Lilaea: Pausanias 10.36.2–3; cf. 4.31.5.

[44] Aeschines 3.146, 147.

[45] Plutarch, *Demosthenes* 19.1, Aeschines 3.130–131, Apollonius, *Argonauica* 4.1284.

[46] Aeschines 3.130, Plutarch, *Demosthenes* 20.1.

[47] Demosthenes 18.156, 158, 218, 221–222.

Although a widespread coalition of Greek states had not formed, Philip still tried to reach a diplomatic solution. He sent an embassy to Athens and to Thebes seeking peace. Phocion spoke in its favor, but Demosthenes would have none of it, dramatically threatening to drag anyone who so much as mentioned peace off to prison by his hair. Demosthenes, who won the Assembly's vote, was right to take this line because Philip's initiative was little more than a face-saving gesture.

Greek and Macedonian troops engaged in guerilla warfare in and around the Cephissus Valley during the winter and into the spring. Demosthenes mentioned two battles, one "by the river" and one "in winter,"[48] which must be the winter of 339/8. If he is to be trusted, it appeared that Philip twice attempted to cross the Cephissus River to dislodge the allied line, but both times he was unsuccessful. In light of those failed attempts, he directed his attention to the Gravia Pass. Rather than attack Chares and Proxenus frontally and risk losing men, he resorted to his "Thracian revolt" trick that had fooled Chares at Byzantium in 340. He arranged for a letter to fall into the hands of the Athenian commanders at the Gravia Pass that announced his immediate departure to deal with a revolt in Thrace. He withdrew soldiers from Cytinium to lend credence to the letter's contents.[49] Chares and Proxenus inexplicably fell for the hoax. Thinking that Philip was packing up, they relaxed the guard at the pass, at which point Philip sent Parmenion into action. He stormed the allied troops, massacring many of the mercenaries, and took the pass.[50] Three hours later he arrived at Amphissa,[51] which immediately surrendered to him, and those whom the Amphictyonic Council declared guilty of sacrilege were banished.[52]

Philip's deception and speed gave him command of the passes through Mount Parnassus to the plain of the Cephissus. The only troops that now blocked his way were those at Parapotamii, and in accordance with their alternate plan they now retreated to Chaeronea. From Elatea, Philip marched easily to Parapotamii, and from there to

---

[48] Demosthenes 18.216.

[49] Polyaenus 4.2.8.

[50] Proxenus was later accused of treachery: Dinarchus 1.74.

[51] Aeschines 3.146–147, Polyaenus 4.2.8, and see Griffith in Hammond and Griffith, *History of Macedonia* 2, pp. 590–595, Worthington, *Philip II*, pp. 146–147.

[52] Strabo 9.419 says that Amphissa was destroyed, but that is extreme, and we would expect to hear about it from Demosthenes; Diodorus 18.38.2 (cf. 18.56.5) implies only anti-Macedonian leaders were exiled and the town survived.

Chaeronea. The Fourth Sacred War might have ended but the fighting in Greece was far from over. Now Philip faced his greatest battle yet, with the prize of Greek autonomy going to its victor.

THE BATTLE OF CHAERONEA

The topography of the plain of Chaeronea made it the only realistic place to block Philip from reaching Thebes. The plain was about two miles wide, with hills on its northern and southern sides, and several rivers flowed through it (Map 4). Its width limited the amount of fighting space, and the rivers and marshy ground to its east, by the Cephissus River, impeded the effective deployment of cavalry. If Philip beat the Greeks, then they could fall back over the Kerata Pass to their homes as his cavalry could not pursue them, thereby allowing them to regroup to fight again.

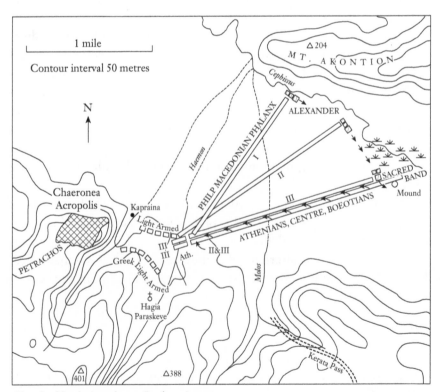

Phase I   Macedonians advance; Greeks stationary
Phase II   Philip retreats, his centre and left advancing; Athenians, Centre and Boeotians advance to
           left front, but the Sacred Band stands firm
Phase III Alexander charges, the centres engage, and Philip drives the Athenian wing up the Haemon Vally

MAP 4. Battle of Chaeronea

The Greeks encamped by the Haemon (Lykuressi) stream. Their army of 30,000 infantry and 3,800 cavalry was under the command of Chares, Lysicles, and Stratocles and the Theban general Theagenes.[53] Boeotia had sent 12,000 hoplites, including the Sacred Band of Thebes, an elite 300-strong infantry corps, possibly commanded by Theagenes.[54] The Athenians deployed at least 6,000 citizen soldiers up to the age of fifty and hired 2,000 mercenaries.[55] Included among them was Demosthenes, whose shield was emblazoned with the phrase "good luck" in gold letters.[56] Achaea sent 2,000 soldiers, and Corinth, Megara, Acarnania, and several islands also sent troops.[57] Philip's camp was to the plain's east, since the eighteen-year-old Alexander pitched his tent next to an oak tree by the Cephissus River, which even in Plutarch's lifetime "was known as Alexander's oak."[58] The Macedonian army numbered 30,000 infantry and 2,000 cavalry, of which 24,000 were Macedonians and the rest provided by Thessaly and Phocis.[59]

The Greek battle line took up a defensive position on the plain. The Boeotians were on the right wing (the Sacred Band to the far right) by the Cephissus River. The Athenians led by Stratocles, together with 5,000 light-armed infantry, were on the left flank by the Haemon River. Demosthenes would have stood here, although his exact position in the line is unknown. The other Greek allies were in the center of the line, facing the bulk of the various battalions that comprised the Macedonian phalanx. Philip arranged his line so that he was on its right flank, facing the Athenians. On his left flank, opposite the Boeotians and the Sacred Band, he stationed the Companion Cavalry, commanded by Alexander, whom he positioned next to his "most seasoned generals," probably Parmenion and Antipater.[60] The phalanx, with each battalion under individual commanders, stood in his center facing the Greek hoplite soldiers.

[53] Diodorus 16.85.2, 85.5, 86.1, Plutarch, *Demosthenes* 17.3, *Alexander* 12.5, Justin 9.3.9.
[54] On the Sacred Band, see Plutarch, *Pelopidas* 18. In detail from its creation in 378 to 338, J. De Voto, "The Theban Sacred Band," *Anc. World* 23 (1992), pp. 3–19. Theagenes as its commander: [Plutarch], *Moralia* 259d, Plutarch, *Alexander* 12.5.
[55] Plutarch, *Demosthenes* 20.2, [Plutarch], *Moralia* 845f.
[56] Plutarch, *Demosthenes* 20.2, [Plutarch], *Moralia* 845f.
[57] Demosthenes 18.237.
[58] Plutarch, *Alexander* 9.3.
[59] For a discussion of both sides' fighting capabilities, see N. G. L. Hammond, *Philip of Macedon* (London: 1994), pp. 149–151; cf. Worthington, *Philip II*, pp. 147–149.
[60] Diodorus 16.86.1.

A little after dawn on either Metageitnion 7 or 9 (August 1 or 4), 338, the two sides did battle.[61] Since the infantry would dictate the outcome of the battle, the Greeks had deliberately extended their line from one side of the plain to the slope of the acropolis of Chaeronea (the city was below the southern hills) on the other so that Philip would have to match it or be outflanked. To meet the line, Philip reduced the depth of his phalanx, thereby weakening the force of its charge. The allies intended their right wing to push its way through the thinner Macedonian line, pivot, and force the Macedonian left into the marshes, where it would become bogged down, or even into the Cephissus itself. Unfortunately for the Greeks, they were facing a master tactician in Philip and a Macedonian army that was battle-hardened from years of fighting in different regions against a variety of foes. The Greeks could not match that experience, and the Athenians had never fought Macedonian troops.

Philip planned a three-phase operation to upset the allied strategy. For the first phase, he directed his entire line to march towards the Greeks at an acute angle, not face on, his right flank closer to the Greek line than its left. When the Macedonian right under Philip came into contact with the Athenians on the Greek left, he put the second phase of his strategy into operation. Rather than engaging the Athenians in hand-to-hand fighting as they expected, he began to lead his wing sideways to the right, and the rest of his line followed suit. The Athenian left moved with him, and as it did so it opened a gap in the allied line. The Greeks stationed in the center and up to the right flank scrambled to plug it, but the Sacred Band on the extreme right followed orders and stood fast. Thinking that Philip was actually retreating, Stratocles yelled to his men to attack and shut him up in Macedonia.[62] His impetuosity proved fatal.

About one hundred feet on, by the Lykuressi stream, Philip stopped his feigned retreat and deployed his third phase. Alexander and the cavalry on the Macedonian left flank now charged at the gap that remained

---

[61] Date: Plutarch, *Camillus* 19.5, 8. Battle: Diodorus 16.86, Plutarch, *Alexander* 9, *Pelopidas* 18.7, Justin 9.3.4–11, Polyaenus 4.2.2, 7; for modern discussions of the battle, see Griffith in Hammond and Griffith, *History of Macedonia* 2, pp. 596–603, Worthington, *Philip II*, pp. 149–151, R. A. Gabriel, *Philip II of Macedon: Greater than Alexander* (Washington: 2010), pp. 214–222. N. G. L. Hammond, "The Victory of Macedon at Chaeronea," in N. G. L. Hammond, *Studies in Greek History* (Oxford 1973), pp. 534–557, but see now J. Ma, "Chaironeia 338: Topographies of Commemoration," *JHS* 128 (2008), pp. 172–191.

[62] The remark is given by Polyaenus 4.2.2 (second century AD), but it is doubtful.

open between the immobile Sacred Band and the rest of the Greek line. Once through it, they wheeled round at speed to encircle the band, cutting it down to the last man, and then quickly reformed to attack the other Boeotian troops.[63] Meanwhile, Philip turned back and charged the startled Athenians, forcing them into the river valley. The Athenians stood no chance as the Macedonians mowed them down and then ploughed into the allied center. The fighting turned into a rout. One thousand Athenians were killed and 2,000 taken prisoner. The other allies also lost substantial numbers, and the Haemon was said to have run red with blood.[64] Perhaps as much as half of the Greek army was killed or captured. In complete shock and disarray, the survivors (including Demosthenes) managed to struggle over the Kerata Pass to Lebadea (Livadhia) in Boeotia, but they were in no mood to regroup to fight Philip again.

Demosthenes had somehow survived the battle, but that good fortune would be used against him. He was later accused of cowardice, an indictable offence that carried with it loss of citizenship.[65] Since he continued his political career after Chaeronea, the charge is clearly a sham. It was actually begun by his enemy Aeschines, who used it to cast aspersions on his character, for Athenian society felt that a man guilty of cowardice was no better than a woman.[66]

A story also circulated that as he fled his cloak caught on a bramble bush. Thinking that one of the enemy had seized him, he begged for his life.[67] Demosthenes lived down these slurs on his character,[68] but other men were not so lucky. The general Lysicles was put on trial, damned by his prosecutor as "a living monument of our country's shame and disgrace," and condemned to death.[69]

<hr>

[63] Diodorus 16.85.5–87, Plutarch, *Alexander* 9.2; see P. A. Rahe, "The Annihilation of the Sacred Band at Chaeronea," *AJA* 85 (1981), pp. 84–87. For the view that Alexander did not charge the Sacred Band and indeed that no cavalry was used in the battle, see J. Buckler, "A Note on the Battle of Chaeronea," in J. Buckler and H. Beck (eds.), *Central Greece and the Politics of Power in the Fourth Century BC* (Cambridge: 2008), pp. 254–258.

[64] Diodorus 16.85.5–86.6, Plutarch, *Alexander* 9.2–3; Acarnanian losses: P. J. Rhodes and R. Osborne (eds.), *Greek Historical Inscriptions, 404–323 BC* (Oxford: 2003), no. 77.

[65] Aeschines 3.152, 159, 175, 181, 187, 244, and 253, Dinarchus 1.12, 71, 81; cf. Plutarch, *Demosthenes* 20.2, [Plutarch], *Moralia* 845f.

[66] On this point, see P. Hunt, *War, Peace, and Alliance in Demosthenes' Athens* (New York: 2010), pp. 118–119.

[67] [Plutarch], *Moralia* 845f.

[68] Cloché, *Démosthène*, p. 204.

[69] Diodorus 16.88.1–2.

AFTERMATH

The battle for Greek freedom was over and Philip was the victor.
The bodies of his men were cremated and the ashes interred under a
large burial mound called a *polyandreion*. He later held a parade and
sacrificed to their memory. As he walked the western part of the battlefield, where the Greek right flank had been stationed, he came
across the corpses of all 300 members of the Sacred Band, who had
fought to the last man. He apparently burst into tears, and then
ordered a statue of a lion to be erected where they died to commemorate their bravery.[70] The restored Lion of Chaeronea could well
mark the very spot (Figure 11).

Another story from a hostile tradition has it that Philip celebrated
his victory by getting drunk and mocking Demosthenes by shouting out
the opening words of his decrees: "Demosthenes son of Demosthenes

FIGURE 11. The Lion of Chaeronea, erected to commemorate the bravery of
the Theban Sacred Band at Chaeronea in 338.

[70] Tears: Plutarch, *Pelopidas* 18.5. Monument: Pausanias 9.40.10.

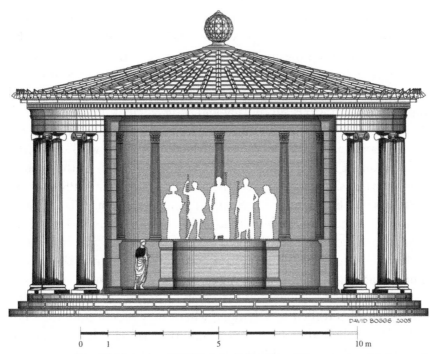

FIGURE 12. The Philippeion ("Philip's building") at Olympia, in which stood statues of the royal family, with Philip at the centre.

of Paeania moved this."[71] One of the Athenian prisoners who heard him was an orator named Demades.[72] Unable to keep quiet at the king's outburst, Demades reputedly asked him, "O King, when Fortune has cast you in the role of Agamemnon, are you not ashamed to act the part of Thersites?" Agamemnon was the leader of the Greeks in the Trojan War and Thersites one of his men who in Homer's *Iliad* berated the king and was beaten for not knowing his place. Philip was immediately sober and repentant. Later it was said that when he thought of Demosthenes he "trembled to think of the power and skill of the orator who had forced him to risk his empire and his life on the outcome of a few hours on a single day."[73]

[71] Story: Theopompus *FGrH* 115 F 236 = Athenaeus 435b–c. Theopompus, *FGrH* 115 F 282, says that Philip rushed into battle drunk, but that is a biased view. Mockery of Demosthenes: Diodorus 16.87.1–2, Plutarch, *Demosthenes* 20.3, [Plutarch], *Moralia* 715c; contra Justin 9.4.1–3. On this story, see Worthington, *Philip II*, pp. 152–154.

[72] Blass, *attische Beredsamkeit*[2] 3.2, pp. 236–247, J. K. Davies, *Athenian Propertied Families* (Oxford: 1971), pp. 99–102.

[73] Plutarch, *Demosthenes* 20.3.

Chaeronea changed Greece forever.[74] Even ancient writers recognized the magnitude of Philip's victory: "with the bodies of those who fell here was buried the freedom of the Greeks," the Athenian orator Lycurgus lamented.[75] Centuries later, Justin epitomized the result of the battle even more soberly: "for the whole of Greece this day marked the end of its glorious supremacy and of its ancient independence."[76] As a sign of his prestige and power, Philip commissioned one of the era's greatest artists, Leochares of Athens (who had worked on the Mausoleum at Halicarnassus, one of the seven wonders of the ancient world), to design and oversee the construction of his Philippeion ("Philip's building") in the sanctuary of Zeus at Olympia (Figure 12).[77]

In this large, circular building (*tholos*) stood statues of Philip, his mother and father (Eurydice and Amyntas), his son and heir Alexander, and Olympias. Philip's statue was in the center of the group. The propaganda of this secular, eye-catching monument in so religious a setting was obvious. Visitors and pilgrims from all over the Greek world travelled to Olympia, where they would now view not only the celebrated statue of Zeus (another wonder of the ancient world) but also the building that overtly proclaimed Philip's supremacy in Greece.[78]

After a hard-fought battle, Philip was master of Greece. However, he knew that he now faced a greater challenge, that of keeping the Greeks subservient to Macedonian rule. To achieve this goal, he resorted to a radical diplomatic initiative that changed the face of Greek politics.

---

[74] G. L. Cawkwell, "The End of Greek Liberty," in W. R. Wallace and E. M. Harris (eds.), *Transitions to Empire: Essays in Honor of E. Badian* (Norman: 1996), pp. 98–121.

[75] Lycurgus 1.50.

[76] Justin 9.3.11.

[77] Pausanias 5.17.4, 5.20.9–10.

[78] On the building and its significance, see Worthington, *Philip II*, pp. 164–166, citing bibliography.

"For the Conqueror, Death"

SETTLING SCORES

Philip first had to deal with the states that had brought him to battle at Chaeronea and those that had not responded to his call to arms.[1] His victory meant that he could dispense with diplomacy and simply impose terms. Since he was already in Boeotia he punished the Thebans first.[2] He abolished their hegemony of the Boeotian League and installed a pro-Macedonian oligarchy of 300 men and a garrison.[3] Further, he authorized the rebuilding of the three cities in Boeotia that the Thebans had earlier destroyed, Plataea and Thespiae (in 373) and Orchomenus (in 371),[4] and returned the border town of Oropus to the Athenians.[5] Against Greek tradition, the Thebans had to pay a ransom for their soldiers killed at Chaeronea (excluding the Sacred Band), and he sold the prisoners from the battle as slaves.

The Athenians, at war with Philip since 340, steeled themselves for similar treatment. After Chaeronea Demosthenes and Hyperides had

---

[1] For Philip's settlements, including his later common peace, see C. Roebuck, "The Settlement of Philip II with the Greek States in 338 B.C.," *CP* 43 (1948), pp. 73–92, N. G. L. Hammond and G. T. Griffith, *A History of Macedonia* 2 (Oxford: 1979), pp. 604–623, Worthington, *Philip II*, pp. 154–163.

[2] Diodorus 16.87.3, Pausanias 4.27.9–10, 9.1.8, 6.5, 37.8, Justin 9.4.6–10, 11.3.8.

[3] Demosthenes 18.282, 284, Aeschines 3.227, Diodorus 16.87.3, 17.8.3–7, 17.13.5, Justin 9.4.7–8, Pausanias 9.1.8, 9.6.5.

[4] Pausanias 4.27.10, 9.1.8.

[5] [Demades] 1.9, Diodorus 18.56.7, Pausanias 1.34.1; see also P. J. Rhodes and R. Osborne (eds.), *Greek Historical Inscriptions, 404–323 BC* (Oxford: 2003), no. 75.

enacted a series of emergency measures to protect the city.[6] These included evacuating the Attic countryside, sending the women, children, and sacred objects to the Piraeus, and deploying all men up to age sixty to guard the walls. To increase manpower in the event of an attack, they mandated that no man leave the city, restored the rights of the *atimoi* (those who had lost their citizenship), and promised citizenship to metics and freedom to slaves who worked in the silver mines and in the countryside. The Assembly had originally appointed Charidemus (one of the generals at Chaeronea) to command the remnants of the Athenian army, but the Areopagus overrode its decision and replaced him with Phocion.[7] Finally, the Athenians formed a special commission to procure grain from abroad and appointed Demosthenes to it.[8] He may have used the pretext of his office to escape Athens because his policy had led to the debacle at Chaeronea, for he was later accused of deserting Athens.[9] On the other hand, it has been suggested that the people needed his diplomatic skills to obtain grain at this crucial time, and he may have been confident that Lycurgus and Hyperides could protect the city.[10]

The Athenians had needlessly panicked. Philip dispatched Demades, the orator who had earned his respect for boldly chastising him after Chaeronea, to assure the Athenians that he wanted peace and did not intend to punish them as he had Thebes. As a mark of his sincerity, he sent his heir Alexander and his generals Antipater and Alcimachus at the head of an official embassy to return the ashes of the Athenian dead from Chaeronea and the 2,000 captives. The Macedonians requested that the people send an embassy to Philip to discuss peace,[11] and Demades, Aeschines, and Phocion were selected to serve on it.[12] Demosthenes, even if he had returned to Athens by this stage, was hardly a viable candidate.

---

[6] Lycurgus 1.16, 36–37, 41, Demosthenes 18.248, [Demosthenes] 26.11, [Plutarch], *Moralia* 848f–849a, 851a.

[7] Plutarch, *Phocion* 16.3.

[8] Aeschines 3.159, 259, Demosthenes 18.248, Lycurgus 1.42.

[9] At his trial in 323: Dinarchus 1.80, 82—for the trial, see Chapter 14.

[10] Pickard-Cambridge, *Demosthenes*, p. 394.

[11] Polybius 5.10.1–5, Justin 9.4.4–5, Diodorus 16.87.3, 32.4.1, 18.56.6–7, Plutarch, *Alexander* 28.1–2.

[12] Cf. T. T. B. Ryder, "The Diplomatic Skills of Philip II," in Ian Worthington (ed.), *Ventures into Greek History: Essays in Honour of N. G. L. Hammond* (Oxford: 1994), pp. 241–243.

The Athenian ambassadors met with the king and returned to Athens with good and bad news.[13] Philip did not intend to establish an oligarchy or install a Macedonian garrison in Athens, nor did he demand the surrender of anti-Macedonian politicians like Demosthenes, and he returned control of Oropus to the city. He also permitted them to retain their "traditional" islands of Lemnos, Imbros, Scyros (which lay on the grain route), and Salamis, and reaffirmed their possession of Delos and Samos.[14] However, he insisted that they disband their Second Athenian Confederacy (though they did not have to decrease the size of their navy), recall their cleruchs from the Chersonese, and relinquish all influence in that area. The Athenians had little choice but to accept Philip's terms and make a treaty with the king, which has been called the Peace of Demades because of his role in effecting it.[15]

Despite Demosthenes' warnings in his speeches, Philip did not destroy Athens or even abolish its democracy. The relieved people bestowed citizenship on Philip and Alexander and erected an expensive equestrian statue of the king in the Agora.[16] These were hollow acts of gratitude, however, as the Athenians' subsequent actions proved. They offered asylum to anyone fleeing from Philip's purges, including Thebans and, since Philip also eroded Athenian interests on Euboea, Callias and Taurosthenes of Chalcis. Further, when Hyperides was impeached for his emergency measures after Chaeronea he was acquitted—at his trial, he vividly said "it was not I that proposed the decree, but the battle of Chaeronea."[17] Finally, the people selected Philip's nemesis Demosthenes to pronounce the funeral oration (*epitaphios*) for the Athenians killed at Chaeronea (see below).[18] Only someone "regarded as best

[13] Diodorus 16.87–88.2, 18.56.7, Pausanias 1.25.3, 34.1, 7.10.5, Justin 9.4.1–5.

[14] Diodorus 18.56.7, Plutarch, *Alexander* 28.2. Samos was important for Athens for military reasons as well as for its use as a granary: G. Shipley, *A History of Samos* (Oxford: 1987), pp. 155–168. Athenian cleruchs had been living on the island since the 360s: J. Cargill, "*IG* II² 1 and the Athenian Kleruchy on Samos," *GRBS* 24 (1983), pp. 321–332 and *The Second Athenian League* (Berkeley: 1981), pp. 148–149 and 168.

[15] Diodorus 16.87.3. The inscription that recorded the treaty may survive: see below. Peace of Demades: Carlier, *Démosthène*, pp. 222–225.

[16] M. N. Tod, *Greek Historical Inscriptions* 2 (Oxford: 1948), no. 180, Plutarch, *Demosthenes* 22.4, Pausanias 1.10.4.

[17] [Plutarch], *Moralia* 849a.

[18] Plutarch, *Demosthenes* 15.2, [Plutarch], *Moralia* 845d.

endowed with wisdom and foremost in public esteem"[19] was selected
for this eulogy, similar to a present-day national address in time of
tragedy. Aeschines was passed over, something he bitterly resented, and
he unsuccessfully challenged Demosthenes' selection.[20] Demosthenes
later said the people chose him because of his patriotism and ability to
perform his duties properly—and Aeschines' dishonesty.[21]

Philip displayed a remarkably different attitude to the Athenians
than the other Greeks, especially in his post-Chaeronea settlements.[22]
He had been at war with Athens for over half of his reign but possessed
a genuine love of Athenian culture—several Macedonian kings, including Philip, had contacts with the leading intellectuals of the day.
When Plato died in 348, for example, Philip "honored him."[23] Yet he
never visited the city. His benevolence to Athens in the 350s and even
the 340s may be explained by his intention to promote Athenian power
over that of Thebes. On the other hand, after Chaeronea he was master of Greece, and therefore the influence of individual cities no longer
concerned him. Possibly he courted the Athenians at this time because
he needed their navy for his projected invasion of Asia. His conquest of
Thrace, which would protect his rear, and the Persian king's torture of
Hermias of Atarneus for information on Philip's Asian plans, testify to
his next grand campaign. Furthermore, one of his reasons for invading
Asia was revenge for Persian troops looting and burning Athens during
the Persian Wars (see below). Philip therefore could not punish the
Athenians as he had the Thebans after Chaeronea and then declare
himself their champion.

After dealing with his opponents in central Greece, the king turned to
the isthmus and the Peloponnese.[24] The Corinthians and the Megarians

[19] Thucydides 2.34. This information relates to the fifth century, when Thucydides was
writing, but nothing seems to have changed by the fourth century.

[20] Demosthenes 18.285; cf. Plutarch, *Demosthenes* 21.2.

[21] Demosthenes 18.285–288.

[22] Worthington, *Philip II*, pp. 84–85, 86, 88, 90, 95, 98–99, 100–101, 142; see also G.
L. Cawkwell, "Philip and Athens," in M. B. Hatzopoulos and L. D. Loukopoulos
(eds.), *Philip of Macedon* (Athens: 1980), pp. 100–110 and Ryder, "Diplomatic Skills
of Philip II," pp. 251–257.

[23] Theopompus, *FGrH* 115 F 294.

[24] Roebuck, "Settlement of Philip," pp. 83–89, Ryder, "Diplomatic Skills of Philip II,"
pp. 241–242, Worthington, *Philip II*, pp. 157–158; cf. C. D. Hamilton, "Philip II and
Archidamus," in W. L. Adams and E. N. Borza (eds.), *Philip II, Alexander the Great,
and the Macedonian Heritage* (Lanham: 1982), pp. 81–83.

immediately surrendered, and he set up pro-Macedonian oligarchies and garrisons in Corinth, Chalcis, Ambracia, and probably Megara.[25] From his base of operations at Corinth, he marched into the Peloponnese to subjugate the troublesome Spartans once and for all. He gave them one chance to yield by asking them whether they preferred him marching to their city as their friend or foe. In typical laconic fashion they said neither.[26] Accordingly, Philip imposed several terms on them, including the surrender of all disputed territories in the Peloponnese, and then burned their land.[27] States sympathetic to Sparta now pledged their loyalty to Philip, effectively blockading Sparta in the Peloponnese as he had intended.

Demosthenes' *Funeral Oration*[28]

Late in the year, Demosthenes delivered his funeral speech (*epitaphios*) over the Athenian dead at Chaeronea.[29] Athens was the only city in Greece with this type of public eulogy and everyone in the city—citizens, metics, and foreigners visiting Athens at the time—gathered in the Agora to hear it.[30] A funeral oration had a rigid structure; its purpose was to glorify the dead and exhort the living by arguing that those who gave their lives in battle had fought for the two ideals Greeks held in the highest regard: freedom and autonomy. They had given the living hope for the future. The speaker praised their bravery and sacrifice, which allowed people to continue living under a democracy with all the rights and freedoms it afforded.

---

[25] Diodorus 17.3.4–5, Polybius 9.8.3, 38.3.3.

[26] [Plutarch], *Moralia* 216b, 235a–b, 513a.

[27] Polybius 9.28.6–7, 33.8, Pausanias 7.10.3, [Plutarch], *Moralia* 219f.

[28] On the speech, see Blass, *attische Beredsamkeit*[2] 3.1, pp. 356–358, S. Usher, *Greek Oratory, Tradition and Originality* (Oxford: 1999), p. 351, MacDowell, *Demosthenes*, pp. 372–377. Translation with notes: Ian Worthington, *Demosthenes: Speeches 60 and 61, Prologues, Letters* (Austin: 2006), pp. 21–37. On authenticity, see Ian Worthington, "The Authorship of the Demosthenic *Epitaphios*," *Museum Helveticum* 60 (2003), pp. 152–157.

[29] The *epitaphios* belonged to the genre of epideictic oratory, on which see C. Carey, "Epideictic Oratory," in Ian Worthington (ed.), *Blackwell Companion to Greek Rhetoric* (Malden: 2007), pp. 236–252; see also N. Loraux, *The Invention of Athens: The Funeral Oration in the Classical City* (Cambridge: 1986), and Usher, *Greek Oratory, Tradition and Originality*, pp. 349–352, who briefly discusses Demosthenes' speech.

[30] Demosthenes 20.141.

Despite the many years in which Athenians lost citizens in fighting throughout the fifth and fourth centuries, only six funeral orations have survived including that of Demosthenes.[31] The *epitaphios* has a long legacy. The most famous ancient funeral speech was that of Pericles, dated to the end of the first year of the Peloponnesian War in 430. It became something of a blueprint for President Lincoln's Gettysburg Address (1863) and President Clinton's eulogy for the fiftieth anniversary of D-Day (1994). Other speeches not dealing with war that have the same themes of honoring the deceased for their actions and providing hope for the future may be traced back to the *epitaphios*—for example, President Reagan's address to the nation after the space shuttle *Challenger* exploded (1986) and that of President Bush following the reentry breakup of the space shuttle *Columbia* (2003).

Demosthenes' funeral oration, which was divided into six parts, survives. He began by talking of the difficulties speakers faced because of the somber occasion and the immeasurable sacrifice of the deceased (1–3):

> I discovered that to speak properly about the dead was an impossible task. Since they scorned the passion for life which is inherent in everyone, preferring to die nobly than live and see Greece suffer misfortune, how can the example of courage left behind not surpass the power of any speech?

Next he outlined the exploits of the fallen men's ancestors from the mythical era to the Persian Wars (4–14). In the third part he brought his speech up to the present day by describing the war against Philip, praising the courage of those who died in it, and the constitution for which they fought and gave their all (15–26):

> In my view, the reason why our land was not invaded by the enemy, besides their own poor judgment, was the courage of these men. This is clear especially from the peace that was made. For you cannot cite a more true or more honorable reason for this than that [Philip] admired the courage of those who died, and wished to be friends with their relatives rather than to endanger all his achievements again. . . . Many

---

[31] Pericles' funeral speech at Thucydides 2.35–46 (delivered 430); that of Gorgias (date unknown); Lysias 2 (392); Demosthenes 60 (338); and Hyperides 6 (322). The sixth was put into the mouth of Socrates in Plato, *Menexenus* 236d–249c, and may simply be a rhetorical set piece. On Hyperides' *epitaphios*, see Chapter 15 pp 332–333.

factors undoubtedly contributed to their character, not least of which was our constitution, which inspired them. For oligarchies run by a few produce fear in their citizens, but do not foster a sense of duty. So, when the test of war comes, every man saves himself to the best of his ability, for he knows that if he wins over his masters with gifts or any other service whatsoever, no matter how shamefully he has acted, only a little blame will attach to him afterwards. But democracies have many noble and just qualities, to which sensible people must be loyal, and in particular freedom of speech, which cannot be prevented from showing the truth because it is based on speaking the truth.

The fourth part of the speech was an excursus on the origins of the ten tribes into which the Athenians were divided (27–31), which led into another eulogy to the dead, who were now living with the gods because of their sacrifice (32–34):

First, in exchange for a short period of life, they leave behind for all time an ageless glory in which their children will be raised in honor, and their parents will be maintained in old age, admired by all, and the glory of these men will console them in their grief. Next, their bodies are free of sickness and their souls know no pain, which the living have to bear as circumstances dictate and they receive the traditional rites with great honor and much admiration.

Demosthenes ended his speech with the customary consolation to the families of the deceased and abrupt dismissal (35–37):

It is difficult, I suppose, to lighten present misfortunes with a speech, but we must try nevertheless to turn our minds to consolation, and realize that it is a fine thing for those who gave birth to men such as these, and were themselves born of similar stock, to be seen bearing these tribulations more gracefully than others, and to remain the same no matter what fortune befalls them . . . It is hard for fathers and mothers to be robbed of their children and to be without their dearest family to care for them in their old age. However, it is a majestic thing to see that they have immortal honor and a public memorial of their virtue, and are thought to deserve sacrifices and games in perpetuity . . . I did not think how I might speak at length, but how I might speak the truth. And now that you have grieved, and properly performed the customary rites, you should depart.

How the Athenians received Demosthenes' speech is unknown. It did not have the rhetorical flourish of that attributed to Pericles, yet he achieved his aims of praising the fallen, lauding the city and its democracy, and encouraging those left behind to take heart. In all, it was a fitting eulogy to those who died at Chaeronea.

PHILIP'S COMMON PEACE

The breakdown of the Peace of Philocrates confirmed that no voluntary diplomatic settlement would keep Greece at peace in the long term. For that, only a military solution would work, and Philip was now in a position to enforce that. Yet simply settling pro-Macedonian oligarchies in Greek cities, for example, would merely encourage resentment and hardly guarantee Macedonia's long-term control of Greece. In any case, even without a forthcoming campaign in Asia, Philip did not have the manpower for a large-scale Macedonian presence in Greece. He needed a settlement that would put the onus on the Greeks to remain passive, to which end he enforced a permanent common peace on them, in contrast to the previous voluntary common peaces that had soon failed.[32]

In the winter of 338/7 Philip ordered all Greek states to send deputations to him at Corinth.[33] Phocion encouraged the Athenians to wait until they knew exactly what Philip was planning, but he was ignored, a positive indication that the people knew this was not the time to refuse Philip.[34] The Spartans, however, did not send envoys, giving the haughty excuse that "what was imposed by a conqueror was not peace but servitude."[35]

Philip treated the ambassadors well.[36] He informed them he intended to establish a common peace, but with some significant differences from

---

[32] On the differences, see T. T. B. Ryder, *Koine Eirene* (Oxford: 1965), pp. 102–106. See also S. Perlman, "Fourth Century Treaties and the League of Corinth of Philip of Macedon," in *Ancient Macedonia* 4 (Institute for Balkan Studies, Thessaloniki: 1986), pp. 437–442 and "Greek Diplomatic Tradition and the Corinthian League of Philip of Macedon," *Historia* 34 (1985), pp. 153–174, and P. Hunt, *War, Peace, and Alliance in Demosthenes' Athens* (New York: 2010), pp, 232–234 (common peaces as part of intestate law, on which see too below).

[33] Diodorus 16.89, Justin 9.5.1–6; cf. [Demosthenes] 17.1. On the historical background, see Worthington, *Philip II*, pp. 158–171, citing bibliography.

[34] Plutarch, *Phocion.* 16.5.

[35] Justin 9.5.3.

[36] Diodorus 16.89.2.

earlier ones.[37] There were the expected provisos that each state was to swear an oath of allegiance not to harm any other member or interfere in another's domestic or foreign policy, nor to make an alliance with a potential enemy, and to assist a member that was attacked. Then the peace went in a completely new direction. First, each state was required to swear an oath of allegiance to Philip and his descendants. Second, Philip created an allied council (*synedrion*), of which Macedonia was not a member, that would meet regularly to oversee military, financial, domestic, and foreign affairs between member states. Greek states were to send elected representatives to this council, which was to be presided over by a hegemon or leader. The embassies returned to their homes, and in the following spring (337) returned to Corinth, where they swore their oaths to Philip and elected him—as he expected— hegemon of the council.[38]

Thus Philip created what the Greeks referred to as the Community of the Greeks (*to koinon ton Hellenon*),[39] but which is more commonly called by its modern name, the League of Corinth.[40] As an interstate institution, the league is an excellent example of an early system of international law.[41] Nonetheless, ancient writers devoted little attention to the league,[42] although because of its revolutionary impact on Greek

---

[37] [Demosthenes] 17. 2, 6, 8, 10, 15–16, 19.

[38] Cf. Demosthenes 18.201, Polybius 9.33.7, [Plutarch], *Moralia* 240a.

[39] *P. Oxy.* 12 (*FGrH* 255), 5, with N. G. L. Hammond, "The *Koina* of Epirus and Macedonia," *ICS* 16 (1991), pp. 183–192.

[40] Diodorus 16.89.1–3, 91.2, Justin 9.5.1–7; cf. [Demosthenes] 17. Ryder, *Koine Eirene*, pp. 102–106 and 150–162 and "Demosthenes and Philip's Peace of 338/7 B.C.," *CQ²* 26 (1976), pp. 85–87.

[41] Hunt, *War, Peace, and Alliance in Demosthenes' Athens*, p. 218, and pp. 217–236 on interstate law in ancient Greece.

[42] Diodorus 16.89, Justin 9.5.1–7: Diodorus discusses the second meeting at Corinth and Philip's plan to invade Persia; Justin mentions the first meeting at Corinth, ignores the second, and jumps to Philip and Asia. A contemporary inscription could be the Athenian copy of the peace: Rhodes and Osborne, *Greek Historical Inscriptions*, no. 76, citing previous publications. However, scarcely half of any line in it exists, and it may even record the peace between Philip and Athens after Chaeronea: Ian Worthington, "*IG* ii² 236 and Philip's Common Peace of 337," in L. G. Mitchell and L. Rubinstein (eds.), *Greek Epigraphy and History: Essays in Honour of P. J. Rhodes* (Swansea: 2008), pp. 213–223. Most information about the league and the common peace comes from [Demosthenes] 17.2, 6, 8, 10, 15–16, 19.

politics it "has been the subject of closer study than any other topic of [Philip's] life and times."[43]

THE LEAGUE OF CORINTH

The League of Corinth was the constitutional mechanism by which Macedonia controlled Greece. The Greeks had some semblance of autonomy in their affairs but, in reality, as hegemon of the council that managed all aspects of league business, Philip had complete control. Knowing that he could never reconcile the Greeks to Macedonian rule, he created a deterrent in his common peace that held them in check by brilliantly exploiting the major flaw in the polis system: the Greeks' hostile attitude toward each other. If one state were to upset the peace in any manner or, worse still, break its oath of allegiance, Philip knew that the other states would be all too ready and willing to unite in punishing it.

At the same spring meeting of the league Philip announced a panhellenic (all-Greek) enterprise: the invasion of Asia.[44] Isocrates' *To Philip* of 346, calling on the king to unite Greece and attack Persia, may originally have put the idea into his head.[45] He explained to the assembled delegates that he intended to liberate the Greek cities in Asia Minor from Persian rule and punish the Persians for what the Greeks, especially the Athenians, had suffered in the Persian Wars of 480–479. His panhellenic reason was, however, a ruse, advanced solely to appeal to Greeks.[46] His real reason may have been the pressing need to acquire

---

[43] Griffith in Hammond and Griffith, *History of Macedonia* 2, p. 623.

[44] Diodorus 16.89, Justin 9.5.4–7. Panhellenism: M. B. Sakellariou, "Panhellenism: From Concept to Policy," in M. B. Hatzopoulos and L. D. Loukopoulos (eds.), *Philip of Macedon* (Athens: 1980), pp. 128–145, J. M. Hall, *Hellenicity: Between Ethnicity and Culture* (Chicago: 2002), pp. 205–220.

[45] Cf. Diodorus 16.60.4–5: Philip in 346 "was ambitious to be designated general of Hellas in supreme command and as such to prosecute the war against the Persians"; J. R. Ellis, "The Dynamics of Fourth-Century Macedonian Imperialism," *Ancient Macedonia* 2 (Institute for Balkan Studies, Thessaloniki: 1977), pp. 103–114 and *Philip II and Macedonian Imperialism* (London: 1976), pp. 91–92, and G. L. Cawkwell, *Philip of Macedon* (London: 1978), p. 111, believe that in 346 Philip planned to invade Persia; contra Worthington, *Philip II*, pp. 166–167.

[46] Diodorus 16.89, Justin 9.5.4–7. Polybius 3.6.12–13 is explicit: Philip masked his true reason for invading Asia with the Panhellenic one. On Philip's aims, see Worthington, *Philip II*, pp. 166–169.

money because of his declining revenues. When Alexander became king the following year (336) he found only 70 talents in the treasury, and on the eve of his Persian expedition he owed 200 talents and had to borrow 800 more.[47] Demosthenes, like most Athenians, was probably not hoodwinked by Philip's professed motive, but he probably did relish the proposed expedition because it would remove Philip from Greece and put him in harm's way.[48]

Philip may not have intended to vanquish the Persian Empire but to campaign only in Asia Minor until he restored his finances.[49] Ultimately the issue is academic because he never saw Asia: the following year, he was assassinated.

PHILIP'S SEVENTH MARRIAGE

In the summer of 337 Philip married for the seventh and final time. The motives for his previous six marriages were military and diplomatic, but now he apparently married for love.[50] His new wife was a teenage noblewoman, Cleopatra, who at some point after her father died had been adopted by the powerful nobleman Attalus.[51] The marriage intensified the tension between Philip and Olympias, Alexander's mother, who was of "bad temper," "jealous and sullen," and "wasted no

[47] Aristobulus, *FGrH* 139 F 4, Duris, *FGrH* 70 F 40, Onesicritus, *FGrH* 134 F 2 = Plutarch, *Alexander* 15.2, Arrian 7.9.6, Curtius 10.2.24, [Plutarch], *Moralia* 327d, 342d.

[48] T. T. B. Ryder, "Demosthenes and Philip II," in Ian Worthington (ed.), *Demosthenes: Statesman and Orator* (London: 2000), p. 84.

[49] Worthington, *Philip II*, pp. 169–170; for the view that he wanted to defeat Darius and establish an absolute monarchy, see E. A. Fredricksmeyer, "On the Final Aims of Philip II," in W. L. Adams and E. N. Borza (eds.), *Philip II, Alexander the Great, and the Macedonian Heritage* (Lanham: 1982), pp. 85–98, N. G. L. Hammond, "The Kingdom of Asia and the Persian Throne," *Antichthon* 20 (1986), pp. 73–85; cf. E. Bloedow, "Why Did Philip and Alexander Launch a War against the Persian Empire?," *L'Ant. Class.* 72 (2003), pp. 261–274.

[50] The order of Philip's wives: A. D. Tronson, "Satyrus the Peripatetic and the Marriages of Philip II," *JHS* 104 (1984), pp. 116–126. Reason for marrying now: Worthington, *Philip II*, pp. 172–174.

[51] Athenaeus 13.557b–e (from Satyrus); cf. 13.560c, Diodorus 16.93.9, Justin 9.5.8–9; see E. Carney, *Women and Monarchy in Macedonia* (Norman: 2000), pp. 70–75.

opportunity criticizing [Philip] to her son."[52] Philip was not especially close to her either.[53] For some reason Olympias took an instant dislike to Cleopatra. Matters came to a head at the wedding feast of Philip and Cleopatra, which quickly turned into a typical Macedonian drinking party as the unmixed wine flowed in abundance. At some point Attalus, now Philip's father-in-law, toasted the newly married couple, but then prayed that their marriage produce a legitimate heir to the throne.[54] His comment was a slur on Alexander and Olympias, who came from Epirus, while Cleopatra most likely hailed from Lower Macedonia.[55] For the insult to work, Olympias was probably present at the banquet, but at some point the women would have withdrawn, leaving the men to continue drinking.

Alexander was enraged at Attalus' words. He threw his drinking cup at him and demanded an apology but Attalus refused. Alexander then besought his father to rebuke him, but inexplicably Philip did not stand up for him. Instead, he bade Alexander apologize, drawing his sword on his son when he refused. As Philip lurched toward the young heir, the alcohol overcame him and he fell over a table, prompting Alexander's famous comment that the man who wanted to cross from Europe to Asia could not even navigate a table without falling over.[56] Alexander and Olympias then left the court for that of her brother Alexander in Epirus, and from there Alexander moved north to Illyria.[57]

Perhaps Attalus' taunting prayer had instilled in Alexander and Olympias a fear that a son born to Cleopatra would be the next king because of his Macedonian blood, even though Philip had made it abundantly clear that Alexander was next in line to the throne. Nonetheless, Olympias attempted to persuade her brother Alexander of

---

[52] Plutarch, *Alexander* 9.5; see also Athenaeus 13.557d and 560c, and W. Heckel, "Philip and Olympias (337/6 BC)," in G. S. Shrimpton and D. J. McCargar (eds.), *Classical Contributions: Studies in Honor of M. F. McGregor* (Locust Valley: 1981), pp. 51–57, Worthington, *Philip II*, pp. 175–176. Olympias during Philip's reign: Carney, *Women and Monarchy in Macedonia*, pp. 62–67 and 79–81; generally: E. D. Carney, *Olympias, Mother of Alexander the Great* (London: 2006).

[53] Plutarch, *Alexander* 9.5.

[54] Plutarch, *Alexander* 9.6–11, Athenaeus 13.557d from Satyrus; cf. Justin 9.7.3–4.

[55] Plutarch, *Alexander* 9.4–11, Athenaeus 13.557d, Justin 9.7.3–5. On the incident and Attalus' remark, see Worthington, *Philip II*, pp. 176–178.

[56] Plutarch, *Alexander* 9.10, Justin 9.7.4; contra Athenaeus 557e, who omits the incident with Philip.

[57] Plutarch, *Alexander* 9.4–5, Athenaeus 13.557d, Justin 9.7.5.

Epirus to make war on Philip,[58] and Alexander may have likewise encouraged the Illyrians. Philip neutralized any potential threats by recalling Alexander to Pella and offering his daughter Cleopatra (by Olympias) in marriage to her uncle, Alexander of Epirus.[59] Alexander (Philip's son) returned to court, but the heir felt more marginalized from his father and his principal advisers with each passing day.[60] Philip and Alexander were estranged for the rest of the king's life.[61] The entire incident may have contributed to the pattern of paranoia that Alexander demonstrated when he was king.

In the late spring of 336 Philip sent a vanguard of 10,000 Macedonians and mercenaries under the command of Parmenion, Attalus (further angering Alexander), and Amyntas (the son of Arrabaeus of Lyncestis) across the Hellespont to Abydus.[62] Its purpose was to win over some of the Greek cities of Asia Minor before Philip brought across the main army in July following the wedding of Cleopatra to Alexander of Epirus at Aegae.

"FOR THE CONQUEROR, DEATH"

The day after Alexander of Epirus married the princess Cleopatra celebratory athletic games were held in the theater at Aegae, one of the largest in Greece (Figure 13).[63] Philip intended the wedding and the games as propaganda, publicizing a new era in history with the League of Corinth and his projected invasion of Asia, and to "show himself to the Greeks as an amiable person and to respond to the honors conferred when he was appointed to the supreme command with appropriate entertainment."[64] This ancient "media event" attracted a huge crowd of attendees from ordinary Macedonians to dignitaries from all the Greek cities.

---

[58] Cf. Justin 9.7.7.

[59] Diodorus 16.91.4, Justin 9.7.7. On this Cleopatra: Carney, *Women and Monarchy in Macedonia*, pp. 75–76.

[60] Cf. Plutarch, *Alexander* 10.1–3; see further, Worthington, *Philip II*, pp. 177–180.

[61] E. A. Fredricksmeyer, "Alexander and Philip: Emulation and Resentment," *CJ* 85 (1990), pp. 300–315, Ian Worthington, *Alexander the Great, Man and God*, rev. ed. (London: 2004), pp. 37–43, Worthington, *Philip II*, pp. 176–180, 182–186.

[62] Diodorus 16.91.2, 17.2.4, Justin 9.5.8.

[63] Diodorus 16.91.4–93.4, Justin 9.6.1–3.

[64] Diodorus 16.91.5 and 6.

FIGURE 13. The theatre at Aegae (modern Vergina), former capital of Macedonia, where Philip II was assassinated in 336.

At dawn the spectators to the games packed into the theater. The entertainment began with a grand procession. First came statues of the twelve Olympian gods, then one of Philip to show he was "enthroned among the twelve gods,"[65] and finally Philip, Alexander the heir, and Alexander of Epirus walked into the theater.[66] The two Alexanders took their seats, at which point Philip told his bodyguard to withdraw so he could "show publicly that he was protected by the goodwill of the Greeks, and had no need of a guard of spearmen. Such was the pinnacle of success that he had attained."[67] He stopped by himself in the middle of the theater's orchestra (performance area) to receive the crowd's cheers and applause. Suddenly, one of his bodyguards, Pausanias of Orestis in western Macedonia, rushed forward and stabbed the forty-six-year-old king in the chest.[68]

[65] Diodorus 16.92.5, 95.1. Philip did not consider himself divine: Worthington, *Philip II*, pp. 228–233.

[66] Justin 9.6.3.

[67] Diodorus 16.93.1–2.

[68] Diodorus 16.93.3–95, Justin 9.6.4. N. G. L. Hammond, "The Various Guards of Philip II and Alexander III," *Historia* 40 (1991), pp 396–417, argues that the assassination occurred in an entry passage, not in the actual orchestra of the theater.

Philip died on the spot. His death brought to pass an earlier oracular pronouncement about the Battle of Chaeronea:

> Let me fly far from the battle at Thermodon (Chaeronea), let me take
>   refuge
> Watching from high in the clouds, as I soar with the wings of an
>   eagle.
> Tears are for the loser, but death for the victor.[69]

Pausanias tried to escape, but he slipped on a vine and three of the other royal bodyguards speared him to death with their javelins. For his treachery his corpse was crucified, and his family, as Macedonian law decreed, was executed.

The reason for Pausanias' action is controversial because of the confused and inconsistent accounts in the ancient sources.[70] The official reason that Alexander circulated was that Pausanias acted out of spite because he was one of Philip's jilted lovers. However, some ancient writers give a very different motive and involve Olympias and even Alexander in a plot to kill Philip.[71] The real motive may never be known, but a conspiracy orchestrated by Olympias that used the disgruntled Pausanias as a pawn is a more plausible option than Pausanias deciding to kill Philip so publicly and expect to escape scot-free. Olympias disliked the new queen Cleopatra and had concerns that if she bore Philip a son he would rival Alexander for the throne.[72] Olympias had worked to elevate her son at court. There is a story that because Alexander was Philip's second son she poisoned Arrhidaeus (born in 357) to ensure that Alexander would become heir.[73] Arrhidaeus suffered from some

[69] Plutarch, *Demosthenes* 19.1.

[70] Aristotle, *Politics* 5.1311b1–3, Diodorus 16.93–94, 17.2.3–6, Plutarch, *Alexander* 10.4–7, [Plutarch], *Moralia* 327c, Justin 9.6.4–7.14; cf. Arrian, *FGrH* 156 FF 9 and 22. For a fuller discussion of the assassination and motives, see Worthington, *Philip II*, pp. 181–186, citing bibliography.

[71] Justin 9.7.1: "it was also believed that Pausanias had been suborned by Olympias, mother of Alexander, and that Alexander was not unaware of the plot to murder his father." See too Plutarch, *Alexander* 10.6: "it was Olympias who was chiefly blamed for the assassination, because she was believed to have encouraged the young man [Pausanias] and incited him to take his revenge, but a certain amount of accusation was also attached to Alexander."

[72] Justin 9.7.1–11.

[73] Plutarch, *Alexander* 77.8.

type of mental illness that the poison may well have induced, prompting Philip to set him aside in favor of Alexander.[74] If Olympias suspected her son's succession was in danger when Philip married Cleopatra, she may well have plotted to kill him, given there was no love lost between them.

Alexander arguably also had motivation. He was increasingly estranged from his father and jealous of men like Attalus, Parmenion, and Antipater, who formed an inner circle that excluded him. More than that, he was eager for military glory. He had tasted battle when regent at age sixteen in 340, had played a decisive role at Chaeronea in 338, and was ready to fight with his father in Asia. Philip, however, needed someone whom he could trust in Greece and intended his son to stay behind and serve as deputy hegemon of the League of Corinth. There may well be truth to this ancient account:[75]

> Whenever [Alexander] heard that Philip had captured some famous city or won an overwhelming victory, Alexander would show no pleasure at the news, but would declare to his friends, "Boys, my father will forestall me in everything. There will be nothing great or spectacular for you and me to show the world." He cared nothing for pleasure or wealth but only for deeds of valour and glory, and this was why he believed that the more he received from his father, the less would be left for him to conquer. And so every success that was gained by Macedonia inspired in Alexander the dread that another opportunity for action had been squandered on his father.

It is significant that six years later Alexander visited the Oracle of Zeus Ammon at the Oasis of Siwah in Egypt (now in the Libyan Desert).[76] There he asked the god a number of questions, including whether all the murderers of his father had been punished, to which the god responded in the affirmative. The question is a curious one unless he wanted to put to rest a lingering suspicion that he or his mother was implicated in his father's assassination.

Certainly the manner of Philip's death was undeserved, given his achievements for Macedonia and his tremendous legacy. In a speech

---

[74] Plutarch, *Alexander* 77.7–8, [Plutarch], *Moralia* 1.3, Justin 9.8.2, 13.2.11, 14.5.2.

[75] Translation: C. A. Robinson, *The History of Alexander the Great*, 2 vols. (Providence: 1953).

[76] Diodorus 17.51.1–2, Curtius 4.7.25, Plutarch, *Alexander* 27.5, Justin 11.1.2–12; cf. Arrian 3.4.5. On the visit, see Worthington, *Alexander the Great*, pp. 83–90.

supposedly given to his mutinous troops at Opis in Mesopotamia in 324, Alexander succinctly expressed what Philip had achieved for the Macedonians:[77]

> Philip took you over when you were helpless vagabonds, mostly clothed in skins, feeding a few animals on the mountains and engaged in their defence in unsuccessful fighting with Illyrians, Triballians and the neighbouring Thracians. He gave you cloaks to wear instead of skins, he brought you down from the mountains to the plains; he made you a match in battle for the barbarians on your borders, so that you no longer trusted for your safety to the strength of your position so much as to your natural courage. He made you city dwellers and established the order that comes from good laws and customs. It was due to him that you became masters and not slaves and subjects of those very barbarians who used previously to plunder your possessions and carry off your persons. He annexed the greater part of Thrace to Macedonia and, by capturing the best placed positions by the sea, he opened up the country to trade; he enabled you to work the mines in safety; he made you the rulers of the Thessalians, who in the old days made you dead with terror; he humbled the Phocian people and gave you access into Greece that was broad and easy instead of being narrow and hard. The Athenians and the Thebans were always lying in wait to attack Macedonia; Philip reduced them so low, at a time when we were actually sharing in his exertions, that instead of our paying tribute to the Athenians and taking orders from the Thebans it was we in our turn who gave them security. He entered the Peloponnese and there too he settled affairs, and his recognition as leader with full powers over the whole of the rest of Greece in the expedition against the Persians did not perhaps confer more glory on himself than on the commonwealth of the Macedonians.

Philip's assassination set off a chain of events from Macedonia to Asia Minor. There was chaos in Macedonia,[78] heightened by a possible Illyrian and Paeonian revolt, which could have taken the kingdom back to its dismal days prior to Philip's reign. A substantial number of Greek states revolted from the League of Corinth. Finally, Parmenion and

---

[77] Arrian 7.9.2–5; the translation is that of P. A. Brunt, *Arrian, History of Alexander*, Loeb Classical Library 2 (Cambridge: 1983), ad loc. On Philip's legacy (compared also to that of Alexander), see Worthington, *Philip II*, pp. 194–208.

[78] Arrian 1.25.2, [Plutarch], *Moralia* 327c, Justin 11.1.1–6.

the advance force in Asia waited to learn whether Alexander had succeeded his father or had fallen victim to an insurrection.

DEMOSTHENES' "GREAT BLESSING"

According to Aeschines, scouts of Charidemus (who may have been in Thrace at the time) secretly told Demosthenes that Philip was dead, thereby indicating the influence the orator still wielded.[79] Demosthenes was politically active after his return to the city from the grain commission in 338.[80] His enemies, however, were relentless in pursuing him; for the rest of 338 and some of 337 he was indicted "every day" in the courts, and he needed his friends, especially Nausicles, to move decrees for him in the Assembly.[81] At some point in 337, a man named Eucrates passed a law checking the Areopagus' recent activities. Demosthenes had enjoyed close contact with this council for some years, and therefore Eucrates' law may well have been intentionally anti-Demosthenic.[82] Yet Demosthenes rode out all the attacks, and in 336 he held two important offices on the boards of the city's wall-repairers or *teichopoioi* and of the Theoric Fund. There was even talk of his becoming one of the Athenian representatives to the council of the League of Corinth, which would have been "an extravagant gesture of defiance."[83] Then came the thunderbolt of Philip's assassination.

Demosthenes may have found out about Philip's death from Charidemus, but news of this momentous event traveled fast throughout the Greek world. Still, Demosthenes proclaimed to the Athenians that

---

[79] Aeschines 3.77; cf. Plutarch, *Demosthenes* 22.1, who says that Demosthenes had "secret intelligence of Philip's death."

[80] Aeschines 3.17, 24, 27, 31, Demosthenes 18.113. Background: Lehmann, *Demosthenes*, pp. 182–186, for example.

[81] Aeschines 3.159, Demosthenes 18.249, 25.37, Plutarch, *Demosthenes* 21.3, [Plutarch], *Moralia* 845f; see also E. M. Harris, "Demosthenes Loses a Friend and Nausicles Gains a Position: A Prosopographical Note on Athenian Politics after Chaeronea," *Historia* 43 (1994), pp. 378–384.

[82] Sealey, *Demosthenes*, p. 201 (cf. pp. 185–187); see in more detail, R. W. Wallace, *The Areopagos Council, to 307 B.C.* (Baltimore: 1989), pp. 179–184 (the law had nothing to do with Athenian relations with Macedonia but was motivated by "democratic ideology"—p. 184).

[83] J. K. Davies, *Athenian Propertied Families* (Oxford: 1971), p. 137—the quote is from Ryder, "Demosthenes and Philip II," p. 83.

he had had a dream in which Zeus and Athena appeared to him, promising a great blessing to Athens. He persuaded the Boule to make a public sacrifice of thanksgiving and to vote a crown for Pausanias, Philip's assassin.[84] His sensational reaction was perhaps to be expected, but a true indication of how absolutely he hated the king was that he "appeared in public dressed in magnificent attire and wearing a garland on his head, although his daughter had died only six days before."[85] His daughter, aged about ten, was his only child in 336, and he was said to have doted on her.[86] Nevertheless, he did not respect the normal mourning period of a month but dressed as if he were going to a festival.

Demosthenes might have thought Greece had been blessed, but Philip's death had further consequences for the orator. In the spring of 336 before Philip was murdered a man named Ctesiphon brought a proposal before the Boule.[87] He wanted the Athenians to bestow a gold crown on Demosthenes for the offices he was holding and for serving the best interests of the city over the years.[88] The crown was to be proclaimed in the theater of Dionysus at the forthcoming Dionysia festival.[89] The Boule approved the recommendation,[90] but before it went to the Assembly for endorsement Aeschines blocked it with a *graphe paranomon*. Demosthenes' crowning therefore could not take place until the case against Ctesiphon was decided. Any anger Demosthenes felt for Aeschines must have intensified when in light of Philip's assassination Aeschines delayed prosecuting Ctesiphon. The case was not heard until 330 (Chapter 13).

With Philip dead and the Greeks in revolt, the Macedonian hegemony of Greece appeared a thing of the past. Phocion's remark, however,

---

[84] Plutarch, *Demosthenes* 22.1–2.

[85] Plutarch, *Demosthenes* 22.3; see also Aeschines 3.77, 160, *Phocion* 16.6, [Plutarch], *Moralia* 847b.

[86] On Demosthenes' children, see Chapter 2 p. 30.

[87] Probably the same Ctesiphon who brought news to the Athenians that Philip wanted to end the first war, and who was one of the envoys on the embassies to him that led to the Peace of Philocrates. Plutarch, *Demosthenes* 24.2, wrongly dates Ctesiphon's proposal before Chaeronea.

[88] Aeschines 3.49–50, 237, Demosthenes 18.57, 118. The actual wording of the proposal is unknown; Demosthenes 18.118 quoted it, but documents in speeches are not often genuine.

[89] Aeschines 3.49–50, 101, 236–237, Demosthenes 18.57–58, 244.

[90] Demosthenes 18.118.

that the army that defeated the Athenians at Chaeronea was now only one man short proved prophetic.[91] Even while Philip's corpse lay on the theater floor at Aegae the general Antipater declared his loyalty to Alexander and led him before the people.[92] His quick action muted any opposition to Alexander's succession,[93] and the throne passed to him as Philip intended. The new king quickly convened an Assembly, encouraging the people to take heart and swearing the customary oath to them that he would rule according to the laws; they in turn swore their oath of allegiance to him.[94]

Thus Alexander III (the "Great") became king of Macedonia at the age of twenty. Demosthenes clearly thought little of him: when he stopped celebrating Philip's death, he nicknamed the new king Margites, the name of a foolish character in an old poem.[95] As events quickly showed, Demosthenes was more deserving of that nickname.

---

[91] Plutarch, *Phocion* 16.6.

[92] Justin 11.1.7–10.

[93] Alexander's friends had armed themselves expecting trouble, and "all Macedonia was seething with discontent, looking to Amyntas and the sons of Aeropus": Arrian 1.25.2, [Plutarch], *Moralia* 327c. His friends might have thought that Alexander was also a target for assassination, hence they prepared to defend him, but the second part is exaggerated. Amyntas was Philip's nephew (the actual heir in 359); Aeropus of Lyncestis had been exiled by Philip (Polyaenus 4.2.3).

[94] Diodorus 17.2.1–2.

[95] Cf. Aeschines 3.160.

Demosthenes and
Alexander the Great

A LEXANDER WENT FROM being a spectator at the games in the theater of Aegae to king of Macedonia within minutes. If that new responsibility was not enough, he also had to deal with potential opponents who threatened the internal stability of his kingdom as well as a widespread Greek revolt that jeopardized Macedonia's control of Greece.

ALEXANDER TAKES CONTROL

Alexander first attended to the funeral of his father. Philip's body, arms, and armor were burned on top of a huge pyre. Afterward, his bones were washed in wine, wrapped in a purple robe, and placed in a gold *larnax* or box. On its lid were emblazoned the Macedonian starburst (a sixteen-rayed star), the emblem of the royal house, and rosettes. The *larnax* was put inside a stone sarcophagus, which was interred in a tomb along with his weaponry and other personal items and a set of small ivory heads (each about one inch high) of the royal family. The tomb was covered with earth to form a large tumulus, thirteen meters high and one hundred meters in diameter. Alexander had to conduct the burial in haste because of the pressing problems he faced, although he swore that one day he would bury his father properly in a tomb that rivaled the pyramids. When the modern village of Vergina, in the shadow of Mount Pieria and fifty miles southwest of Thessaloniki, was

FIGURE 14. The tumulus at Vergina (ancient Aegae) containing four royal tombs, including that believed to be Philip's.

identified as ancient Aegae,[1] the Greek archaeologist Manolis Andronikos excavated a large tumulus there in 1977 (Figure 14). He discovered four tombs within it, of which Tomb II, consisting of a main chamber and a smaller, separate antechamber, excited the most interest.[2] The main chamber contained various military and personal artifacts, including a set of small, ivory heads. One of them is of a bearded man with a disfigured right eye (Figure 7, p. 69), evoking Philip's blinding wound at the siege of Methone in 355/4 (Chapter 3 pp. 68–69). The skeletal remains interred in the tomb were tested and revealed to have been burned and washed in wine, consistent with Philip's burial. The antechamber contained bones and weaponry that suggest Philip's sixth wife Meda of Thrace, whom he married in 342 and who may have committed *suttee* (ritual suicide) when her husband

[1] N. G. L. Hammond, *A History of Macedonia* 1 (Oxford: 1972), pp. 156–157 and "The Location of Aegae," *JHS* 117 (1997), pp. 177–179.

[2] M. Andronikos, *Vergina: The Royal Tombs and the Ancient City* (Athens: repr. 2004) and "The Royal Tombs at Aigai (Vergina)," in M. B. Hatzopoulos and L. D. Loukopoulos (eds.), *Philip of Macedon* (London 1980), pp. 188–231; cf. S. Drougou and C. Saatsoglou-Paliadeli, *Vergina: Wandering through the Archaeological Site* (Athens: 2004).

was assassinated. It appears, then, that the tomb of Philip had been found. Although there are plenty of skeptics, the forensic evidence, including the condition of the bones and the rebuilding of the skull and face (Figure 2, p. 4), has never been compellingly refuted.[3]

Alexander had already overseen the execution of the three sons of his father's assassin Pausanias. Now he gave orders to eliminate potential and real enemies to his kingship in a purge that lasted for the rest of 336 and the next year.[4] Two of the sons of Aeropus, who appeared to have posed a threat to Alexander, were quickly executed[5]—the third (named Alexander) proclaimed his loyalty to the new king and was spared. Alexander also had Amyntas, son of Perdiccas III, the true heir to the throne in 359, put to death. Attalus, who was still with the advance force in Asia Minor, was also not spared. Alexander sent a letter to Parmenion instructing him to execute his co-commander. Parmenion did so without hesitation, thereby proving his loyalty to the new king.[6] One person against whom Alexander took no action was his half-brother Arrhidaeus, who lived comfortably at Pella throughout Alexander's reign.[7] Possibly the king let him live because of the blood tie between them.

With Macedonia secured, Alexander turned to Greece, where the revolt had spread from Thessaly to the Peloponnese. Some rebellious cities had even overthrown the Macedonian garrisons and oligarchies that Philip had installed after Chaeronea. Demosthenes' dancing in the streets at the news of Philip's assassination would not last long. Alexander quickly ended the Greek revolt, winning over "some cities by diplomacy, others by striking fear into them, and others by the actual use of force."[8] He marched first into Thessaly, cowing it into

---

[3] See Worthington, *Philip II*, pp. 234–241, for the evidence and citing bibliography for the arguments for and against the occupant being Philip, to which add E. N. Borza and O. Palagia, "The Chronology of the Royal Macedonian Tombs at Vergina," *Jahrbuch des Deutsche Archaeologischen Instituts* 122 (2007), pp. 81–125 (not Philip).

[4] J. R. Ellis, "The First Months of Alexander's Reign," in B. Barr-Sharrar and E. N. Borza (eds.), *Macedonia and Greece in Late Classical and Early Hellenistic Times* (Washington: 1982), pp. 69–73.

[5] See Chapter 11 note 93.

[6] Diodorus 17.2.4–6, 5.1–2, Curtius 7.1.3, Justin 11.5.1.

[7] Arrian, *Successors* 1.22; W. S. Greenwalt, "The Search for Arrhidaeus," *Anc. World* 10 (1985), pp. 69–77.

[8] Diodorus 17.3.6–4.9, Arrian 1.1.2–3. Historical background: A. B. Bosworth, *Conquest and Empire, The Reign of Alexander the Great* (Cambridge: 1988), pp. 188–192 and Ian Worthington, *Alexander the Great, Man and God*, rev. ed. (London: 2004), pp. 50–53.

submission, and, like Philip, was elected its archon.[9] Probably when he arrived at Thermopylae he received his father's two votes on the Amphictyonic Council. From there Alexander moved to Thebes, where an Athenian embassy met him. Demosthenes had been one of the ambassadors, but at Mount Cithaeron he seems to have had second thoughts and returned home.[10] Alexander was ominously brusque with the embassy at first, but then he had a change of heart and offered Athens his friendship. Finally, he traveled to Corinth, summoning envoys from all the Greek states to him. The Spartans defied him, as they had done with Philip, haughtily proclaiming they did not accept him as master of the Greeks.[11] The envoys swore an oath of allegiance to him on behalf of their states, thereby reinstituting the League of Corinth. Alexander was elected its hegemon. Then, in keeping with his father's final plan, he was chosen commander-in-chief of the Greek forces to invade Asia.[12] Satisfied with his settlement of Greece, Alexander returned to Pella.

The following year (335) the young king successfully campaigned in the Danube basin against the Triballi, the tribe that had defeated his father in 339. He killed 3,000 of them (losing only 11 cavalry and 41 infantry), and then attacked the Illyrians.[13] He had requested the Athenians send him ships and troops for both campaigns, but Demosthenes and Hyperides persuaded the Assembly to refuse him.[14] Then, in the middle of his Illyrian campaign, Alexander received news that the Thebans had besieged the Macedonian garrison on the Cadmea and were calling on the other Greeks to resist the "Macedonian tyrant."[15]

---

[9] Diodorus 17.4.1, Aeschines 3.161; cf. Justin 11.3.2.

[10] Diodorus 17.4, Aeschines 3.161, Dinarchus 1.82, Plutarch, *Demosthenes* 23.3.

[11] Diodorus 17.4.9, Arrian 1.1.2, [Plutarch], *Moralia* 240a–b, Justin 11.2.5. 9.5.3.

[12] Renewal of the league and Persian invasion: Aeschines 3.161, Diodorus 17.3–4, 17.4.9, Arrian 1.1.1–3. P. A. Brunt, "The Aims of Alexander," *Greece & Rome* 12 (1965), pp. 205–215, argues that Alexander's invasion was merely an inheritance from Philip. E. A. Fredricksmeyer, "On the Final Aims of Philip II," in W. L. Adams and E. N. Borza (eds.), *Philip II, Alexander the Great, and the Macedonian Heritage* (Lanham: 1982), pp. 85–98 and "Alexander the Great and the Kingship of Asia," in A. B. Bosworth and E. J. Baynham (eds.), *Alexander the Great in Fact and Fiction* (Oxford: 2000), pp. 136–166, argues that Philip wanted to establish an absolute monarchy. If this is true, then Alexander's invasion was not for panhellenic but personal reasons.

[13] Diodorus 17.8.1–2, Arrian 1.1.4–6.11, Plutarch, *Alexander* 11.5, Justin 11.2.8.

[14] [Plutarch], *Moralia* 847c, 848e; cf. Plutarch, *Phocion* 21.1.

[15] Arrian 1.7.2, Justin 11.2.

THE REVOLT OF THEBES

When a rumor circulated in Greece that Alexander had died in Illyria, Theban democrats, whom Philip had expelled from the city after Chaeronea, returned home.[16] They persuaded the people to revolt from the League of Corinth and may also have promised to support a bid for the throne by Amyntas.[17] Alexander knew he needed to act quickly before the other Greeks, especially Athens and Sparta, answered the Theban call to arms.[18] He made terms with the Illyrian king, and with 30,000 infantry and 300 cavalry marched to Thebes, covering 250 miles through rugged terrain in just 13 days.[19] He had marched so quickly that the Thebans believed it was not Alexander before their gates but Antipater from Macedonia. When the Thebans refused to surrender, Alexander besieged the city.[20]

The Greeks carefully considered the Theban predicament. However, as Philip had originally intended, reprisals from the other members of the League of Corinth for breaking the peace proved enough of a deterrent. In the end, virtually every state ignored Thebes' call for help. The Arcadians mobilized troops, but their commander Astylus waited at the isthmus once it became clear Alexander was alive. Although Demosthenes' speeches from this period do not survive, it appears that he initially sided with the Thebans, perhaps supposing Alexander was dead, and even advocated an alliance with Darius III of Persia.[21] The Persian king was said to have sent 300 talents to Demosthenes to help Thebes and foster a wider Greek revolt (see below). Then Demosthenes had a change of heart and successfully persuaded the Athenians to remain neutral.[22]

---

[16] Arrian 1.7.2; cf. 1.7.6. Justin 11.2.8 for the view that Demosthenes told the Greeks Alexander died fighting against the Triballi.

[17] Ian Worthington, "Alexander's Destruction of Thebes," in W. Heckel & L. A. Tritle (eds.), *Crossroads of History. The Age of Alexander the Great* (Claremont: 2003), pp. 65–86.

[18] Arrian 1.7.4; cf. Plutarch, *Alexander* 11.6.

[19] Arrian 1.7.5.

[20] Siege: Diodorus 17.8.3–14, Arrian 1.7–9, Plutarch, *Alexander* 11.6–13, *Demosthenes* 23.1–3, Justin 11.3.6–4.8; see also Bosworth, *Conquest and Empire, The Reign of Alexander the Great*, pp. 32–33, 194–196, Worthington, *Alexander the Great*, pp. 58–63.

[21] Diodorus 17.8.6, Arrian 2.15, Dinarchus 1.19, Plutarch, *Demosthenes* 23.1, [Plutarch], *Moralia* 850.

[22] Cf. Carlier, *Démosthène*, pp. 238–242.

The siege was difficult for the Macedonians. They needed to liberate the Macedonian garrison on the Cadmea, but the Thebans had constructed a double palisade to reinforce the southern section of their defensive wall, which formed part of the Cadmea. At one point the Thebans held off a Macedonian attack on the walls and 70 Macedonian archers, including their commander Eurybotas the Cretan, were killed. Eventually, Alexander's men were able to push through the city gates and pour into the city, at which point the Theban cavalry deserted, leaving street fighting to decide the city's fate. Alexander freed his garrison and then systematically massacred the Thebans—6,000 were killed and 30,000 were taken prisoner, against Macedonian losses of 500 men.

Joining Alexander at Thebes were representatives from the Thespiaeans, Plataeans, Phocians, and Orchomenians, all members of the League of Corinth.[23] They had suffered at Theban hands in the past, and the Phocians, Plataeans, and other Boeotians actually fought with the Macedonians in the city.[24] Knowing they would eagerly seize the opportunity for revenge, Alexander cynically turned the Theban punishment over to them. On behalf of the league, they directed him to raze Thebes to the ground, ostensibly because the city had medized during the Persian Wars.[25] Alexander complied, sparing only the temples and the house of the famous fifth-century poet Pindar, who had written an encomium for Alexander I of Macedonia.[26] Thebes was not rebuilt until 316.

The king had wanted Thebes destroyed for harboring Amyntas and to present "possible rebels among the Greeks with a terrible warning" that he would not tolerate rebellion.[27] His action achieved its purpose. Apart from a brief attempt by the Spartans to resist Macedonian rule in 331 (see below), Greece remained passive until Alexander died in 323.

[23] Diodorus 17.13.5; cf. 17.14.2, Arrian 1.8.8, Plutarch, *Alexander* 11.11, Justin 11.3.8.

[24] Arrian 1.8.8 (from Ptolemy, *FGrH* 138 F 3).

[25] Diodorus 17.14.1–3, Justin 11.3.8–10; cf. Arrian 1.9.6–9.

[26] Arrian 1.9.10, Plutarch, *Alexander* 11.12, Pliny, *NH* 7.109, Dio Chrysostrum, *Oration* 2.33, with W. J. Slater, "Pindar's House," *GRBS* 12 (1971), pp. 146–147.

[27] Diodorus 17.14.4. See also Plutarch, *Alexander* 11.12 (Alexander "wanted to frighten the rest of the Greeks into submission by making a terrible example"), Polybius 38.2.12, 4.23.8 (to cow the Greeks into submission); contra Arrian 1.9.6–8: Thebes was destroyed because of divine wrath.

SURRENDERING SHEEPDOGS TO WOLVES

News of Thebes' fate spread quickly. The Athenians interrupted their celebration of the festival of the Eleusinian Mysteries to hold an emergency Assembly. Demosthenes was clearly out of favor, for Demades dominated its proceedings. The Athenians boldly decided to offer Theban fugitives asylum in Athens and to send an embassy of ten men, led by Demades, to Alexander.[28] They were to take a letter expressing relief that the king had not suffered harm in Illyria and—contemptibly—congratulating him for punishing the Thebans. Because of his history of defying Macedonian kings, Demosthenes was not a member of the embassy.

At first Alexander refused to see the Athenians and threw their letter away, but then because he respected the skills of their general Phocion he changed his mind.[29] He told the Athenian envoys he would take no formal action against the city, but he insisted on the expulsions of the Theban refugees and the surrender of several prominent anti-Macedonian politicians, including Demosthenes, Lycurgus, Polyeuctus, and Ephialtes, as well as the general Charidemus.[30] At an Assembly discussing Alexander's demands, Phocion proposed that the people hand over these men—it was because of them, he said, that the Athenians were in this sorry state of affairs in the first place. Hyperides and Lycurgus spoke in Demosthenes' defense, but Demosthenes "compared himself and his colleagues to sheepdogs who fought to defend the people, and referred to Alexander as the lone wolf of Macedonia."[31] If the people, he continued, gave up these men to Alexander, then, like sheep that surrendered their sheepdogs to wolves, they would be yielding to Macedonia.

An impasse was reached, so Demades recommended sending another embassy to Alexander. It would ask him to reconsider his decision

---

[28] Plutarch, *Alexander* 13.1.

[29] Plutarch, *Phocion* 17.4.

[30] Diodorus 17.115, Arrian 1.10.4–6, Plutarch, *Demosthenes* 23.4, *Phocion* 17.2, [Plutarch], *Moralia* 841e, 847c, 848e, Justin 11.4.10–11. The sources give differing numbers but five names are common to all accounts: Demosthenes, Lycurgus, Polyeuctus, Ephialtes, and Charidemus; see A. B. Bosworth, *A Historical Commentary on Arrian's History of Alexander* 1 (Oxford: 1980), pp. 92–96, Sealey, *Demosthenes*, pp. 204–205, Lehmann, *Demosthenes*, pp. 190–191.

[31] Aristobulus, *FGrH* 139 F 3 = Plutarch, *Demosthenes* 23.5–6.

and inform him that the people would investigate each of the men he
had stipulated and prosecute anyone guilty of misconduct. Demades
again led the embassy, but Phocion was also elected to it because of
Alexander's admiration for the old general. The meeting with Alexander was short. Phocion implored him to put the past behind him and
focus on attacking the barbarians in Asia, not other Greeks. The young
king, anxious to invade Asia and with Greece again under Macedonian
rule, relented, but insisted on the expulsion of Charidemus.[32] The
relieved Athenians rewarded Demades for his role in these negotiations with a statue and *sitesis* (free public meals in the Prytaneum or
city hall). Demosthenes the sheepdog was thus free to continue railing
against the lone wolf of Macedonia, but for the next decade he kept a
low profile in politics.

A postscript to the revolt of Thebes is the issue of the 300 talents
Darius III supposedly sent to Athens. Evidently the entire amount
went missing, for the Areopagus undertook an enquiry into its dis-
appearance, but abandoned it when Alexander left Greece for Asia in
the spring of 334.[33] Demosthenes was later accused of treacherously
keeping all the money, not even spending 10 talents that the Arcadian leader Astylus demanded to take his troops from the isthmus to
Thebes, and so betraying Thebes to destruction.[34] The charge,
found in the later prosecution speeches of Aeschines and Dinarchus,
is unfounded.[35] Among other things, these speeches are inconsistent
and contradictory: Aeschines in 330 stated that Demosthenes embezzled only 70 talents, whereas Dinarchus in 323 accused him in
different parts of his speech of taking either all 300 talents or only
150 talents, and even of sharing the money with other men.[36] Furthermore, no ancient historical writer related that Demosthenes
kept Persian money or blamed him for Thebes' destruction.[37] They

---

[32] Charidemus fled to Persia but was killed two years later: Arrian 1.10.1–6, Diodorus
17.15.1–5, Plutarch, *Demosthenes* 23.6, Justin 11.4.12.

[33] Dinarchus 1.10.

[34] Aeschines 3.239–240; cf. 133, 155–156, Dinarchus 1.10, 18–20, 24–26.

[35] See Ian Worthington, *A Historical Commentary on Dinarchus* (Ann Arbor: 1992), ad
1.18–21 on pp. 139–143 and 160–170 and "Intentional History: Alexander, Demosthenes and Thebes," in L. Foxhall and H.-J. Gehrke (eds.), *Intentional History:
Spinning Time in Ancient Greece* (Stuttgart: 2010), pp. 239–246.

[36] Aeschines 3.239–240, Dinarchus 1.10, 18, 70.

[37] Plutarch, *Demosthenes* 14.2 and 20.4–5, [Plutarch], *Moralia* 848a, Diodorus 17.4.8,
Justin 11.2.7.

mention only that at first he supported the revolt but then he and the Assembly decided otherwise. Aeschines and Dinarchus were simply inventing a connection between Demosthenes, the Persian money, and the razing of Thebes to cast aspersions on Demosthenes' character.

ALEXANDER THE GREAT

In the spring of 334, Alexander crossed the Hellespont with an army of 48,100 soldiers, 6,100 cavalry, and 120 warships and transport vessels.[38] He left behind Antipater as guardian (*epitropos*) of Macedonia and deputy hegemon of the League of Corinth.[39] Alexander had bigger fish to fry in Asia, but he was always aware of events on the Greek mainland.[40] Although he had visited Athens only once, after Chaeronea in 338, he attempted to remain on amicable terms with the Athenians. For example, after his first battle against the Persians in 334, at the Granicus River, he sent back 300 Persian panoplies (sets of armor) in dedication to Athena at Athens. There is a story that in 326, as he struggled across the raging Hydaspes River in India to do battle with the Indian prince Porus, he called out "O Athenians, can you possibly believe what perils I am undergoing to win glory in your eyes?"[41] He cared little about Demosthenes, however, and after his demand for the orator's surrender in 335 never seems to have bothered about him again.

Alexander never returned to Greece, dying in Babylon in June 323 a few months short of his thirty-third birthday. By that time, he had conquered the entire Persian Empire, including Egypt, Syria, and the

[38] D. Engels, *Alexander the Great and the Logistics of the Macedonian Army* (Berkeley and Los Angeles: 1978), pp. 146–147 (Table 4).

[39] Arrian 1.11.3. On Antipater, see E. Baynham, "Antipater, Manager of Kings," in Ian Worthington (ed.), *Ventures into Greek History: Essays in Honour of N. G. L. Hammond* (Oxford: 1994), pp. 331–356.

[40] Alexander and the Greeks: M. Faraguna, "Alexander and the Greeks," in J. Roisman (ed.), *Brill Companion to Alexander the Great* (Leiden: 2003), pp. 99–130 and E. Poddighe, "Alexander and the Greeks," in W. Heckel and L. Tritle (eds.), *Alexander the Great. A New History* (Oxford: 2009), pp. 99–120.

[41] Onesicritus, *FGrH* 134 F 19 = Plutarch, *Alexander* 60.1, 5–7.

FIGURE 15. Early Hellenistic portrait of Alexander the Great found at Pella.

Levantine coast. When he died he was preparing to invade Arabia, and after that probably the western Mediterranean.[42] Alexander did not merely extend Macedonia's empire from Greece in the west to what the Greeks called India (now Pakistan) in the east, but helped spread Greek culture in the eastern half of his empire.

[42] Alexander's reign: Bosworth, *Conquest and Empire*, Worthington, *Alexander the Great* and *By the Spear. Philip II, Alexander the Great, and the Rise and Fall of the Macedonian Empire* (New York: 2014), P. Cartledge, *Alexander the Great: The Hunt for a New Past* (London: 2003), and see also Major General J. F. C. Fuller, *The Generalship of Alexander the Great* (repr. New Brunswick: 1960). Succinct surveys and discussions: B. Strauss, "Alexander: The Military Campaign," in J. Roisman (ed.), *Brill Companion to Alexander the Great* (Leiden: 2003), pp. 133–156, D. L. Gilley and Ian Worthington, "Alexander the Great, Macedonia and Asia" and M. J. Olbrycht, "Macedonia and Persia," in J. Roisman and Ian Worthington (eds.), *Blackwell Companion to Ancient Macedonia* (Malden: 2010), pp. 186–207 and 342–369, respectively, and Ian Worthington, "The Battles and Sieges of Alexander the Great," in H. Sidebottom and M. Whitby (eds.), *Blackwell Encyclopaedia to Ancient Battles* (Malden: forthcoming).

KEEPING A LOW PROFILE

"To explain why little is known of what Demosthenes was doing during the reign of Alexander, the best hypothesis is that he was not doing much."[43] Demosthenes was certainly less active in Athenian politics during Alexander's reign in contrast to that of Philip, but he had not abandoned his attempts to defy Macedonia.[44] Moreover, although none of the political speeches he gave in this period survive, he addressed the Assembly on at least two significant occasions for Athens in 331 and 324.

Demosthenes' relative inactivity may be attributed in part to his traumatic experience of 335, when he had escaped Alexander's wrath by the skin of his teeth. If Alexander could insist on his surrender once, he could do so again. Next time the king might not be so forgiving—or the Athenians so willing to protect him. Moreover, no major issues plagued the Athenians after Alexander departed Greece because of Macedonia's tight control, so there was no need for Demosthenes to speak in public. He had achieved his dizzying political height by exploiting Philip's perceived threat to Athens and Greek autonomy. After Chaeronea, Demosthenes could no longer worry the Athenians over potential threats from Macedonia—they had been realized.

Philip's death ultimately had little effect on the Macedonian hegemony of Greece, which continued under Alexander. The revolt of Thebes and Alexander's merciless punishment of the city proved to Demosthenes what he already knew: Macedonian power was absolute. The new situation in Greece no longer permitted fiery anti-Macedonian speeches in the Assembly. Demosthenes had expected Alexander to stay at Pella,[45] but when he led his army to Asia in 334, Demosthenes changed tactics. He began writing letters to Persian generals encouraging them to defeat Alexander,[46] wanting him to be "trampled under the hoofs of the Persian cavalry," as Aeschines later stated.[47] In 333,

---

[43] Sealey, *Demosthenes*, p. 208.

[44] Ian Worthington, "Demosthenes' (In)activity During the Reign of Alexander the Great," in Ian Worthington (ed.), *Demosthenes: Statesman and Orator* (London: 2000), pp. 90–113. This chapter and the following ones have their genesis in that essay.

[45] Aeschines 3.160.

[46] Plutarch, *Demosthenes* 23.2.

[47] Aeschines 3.164; cf. G. L. Cawkwell, "The Crowning of Demosthenes," CQ^2 19 (1969), pp. 174–180, Lehmann, *Demosthenes*, pp. 192–194.

however, the futility of his hope manifested itself when Alexander decisively defeated Darius at the Battle of Issus (modern Iskenderun, on the Gulf of Issus), after which he declared himself Lord of Asia.[48] Alexander's second and final battle against Darius was at Gaugamela in 331, and again ended in a Persian rout.[49] By late 330 all of the great Persian capitals had fallen to Alexander and Darius had been treacherously murdered by some of his satraps. Alexander to all intents and purposes was now the Great King, though he never took that title, and he prepared to invade Bactria and Sogdiana. Demosthenes now knew that it would take a miracle to end Macedonian hegemony and restore Greek autonomy, so he was left with no choice but to adjust to the new Greece.

Demosthenes might not have been "doing much" politically during Alexander's reign, but he was still active in the courts. Several of his private speeches were written in the 320s so he likely returned to his career as a speechwriter.[50] He also teamed up with Lycurgus in 325/4 to prosecute a man named Aristogeiton, a second-rate and venal orator who illegally exercised his citizen rights while in debt to the state.[51] Demosthenes' successful speeches against Aristogeiton survive, although there is some doubt about the authenticity of the second one.[52] Also in this period, Demosthenes might have prepared for

---

[48] Diodorus 17.31–36, Arrian 2.6–11, Curtius 3.3–4, 7–11, Plutarch, *Alexander* 20, Justin 11.9, with Fuller, *Generalship of Alexander*, pp. 154–162, Bosworth, *Conquest and Empire*, pp. 58–64, Worthington, *Alexander the Great*, pp. 95–102. Alexander fought three battles against the Persians, at the Granicus river (334), Issus (333) and Gaugamela (331), but the Persian king was not present at the first one.

[49] Diodorus 17.56–61, Arrian 3.8–15, Curtius 4.9–10.12, 4.12–16.33, Plutarch, *Alexander* 31–33, Justin 11.13–14.7, with Fuller, *Generalship of Alexander*, pp. 163–180, Bosworth, *Conquest and Empire*, pp. 76–85, Worthington, *Alexander the Great*, pp. 126–135.

[50] For example, a speech against Phormion (34) can be dated to 327/6: Blass, *attische Beredsamkeit*[2] 3, p. 578, MacDowell, *Demosthenes*, pp. 279–284. Other speeches include *Against Dionysodorus* (56), and the two speeches against Aristogeiton (25 and 26), on which see MacDowell, *Demosthenes*, pp. 284–287 and 298–313, respectively.

[51] Athenaeus 13.591e, Plutarch, *Phocion* 10.2; cf. [Demosthenes] 25.42, 47, 53, 67 and 70–73, and see R. Sealey, "Who Was Aristogeiton?," *BICS* 7 (1960), pp. 33–43. See previous note.

[52] R. Sealey, "Pseudodemosthenes xiii and xxv," *REG* 80 (1967), pp. 250–255; for the case for authenticity, see MacDowell, *Demosthenes*, pp. 298–313: Speech 25 was Demosthenic but another prosecutor from the trial composed speech 26.

circulation the fifty-five *prooemia*, or rhetorical openings of political speeches, that have survived in his corpus.[53] Since some of these preludes mirror several of his extant speeches,[54] the others may be from speeches that did not survive. Alternatively, he may have intended his *prooimia* to provide a "bank" of openings from which other orators might borrow.[55]

Demosthenes returned to the political limelight in 331 when the inevitable confrontation between Sparta, which had refused to join the League of Corinth, and Antipater took place.

SPARTA GOES TO WAR

In the late spring of 331 the Spartans under their king Agis III attacked Megalopolis and urged the rest of the Greek cities to rebel against Macedonian rule.[56] Two years earlier, Agis had sailed to the island of Siphnos to seek money and military support from the Persian satraps

---

[53] Blass, *attische Beredsamkeit*² 3.1, pp. 281–287. There are fifty-six *prooimia* but the fifty-fourth was included in them by mistake as it is an account of state sacrifices performed in honor of various gods. Translation with notes: Ian Worthington, *Demosthenes: Speeches 60 and 61, Prologues, Letters* (Austin: 2006), pp. 55–98. See also Ian Worthington, "Oral Performance in the Athenian Assembly and the Demosthenic *Prooemia*," in C. M. Mackie (ed.), *Oral Performance and Its Context* (Leiden: 2004), pp. 129–143.

[54] For example, *Prooemion* 1 is very close to *Philippic* 1 and *Prooemion* 3 to *Olynthiac* 1. *Prooemion* 7 is almost exactly the opening of *On the Symmories*, as is *Prooemion* 8 to *For the People of Megalopolis* and *Prooemion* 27 to *For the Liberty of the Rhodians*. Parts of other *prooimia* correspond to some of Demosthenes' other speeches; thus 21.4 is very similar to Demosthenes 4.14–15; 23.2 is similar to the epilogue of Demosthenes 4 (51); 30 has similar arguments to Demosthenes 4.2 and 9.5; 35 has some similarity to Demosthenes 2.25; and 41 is similar to Demosthenes 3.35–36. In 48.2 the expression "the office reveals the man" echoes Demosthenes 19.247, while 49.3 is very similar to Demosthenes 19.2, and 53.4 echoes Demosthenes 3.33.

[55] That may explain why Alexandrian scholars copied his public speeches along with his *prooimia*: see Ian Worthington, "Why We Have Demosthenes' Symbouleutic Speeches: A Note," in F. C. Gabaudan and J. V. M. Dosuna (eds.), *Dic mihi, Musa, virum: Homenaje al profesor Antonio López Eire* (Salamanca: 2010), pp. 709–713.

[56] On the war: Bosworth, *Conquest and Empire*, pp. 198–204; see also E. Badian, "Agis III: Revisions and Reflections," in Ian Worthington (ed.), *Ventures into Greek History: Essays in Honour of N. G. L. Hammond* (Oxford: 1994), pp. 258–292.

Pharnabazus and Autophradates. Pharnabazus gave Agis 10 triremes
and 30 talents, which he sent to his brother Agesilaus in Crete, a strategic base for the Persian fleet and also a mercenary refuge. When in
the same year Alexander defeated Darius at the Battle of Issus, about
8,000 mercenaries from the Persian army fled to Crete, where Agesilaus hired them for his brother.[57]

Most of the Peloponnese and some northern Greeks responded to
Agis' call in 331.[58] He thus posed no small threat to Antipater because
of his resources and the natural Greek resentment to Macedonian rule
not to mention the fact that Antipater was then in Thrace putting
down a revolt.[59] Because he had recently dispatched troops from Macedonia to Alexander in Asia, he did not have the manpower to fight in
both Thrace and the Peloponnese. In some desperation Alexander
hurriedly sent him 3,000 silver talents to hire mercenaries.[60]

The Athenian Assembly met to debate the pros and cons of taking
Agis' side, an issue pressing enough for Demosthenes to emerge from
the political shadows and address his fellow citizens. He may have
prompted the people to deploy their fleet to assist Sparta, based on the
implication of Demades' warning that they would need to meet this
expense by using money budgeted for an approaching festival.[61] Only
the speech *On the Treaty with Alexander*, which was erroneously included among Demosthenes' works, survives from this debate.[62] Its
speaker is unknown, but the speech accused Alexander of breaking
many of the terms of the League of Corinth by supporting various
tyrants (unconstitutional leaders) in several Greek cities[63] and helping
to overthrow democracy at Pellene.[64] He furnished information that

---

[57] Diodorus 17.48.2, Curtius 4.1.39.

[58] Diodorus 17.62.7. See E. I. McQueen, "Some Notes on the Anti-Macedonian Movement in the Peloponnese in 331 B.C.," *Historia* 37 (1978), pp. 52–59.

[59] Diodorus 17.62.4–6.

[60] Arrian 3.16.9–10; cf. Diodorus 17.64.5, Curtius 5.1.43.

[61] [Plutarch], *Moralia* 818e–f.

[62] [Demosthenes] 17, on which see Schaefer, *Demosthenes²* 3, pp. 203–206, Blass,
attische Beredsamkeit² 3.2, pp. 121–126, MacDowell, *Demosthenes*, pp. 379–381. See
also G.L. Cawkwell, "A Note on Ps.-Demosthenes 17.20," *Phoenix* 15 (1961),
pp. 74–78. Translation with notes: J. Trevett, *Demosthenes, Speeches 1–17* (Austin:
2011), pp. 286–300.

[63] [Demosthenes] 17. 4–7, 15–16.

[64] [Demosthenes] 17.10–11.

Macedonian ships had preyed on Athenian and other trading vessels sailing from the Black Sea and that enemy vessels had even put into the Piraeus.[65] For these exploitive actions the Athenians had to throw their weight behind Agis, and the speaker ended his speech on a rousing note: "if you bid me do so, men of Athens, I shall move a proposal, just as the agreement requires, that we wage war on the transgressors."[66]

Demosthenes then appears to have had second thoughts and he persuaded the Athenians to ignore Agis' call.[67] At his trials in 330 and 323, his prosecutors seized on this volte-face to accuse him of bringing discredit to Athens for missing a golden opportunity to resist Macedonia. Yet his advice was prudent.[68] Agis enjoyed some initial military successes, but in early 330 Antipater, newly returned from Thrace, brought him to battle at Megalopolis, where he defeated his troops and killed him.[69] Antipater fined Agis' allies heavily and instructed the Spartans to surrender fifty noblemen to him, which he held as hostages.[70] He charged the League of Corinth to decide Sparta's actual punishment, as was its right, but for some reason it transferred the matter to Alexander. Surprisingly, the king merely ordered the Spartans to pay the Megalopolitans 120 talents for besieging their city and probably now insisted that Sparta join the league.[71]

Alexander's leniency may well have been prompted by a Spartan embassy that met him to plead for mercy and, significantly, to report that the Spartans had voted him divine honors.[72] Alexander's pretensions to personal divinity are controversial, but as his reign progressed he came to believe he was a god and openly referred to himself as the

---

[65] [Demosthenes] 17.19–22, 26–28.

[66] [Demosthenes] 17.30.

[67] Aeschines 3.165–166, Dinarchus 1.34–35; cf. Plutarch, *Demosthenes* 24.1.

[68] Cf. Carlier, *Démosthène*, p. 246, Lehmann, *Demosthenes*, p. 195.

[69] Dinarchus 1.34, Diodorus 17.63.1–3, Curtius 6.1, and see Worthington, *Alexander the Great*, pp. 77–78, 105–106 and 111. Date: Badian, "Agis III: Revisions and Reflections," pp. 272–277.

[70] On the settlements and especially punishment of Sparta: McQueen, "Some Notes on the Anti-Macedonian Movement in the Peloponnese in 331 B.C.," pp. 52–58.

[71] Aeschines 3.133, Diodorus 17.63.1–3, 73.5–6, Curtius 6.1.19–21. Fine: Diodorus 17.73, Curtius 6.1; membership: Sealey, *Demosthenes*, p. 206.

[72] [Plutarch], *Moralia* 219e, Aelian, *VH* 2.19.

son of Zeus.[73] That explains why his portraits usually depicted him with his eyes upturned toward heaven (Figure 15). The Spartans' flattery may indeed have mitigated their punishment. It is not a coincidence that to strengthen their protests over Alexander's Exiles Decree in 324 embassies from the Greek states announced that they too recognized his divinity (Chapter 14 pp. 314–315).

DEMOSTHENES AND AGIS

With Antipater hard pressed in Thrace and Alexander deep in the heart of the Persian Empire in 331, Demosthenes has been criticized for misjudging the opportunity afforded by Agis' war to liberate Greece from Macedonia—he had done "nothing, and worse than nothing. He had seen to it that nothing was done."[74] However, Demosthenes had simply recognized that resistance to Macedonian rule was futile, as the Theban revolt of 335 attested. Worse was the punishment that Alexander could have inflicted on Athens if the city had supported his enemy. For example, he could have closed the Hellespont, depriving Athens of its major source of grain, or he could have called on the Macedonian garrisons at Thebes, Corinth, and Chalcis to attack the city.[75] The risks of rebellion were simply too great. Twenty years had passed since Demosthenes' first *Philippic*, during which period he had consistently advocated opposition to Macedonia. Now he had to live with the realization that those days were well and truly over.

Thousands of miles away at Persepolis, the last of Persia's ceremonial capitals to fall to Alexander, an event occurred that proved Demosthenes' wisdom. Persepolis, "the most hateful city in Asia,"[76] was home to the monumental palace of Xerxes, with its soaring columns,

[73] Alexander's divinity is a contentious issue: for two contrasting views see, for example, Worthington, *Alexander the Great* and E. A. Fredricksmeyer, "Alexander's Religion and Divinity," in J. Roisman (ed.), *Brill Companion to Alexander the Great* (Leiden: 2003), pp. 253–278.
[74] Cawkwell, "Crowning of Demosthenes," p. 176; for a critical evaluation of Demosthenes' policy as one of missed chances after Chaeronea (especially by not supporting Agis of Sparta), see pp. 163–180.
[75] Sealey, *Demosthenes*, p. 207, suggests that the Macedonian garrison at Thebes was the reason why the Athenians stayed aloof.
[76] Diodorus 17.70.

enormous audience halls, and friezes depicting embassies from Ethiopia, the Indus Valley, Central Asia, and Asia Minor bringing tribute to the Great King. Alexander arrived there in January 330 and occupied the palace as his headquarters. When the Macedonians left four months later, they looted the city, and the huge palace was burned to the ground.[77] The palace's destruction is controversial: it may have been a deliberate panhellenic act, symbolizing the downfall of the Persian Empire, or the accidental result of a fire started during a drunken party one night, which Alexander exploited for propaganda purposes.[78] Either way, the conflagration also sent a message to the mainland Greeks about Agis' war.[79] The Athenian Acropolis had been looted and burned during the Persian Wars—Demosthenes did not want that to happen again, this time at the hands of Macedonians.[80] Far from doing "nothing, and worse than nothing," he had done the right thing for Athens.

REGARDING MACEDONIA

None of the Athenians' actions in the later 330s indicate they had undergone a change of heart regarding Macedonia. Shortly after Agis' defeat, Macedonian sympathizers in Athens were indicted. One famous case was that of the politician Polyeuctus, who impeached Euxenippus for giving bad advice to the people, taking bribes from the city's enemies, and flattering Macedonians, especially Alexander's mother Olympias.[81] Polyeuctus' prosecution speech has not survived, but fragments exist of

---

[77] Diodorus 17.72, Curtius 5.7.3–8, Plutarch, *Alexander* 38.1–8.

[78] For example, see Worthington, *Alexander the Great*, pp. 149–151; on the destruction, see also E. N. Borza, "Fire from Heaven: Alexander at Persepolis," *CP* 67 (1972), pp. 233–245, N. G. L. Hammond, "The Archaeological and Literary Evidence for the Burning of the Persepolis Palace," *CQ*² 42 (1992), pp. 358–364, A. Shapur Shahbazi, "Iranians and Alexander," *AJAH*² 2 (2003), pp. 5–38.

[79] Cf. Bosworth, *Conquest and Empire*, p. 93, Badian, "Agis III: Revisions and Reflections," p. 284, Worthington, *Alexander the Great*, pp. 110–111.

[80] Alexander's release of Athenian prisoners from his first battle against the Persians, at the Granicus River in 334, while Agis was still besieging Megalopolis, was also meant to preserve Athenian loyalty: Diodorus 17.22.5, Arrian 1.16.6, 29.5–6, 3.6.2.

[81] The precise date for the trial is unknown, but it had to have been in the 330–324 period: Blass, *attische Beredsamkeit*² 3.2, p. 54, D. Whitehead, *Hyperides, The Forensic Orations* (Oxford: 2000), pp. 155–157.

Euxenippus' defense speech, written by Hyperides, which indicate the level of anti-Macedonian feeling in the city.[82] That the Athenians were able to pursue such cases shows that Alexander and Antipater were tolerating the seeming autonomy that the League of Corinth afforded the Greeks; that would change within a few short years.

Two higher profile cases also took place in 330, the most famous being the so-called Crown trial in which Aeschines strove to discredit Demosthenes' entire anti-Macedonian policy (Chapter 13). Before that, Lycurgus indicted Leocrates for treason (*prodosia*). Leocrates had fled Athens soon after Chaeronea in 338, thereby contravening the emergency decree that no person was to leave the city except on official business. He first went to Rhodes and then to Megara, but eventually returned to Athens, possibly even in the year of his prosecution.[83] Lycurgus' lengthy prosecution speech from the trial survives—the only one of his speeches to do so despite his importance in public affairs.[84]

Lycurgus insisted on Leocrates' execution for betraying Athens in its hour of need and so being a disloyal citizen. He contrasted Leocrates' cowardly and treacherous actions with patriotic appeals to the exploits of the Athenians' ancestors and the Greeks who died fighting for freedom at Chaeronea.[85] If, declared Lycurgus sensationally, everyone in Athens had been a Leocrates and fled, the city would have been deserted and easy prey for Philip.[86] Lycurgus had an open-and-shut case. There was no question that Leocrates had left the city illegally, and his defense that he had not deserted the city but merely left it to engage in trade was most likely a lie. The minimum age for a juror in Athens was thirty, so even the youngest of them at Leocrates' trial would have remembered the panic following Chaeronea eight years before. Yet despite Leocrates' weak defense, the jury acquitted him, although only by a single vote.[87]

---

[82] Blass, *attische Beredsamkeit*[2] 3.2, pp. 54–58. Translation with notes: C. Cooper in Ian Worthington, C. Cooper and E. M. Harris, *Dinarchus, Hyperides, Lycurgus* (Austin: 2001), pp. 102–114. Translation and commentary: Whitehead, *Hyperides, The Forensic Orations*, pp. 151–262.

[83] Rhodes: Lycurgus 1.14–15, 16–19; Megara: Lycurgus 1.21–27.

[84] Translation with notes: E. M. Harris in Ian Worthington, C. Cooper and E. M. Harris, *Dinarchus, Hyperides, Lycurgus* (Austin: 2001), pp. 159–203. Lycurgus wrote fifteen speeches in his career: see Blass, *attische Beredsamkeit*[2] 3.2, pp. 72–111.

[85] Lycurgus 1.46–51.

[86] Lycurgus 1.59–62.

[87] Aeschines 3.252.

The jurors' surprising verdict may have been because Lycurgus only convinced half of them that Leocrates' desertion was actually treason.[88] Possibly the Athenian attitude to Macedonia accounted for the vote. Lycurgus may perhaps have exploited anti-Macedonian sentiment when he indicted Leocrates for contemptibly fleeing the city rather than defending it.[89] Yet the vote indicated that any such predilection was less of an issue for at least half of the jurors. What the vote arguably indicated was a reaction against Lycurgus that he did not anticipate. Like Demosthenes, the Athenians recognized the new Greece. They might be anti-Macedonian in spirit, but they had to live their lives under Macedonian rule. Leocrates was thus acquitted not because he was innocent but because of a reaction against Lycurgus for reminding the people that they had lost their autonomy. Eight years after Leocrates' crime, Lycurgus rubbed salt into the Greek wound, and it cost him in court.

Not everyone in Athens held the opinion that Demosthenes' advice to resist Agis was sound. Shortly after the trial of Leocrates, Aeschines felt there was enough hostility against Demosthenes to render him vulnerable to attack. He therefore rekindled his indictment of Ctesiphon from six years ago for proposing Demosthenes be crowned. The ensuing highly political trial, which (unusually) attracted spectators from all over Greece,[90] marked the inevitable showdown between Demosthenes and Aeschines that had been brewing since the false embassy trial of 343.

---

[88] Lycurgus 1.68.

[89] E. M. Burke, "*Contra Leocratem* and *De Corona*: Political Collaboration?," *Phoenix* 31 (1977), pp. 330–340, argues that Leocrates' trial and that of Demosthenes, which followed soon after, are connected, and that Lycurgus and Demosthenes used both to rid Athens of anti-Macedonians. The connection is strained: see N. Sawada, "Athenian Politics in the Age of Alexander the Great: A Reconsideration of the Trial of Ctesiphon," *Chiron* 26 (1996), pp. 57–82; see too J. E. Atkinson, "Macedon and Athenian Politics in the Period 338 to 323 BC," *Acta Classica* 24 (1981), pp. 37–48.

[90] Aeschines 3.56. Demosthenes refers to spectators at the trial, for example 18.196: "I intend this entire long discussion for your benefit, jurors, as well as for that of the surrounding audience."

13

The Crown Trial

THE CROWN AFFAIR

The Assembly had never ratified Ctesiphon's proposal of 336, that Demosthenes be awarded a gold crown in the theater of Dionysus for his recent civic activities and for the way he had served Athens' best interests over the years, because Aeschines had brought a *graphe paranomon* against him. He had let the matter drop until now, the late summer of 330.[1] Some scholars have argued that Demosthenes forced Aeschines to rekindle his indictment because the original one was still outstanding and under Athenian law a prosecutor who did not proceed with a case lost his citizenship (*atimia*).[2] If Demosthenes intended to make the lapse of time public knowledge, then Aeschines had no choice but to revisit his charge. Yet Demosthenes could have forced Aeschines to do so at any stage after 336, and there is no evidence that he was pressuring him in that year. It is more likely that Aeschines saw a vulnerability in Demosthenes'

---

[1] Date: Dionysius of Halicarnassus, *To Ammaeus* 1.12, Plutarch, *Demosthenes* 24.2 (archonship of Aristophon, 330/29)—a few days before the Pythian Games (Aeschines 3.254), which were held in the late summer; cf. H. Wankel, *Demosthenes: Rede für Ktesiphon über den Kranz* (Heidelberg: 1976), pp. 25–37.

[2] E. M. Burke, "*Contra Leocratem* and *De Corona*: Political Collaboration?," *Phoenix* 31 (1977), pp. 330–340, N. Sawada, "Athenian Politics in the Age of Alexander the Great: A Reconsideration of the Trial of Ctesiphon," *Chiron* 26 (1996), pp. 60–71.

handling of Agis of Sparta's abortive war and thought he might finally overcome his hated adversary. For personal reasons, then, he went on the offensive.[3]

Because Aeschines had indicted Ctesiphon his prosecution speech is titled *Against Ctesiphon*, and Ctesiphon had to answer the charge. However, a *graphe paranomon* invited jurors to consider both legal issues and any political implications presented by the recommendation.[4] Ctesiphon had wanted to honor Demosthenes for his advice over the years—specifically, "because he consistently speaks and acts in the best interests of the people."[5] Aeschines was therefore able to focus his attention on Demosthenes because the jurors would need to review his entire career to decide whether Ctesiphon's reason was appropriate. If they voted in favor of Aeschines, then they would judge Demosthenes' anti-Macedonian policy a failure, thereby vindicating that of Aeschines. Ctesiphon therefore gave only a short defense speech after which Demosthenes responded more formally with what is universally regarded as his masterpiece: *On the Crown*. The prosecution and defense speeches from the crown trial survive, although they were revised after oral delivery.[6]

[3] See G. L. Cawkwell, "The Crowning of Demosthenes," *CQ*² 19 (1969), pp. 170–180, Wankel, *Demosthenes: Rede für Ktesiphon*, pp. 18–25, S. Usher, *Demosthenes: On the Crown* (Warminster: 1993), pp. 14–15. E. M. Harris, *Aeschines and Athenian Politics* (New York: 1995), pp. 140–142, 173–174, does not discount the effect of Agis' defeat on Aeschines' decision, but argues that Darius III's final defeat at Alexander's hands at the Battle of Gaugamela in 331 also influenced Aeschines. Since Demosthenes had hoped the Persians would defeat and kill Alexander, the latter's victory led to the demise of the Persian Empire, and was evidence of yet another of Demosthenes' failed policies. However, Demosthenes' Persian hopes were hardly policy; cf. Lehmann, *Demosthenes*, pp. 192–194.

[4] H. Yunis, "Law, Politics, and the *Graphe Paranomon* in Fourth-Century Athens," *GRBS* 29 (1988), pp. 361–382, MacDowell, *Demosthenes*, pp. 152–155.

[5] Aeschines 3.49. The language of Ctesiphon's decree praising Demosthenes for his merit and virtue was taken up by both Aeschines and Demosthenes against the backdrop of democratic ideals: see further, B. L. Cook, "Athenian Terms of Civic Praise in the 330s: Aeschines vs. Demosthenes," *GRBS* 49 (2009), pp. 31–52; cf. D. Whitehead, "Cardinal Virtues: The Language of Public Approbation in Democratic Athens," *Class. & Med.* 44 (1993), pp. 37–75.

[6] See J. Buckler, "Demosthenes and Aeschines," in Ian Worthington (ed.), *Demosthenes: Statesman and Orator* (London: 2000), pp. 148–154, Wankel, *Demosthenes: Rede für Ktesiphon*, pp. 48–51.

Against Ctesiphon

Aeschines brought three charges against Ctesiphon. First, a serving public official could not receive an award until his office ended and he had passed the customary enquiry (*euthune*) into his conduct.[7] In 337/6 Demosthenes had been a *teichopoios* and had served on the theoric board. Second, if the Boule approved a crown, it had to be proclaimed in the Bouleuterion (where the Boule met)—likewise, if the Assembly authorized a crown, it had to be proclaimed in the Assembly.[8] Ctesiphon had submitted his proposal to the Boule. In both of these charges Aeschines had the law on his side and ought to have won his case against Ctesiphon, thereby denying Demosthenes his crown.[9] However, he wanted more. He alleged that Ctesiphon's reason for the crown was flawed because Demosthenes had not acted in the people's best interests, as evidenced by the Greeks' defeat at Chaeronea. Aeschines' third charge moved away from the law and into the realm of interpretation and speculation—it would be his undoing.[10]

As prosecutor Aeschines spoke first.[11] There is some evidence that a man named Diodotus assisted him but nothing is known about him.[12] Aeschines opened his speech by calling on the jury to punish men who put forward illegal recommendations, then quickly moved to the law that prevented a serving magistrate from being crowned.[13] Next, he cited the law that did not permit Demosthenes to be crowned in the theater.[14] Now, about one-fifth of the way through his speech, he turned to his

---

[7] Aeschines 3.11.

[8] Aeschines 3.32.

[9] For the law that Ctesiphon contravened, see P. J. Rhodes, *The Athenian Boule* (Oxford: 1972), pp. 15–16. Aeschines' winning: W. E. Gwatkin, "The Legal Arguments in Aischines' *Against Ktesiphon* and Demosthenes' *On the Crown*," *Hesperia* 26 (1957), pp. 129–141. Against the view: E. M. Harris, "Law and Oratory," in Ian Worthington (ed.), *Persuasion: Greek Rhetoric in Action* (London: 1994), pp. 141–148; cf. Harris, *Aeschines and Athenian Politics*, pp. 142–145; see further, below.

[10] See Harris, *Aeschines and Athenian Politics*, pp. 145–148.

[11] Translation of Aeschines' *Against Ctesiphon* with notes: C. Carey, *Aeschines* (Austin: 2000), pp. 159–251; see also Schaefer, *Demosthenes*[2] 3, pp. 228–250, Blass, *attische Beredsamkeit*[2] 3.2, pp. 182–193, S. Usher, *Greek Oratory: Tradition and Originality* (Oxford 1999), pp. 287–293.

[12] [Plutarch], *Moralia* 846a.

[13] Aeschines 3.1–31.

[14] Aeschines 3.32–48.

third charge, to which he devoted most attention. He divided his critique of Demosthenes' anti-Macedonian policy into four sections.[15] The first dealt with Demosthenes' career from the outbreak of the war over Amphipolis in 357 to the Peace of Philocrates in 346, the second with the period from that peace to the outbreak of the second war between Athens and Philip in 340, the third with the events leading to the alliance with Thebes in 339 and its aftermath, and the fourth and final section covered the period from Chaeronea in 338 to the present trial.

Aeschines rightly argued that Demosthenes and Philocrates were responsible for the Peace of Philocrates. Demosthenes could not shy away from his role in the affair, despite his attempts to distance himself from it in the second half of the 340s. To Aeschines, therefore, Demosthenes was untrustworthy and inconsistent, and his reckless policy brought down not only Athens but also Greece. He was especially critical of Demosthenes' role in securing the alliance with Thebes, accusing him of surrendering strategy to Thebes while Athens paid its costs. Aeschines was on weaker ground when he insisted that Demosthenes' policy did not merely end Greek liberty at Chaeronea but caused Thebes' destruction in 335 and was responsible for the punishment inflicted on the Spartans in 330.

Aeschines also lambasted Demosthenes for taking bribes from many individuals, including Callias of Euboea, Philip, and the Persian King. In exaggerated terms, he described how Demosthenes had withheld money from the Great King in 335 and so allowed Thebes to be destroyed.[16] He also claimed Demosthenes was a coward and accused him of fleeing the battlefield at Chaeronea,[17] defending his allegations with striking emotional rhetoric. For example, his lament over the fates of Sparta and Thebes:[18]

> And Thebes, Thebes our neighbor city, has been snatched from the middle of Greece in a single day . . . And the poor Spartans . . . who once claimed to be leaders of Greece, are about to be sent to Alexander as hostages and make an exhibition of their calamity, to suffer, both

---

[15] Aeschines 3.49–167.

[16] See Chapter 12 pp. 279–280.

[17] Aeschines 3.142–146, 152, 168–198; on this aspect of Aeschines' ideology, cf. R. Lane Fox, "Aeschines and Athenian Politics," in R. Osborne and S. Hornblower (eds.), *Ritual, Finance, Politics: Athenian Democratic Accounts Presented to David Lewis* (Oxford: 1994), pp. 135–155.

[18] Aeschines 3.133.

individually and as a country, whatever he chooses, and to have their fate decided by the mercy of a victory they have wronged.

Equally vivid is the tragic scene he conjured up of Demosthenes hypocritically receiving his gold crown at the Dionysia when his policy had resulted in the deaths of many young men and turned many children into war orphans.[19]

After his long narrative, Aeschines turned to his arguments. Among other things, he criticized awards that the city now bestowed willy-nilly, in contrast to previous eras when they were harder to obtain and therefore meant more. The present generation of Athenians should return to the strictness of the earlier age, Aeschines lectured, and so deny Ctesiphon's proposal now.[20] As he moved to the conclusion of his speech, he urged the jurors not to be beguiled by Demosthenes' rhetoric.[21] He concluded by calling on them to put an end to the excessive power and corruption of a few individuals and not to disregard recent events.[22]

Aeschines sat down, and Ctesiphon gave a brief defense speech, which does not survive. Then Demosthenes rose. He spent only moments on the laws Aeschines cited to substantiate his first two charges before focusing primarily on his adversary's third charge. His lengthy defense speech (ninety-three pages of Greek text) is a forceful justification of his policy toward Macedonia and of why he deserved his crown. He had conveniently forgotten his first public speech of twenty-five years earlier, when in moral indignation he attacked Androtion for casting aside the law in order to receive a crown (Chapter 4 pp. 72–77)!

There is no question that Demosthenes' speech is "generally regarded as the greatest achievement of Greek oratory,"[23] and that it "encompasses the whole of his art, transcending genre, and defining his position in both literature and history."[24]

---

[19] Aeschines 3.152–158; cf. H. Yunis, *Demosthenes, On the Crown* (Cambridge: 2001), pp. 12–13.

[20] Aeschines 3.167–200.

[21] Aeschines 3.192–242.

[22] Aeschines 3.243–259.

[23] MacDowell, *Demosthenes*, p. 382. Structure of the speech: Usher, *Demosthenes: On the Crown*, pp. 17–19, Yunis, *Demosthenes, On the Crown*, pp. 30–31, and especially F. P. Donnelly, "A Structural Analysis of the Speech on the Crown," in J. J. Murphy (ed.), *Demosthenes' On the Crown: A Critical Case Study of a Masterpiece of Ancient Oratory* (New York: 1967), pp. 137–144. MacDowell, *Demosthenes*, pp. 386–396, details the parts of the speech in his discussion.

[24] Usher, *Greek Oratory: Tradition and Originality*, p. 270.

On the Crown[25]

Demosthenes began with a solemn oath and a plea to be judged fairly, then condemned Aeschines for wrongfully prosecuting Ctesiphon and telling a multitude of lies about him (1–16). He wove together Aeschines' three charges against Ctesiphon into a spirited and varied defense of his career, arranged chronologically in the largest section of his speech (17–251), concluding with a justification of the Theban alliance (160–226) and a summary of his leadership (227–251). Demosthenes countered the character denigration Aeschines threw at him in his speech by attacking his poor upbringing, suspect parents, lack of education, and treachery (126–131, 132–159; cf. 258–262). He compared and contrasted his own political capabilities and his integrity to those of Aeschines, which paled by comparison (252–323). To Demosthenes, Aeschines was a criminal and traitor (276–296), who inflicted inordinate harm on Athens (306–313) and was the antithesis of a patriot like Demosthenes (314–323). In like fashion to his opening, Demosthenes ended on a short prayer (324).

Demosthenes could not rebut Aeschines' first charge about receiving a crown while in office. Ctesiphon's proposal may not have included the offices Demosthenes currently held in 336 but a voluntary monetary donation he had contributed when he was a *teichopoios*.[26] Yet Aeschines' speech does not countenance that view, and in any case all Demosthenes needed to do was distinguish between holding an office and making a donation. He did not, instead distracting the jury from his legal predicament by citing examples of other men who were crowned by popular vote (113–114):

[25] On the speech, see Schaefer, *Demosthenes*[2] 3, pp. 253–287, Blass, *attische Beredsamkeit*[2] 3.1, pp. 364–383, Pickard-Cambridge, *Demosthenes*, pp. 430–445, Jaeger, *Demosthenes* pp. 193–196, G. Kennedy, *The Art of Persuasion in Greece* (Princeton 1963), pp. 230–236, L. Pearson, *The Art of Demosthenes* (Meisenheim am Glan: 1976), pp. 178–199, Carlier, *Démosthène*, pp. 249–256, Usher, *Greek Oratory: Tradition and Originality*, pp. 270–276, Lehmann, *Demosthenes*, pp. 197–203, MacDowell, *Demosthenes*, pp. 382–397. See also the essays in Murphy, *Demosthenes' On the Crown*. Translation of the speech with notes: J. J. Keaney in Murphy, *Demosthenes' On the Crown*, pp. 59–125, H. Yunis, *Demosthenes, Speeches 18 and 19* (Austin: 2005), pp. 23–113; translation and commentary: Usher, *Demosthenes: On the Crown*; text and commentary: W. W. Goodwin, *Demosthenes, On the Crown* (Cambridge: 1953), Wankel, *Demosthenes: Rede für Ktesiphon*, Yunis, *Demosthenes, On the Crown*.

[26] Harris, "Law and Oratory," pp. 143–148, echoed at *Aeschines and Athenian Politics*, pp. 142–145; contra MacDowell, *Demosthenes*, p. 388.

Gifts merit thanks and commendation, which is the very reason that Ctesiphon proposed the measure on my behalf. Many examples make it abundantly clear that this principle is based not only on the laws, Athenians, but also on your values. First, you bestowed several crowns on Nausicles for voluntary contributions from private resources while he was a general. Then Diotimus received a crown for a donation of shields, as did Charidemus. And Neoptolemus, right here, was publicly honored for private contributions while in charge of several public tasks. It would be appalling if while holding some office, a citizen cannot give his own money to the city because of that office or else must undergo an audit for his gifts rather than receive thanks.

Demosthenes may have countered Aeschines' second charge by quoting a law allowing a crown to be proclaimed in the theater, subject to the Assembly's approval (120–121):

The next point concerns the theater as a place of proclamation. I leave aside the fact that thousands of people on thousands of occasions have received their crowns in the theater, as I myself have done on several previous occasions. Yet, by god, Aeschines, are you so stupid and obtuse as to be unable to comprehend that the crown brings the recipient the same admiration wherever it is announced, but it is proclaimed in the theater because that is to the advantage of those who bestow it? All those in attendance are motivated to do the city some good, and they praise those who display gratitude more than they do the honoree. For that reason, the city instituted the following law. Clerk, take the law and please read it. [The law is read, but it did not survive with the speech.] Do you hear the clear voice of the law, Aeschines: "except any whom the People or Council specify in a decree: these are to be proclaimed by the herald"? Why do you prosecute on false premises, you wretch? Why do you make up lies? Why don't you take some hellebore [a remedy for madness] for your trouble? But you're not ashamed to bring suit out of envy rather than for an actual offense and to rewrite laws or snip off parts of them, even though citizens sworn to render judgment according to the laws should hear them in their entirety.

Demosthenes was guilty of rhetorical exaggeration when he spoke of "thousands of people on thousands of occasions" being crowned and of receiving a crown himself on "several previous occasions." He had been crowned only twice before, in 340 and 338. Nevertheless, as he pointed out elsewhere in his defense speech, Aeschines had issued no challenges at those times (23, 223), so he was being inconsistent now.

The law that Aeschines accused Ctesiphon of breaking may have been still "on the books" but was simply no longer observed.[27] Ctesiphon was technically guilty but according to Demosthenes his motive was honorable, in which case a fine was a better penalty to impose on him than what Aeschines intended him to suffer.[28]

Aeschines' third charge most occupied Demosthenes' attention. He built his rebuttal around the premise that the defeat at Chaeronea was not due to him but to the gods (fate), bad generalship, and the people's reluctance to fight Philip until it was too late.[29] He defiantly, and unconventionally by modern expectations, insisted that his policy toward Philip had always been the correct one, excusing himself of blame for how it eventuated because of matters beyond his control. He claimed that he had recognized from the outset that the king was a tyrant who wanted only to dominate Greece, although he had misrepresented the extent of his involvement in Greece in the period 346 to 340 and falsely accused him of breaking the Peace of Philocrates a number of times.[30] People, Demosthenes announced, either had to fight or meekly surrender to tyrants, for diplomacy was not an option (60–78). Demosthenes justified his anti-Macedonian policy by saying he had scrupulously acted only in the best interests of Athens and Greek freedom (174–178, 190–191, 195). Indeed, he stressed he had had no choice as a patriot and a statesman but to develop and fight for the policy he did (66):

> What, Aeschines, should the city have done when it saw Philip building toward empire and tyranny over the Greeks? And what was an adviser in Athens—for that makes all the difference—obliged to say and propose? During all my time until the day I myself stepped onto the speaker's platform, I knew that our country always fought for the first prize in honor and glory and had expended more money and men in pursuit

---

[27] See Gwatkin, "Legal Arguments," pp. 138–140, Harris, "Law and Oratory," p. 142 and *Aeschines and Athenian Politics*, pp. 142–145, MacDowell, *Demosthenes*, p. 389, 396.

[28] MacDowell, *Demosthenes*, p. 396.

[29] For example, Demosthenes 18.63, 66–68, 192–195, 199, 206, 245–246, 270–275; see also 60.19–22. G. Clemenceau, *Démosthènes* (Paris: 1926), p. 10, for example, blamed the Athenian people for their demise because they did not listen to Demosthenes from the outset! Pickard-Cambridge, *Demosthenes* and Jaeger, *Demosthenes*, have similar sentiments.

[30] For example, see G. L. Cawkwell, "Demosthenes' Policy after the Peace of Philocrates II," *CQ²* 13 (1963), pp. 200–205.

of honor and the common good than all the other Greeks had expended on their own behalf.

Demosthenes argued that factors beyond his control disabled his policy, and therefore that Ctesiphon's proposal to award him a crown was both legal and deserved (199–203, 208, 246, 297–298, 303, 322).

Aeschines' condemnation of his opponent's career was met with bold defiance, contempt—and a manipulation of the facts. He distorted Aeschines' role in the events leading to the Peace of Philocrates to distance himself from the peace (17–52), stating that it was "not, as Aeschines maliciously claimed, my actions that brought about the peace we reached at that time" (20–21). In dealing with the aftermath of the peace, Demosthenes even charged Aeschines with treachery by alluding to his support of Python's embassy in 344 and of Antiphon, who planned to burn the Piraeus dockyards for Philip in 343 (132–159). Even more sensationally, Demosthenes falsely accused Aeschines of conspiring with Philip to provoke the Fourth Sacred War in 339, thereby permitting the king to lead his army into Greece. He impressed his claims on the jury in a series of rhetorical questions (158–159):

> You see how Philip shrinks from his own motives and seeks shelter in the pretext afforded by the Amphictyons. Who assisted him in this matter? Who supplied him with the pretext? Who is most responsible for the troubles that ensued? Is it not this man? Do not, Athenians, go around saying that disaster befell Greece because of one individual. Not because of one, but because of many corrupt people from all over, O earth and gods, and among them is this man here, whom I at least, if the truth must be uttered freely, would not hesitate to call a universal villain who caused all the ensuing destruction of people, places, cities. For he who sows the seed is responsible for the evils that sprout. I wonder that you did not turn away as soon as you saw him. But a great deal of darkness, it seems, hangs about you, screening off the truth.

One of Aeschines' principal accusations was that Demosthenes' alliance with Thebes was flawed because it was costly to the city and brought about the defeat at Chaeronea.[31] Demosthenes responded in a lengthy part of his speech (160–226). He brilliantly (and falsely) turned Aeschines' charge on its head by making *him* out to be a traitor and forcing the Athenians into a situation where the only recourse to save

---

[31] Aeschines 3.140–151.

Greece was to ally with Thebes, regardless of the unpalatable terms of the alliance.[32] After describing the panic that gripped the Athenians when Philip seized Elatea in 339 (quoted on pp. 242–243), Demosthenes portrayed himself as the only man who acted for the city's benefit, unlike Aeschines (196–197):

> I intend this entire long discussion for your benefit, jurors, as well as for that of the surrounding audience, since for this contemptible man a short, simple statement suffices. If what was going to happen was clear in advance to you alone, Aeschines, you were obliged to speak out then, when the city was debating it. But if you did not know in advance, you are answerable for the same ignorance as anyone else, so why should you censure me for this more than I you? I am a better citizen than you for the following reason (speaking with regard just to the point at issue since I'm not yet discussing the rest): while I devoted myself to the policy decided by all as expedient and did not hesitate or even consider any risk to myself, you neither proposed a policy better than mine (otherwise mine would not have been adopted) nor played any useful role to support it. Instead, it is now confirmed that afterward you committed an act worthy of the meanest, most treacherous citizen ... [you are] accusing Demosthenes in Athens.

Acknowledging that the battle of Chaeronea was a tragedy for the Greeks, Demosthenes nonetheless crafted it as their most renowned triumph because of why they fought it. Instead of bowing to Philip's steady advance into Greece the Athenians stood fast with their fellows for the noblest of causes: freedom. Previously in his speech, Demosthenes had tried to convince the people they had the potential to defeat Philip by reminding them of their successes against him prior to Chaeronea, in places like Euboea and the Chersonese (79–94). Although they lost the battle, they had nevertheless lived up to the glorious example set by their ancestors who in a similar fight for freedom had confronted the Persians in the Persian Wars (208):

> But you were not wrong, no, you were not, Athenians, to take on danger for the sake of the freedom and safety of all—I swear by your forefathers who led the fight at Marathon, by those who stood in the ranks at Plataea, by those who fought aboard ship at Salamis and Artemisium, and by the many other brave men who lie in the public tombs, all of

---

[32] Demosthenes 18.150–152, 156, 159, 163, Buckler, "Demosthenes and Aeschines," p. 144. Demosthenes' allegations are ably rebutted by J. Roisman, *The Rhetoric of Conspiracy in Ancient Athens* (Berkeley and Los Angeles: 2006), pp. 133–145.

whom the city buried, deeming them all equally worthy of the same honor, Aeschines, not just those among them who were successful or victorious. Rightly so, for they all performed the task required of brave men, and they each met with the fortune conferred on them by god.

Not only was the bond between father and son strong in Greek society but also Greeks felt deeply about their ancestors, hence Demosthenes' evocation of the bravery of the Athenians' forefathers was rhetorically very powerful here.[33] Aeschines' ignoble comparison of Demosthenes to the heroes of fifth-century Athens was demolished by Demosthenes' rousing analogy. He could thus take credit not just for fighting in the battle with his fellow Greeks, but especially for his policy that brought together the Greeks for all the right reasons (195, 244–247, 253–254), something that would not have occurred if they had followed Aeschines' conciliatory policy.[34] Demosthenes thus made the symbolism of the battle its most important aspect—that the Greeks were defeated is all but lost on the jury.

Demosthenes did not shy from retaliating against Aeschines' "outrageous slanders" (10) about his personal life (122–159, 252–296).[35] Calling him an "abominable, deformed little clerk" (209), he accused him of being politically naive, venal, ignoble, and a man who never honored his city because of his friendship to Philip the tyrant. He ridiculed Aeschines' family and lack of formal education, and made him out to be depraved and even a deviant because he and his mother allegedly took part in secret orgiastic cults (258–259):

But you, you pretentious and haughty man, compare my lot with that enjoyed by you: as a boy raised in great poverty, serving at the school alongside your father, you rubbed the ink, wiped the benches, and swept the schoolroom, relegated to the status of a household slave, not that of a freeborn youth. Grown to manhood, you used to read aloud from books for your mother as she conducted initiation rites, and you colluded with her in other ways. By night, you clothed the initiates in

[33] P. Hunt, *War, Peace, and Alliance in Demosthenes' Athens* (New York: 2010), pp. 123–132.

[34] Cf. T. T. B. Ryder, "Demosthenes and Philip II," in Ian Worthington (ed.), *Demosthenes: Statesman and Orator* (London: 2000), p. 82.

[35] See also G. O. Rowe, "The Portrait of Aeschines in the Oration *On the Crown*," *TAPA* 97 (1966), pp. 397–406, A. R. Dyck, "The Function and Persuasive Power of Demosthenes" Portrait of Aeschines in the Speech *On the Crown*', *G&R²* 32 (1985), pp. 42–48.

fawn skins, plied them with wine, purified them, and scrubbed them down with clay and bran.

He then succinctly and in dramatic staccato fashion compared Aeschines' life and career to his own (265):

> So examine my life and yours in comparison with each other, and do it sympathetically and without bitterness, Aeschines. Then ask each member of the audience whose fortune in life he would prefer. You taught school, I was a student; you conducted initiation rites, I was initiated; you served as a public scribe, I attended the Assembly; you played bit parts on stage, I sat in the audience; you were hissed offstage, I was hissing. All your policies helped the enemy; mine helped our country.

Demosthenes ended his speech on a pious note by uttering a short prayer calling on the people to destroy their enemies (324):

> Best would be to inspire better thoughts and intentions even in them, but if they are indeed incurable, destroy every last one of them utterly and thoroughly on earth and sea. And grant the rest of us as soon as possible release from the fears that threaten and salvation that endures.

Demothenes' stirring version of events took the jurors by storm—Aeschines did not even win one-fifth of their votes. Demosthenes' rhetoric and style were certainly more powerful than those of Aeschines, which is why, even today, the speech is considered his masterpiece.[36]

Aeschines misjudged the situation by giving the jury only a picture of doom and gloom.[37] In rehearsing the details of the very recent past he had reminded the jury too often that the Greeks' most cherished ideals—*eleutheria* (freedom) and *autonomia* (autonomy)—were no more.[38] It has been said that Demosthenes deliberately concentrated on his actions in the 340s and early 330s because he knew that the Athenians should have rallied to Agis' cause in 331.[39] He has even been accused of wanting to mask his ineptitude at that time, which rendered him vulnerable. Sparta,

---

[36] There are very good analyses of both at MacDowell, *Demosthenes*, pp. 386–397 (see also pp. 398–407), Usher, *Demosthenes: On the Crown*, pp. 19–28, Yunis, *Demosthenes, On the Crown*, pp. 17–26.

[37] See also Harris, *Aeschines and Athenian Politics*, p. 142, who criticizes Aeschines' political myopia.

[38] On these ideals, cf. Sealey, *Demosthenes*, pp. 241–244.

[39] Cawkwell, "Crowning of Demosthenes," pp. 173–180; the quotation is from p. 180. Contra Sealey, *Demosthenes*, pp. 207–208.

however, was not an issue at this trial. Demosthenes intended to create a link between the patriotic idealism of the Persian Wars and Chaeronea. His policy had not achieved its objective, which he argued was not his fault, but had provided the Athenians with another glorious episode in their history that would have made their forebears proud. By likening the Athenians at Chaeronea to their ancestors, the jury would have found it practically impossible to convict him without denigrating anyone who fought for freedom against tyranny.

As Athenian law dictated, for gaining less than one-fifth of the jury vote Aeschines was fined 1,000 drachmas and banned from lodging similar cases in future.[40] Worse still, his bitter enemy had been vindicated. Whenever he saw Demosthenes in the city he would relive the humiliation of his defeat. Therefore Aeschines decided to leave Athens. He first traveled to Ephesus, and then to Rhodes, where he founded a school of rhetoric, and at some point moved to Samos, where he died (the year is unknown).[41] There is a story that he would recite his speech against Ctesiphon to his students at his school, who were always amazed he lost. His response was that if they had heard Demosthenes' speech that day, they would know why.[42]

RETREAT FROM THE LIMELIGHT

When Aeschines was leaving Athens the story goes that Demosthenes rode after him and "Aeschines, thinking he was arresting him, fell at his feet and covered his head, but Demosthenes raised him up, encouraged him, and gave him a talent of silver."[43] It is hard to accept the veracity of this account, given the hatred that the two men had had for each other over the previous two decades. "Neither Demosthenes nor Aeschines was a high-minded man whose ideals transcended the political cause that he espoused at the moment. Both men were mean, meretricious, and scurrilous."[44] They were both patriots, but their differing interpretations

---

[40] Plutarch, *Demosthenes* 24.2.

[41] Plutarch, *Demosthenes* 24.3, [Plutarch], *Moralia* 840c. Aeschines as an orator: Blass, *attische Beredsamkeit*[2] 3.2, pp. 129–236, J. F. Kindstrand, *The Stylistic Evaluation of Aeschines in Antiquity* (Upsala: 1982), Usher, *Greek Oratory: Tradition and Originality*, pp. 279–295.

[42] [Plutarch], *Moralia* 840d–e.

[43] [Plutarch], *Moralia* 845f.

[44] Buckler, "Demosthenes and Aeschines," pp. 114–115.

of Philip's aims placed them at different ends of the political spectrum, and their personal enmity merely intensified and perhaps even deliberately misguided their interpretations.[45] Still, Aeschines did not "deserve to be grouped with those who had betrayed the freedom of the Greeks."[46]

Whether Demosthenes received his crown after a six-year delay is unknown—no ancient writer, not even his biographer Plutarch, stated that he did. After the trial, Demosthenes retired from the public spotlight, leaving Lycurgus, Phocion (who was reelected general every year), and Demades to dominate politics.[47] In these years the Athenians, like the other Greeks, benefited from the peace that Macedonia enforced on them.[48] Lycurgus had almost total control of Athenian finances for a dozen years, the first four as treasurer of the theoric board and the remaining eight thanks to his supporters on it.[49] He increased the city's financial reserves sufficiently to inaugurate a building program, which included a naval arsenal, 400 new triremes, the Panathenaic Stadium, and the theater of Dionysus.[50] He also improved the

---

[45] Buckler, "Demosthenes and Aeschines," p. 148.

[46] Harris, *Aeschines and Athenians Politics*, p. 148.

[47] Demades was one of the more active politicians as his numerous decrees testify: J. M. Williams, "Demades' Last Years, 323/2–319/8 B.C.: A 'Revisionist' Interpretation," *Anc. World* 19 (1989), pp. 19–30.

[48] See Ian Worthington, "The Harpalus Affair and the Greek Response to the Macedonian Hegemony," in Ian Worthington (ed.), *Ventures Into Greek History: Essays in Honour of N. G. L. Hammond* (Oxford 1994), pp. 307–330, G. Shipley, "Between Macedonia and Rome: Political Landscapes and Social Changes in Southern Greece in the Early Hellenistic Period," *BSA* 100 (2005), pp. 315–330.

[49] Lycurgus' twelve-year headship is commonly thought to have been from 338 to 326. J. J. Buchanan, *Theorika* (New York: 1962), pp. 75–77, however, believes he ran the fund from 337/6 to 326/5, when Menesaechmus succeeded him (Dionysius of Halicarnassus, *Dinarchus* 11). See also J. K. Davies, *Athenian Propertied Families* (Oxford: 1971), p. 351, for Lycurgus' twelve-year headship running from 336–324. See further, M. Faraguna, *Atene nell' età di Alessandro: Problemi politici, economici, finanziari* (Rome 1992). The tenure of office is controversial because it is not known whether officials served for one year or four: see R. Develin, "From Panathenaia to Panathenaia," *ZPE* 57 (1985), pp. 133–138, citing bibliography.

[50] See E. M. Burke, "Lycurgan Finances," *GRBS* 26 (1985), pp. 251–264 with F. W. Mitchel, "Athens in the Age of Alexander," *G&R²* 12 (1965), pp. 189–204 and "Lykourgan Athens: 338–322," *Semple Lectures* 2 (Cincinnati: 1970), A. B. Bosworth, *Conquest and Empire, The Reign of Alexander the Great* (Cambridge: 1988), pp. 204–215, J. Engels, "Anmerkungen zum 'Ökonomischen Denken' im 4. Jahrh. v. Chr. und zur wirtschaftlichen Entwicklung des Lykurgischen Athen," *MBAH* 7 (1988), pp. 90–132, Sealey, *Demosthenes*, pp. 209–211, Faraguna, *Atene nell' età di Alessandro: Problemi politici, economici, finanziari*.

ephebic system, which was meant to promote a new policy of educating the youth.[51] Lycurgus' reforms heralded a fresh era for Athens after the recent miserable decades, and to celebrate his new age he produced a standard edition of the fifth-century tragedies of Aeschylus, Sophocles, and Euripides and had bronze statues of them set up in the city.[52]

At some point before 330 a dramatic surge in the price of grain led to shortages.[53] In response, the Athenians established a special fund to buy grain, and in 325/4 founded a colony in the Adriatic to deter pirates from preying on merchant vessels loaded with that cargo.[54] The people bestowed honors, including citizenship, on a number of individuals for supplying grain,[55] and Demosthenes generously contributed a talent to help meet costs. For that he was appointed one of the grain fund's commissioners,[56] although he was later accused of embezzlement but acquitted.[57]

[51] See Sawada, "Athenian Politics in the Age of Alexander," pp. 77–78. Sealey, *Demosthenes*, pp. 211–212, believes the ephebes were meant to be ready for military service if dissension amongst the Macedonians occurred, but that view is unlikely given the tight control the Macedonians exercised until Alexander's death in 323: see Chapter 14.

[52] [Plutarch], *Moralia* 841f.

[53] Demosthenes 18.89, [Demosthenes] 7: P. J. Rhodes and R. Osborne, *Greek Historical Inscriptions, 404–323 BC* (Oxford 2003), no. 96 with commentary.

[54] Rhodes and Osborne, *Greek Historical Inscriptions*, no. 100 with commentary.

[55] For example, Diphilus was given the VIP treatment of *sitesis* in the Prytaneum (meals at state expense in the city hall, often combined with *proedria*, a front seat at the theater) and a statue in the Agora (Dinarchus 1.43). The salt-fish sellers Chaerephilus and his sons were given citizenship (Dinarchus 1.43). So also were the bankers Epigenes and Conon (Dinarchus 1.43). Paerisades I, ruler of the Bosporus, and his sons were given statues (Dinarchus 1.43)—Demosthenes seems to have negotiated grain from them on behalf of Athens: S. M. Burstein, "*IG* II² 653, Demosthenes and Athenian Relations with Bosporus in the Fourth Century B.C.," *Historia* 27 (1978), pp. 428–436. On these men, see Ian Worthington, *A Historical Commentary on Dinarchus* (Ann Arbor: 1992), *ad* 1.43, pp. 201–207, citing bibliography.

[56] [Plutarch], *Moralia* 845c-f, 851b. However, see Davies' reservation, *Athenian Propertied Families*, p. 137.

[57] [Plutarch], *Moralia* 845e. This charge is not to be confused with the one Demosthenes faced for leaving the city after Chaeronea to procure grain.

As the 320s continued more militant politicians such as Hyperides and Menesaechmus, who in 326 succeeded Lycurgus as treasurer of the Theoric Fund, came to the fore.[58] Still, the city maintained amicable relations with Antipater. Then unexpectedly in 324 Alexander's imperial treasurer Harpalus fled from his headquarters in Babylon to Athens. He intended to incite rebellion against Macedonia. As the next chapter discusses, his flight and the Athenian reaction to it brought about Demosthenes' political disgrace and exile.

---

[58] Dionysius of Halicarnassus, *Dinarchus* 11. Lycurgus' twelve-year tenure of the fund had ended by 326.

14

Decline and Fall

HARPALUS

Harpalus and Alexander had been friends since childhood. Because of a physical affliction, possibly a limp, which debarred Harpalus from military service, Alexander appointed him imperial treasurer. While the king was campaigning in India from 327 to 325, Harpalus embezzled funds and lived a debauched life in Babylon, even enjoying the company of two Athenian mistresses at the same time. He was not the only one of Alexander's satraps and senior officials to have been openly exploitive, prompting Alexander on his return from India to conduct a purge of corrupt individuals. To escape execution Harpalus fled to Athens with 6,000 mercenaries, 5,000 talents of stolen money, and 30 ships.[1] His intention was to incite a revolt against Alexander that would distract the king from tracking him down for punishment. Athens was the logical city to which to flee because of its military strength and because of the citizenship the city had conferred on him for his gift of grain during the recent famine.[2]

---

[1] Theopompus, *FGrH* 115 FF 244, 245, Diodorus 17.108.6, Curtius 10.2.1; cf. Plutarch, *Demosthenes* 25.1. On Alexander's purges and the background to Harpalus' flight, see E. Badian, "Harpalus," *JHS* 81 (1961), pp. 16–25. This was the second time that Harpalus had fled Alexander: the first was in 333, before the Battle of Issus, after which Alexander forgave him and he returned as treasurer: Ian Worthington, "The First Flight of Harpalus Reconsidered," *G&R*[2] 31 (1984), pp. 161–169.

[2] Athenaeus 13.586d and 596a–b, with M. J. Osborne, *Naturalization in Athens* 3 (Brussels: 1983), T82.

Harpalus' armada appeared off Attica in June of 324.[3] In Philip's day, the Athenians would have welcomed him with open arms, but the Greece of 324 was far different from that of the 350s and 340s. Demosthenes, who fully understood the futility of resisting Macedonia, persuaded the people at an Assembly to deny Harpalus admittance into Athens.[4] The general Philocles was instructed to enforce their decision.[5] Harpalus therefore sailed to a mercenary base at Taenarum, on the southern tip of the Peloponnese, where he left most of his troops and money. He cunningly returned to Athens as a suppliant, taking with him a handful of ships and some money.[6] Faced with a citizen claiming refuge, Philocles had no choice but to admit him. Thus began the so-called Harpalus affair.[7]

The Athenians were in a serious dilemma. They were sheltering Harpalus, as was their moral duty, but that meant protecting a fugitive from Alexander. Demands for his surrender from Antipater, Olympias, and Philoxenus (Alexander's commander in southern Asia Minor) added to the gravity of the situation.[8] Demosthenes may even have been in favor of handing Harpalus over, possibly to Antipater, but Hyperides successfully persuaded the people that betraying a citizen was morally reprehensible. Adding to the Athenians' concerns was a directive from Alexander, commonly called the Exiles Decree, which detrimentally affected all Greek cities and played a role in the Harpalus affair.

---

[3] Chronology of the affair: Ian Worthington, "The Chronology of the Harpalus Affair," *SO* 61 (1986), pp. 63–76.

[4] Note the suggestion of Sealey, *Demosthenes*, p. 208, that Demosthenes was inactive after 330 because he knew that only when Alexander's power was challenged and the Macedonians became divided was there any real chance of opposing the Macedonian hegemony, as was the case in 324. However, Alexander's power was hardly challenged in 324 nor were the Macedonians as divided as Sealey contends.

[5] Dinarchus 3.1, Plutarch, *Demosthenes* 25.3, [Plutarch], *Moralia* 846a.

[6] Number of ships: Ian Worthington, "*I.G.* ii² 1631, 1632 and Harpalus' Ships," *ZPE* (1986), pp. 222–224.

[7] On the affair, see J. A. Goldstein, *The Letters of Demosthenes* (New York: 1968), pp. 37–94, Ian Worthington, *A Historical Commentary on Dinarchus* (Ann Arbor: 1992), pp. 41–77, and C. W. Blackwell, *In the Absence of Alexander: Harpalus and the Failure of Macedonian Authority* (New York: 1998); cf. Carlier, *Démosthène*, pp. 261–268, Lehmann, *Demosthenes*, pp. 206–216.

[8] Hyperides 5.8, Diodorus 17.108.7, [Plutarch], *Moralia* 846b.

THE EXILES DECREE

As part of his draconian measures against corrupt officials, Alexander issued what is generally referred to as the Dissolution Decree, which commanded them to stand down the mercenaries in their armies.[9] The decree immediately depleted their manpower, and so countered any military threat to Alexander's position. However, tens of thousands of mercenaries were now unemployed and to survive they turned to robbery and intimidation, thereby causing instability in the eastern part of the Macedonian empire. Furthermore, the Athenian general Leosthenes transported 8,000 of them to Taenarum in Greece, where they represented a ready supply of soldiers to anyone with money, like Harpalus. Thus they now also threatened stability in the western half of the empire.

When Alexander reached Susa in 324 he decided on a simple solution to combat the problem: send the men home. His Exiles Decree authorized all Greek exiles (not just mercenaries), apart from murderers, antidemocrats, and Thebans, to return to their home cities, and empowered Antipater to use force against any city unwilling to take them back.[10] Nicanor of Stageira was dispatched to Greece to proclaim the royal directive at the Olympic Games of July 31 to August 4, 324. News of it had leaked out well in advance, however, and 20,000 exiles were waiting for him there. Diodorus included the text of the decree in his account of Alexander's reign:[11]

> King Alexander to the exiles from the Greek cities. We have not been the cause of your exile, but, apart from those of you who are under a curse, we shall be the cause of your return to your own native cities. We have written to Antipater about this so that if any cities are not willing to restore you, he may force them.

---

[9] Diodorus 17.106.3, 111.1–2, Curtius 10.1.45.

[10] Hyperides 5.18, Diodorus 17.109.1, 18.8.2–7, Curtius 10.2.4–7, [Plutarch], *Moralia* 221a, Justin 13.5.2–6. Background and discussion: A. B. Bosworth, *Conquest and Empire. The Reign of Alexander the Great* (Cambridge: 1988), pp. 220–228, S. Dmitriev, "Alexander's Exile's Decree," *Klio* 86 (2004), pp. 348–381, Ian Worthington, "From East to West: Alexander and the Exiles Decree," in E. Baynham (ed.), *East and West in the World of Alexander: Essays in Honour of A. B. Bosworth* (Oxford: forthcoming). See P. J. Rhodes and R. Osborne, *Greek Historical Inscriptions, 404–323 BC* (Oxford 2003), no. 83, for anti democrats not being allowed to return to Eresus.

[11] Diodorus 18.8.4.

Exiles had been allowed to go back to their homes at other stages in Alexander's reign, but never on this scale.[12] The return of so many thousands of men had the potential to create significant economic problems for the mainland states still recovering from the famine, not to mention political and social unrest because Alexander had enforced their return. The League of Corinth theoretically protected its members from outside interference, and only they had the right to recall their exiles. Alexander's roughshod action emphasized the difference between reality and theory, and to protest the decree's implementation the Greek states refused to readmit their exiles and sent embassies to the king at Babylon about the matter.

DEMOSTHENES AND THE HARPALUS AFFAIR

Despite the activist rhetoric of Hyperides, Demosthenes successfully prescribed that Harpalus be imprisoned, his money confiscated, and an embassy dispatched to Alexander requesting instructions about him.[13] When Demosthenes asked Harpalus the amount of money he had brought back to Athens, he replied 700 talents, significantly less than the amount he had embezzled from Babylon.[14] Harpalus was subsequently arrested and imprisoned, but a special guard had to move his money to the Acropolis, which Demosthenes could not arrange until the next day. For that intervening night Harpalus' money was unaccounted for, much to Demosthenes' later detriment.

With Harpalus incarcerated, Demosthenes traveled to Olympia, officially as the city's *archetheoros*, the man who funded the Athenian team in the Olympic Games.[15] Unofficially, however, he went there to discuss the Exiles Decree with Nicanor,[16] despite the fact that he was simply a messenger who could not negotiate on Alexander's behalf.[17]

---

[12] See further, Dmitriev, "Alexander's Exile's Decree," pp. 349–372.

[13] Dinarchus 1.70 and 89 (cf. 90); cf. Hyperides 5.9 and [Plutarch], *Moralia* 846b.

[14] Hyperides 5.9–10; cf. [Plutarch], *Moralia* 846b.

[15] Dinarchus 1.81–82.

[16] Dinarchus 1.81, Hyperides 5.18, Plutarch, *Demosthenes* 9.1, [Plutarch], *Moralia* 845c.

[17] Badian, "Harpalus," p. 33.

Nonetheless, Nicanor may well have given Demosthenes advice about how to respond to the king over the decree, perhaps even cautioning him against continuing to harbor Harpalus in the city. Certainly, when Demosthenes returned to Athens he arranged for Harpalus to flee Athens, thereby relieving the tensions between the city and Alexander. Harpalus went to Crete, where he was murdered.[18]

Demosthenes also persuaded the Athenians to recognize Alexander as a god. The Greeks had been scornful of Alexander's pretensions to personal divinity, and the ancient writer Polybius praised Demosthenes and other orators for their opposing stance.[19] Now Demosthenes altered his opinion, for which he was later accused of bribery.[20] Demosthenes never seriously considered Alexander divine, as his contemptuous comment that he "could be the son of Zeus and Poseidon if he wanted" proved.[21] His volte-face, however, was simply to support the Athenian embassy imploring Alexander to revoke his Exiles Decree.[22] The Athenians faced not only the unwelcome return of their exiles but also losing Samos. Philip had given them the island after Chaeronea, and they had a large number of cleruchs living on it. A number of displaced Samians had begun to return home in light of the Exiles Decree, which had led to warfare between them and the Athenians.[23] Demades had remarked that the Athenians were so concerned about heaven that they stood to lose the earth, meaning that their ridicule of Alexander's divine pretensions stood to lose them Samos.[24] Therefore, on Demosthenes' urging, Demades proposed that the Athenians recognize Alexander as the thirteenth god on Olympus under the name of Dionysus

---

[18] Diodorus 17.108.18, 18.9.2, [Plutarch], *Moralia* 846c, Curtius 10.2.3.

[19] Polybius 12.12b3. There had also been opposition from Lycurgus ([Plutarch], *Moralia* 842d) and Pytheas ([Plutarch], *Moralia* 804b), and Sparta simply acknowledged the request ([Plutarch], *Moralia* 219e, Aelian, *VH* 2.19).

[20] Dinarchus 1.94, 103, Hyperides 5.31–32.

[21] Hyperides 5.31. Compare the similar sarcastic comment of Damis of Sparta at [Plutarch], *Moralia* 219e. See also K. M. T. Atkinson, "Demosthenes, Alexander and Asebeia," *Athenaeum* 51 (1973), pp. 310–335.

[22] Schaefer, *Demosthenes*² 3, pp. 318–319; cf. Pickard-Cambridge, *Demosthenes*, pp. 458–459.

[23] G. Shipley, *A History of Samos* (Oxford: 1987), pp. 166–168, R. M. Errington, "Samos and the Lamian War," *Chiron* 5 (1975), pp. 51–57.

[24] Lehmann, *Demosthenes*, p. 209.

and erect a temple to him.[25] The other Greeks followed suit for the same reasons.[26]

Demosthenes may, however, have jeopardized the embassy's chances of success because of his behavior at the Olympic Games. During them, a man named Lamachus from Myrina publicly eulogized Philip and Alexander and mocked the Thebans and Olynthians. An angry Demosthenes so vehemently censured Lamachus that he "took fright at the uproar which arose against him and slunk away from the festival."[27] Demosthenes' reaction may have been understandable, but it was foolhardy, not least because Nicanor would surely have reported the incident to Alexander.

More pressing problems presented themselves for Demosthenes when the Athenians discovered only half of Harpalus' 700 talents on the Acropolis.[28] Demosthenes and several other men (including Philocles) were accused of taking bribes from Harpalus to arrange his escape, prompting Demosthenes to order the Areopagus to investigate the matter under the *apophasis* procedure.[29] He also issued a *proklesis* (challenge) to the people to provide evidence for their accusation, and voluntarily submitted himself to the death penalty if the Areopagus' enquiry found him guilty. Many of the other accused men followed suit.[30] To protest his innocence Demosthenes also authorized the execution of two men at this time who had either moved Harpalus' money to the Acropolis or guarded it.[31]

Demosthenes likely initiated the *apophasis* in the expectation that his positive relationship with the Areopagus since the 340s would benefit

[25] Valerius Maximus 7.2, Aelian, *VH* 5.12, Athenaeus 6.251b, Diogenes Laertius 6.63; cf. Hyperides 6.8. Hyperides 1.21 and 6.21 suggest statues of Alexander and shrines and altars to him in Athens; cf. [Demades] 48.

[26] For the idea that it was the Greeks who first recognized Alexander's divinity rather than it being an order from him, see G. L. Cawkwell, "The Deification of Alexander the Great: A Note," in Ian Worthington (ed.), *Ventures Into Greek History: Essays in Honour of N. G. L. Hammond* (Oxford: 1994), pp. 293–306.

[27] [Plutarch, *Demosthenes* 9.1, [Plutarch], *Moralia* 845c.

[28] [Plutarch], *Moralia* 846b, citing Philochorus.

[29] Dinarchus 1.1; cf. Plutarch, *Demosthenes* 26.1; cf. R. W. Wallace, *The Areopagos Council, to 307 B.C.* (Baltimore: 1989), pp. 199–200.

[30] Dinarchus 2.3, 4, 11, 17, and 20, 3.2, 5, 16, 21; cf. Hyperides 5.34 (unnamed others).

[31] Dinarchus 1.62 and 83, Pickard-Cambridge, *Demosthenes*, 461.

him.[32] He would certainly have remembered that in 335 the Areopagus had abandoned its enquiry into the Persian money he had allegedly taken. His hope for similar treatment now appeared fulfilled because six months went by with no report from the Areopagus. The people thought differently, however – refusing to let the matter fall by the wayside, in March 323 the Assembly ordered the Areopagus to declare its findings.[33] The resulting report (*apophasis*) was simply a list of men accused of taking bribes (*dorodokia*): Demosthenes, Aristogeiton, Aristonicus, Cephisophon, Charicles (the son-in-law of Phocion), Demades, Hagnonides, Philocles, and Polyeuctus of Sphettus.[34] Next to each man's name was the suspected amount.[35] As was the custom in the *apophasis* procedure, the Areopagus issued no evidence to sustain its findings.[36]

Demosthenes, who was accused of taking the enormous sum of 20 talents, immediately issued a second *proklesis*, which challenged the members of the Areopagus to produce their evidence.[37] None was submitted, so the accused men were sentenced to the courts and put on trial in the same month. The charge was a serious one, and the penalty was either a fine ten times the amount of bribe taken (with loss of citizen rights until it was paid) or death.[38]

DEMOSTHENES ON TRIAL

Demosthenes was tried first before a jury of 1,500 men.[39] He faced no fewer than ten state prosecutors, including Himeraeus, Hyperides, Menesaechmus, Patrocles (or Procles), Pytheas, and Stratocles.[40] The

---

[32] Badian, "Harpalus," p. 33; cf. Sealey, *Demosthenes*, pp. 185–187, 214, and Wallace, *Areopagos Council*, pp. 199–200.

[33] Hyperides 5.5.

[34] On all the accused: Worthington, *Commentary on Dinarchus*, pp. 54–55.

[35] Dinarchus 2.21, Hyperides 5.6, Demosthenes, *Letter* 2.1, 15 and 3.42.

[36] On the accused and the amounts: Worthington, *Commentary on Dinarchus*, pp. 54–56.

[37] On ancient coinage, see the Appendix.

[38] [Aristotle], *Athenian Constitution* 54.2, Dinarchus 1.60, Hyperides 5.24; cf. Andocides 1.73–79.

[39] Dinarchus 1.105–106; cf. 113, Hyperides 5.6–7, Demosthenes, *Letter* 2.14; cf. Plutarch, *Demosthenes* 26.2.

[40] [Plutarch], *Moralia* 846c. On the prosecutors, see Worthington, *Commentary on Dinarchus*, pp. 52–54.

political amity and even collaboration shared by Demosthenes and Hyperides over the years had been shattered by their recent clashes in the Assembly over Harpalus' troops and money,[41] and Hyperides welcomed the opportunity to prosecute Demosthenes. Most of the prosecutors composed their own speeches, but either Himeraeus or Menesaechmus employed a speechwriter named Dinarchus, who was originally from Corinth and lived and worked in Athens as a metic.[42] Stratocles was the first prosecutor to speak, followed by Dinarchus' client, but the remaining order is unknown. Only Dinarchus' speech against Demosthenes, some substantial fragments of that written by Hyperides, and scraps from what Stratocles delivered have survived.[43]

Dinarchus and Hyperides constructed their cases around the premise that the reputation of the venerable Areopagus was sufficient for the jury to accept its report without question. Their arguments attempted to cloud the fact that Demosthenes had twice asked for the evidence to substantiate the bribery charges leveled against him but none had been forthcoming. Dinarchus also reminded the jury that Demosthenes had offered to submit to the death penalty if the Areopagus found him guilty and urged the jurors to act accordingly.[44] However, the lack of proof undermined the cases of the prosecutors, forcing them to resort to character attacks similar to those

---

[41] Collaboration: implication of Hyperides' *Against Diondas*: C. Carey, M. Edwards and Z. Farkas, "Fragments of Hyperides' *Against Diondas* from the Archimedes Palimpsest", *ZPE* 165 (2008), pp. 1–19, especially p. 3.

[42] Worthington, *Commentary on Dinarchus*, pp. 53–54; cf. Pickard-Cambridge, *Demosthenes*, p. 463. On Dinarchus, see Worthington, *Commentary on Dinarchus*.

[43] Dinarchus' speech: Schaefer, *Demosthenes*² 3, pp. 330–340, Blass, *attische Beredsamkeit*² 3.2, pp. 278–283; Hyperides' speech: Blass, *attische Beredsamkeit*² 3.2, pp. 64–68. Translation of Dinarchus' speech with notes: Ian Worthington, in Ian Worthington, C. Cooper and E. M. Harris, *Dinarchus, Hyperides, Lycurgus* (Austin: 2001), pp. 11–44; text, translation, and commentary: Ian Worthington, *Greek Orators 2, Dinarchus 1 and Hyperides 5 & 6* (Warminster: 1999), pp. 44–93 and 133–183; detailed commentary: Worthington, *Commentary on Dinarchus*, pp. 121–285. Translation of Hyperides' speech with notes: C. Cooper, in Worthington, Cooper and Harris, *Dinarchus, Hyperides, Lycurgus*, pp. 115–127; text, translation, and commentary: Worthington, *Greek Orators 2*, pp. 94–113 and 184–204; translation and detailed commentary: D. Whitehead, *Hyperides, The Forensic Orations* (Oxford 2000), pp. 355–472. On Stratocles' speech, see Schaefer, *Demosthenes*² 3, p. 330, Blass, *attische Beredsamkeit*² 3.2, pp. 302–304, Worthington, *Commentary on Dinarchus*, p. 54. The following translations are taken from Worthington, Cooper and Harris, *Dinarchus, Hyperides, Lycurgus*.

[44] Dinarchus 1.1,40, 61, 63, 83–84, 86, 104, 108, and Hyperides 5.1.

that Aeschines had employed unsuccessfully in his speech against Ctesiphon (Chapter 13). For example, they criticized Demosthenes' policy toward Macedonia, especially after Chaeronea, and his alleged venality throughout his career. Dinarchus, for example, accused him of taking money from the Persian king and keeping it while Thebes was razed to the ground:[45]

> But thanks to this traitor [Demosthenes], the children and wives of the Thebans were divided among the tents of the barbarians, a neighboring and allied city has been torn from the middle of Greece, and the city of Thebes, which shared the war against Philip with you, is being ploughed and sown. I repeat: it is being ploughed and sown!

Stratocles' speech also lamented the fate of Thebes as a surviving fragment testified: "the city of the Thebans, which fought on the same side in the war against Philip with you, is being ploughed and sown."[46]

Dinarchus also blamed Demosthenes for the ill-fated attempt of Agis to defy Macedonia, although he exaggerated the support the Spartan king had received:[47]

> Is it not necessary for us to raise up another force such as we had in the time of Agis, when all the Spartans had taken the field, joined by the Achaeans and Eleans and ten thousand mercenaries? Alexander, so they said, was in India, and because of traitors in each city, the whole of Greece was unhappy with the situation and was hoping for some relief from misfortunes?

Ultimately, Dinarchus claimed, Demosthenes' policies and actions did not only cost Athens dearly but also all Greece:[48]

> When he began to advise the people, and would he had never done so—I will pass over his private affairs, for time does not allow me to speak at length—is it not true that absolutely no good has come to the city and that not only the city but all Greece has fallen into danger, misfortune, and disgrace?

He also attacked Demosthenes personally, accusing him of cowardice for fleeing the battlefield at Chaeronea:[49]

[45] Dinarchus 1.24.
[46] Blass, *attische Beredsamkeit*[2] 3.2, pp. 302–304.
[47] Dinarchus 1.34.
[48] Dinarchus 1.31.
[49] Dinarchus 1.12.

Demosthenes nevertheless goes around slandering the Council and telling stories about himself . . . "I brought everyone into line at Chaeronea." No again; on the contrary, you yourself and no one else fled from the line there.

Demosthenes' defense speech is not extant, although in antiquity it was said to have had two titles: *Concerning the Gold* and *Apology [Defense] for the Bribe*.[50] The first is the most likely as the second smacks of a confession. Demosthenes' prosecutors attempted to counter some of his anticipated arguments, thereby affording a glimpse into what he may have said. Dinarchus assumed he would argue that because the Areopagus cited no evidence against him, its report was flawed and therefore to be rejected.[51] He was also expected to cast aspersions on the character of his prosecutors,[52] and even return to the theme of *On the Crown* with examples of how well he had served the city and did not deserve unjust treatment now.[53] Hyperides attempted to rebut Demosthenes' likely claim that he could not be held responsible for the missing money because its guards had not discharged their duty properly.[54] The same prosecutor also beseeched the jury to disregard any case Demosthenes might make that he was being sacrificed to appease Alexander and, further, that he did not take money from Harpalus as a bribe but for the Theoric Fund.[55] Apparently Demosthenes also paraded his (illegitimate) children before the jurors to earn their sympathy, something that was permitted in Athenian courts.[56]

All of Demosthenes' defense strategies were to no avail because the jury found him guilty. He was fined fifty talents and imprisoned, but shortly afterward he fled into exile, perhaps because as a state debtor he lost his civic rights and was too ashamed to live in the city.[57] His fine was far less than the legal penalty of 200 talents or execution, as his prosecutors had sought. In fact, Demosthenes may have been fined 200 talents, a sum beyond his means, so the state confiscated his property

[50] Athenaeus 13.592e (first title) and Dionysius of Halicarnassus, *Demosthenes* 57 (second).
[51] Dinarchus 1.1.1.7, 12.
[52] Dinarchus 1.48 ff.
[53] Dinarchus 1.12.
[54] Hyperides 5.12.
[55] Hyperides 5.12–14.
[56] Athenaeus 13.592e.
[57] Plutarch, *Demosthenes* 26.2, Demosthenes, *Letter* 2.2, 14–16, 21, 26, 3.37–8 and 43.

to pay down his debt, leaving 50 talents outstanding.[58] Demosthenes was wealthy, but whether his net worth totaled 150 talents is unknown.

In the trials of the other accused men, Philocles was found guilty[59]— as possibly was Demades, who may have fled the city before his trial, thereby admitting his culpability—and was fined.[60] At least Aristogeiton, Hagnonides, and Polyeuctus, however, were acquitted.[61]

GUILTY AS CHARGED?

The nature of the evidence precludes a definite answer as to Demosthenes' guilt or innocence. There are, however, enough indications to theorize that he was the victim of a political conspiracy.[62] For one thing, while the Areopagus was not legally bound to furnish evidence in an *apophasis*, its failure to do so when Demosthenes challenged it is suspicious.[63] Second, since no proof was submitted against any of the accused men, the jury at their trials ought to have either condemned or acquitted all of them—a fact that Demosthenes' prosecutors recognized when they stressed the need for consistency.[64]

Further, Hyperides commented in his speech that Demosthenes walked around the city "speaking and making accusations that the Council was seeking Alexander's favor and so wanted to destroy him."[65] Demosthenes' reaction may not have been sour grapes in view of the timing of the Greek embassies to Alexander over the Exiles Decree. The king rejected all appeals and to add to the Athenians' resentment restored Samos to its native inhabitants.[66] The Athenian embassy had

---

[58] J. A. Goldstein, "Demosthenes' Fine and its Payment," *CJ* 67 (1971), pp. 20–21; cf. *Letters of Demosthenes*, pp. 48–49, 66–68 and 233.

[59] Demosthenes, *Letter* 3.31–32.

[60] Dinarchus 1.29, 104, 2.14.

[61] Demosthenes, *Letter* 3.37, 42, [Plutarch], *Moralia* 846c–d, Plutarch, *Phocion* 29.3. A fragment of a lost play by Timocles called the *Delos* (Athenaeus 8.341e–342a) implicated Hyperides in the affair. However, that must be wrong because he was one of Demosthenes' prosecutors in 323.

[62] Schaefer, *Demosthenes*² 3, p. 347 and Blass, *attische Beredsamkeit*² 3.2, p. 316, believe that Philocles was also a political victim.

[63] Dinarchus 1.6, 61, Hyperides 5.3, Schaefer, *Demosthenes*² 3, pp. 330–340.

[64] Dinarchus 1.113, 2.21, Hyperides 5.5–7.

[65] Hyperides 5.14.

[66] See Errington, "Samos and the Lamian War," pp. 51–57, for the view that Alexander decided on Samos at Babylon, not at Susa, just before Nicanor went to Greece.

prepared for its mission to Babylon while Harpalus was incarcerated in Athens, so its return would have been about six months later, coincidentally when the Assembly forced the Areopagus to release its *apophasis*. Given the popular anger over Demosthenes' failed strategy to resist the Exiles Decree the report may well have been finessed to curry favor with Alexander should the Athenians try again—they were, after all, still refusing to readmit their exiles, who had gathered at Megara.[67]

Demosthenes may also have unwittingly contributed to his own political demise if, as Hyperides claimed, he admitted he took money from Harpalus for the Theoric Fund:[68]

> Such, gentlemen of the jury, is the extent of Demosthenes' contempt for the matter, or, if I must be frank, for you and for the laws, that at the very outset, so it seems, he admitted to taking the money but claimed to have used it for your benefit, borrowing it for the Theoric Fund. Cnosion and his other friends went around saying that Demosthenes' accusers would force him to disclose facts he wanted to keep secret and to admit that he had borrowed the money on your behalf to meet government expenses.

Demosthenes could easily have rebutted Hyperides' claim in his defense speech and therefore this admission merits consideration.[69] The Theoric Fund, one of the most important repositories of money in the city, was funded by surplus taxation, but surpluses did not occur on a regular basis, causing shortfalls.[70] When there was no budget surplus for the fund, distributions from it for the following year could not take place.[71] Since taxes were not collected until the penultimate month of the

---

[67] Dinarchus 1.58, 94, Curtius 10.2.6–7.

[68] Hyperides 5.12–13. In the passage, Hyperides uses the verb *prodaneizein*, meaning to negotiate a loan in advance or to negotiate a loan for (the people): W. Wyse, "On the Use of προδανείζειν," *CR* 6 (1892), pp. 254–257.

[69] See in more detail, Worthington, *Commentary on Dinarchus*, pp. 58–73.

[70] [Aristotle], *Athenian Constitution* 47.4; cf. Demosthenes 20.115, 24.96–98. M. H. Hansen, "The Theoric Fund and the *Graphe Paranomon* against Apollodorus," *GRBS* 17 (1976), pp. 214–243, E. M. Burke, "Lycurgan Finances," *GRBS* 26 (1985), p. 253; cf. G. L. Cawkwell, "Demosthenes and the Stratiotic Fund," *Mnemosyne* 15 (1962), p. 382: "Faced with the usual shortage as the ninth prytany drew near . . ." and "Eubulus," p. 63: "there always was a temporary shortage in the latter part of the year until the taxes due in the tenth prytany were paid."

[71] Hansen, "Theoric Fund," p. 243.

year, the people would not be able to determine until then whether there was a surplus, and in times of deficit they took drastic measures—after the Euboean campaign of 349/8, for example, they suspended jury duty.

The state lacked the means to meet monetary shortages. Lycurgus' public works program had cost between 750 and 1,000 talents,[72] and voluntary contributions of ships were solicited, as were loans from private citizens to meet the expenses of the new stadium and theatre of Dionysus.[73] In his speech against Demosthenes, Dinarchus alarmingly asked the jurors what would happen if Alexander demanded the return of the money Harpalus had brought with him, the assumption being the city could not repay it.[74] Money therefore was scarce, and as a former member of the theoric board Demosthenes had insight into its financial situation.[75] If the state faced a budget deficit in 325/4, Harpalus' money thus afforded the means to bail out the fund and authorize its disbursements in 324/3. Hyperides' claim about Demosthenes taking money for the fund would therefore be substantiated.

The amount of Harpalus' missing money also plays a role in Demosthenes' guilt or innocence. Of the 700 talents that Harpalus told the Athenians he had brought back with him, 350 were found on the Acropolis, and the Areopagus could track down only 64 more during its investigation.[76] Unaccounted for were 286 talents, of which some may have been distributed as bribes—including the 20 attributed to Demosthenes—thus taking the missing sum to about 200 talents. Yet to spend that huge sum Harpalus must have bribed half of Athens. Possibly the two men who guarded the money stole some of it, yet there are no allusions to this in the surviving prosecution speeches.

---

[72] Burke, "Lycurgan Finances," pp. 254–255; see pp. 251–264 on Lycurgus' economic legislation, with F. W. Mitchel, "Lykourgan Athens: 338–322," *Semple Lectures* 2 (Norman: 1973), pp. 190–211, and see also M. Faraguna, *Atene nell' età di Alessandro: Problemi politici, economici, finanziari* (Rome 1992). For other instances of cash problems, see P. J. Rhodes, "Athenian Democracy after 403 B.C.," *CJ* 75 (1980), pp. 306 with n. 13 and 310–311.

[73] [Plutarch], *Moralia* 852b, Rhodes and Osborne, *Greek Historical Inscriptions*, no. 94, a honorary decree of 330/29 for Eudemus of Plataea, for supplying 1,000 oxen for the building of the stadium and theatre of Dionysus. See also A. J. Heisserer and R. A. Moysey, "An Athenian Decree Honoring Foreigners," *Hesperia* 55 (1986), pp. 177–182, for a honorary decree for gifts for the *skene* of the theatre of Dionysus.

[74] Dinarchus 1.68; cf. Plutarch, *Demosthenes* 25.7.

[75] Aeschines 3.17, 24, 31, Demosthenes 18.113.

[76] Dinarchus 1.89.

One possibility is that Demosthenes used the money as a retainer fee for the 8,000 mercenaries that Leosthenes had brought from Asia to Taenarum the previous year, thereby providing the city with a ready supply of soldiers.[77] The precarious situation with Macedonia over the Exiles Decree prevented Demosthenes from making his agreement with the exiles public knowledge, so instead he chose political disgrace. Yet 8,000 mercenaries would cost about 480 talents to hire—as a retainer fee, the missing 200 talents may have been enough, but the state could not afford more than that to pay the full fee.[78] Moreover, with so many thousands of men involved this type of arrangement would have quickly become common knowledge, endangering Demosthenes' strategy to resist the Exiles Decree. Finally, it was only when Alexander died in 323 that the Athenians gave the remnants of Harpalus' money to Leosthenes to hire the Taenarum mercenaries (Chapter 15 p. 329).[79]

It is more reasonable to conjecture that the missing 350 talents never existed.[80] In other words, Harpalus returned with perhaps 450 talents, of which only the more realistic sum of 36 could not be traced because 20 were given to Demosthenes for the Theoric Fund and the remainder as bribes. Harpalus thus lied in the Assembly when he was asked the amount of his money, presumably to cause conflict with Alexander. If the king insisted on the return of money that the Athenians could ill afford, as Dinarchus insinuated, Harpalus hoped to create a situation that the militant Hyperides could exploit to gain the upper hand over the pacifist Demosthenes.

Demosthenes' carefully crafted strategy to resist the Exiles Decree had backfired on him through no fault of his own. As in 331 with Agis' war, Demosthenes realized again the futility of aggressively defying the Exiles Decree, despite the temptation of Harpalus' money and troops. Instead, he resorted to diplomacy. His plan was complex, even a gamble, yet it was also a testament to his political cunning—his one slip arguably

---

[77] Badian, "Harpalus," pp. 37–40, based on Hyperides 5.13.

[78] Demosthenes' figures in *Philippic* 1 suggest that a force of 8,000 mercenaries in 351 cost about 240 talents per year at half pay (the soldiers were expected to get the balance form plundering). Inflation over the years would have increased mercenary pay so by 324 the figure would be far higher than three decades earlier, perhaps even double. On costs generally, see M. L. Cook, "Timokrates' 50 Talents and the Cost of Ancient Warfare," *Eranos* 88 (1990), pp. 69–97.

[79] Diodorus 18.8.4.

[80] See in detail, Worthington, *Commentary on Dinarchus*, pp. 65–69.

was taking money from Harpalus for the Theoric Fund, which exposed him to attack when the embassy to Alexander failed on its mission.

The Harpalus affair became the bête noire of Demosthenes' post-humous reputation. In Plutarch's biography, for example, there is the curious anecdote of Harpalus bribing Demosthenes with a golden cup that he was admiring while preparing an inventory of Harpalus' treasure.[81] When Demosthenes asked how much it cost, Harpalus smiled at him and replied "it would fetch you twenty talents." In return for the cup, Demosthenes "lost" his voice the next day during a debate on Harpalus in the Assembly. The story is dubious, not least because Dinarchus and Hyperides did not mention it and Demosthenes spoke at all the Assemblies on the issue of Harpalus.[82]

EXILE

As Demosthenes was fleeing Athens into his self-imposed exile, a group of men apparently followed him.[83] He hid from them because they had all crossed swords in the past, but they found him and tried to cheer him up, even giving him some of their own money so that he could live comfortably in exile. At their kindness he wept, and said: "What comfort can I have at leaving a city where even my enemies treat me with a generosity I shall hardly find among friends anywhere else?" Later, when some young men came to visit him, he told them in no uncertain terms never to get involved in politics: if, recounted Plutarch, "at the beginning of his political career, he had been offered two roads, the one leading to the rostrum and the Assembly, and the other to certain death, and if he could have foreseen the innumerable evils which lie in wait for the politician—the fears, the jealousies, the slanders, and the struggles—he would have chosen the path which led directly to destruction."[84] If this exchange is true, Demosthenes' scorn was understandable.

[81] Plutarch, *Demosthenes* 25.3–6.

[82] See Ian Worthington, "Plutarch *Dem.* 25 and Demosthenes' Cup," *CP* 80 (1985), pp. 229–233; cf. Carlier, *Démosthène*, pp. 263–265. There is also a story that Harpalus' assistant revealed to Philoxenus the names of the men Harpalus bribed, and Demosthenes was not one of them: Pausanias 2.23.4–5. That is also fiction: Ian Worthington "Pausanias II 33, 4–5 and Demosthenes," *Hermes* 113 (1985), pp. 123–125.

[83] Plutarch, *Demosthenes* 26.3–4.

[84] Plutarch, *Demosthenes* 26.7.

With a disgraced Demosthenes no longer living in Athens, Hyperides eclipsed the moderate Phocion to become the dominant person in politics. Then in June 323 came the news that Alexander the Great had died. His Exiles Decree was abandoned, and only Tegea in the Peloponnese allowed its exiles to return.[85] Hyperides immediately persuaded the Athenians to lead a full-scale revolt against Macedonian rule, during which Demosthenes was able to return in triumph to Athens.

---

[85] Rhodes and Osborne, *Greek Historical Inscriptions*, no. 101, Ian Worthington, "The Date of the Tegea Decree (Tod ii 202): A Response to the *Diagramma* of Alexander III or of Polyperchon?," *AHB* 7 (1993), pp. 59–64, Dmitriev, "Alexander's Exile's Decree," pp. 351–354.

15

Poison from the Pen

DEMOSTHENES IN EXILE

After Demosthenes fled into his self-imposed exile in 323 he went first to the island of Aegina and thence to Troezen (on the coast of the Peloponnese).[1] From there he could look across the sea to his beloved Attic coastline.[2] During his self-imposed exile he wrote several letters to the Athenians, which he intended to be read out in the Assembly.[3] They protested his condemnation in the Harpalus affair and pleaded for his return, but all were to no avail.

Shortly after Demosthenes left Athens the militant politicians in the city struck again by prosecuting Lycurgus' sons. A year earlier, a politician named Menesaechmus had indicted the former treasurer of the Theoric Fund and orator Lycurgus. The charge is not known, but it may have had something to do with misappropriation of funds. Lycurgus' name was a byword for honesty, however, so Menesaechmus may well have concocted a criminal act on Lycurgus' part. Lycurgus was so old and feeble by then that he had to be carried into court on his bed, but he put up enough of a defense for the jury to acquit him. Not long

---

[1] [Plutarch], *Moralia* 846e.

[2] Plutarch, *Demosthenes* 26.5, Demosthenes, *Letter* 2.17–20.

[3] There are six letters in the Demosthenic corpus: see Blass, *attische Beredsamkeit*[2] 3.1, pp. 383–398, MacDowell, *Demosthenes*, pp. 408–409, 414–423. Translation with notes: Ian Worthington, *Demosthenes: Speeches 60 and 61, Prologues, Letters* (Austin: 2006), pp. 99–134; translation with commentary: J. Goldstein, *The Letters of Demosthenes* (New York: 1968).

after his trial he died. Menesaechmus, however, was not prepared to let the matter drop. By law he could not himself bring the same charge against another person so he arranged for a certain Thrasycles to indict Lycurgus' sons for their father's alleged crime.[4] Menesaechmus prosecuted them and won his case, and they were imprisoned.[5]

The sons' fate polarized the Athenians. Some of them, aghast at their treatment, demanded their release.[6] When Demosthenes heard the news, he wrote immediately to the Athenians on the matter. His letter, which survives, was addressed to the "Council and People of Athens," so it would have been first discussed in the Boule, then read out in the Assembly.[7] The letter is a rhetorical masterpiece, not least because Demosthenes brilliantly turned the sons' cause into a petition for his recall.[8] He used the arguments in his letter—that the people had treated men who served the city well (like Lycurgus) shamefully and unfairly condemned them, that the people's reputation for fairness among the Greeks was detrimentally affected, and that democrats were men of honor—to insist on his return because he was a democrat and had been abominably treated.

Demosthenes rebuked the Athenians for behaving in a shameful, undemocratic fashion towards Lycurgus the democrat and his sons and called for their release. Likewise, their treatment of himself was unjust: despite the lack of evidence against the men accused of taking bribes from Harpalus, the jury acquitted some of them, yet not him. He scorned the people, among other things, for being "thoughtless, you feel no shame before others or even before yourselves, for banishing Demosthenes on the same charge on which you acquitted Aristogeiton" (37), and stressed his innocence in the Harpalus affair with this challenge (42–43):

[4] Perhaps Lycurgus had been fined after all, and his sons inherited their father's debt, did not pay the fine, and so were indicted: Schaefer, *Demosthenes*[2] 3, p. 349.

[5] [Plutarch], *Moralia* 842e–f, Demosthenes, *Letter* 3.7, 10, 12–13, 16–17, 22, 24, 28.

[6] [Plutarch], *Moralia* 842e.

[7] The letter (number 3) was a *demegoria*, like a political speech, in which advice was given to the people, although rhetorically it was classed as "coming to the aid of the distressed, whether private individuals or city states": Anaximenes, *Rhetorica ad Alexandrum* 34. Translation with notes: Worthington, *Demosthenes: Speeches 60 and 61, Prologues, Letters*, pp. 113–127. The following translations are from this book.

[8] For a stylistic evaluation of the arguments and structure of the letter, see Goldstein, *Letters of Demosthenes*, pp. 211–234.

You will never show that I took money from Harpalus; for neither was I convicted of guilt nor did I take any money. But if you look to the famous prestige of the Areopagus Council, remember the trial of Aristogeiton [one of the men accused of taking a bribe from Harpalus] and hide your heads in shame—I have no milder advice for those who wronged me. For surely you cannot say it was right, after information was given in the same words by the same Council, that he was acquitted and I was condemned—you are not so irrational as that! I do not deserve it; it is not right for me; I am no worse than he, though I admit I am unlucky thanks to you. How could I not be unlucky, for, on top of my other troubles, it turns out that I must compare myself to Aristogeiton, and worse still I am condemned and he got away safely?

Demosthenes' letter helped to free Lycurgus' sons from prison, but his own entreaties fell on deaf ears.

THE KING IS DEAD

Alexander the Great died at Babylon on either June 10 or 11, 323.[9] Demades was supposed to have said that if he were really dead the whole world would smell of his corpse.[10] There was no smell, but the superhuman king really had breathed his last. Then the problems began for the Macedonian empire. Alexander had not left an heir to the throne. His wife Roxane was still pregnant when he died, and when his generals asked him on his deathbed to whom he was leaving his empire, there is a tradition that he replied enigmatically "to the best."[11] Needless to say, each general thought he was the best. One of them, Perdiccas, the commander of the companion cavalry, thought he was the chosen one because Alexander had earlier given him his signet ring.[12] The other generals, none of whom were close friends, did not agree, and while still at Babylon they proceeded to carve up the empire among themselves (Ptolemy, for example, took Egypt and founded the Ptolemaic dynasty). The Macedonian empire ruled by a single king was no more.

---

[9] Most likely on the eleventh: L. Depuydt, "The Time of Death of Alexander the Great," *Welt des Orients* 28 (1997), pp. 117–135.

[10] Plutarch, *Phocion* 22.3.

[11] Ptolemy, *FGrH* 138 F 30 = Arrian 7.26.3.

[12] Diodorus 17.117.3, 18.2.4, Curtius 10.5.4, Justin 12.15.12.

Not long after Alexander's death, his wife Roxane gave birth to a son, Alexander (IV). Some of the generals supported the claim of Alexander IV to the throne, but others proclaimed Alexander the Great's half-brother Arrhidaeus (the son of Philip and Philinna of Larisa) king as Philip III Arrhidaeus. For a time there was a dual monarchy, but both kings were merely used as pawns in the lengthy power struggles the generals waged against each other, and both were eventually put to death. The clashes between the rival generals who were still alive in 301 came to an end at the Battle of Ipsus in that year. In its aftermath the great kingdoms of the Hellenistic period came into being—Antigonid Macedonia, Ptolemaic Egypt, and Seleucid Syria.[13]

Alexander's legacy was undeniably far worse than that of his father. Even ancient writers thought Philip was the better king for Macedonia, despite Alexander's spectacular military successes in Asia.[14] However, the dynastic upheaval and bitter personal rivalries that surfaced when Alexander died in 323 played a major role in encouraging the Greeks to revolt again from Macedonian rule, affording Demosthenes the means to return home.

Once the Greeks heard of Alexander's death, Rhodes, Chios, and Ephesus revolted from the League of Corinth, followed by many cities on the mainland.[15] The Athenian Boule, at Hyperides' bidding, secretly gave the general Leosthenes fifty talents from what was left of Harpalus' money on the Acropolis to recruit mercenaries at Taenarum. Leosthenes already had contacts with them because he had transported 8,000 of their number from Asia in 324. His mission was not publicized until Alexander's death was officially confirmed, probably in about September, when Hyperides formally recommended to the Assembly that Athens revolt from Macedonia.[16]

---

[13] On this period, see W. L. Adams, "Alexander's Successors to 221 BC," in J. Roisman and Ian Worthington (eds.), *Blackwell Companion to Ancient Macedonia* (Malden: 2010), pp. 208–224 and R. Waterfield, *Dividing the Spoils: The War for Alexander the Great's Empire* (Oxford: 2011).

[14] In particular, Justin 9.8 and Diodorus 16.95 on Philip, and Diodorus 17.117 on Alexander: see further, Ian Worthington, "'Worldwide Empire' versus 'Glorious Enterprise': Diodorus and Justin on Philip II and Alexander the Great," in E. Carney and D. Ogden (eds.), *Philip II and Alexander the Great: Lives and Afterlives* (Oxford: 2010), pp. 165–174. On the legacy of Philip, see also Worthington, *Philip II*, pp. 194–208.

[15] Diodorus 18.8, Strabo 14.645, Polyaenus 6.49.

[16] Hyperides 6.2, [Plutarch], *Moralia* 849f.

The ever-cautious Phocion urged the people to sustain amicable relations with Antipater, who had been Alexander's deputy in the League of Corinth but who was now in total control of Greece. Phocion's advice was disregarded and the people voted overwhelmingly for resistance.[17] The Assembly resolved that all men under the age of 40 were to serve in the army and deployed a fleet of 240 vessels to protect Athenian security at sea. Embassies to the other Greeks successfully called many of them to arms in the name of freedom.[18] Thus began what the Greeks for panhellenic reasons called "the Hellenic War" to show they were fighting a foreign foe,[19] but what is more commonly referred to as the Lamian War, named after the small town in central Greece in which Greek forces blockaded Antipater (see below).[20]

THE LAMIAN WAR

The Greek revolt of 323 was very different from that of 336. In that year Alexander had succeeded to the throne without opposition and had stormed into Greece and reimposed Macedonian hegemony by the end of the year. In 323, however, there was dynastic chaos arising from the dual monarchy and the disputes among Alexander's generals. To make matters worse Antipater lacked manpower. The Greeks could field 30,000 men to Antipater's 13,000 infantry and 600 cavalry, supplemented by 2,000 Thessalian cavalry.[21] Moreover, the Greek fleet was probably double the size of the Macedonian,[22] and Leosthenes, commander of the entire Greek army, was a formidable opponent.

---

[17] Plutarch, *Phocion* 23.1–2, *Timoleon* 6.5.

[18] Diodorus 18.10.2, 11, Pausanias 1.25.4.

[19] P. Hunt, *War, Peace, and Alliance in Demosthenes' Athens* (New York: 2010), p. 82.

[20] War: N. G. L. Hammond and F. W. Walbank, *A History of Macedonia* 3 (Oxford: 1988), pp. 107–117. Nomenclature: N. G. Ashton, "The Lamian War—*stat magni nominis umbra*," *JHS* 94 (1984), pp. 152–157.

[21] Diodorus 18.12.2. Alexander's demands for reinforcements may have depleted Antipater's manpower. Diodorus 18.12.2 says that he lacked "citizen soldiers" (i.e., Macedonians): Hammond and Walbank, *History of Macedonia* 3, p. 109 and A. B. Bosworth, "Alexander the Great and the Decline of Macedon," *JHS* 106 (1986), pp. 1–12; cf. his "Macedonian Manpower under Alexander the Great," in *Ancient Macedonia* 4 (Institute for Balkan Studies, Thessaloniki: 1986), pp. 115–122; against this view: R. Billows, *Kings and Colonists* (Leiden: 1995), pp. 183–212.

[22] Diodorus 18.9.2.

Leosthenes' first objective was to secure Thermopylae to prevent Antipater from entering central Greece. With his 8,000 mercenaries from Taenarum Leosthenes marched first to Aetolia. There 7,000 Aetolian troops were to meet him and occupy Thermopylae, where a further 7,500 troops from Athens (5,000 citizens, 2,000 mercenaries, and 500 cavalry) would join him. However, Boeotian and Euboean troops, who had remained loyal to Antipater, blocked the Athenian force in Boeotia. Leosthenes went to the Athenians' rescue. He defeated the opposing army and the Athenian troops escaped safely to Thermopylae.[23] In blocking off the pass to Antipater, the Greeks scored the first victory in the Lamian War.

Leosthenes' success at Thermopylae probably explains why several Macedonian sympathizers in Athens were now indicted. One of them was Demades, who had been used as an intermediary between Athens and both Philip and Alexander since Chaeronea in 338. He was now indicted for his proposal in 324 to recognize Alexander as a god, despite its political motivation. He was put on trial, convicted, fined heavily—anything from ten talents to as many as one hundred—and lost his citizenship.[24]

Since the outbreak of the Lamian War, Demosthenes had taken it upon himself to travel to several states encouraging them to unite under Athens against Macedonia. He also wrote to the Athenians endorsing the militant policies of Hyperides and Polyeuctus, although they had prosecuted him in the Harpalus affair. Whether Demosthenes genuinely supposed the Greeks could successfully shake off Macedonian rule or was simply exploiting the situation to effect his return is unknown—probably a bit of both. At any rate, because of his actions his cousin Demon appealed to the Assembly to pardon and recall him, and the people agreed.[25] The Assembly dispatched a trireme to Aegina to transport him back to Athens. He arrived at the Piraeus, where "every archon and priest was present and the entire citizen body gathered to watch his arrival and give him an enthusiastic welcome."[26] When he disembarked and felt his native soil beneath his feet, he raised his hands towards heaven, remarking he returned home in a more

---

[23] Diodorus 18.9.11, Diodorus 18.11.3–5.

[24] Diodorus 18.18, Plutarch, *Phocion* 26, Athenaeus 6.251b, Aelian, *VH* 5.12; cf. K.M.T. Atkinson, "Demosthenes, Alexander and Asebeia," *Athenaeum* 51 (1973), pp. 310–335, J. M. Williams, "Demades' Last Years, 323/2–319/8 B.C.: A 'Revisionist' Interpretation," *Anc. World* 19 (1989), pp. 23–24.

[25] Plutarch, *Demosthenes* 27.6, [Plutarch], *Moralia* 846d.

[26] Plutarch, *Demosthenes* 27.7.

honorable fashion than Alcibiades. During the Peloponnesian War the general Alcibiades was declared a traitor for defecting to the Spartan side. He eventually orchestrated a pardon for himself, but when he returned to Athens in 407 supposedly the entire Athenian population stood in hostile silence as his ship docked at the Piraeus.[27]

Demosthenes still had to pay his outstanding fine of fifty talents, which by law could not be waived. To solve the dilemma, the Assembly selected him to prepare and decorate the altar of Zeus the Savior for a future sacrifice. His personal outlay for this expense was minimal, but to meet it the Assembly voted him fifty talents, which he promptly used to discharge his fine.[28]

In the meantime, events in the Lamian War still favored the Greeks. A desperate Antipater sent urgent demands to two other Macedonian generals, Craterus and Leonnatus, as well as to Philotas, satrap of Hellespontine Phrygia, to bring their armies to him. They were unable to do so because of the Athenians' tight control of the seas. Antipater therefore tried to take Thermopylae himself. In the ensuing battle the Thessalian cavalry immediately defected to Leosthenes, who forced Antipater and his troops to flee for refuge to the nearby town of Lamia. The Greek force besieged the Macedonians throughout the winter, but then their good fortune changed.[29] During one of several frontal attacks on Lamia in late 323 Leosthenes was killed.[30] Antipater offered to surrender on terms, but Antiphilus, the new Athenian commander, refused.

At the end of 323, the Athenians chose Hyperides to deliver the *epitaphios* (funeral oration) over those Athenians who had died thus far in the war. They chose him because he had persuaded them to go to war in the first place.[31] Demosthenes would not have been considered for the eulogy because he had been in exile for much of the year. Hyperides' funeral oration survives.[32] It followed the conventional

---

[27] Plutarch, *Alcibiades* 32, however, describes an enthusiastic welcome for Alcibiades.

[28] Plutarch, *Demosthenes* 27.8, [Plutarch], *Moralia* 846d, Justin 13.5.

[29] Hyperides 6.12, Diodorus 18.12.4–13.5, Plutarch, *Demosthenes* 27.1, *Phocion* 23.4–5, Polyaenus 4.4.2.

[30] Diodorus 18.13.5, Justin 13.5.12.

[31] Cf. Schaefer, *Demosthenes²* 3, p. 374.

[32] Hyperides 6, Blass, *attische Beredsamkeit²* 3.2, pp. 68–72. Translation with notes: C. Cooper in Ian Worthington, C. Cooper and E. M. Harris, *Dinarchus, Hyperides, Lycurgus* (Austin: 2001), pp. 128–136; text, translation, and commentary: Ian Worthington, *Greek Orators 2, Dinarchus 1 and Hyperides 5 & 6* (Warminster: 1999), pp. 114–127 and 205–225. The following quotations are taken from Worthington, *Greek Orators 2*, ad loc.

formula,[33] but unusually contained a lengthy eulogy to Leosthenes. For example (10):

> Leosthenes saw that the whole of Greece was humiliated and cowed, corrupted by those accepting bribes from Philip and Alexander to the detriment of their own countries. Realising that our city needed a man, and the whole of Greece a city, able to undertake the role of leader, he gave himself to his country and the city to the Greeks for the sake of freedom.

Hyperides could not make Leosthenes the hero of his speech, so he refocused on the men who had lost their lives fighting on behalf of the city and Greek freedom (as at 15):

> Let no one think that in making my speech I am ignoring the other citizens and eulogising Leosthenes alone. For the praise heaped on Leosthenes for these battles is also a eulogy for the other citizens. A general is responsible for the right battle strategy, but those willing to put their lives at risk ensure victory in the actual fighting. Consequently, when I praise the victory that was gained, I am paying tribute at the same time to the leadership of Leosthenes and the courage of his men.

The battle at Thermopylae was the high point for the Greeks in the Lamian War. Leonnatus braved the rough wintry weather that kept the Athenian fleet in harbor to cross to Macedonia with more than 20,000 troops and 1,500 cavalry. In the early spring of 322 he marched to Lamia to free Antipater. Although Antiphilus defeated and killed Leonnatus in a bitter cavalry engagement, Antipater was able to force his way out of Lamia and return to Macedonia.[34] His escape was the turning point in the war for the Macedonians. In the summer of 322 the Macedonian admiral Cleitus defeated the Greek fleet, allowing Craterus and his substantial army of 10,000 infantry, 1,500 Persian archers, and 1,500 cavalry to sail from Cilicia to Macedonia.[35]

At that point many Greeks began to desert Antiphilus and Antipater staked everything on a pitched battle. In August, with 43,000 infantry and 5,000 cavalry, he marched to Crannon in central Thessaly and crushed the Greek army of 25,000 infantry and 3,500 cavalry.[36] He

---

[33] See Chapter 11 p. 259.

[34] Diodorus 18.15.1–7, Plutarch, *Phocion* 25; cf. Justin 13.5.14–16.

[35] Diodorus 18.16.4–5.

[36] Diodorus 18.17.1–5. Date: Plutarch, *Camillus* 19.8.

followed his victory by forcing the surrender of all the Thessalian towns that had earlier deserted him, and then took control of Thermopylae. Athens the ringleader was next.

ATHENS IN DEFEAT

In panic, the Athenians restored Demades' citizenship because of his previous diplomatic successes with Macedonian rulers, and sent him, Phocion, and Demetrius of Phalerum to negotiate terms with Antipater and Craterus.[37] The Macedonians were in no mood for diplomacy, however. Craterus was eager to march into Attica and attack Athens but Antipater dissuaded him because of his professional respect for Phocion.[38] The two Macedonians insisted on the Athenians' unconditional surrender, and the Athenian embassy reported this glum news to the Assembly.[39] Demochares, Demosthenes' nephew, attempted to persuade the people to continue fighting, dramatically entering the Assembly with his sword, but the people knew that resistance was pointless.[40] Hoping that Antipater's friendship with Phocion and the philosopher Xenocrates (the head of the Academy) would persuade him to mitigate their punishment, the people sent Demades, Phocion, and Xenocrates to hear his terms.

Antipater had already begun to face threats to his position in Macedonia and Greece from some of Alexander's other generals. He could not permit the Athenians to challenge his power again and did not even listen to Xenocrates.[41] Diodorus curiously stated that the Athenians were "humanely treated beyond their hopes,"[42] but Xenocrates was closer to the mark when he characterized Antipater's terms as reasonable for slaves but harsh for free men.[43] Antipater set up a garrison on the Munychia (a hill in the Piraeus) to control Athens' port, imposed a heavy war indemnity on the city, and insisted on the surrender of the men who had declared war the previous year, including Demosthenes.

---

[37] Diodorus 18.18.1–2, Plutarch, *Phocion* 26, Nepos, *Phocion* 2.

[38] Diodorus 18.18, Plutarch, *Phocion* 26.5–7.

[39] Diodorus 18.18.3, Plutarch, *Demosthenes* 28.1, *Phocion* 26–29.

[40] [Plutarch], *Moralia* 847c–d.

[41] Plutarch, *Phocion* 27.

[42] Diodorus 18.18.6.

[43] Antipater's terms: Diodorus 18.18.3–6, Plutarch, *Demosthenes* 28–30 and *Phocion* 29 and 33, [Plutarch], *Moralia* 846e–847b, 847d, 849a–d, Pausanias 1.43.1 and 7.10.1.

These punishments were harsh enough but worse was to come. Antipater imposed a wealth requirement of 2,000 drachmas for Athenian citizenship.[44] Exactly how many citizens (that is males over the age of eighteen) were disfranchised is unknown, but it could have been as many as 3,000 out of a total of 12,000.[45] Those who lost their citizenship either continued to eke out a miserable existence in Athens or, apparently, fled to Thrace. Antipater's settlement created a narrower type of democracy, in which men sympathetic to Macedonia dominated politics. From 319 (the year of Antipater's death) until 307 Athens was effectively controlled by Demetrius of Phalerum, a puppet ruler installed by Antipater's son Cassander.[46] During that period, Cassander killed Demades in 319, and in 318 even the much-admired Phocion was condemned to death.[47]

Macedonian troops garrisoned the Munychia on Boedromion 20 (mid-September) of 322, the same day that the annual festival of the Eleusinian Mysteries began. There were no customary celebrations that day.

THE DEATH OF DEMOSTHENES

When Antipater's terms were reported to the Assembly, or possibly even after the Battle of Crannon, Demosthenes, Hyperides, and other anti-Macedonian speakers fled into exile. Demades dubbed them all traitors and passed a decree for their executions.[48] Antipater wanted more: he instructed one of his officers named Archias, "the so-called Exile-hunter," to hunt them down and send them to him.[49]

---

[44] Diodorus 18.18.5, Plutarch, *Phocion* 28.4.

[45] The figures in the sources are problematic because Diodorus says that 9,000 citizens met the wealth requirement but 12,000 citizens were disfranchised. Adding these two figures (21,000) would mean over half of the population lost its citizenship, which seems on the high side. However, the 12,000 citizens may represent the total number of citizens before Antipater's action. Thus 3,000 lost their citizenship, but the bulk of the citizens (9,000) did not.

[46] On the period, see most conveniently C. Habicht, *Athens from Alexander to Antony*, trans. D. L. Schneider (Cambridge: 1997), pp. 36–66.

[47] See Williams, "Demades' Last Years, 323/2–319/8," pp. 19–30, for example.

[48] Plutarch, *Demosthenes* 28.2; see E. Bianchi, "Nota sulla morte degli oratori nel 322 a.C.," *Prometheus* 30 (2004), pp. 129–138.

[49] [Plutarch], *Moralia* 846f, Polybius 9.29.

Archias captured Hyperides and two other exiles, Himeraeus and Aristonicus, in the temple of Aeacus on Aegina. He sent them to Antipater, who executed them on Pyanepsion 9 (mid-October).[50] There are three different versions of how Hyperides died:[51] first, that he bit off his tongue and died when he came before Antipater at Corinth, second, that Antipater executed him at Cleonaea, after which his tongue was cut out and his body returned to Athens, and third, that he was taken to Macedonia and executed, had his tongue cut out, and was left unburied until a relative took his body back to Athens.

A week later Archias caught up with Demosthenes on the island of Calauria (Poros), where he had taken refuge in the temple of Poseidon.[52] Archias assured Demosthenes that if he surrendered he would not harm him, and further, that Antipater was his friend. Demosthenes did not believe any of this, and said so: "your acting in tragedy [Archias was a former actor] was never convincing to me, nor will your advice be convincing now."[53] Archias tried to force him out, but Demosthenes went back into the sanctuary, saying he needed to write a message to his family. Once inside, he "picked up his tablets as if he were about to write, put his pen to his mouth, and bit it, as was his habit when he was thinking out what to say. He kept the reed between his lips for some while, then covered his head with his cloak and bent down."[54]

What Archias' men did not realize was that Demosthenes was not writing a letter but had taken poison, preferring suicide to capture. When they went inside the temple and saw the orator in that posture, they thought he was surrendering, and mocked him. Archias repeated his promise about Demosthenes' safety, at which point Demosthenes lifted the cloak, alluded to Archias as Creon, and talked of himself as being unburied. The literary allusion was to Sophocles' *Antigone*, in which Creon tyrannically ordered that the corpse of Antigone's treacherous brother be left unburied. Still, Demosthenes had no wish to pollute the temple by dying in it. With the help of the Macedonians he stumbled from it and died a few feet from the altar on Pyanepsion 16 (late October); he was sixty-two years old.

The ancient accounts disagree on where Demosthenes kept his poison. Some relate that he drank the poison from his pen, others from a

[50] Plutarch, *Demosthenes* 28.4.

[51] Plutarch, *Demosthenes* 28.4, *Phocion* 29.1, [Plutarch], *Moralia* 849b–c.

[52] Plutarch, *Demosthenes* 29, [Plutarch], *Moralia* 846f.

[53] Plutarch, *Demosthenes* 29.2.

[54] Plutarch, *Demosthenes* 29.4.

bracelet on his arm, and still others from a signet ring or a pouch he kept around his middle.[55] All agree that he poisoned himself. What Demosthenes wrote before he died is also disputed. It was either "Demosthenes to Antipater, greetings," which was the regular opening of a letter, or the words that were later inscribed on his statue:

> If only your strength had been equal, Demosthenes, to your wisdom
> Never would Greece have been ruled by a Macedonian Ares.

A STATUE FOR DEMOSTHENES

Forty years later, in 280/79, Demosthenes' nephew Demochares, by then an influential politician, persuaded the Athenians to grant his uncle a statue as well as the right for his eldest descendants to eat free in the Prytaneum and have a front seat in the theatre.[56] The famous sculptor Polyeuctus cast the statue in bronze, depicting a mature, noble man, pensively gazing into the distance, whose hands clasped papyrus rolls representing his speeches. It was set up in the Agora, where everyone could see it (Figure 1). Plutarch tells the story that a soldier hurriedly hid all his money in the hollow formed by the hand and when he later returned it was still there, thereby illustrating Demosthenes' incorruptibility.[57] The original statue is lost, but two Roman copies of it survive (in the Vatican and Sweden). The hands in both copies were lost but have been restored.

The Athenians wanted a statue of Demosthenes for a political reason. By 280 they had lived under the rule of several exploitive Macedonian leaders. One of them, Demetrius Poliorcetes, had even moved into the Parthenon and turned it into a brothel. Demetrius was expelled from Greece in 287, and by 280 the Athenians had restored some semblance of their former democracy.[58] Thus, they "might well be under the illusion that they had regained their former independence, and the erection of a statue in honour of Demosthenes in 280/79 shows that they now considered themselves free from Macedonian control."[59]

---

[55] Plutarch, *Demosthenes* 30.1–4, [Plutarch], *Moralia* 847b, [Lucian], *Enc. Dem.* 28, 43–9.

[56] Plutarch, *Demosthenes* 30.5, [Plutarch], *Moralia* 847a–c, Cicero, *Brutus* 286.

[57] Plutarch, *Demosthenes* 30–31, [Plutarch], *Moralia* 847a, 850f.

[58] Habicht, *Athens from Alexander to Antony*, pp. 67–97; generally on the period: C. Mossé, *Athens in Decline*, trans. J. Sewart (London: 1973).

[59] Mossé, *Athens in Decline*, p. 125.

Later generations, then, still exploited everything Demosthenes sym-
bolized in defying Macedonian imperialism. Unfortunately for the
Athenians, their illusion was shattered in 276 when Demetrius
Poliorcetes' son Antigonus Gonatas established the Antigonid dynasty,
which controlled Greece until the Roman occupation in the second
century.

Demochares' lengthy decree justifying the honors for his uncle survives. Demosthenes the democrat shines through its rhetoric, and in
succinctly summing up his political career and donations to the city, it
makes a fitting conclusion to the orator's life:[60]

> Demochares of Leuconoë, son of Laches, asks for Demosthenes of
> Paeania, son of Demosthenes, the grant of a bronze statue in the Mar-
> ket-place and maintenance in the Prytaneum and the privilege of front
> seats at the public spectacles for him and for the eldest of his descen-
> dants in perpetuity, because he has shown himself as a public bene-
> factor and counsellor, and has brought about many benefits for the
> people of the Athenians, not only having relinquished his property for
> the common weal but also having contributed eight talents and a tri-
> reme when the people freed Euboea, and another trireme when [Ceph-
> isodotus][61] sailed to the Hellespont, and another when Chares and
> Phocion were sent as generals to Byzantium by the vote of the popular
> assembly, and having ransomed many of those who were taken pris-
> oners by Philip at Pydna, Methone, and Olynthus, and having contrib-
> uted the expense of a chorus of men because when the members of the
> tribe of Pandionis failed to furnish this chorus, he contributed the
> money and, besides, furnished arms to citizens who lacked them; and
> when elected Commissioner of the Fortifications by the popular as-
> sembly he supplied the money for the work, himself contributing three
> talents in addition to the cost of two trenches about the Piraeus, which
> he dug as his contribution. And after the battle of Chaeronea he con-
> tributed a talent, and in the scarcity of food he contributed a talent for
> the food supply. And because, through persuasion, benefactions, and
> the advice by which he moved them, he brought into alliance with the

---

[60] [Plutarch], *Moralia* 850f—accepted as genuine by MacDowell, *Demosthenes*,
p. 425. Translation: H. N. Fowler, *Plutarch's Moralia*, Loeb Classical Library 10
(Cambridge and London: 1969), pp. 449–451.

[61] The Greek text has "Cephisodorus," but that is probably a copyist error: MacDowell,
Demosthenes, p. 425. Cephisodotus sailed on Demosthenes' ship when he was trierarch to the Chersonese in 360/59: see Chapter 3 p. 70.

people the Thebans, Euboeans, Corinthians, Megarians, Achaeans, Locrians, Byzantines, and Messenians and gained troops for the people and its allies, namely ten thousand foot, one thousand horse, and a contribution of money which he as envoy persuaded the allies to give for the war—more than five hundred talents—and because he prevented the Peloponnesians from going to the aid of the Boeotians, giving money and going in person as envoy. And he advised the people to adopt many other excellent measures and of all his contemporaries he performed the best public actions in the cause of liberty and democracy. And having been exiled by the oligarchy when the democracy had been destroyed, and having died at Calauria on account of his devotion to the democracy, when soldiers were sent against him by Antipater, persisting in his loyalty and devotion to the democracy and neither surrendering it to its enemies nor doing anything in his time of danger that was unworthy of the democracy.

"THE BEST PUBLIC ACTIONS IN THE CAUSE OF LIBERTY AND DEMOCRACY"?

Demosthenes the democrat shines through the rhetoric of Demochares' decree, which stands in contrast to a modern view that "the life of Demosthenes and the history of Demosthenic Athens are a story of failure."[62] Bleak though this statement is, at first sight it is hard to discredit it, given that Demosthenes' anti-Macedonian policy was decisively defeated on the battlefield of Chaeronea in 338. Failure, then, is an apposite description, yet it does a disservice more to Demosthenes than to Demosthenic Athens. The truth of the matter is that no single policy or single person could have saved Athens or Greece from Philip once he had decided to conquer it.

Demosthenes advocated a policy that may well have been doomed to failure but the argument is made that his intention of rallying the Greeks to defeat Philip, a policy that cost him his life, was patriotic and far from self-serving.[63] Yet at least one contemporary of Demosthenes thought differently, to the extent that Plutarch later was forced to reject his view:

[62] Sealey, *Demosthenes*, p. 3.

[63] For example, Pickard-Cambridge, *Demosthenes*, G. Clemenceau, *Démosthènes* (Paris: 1926), P. Cloché, *Démosthène et la fin de la démocratie athénienne* (Paris: 1957).

I do not know what evidence Theopompus had for his statement that Demosthenes was of fickle and unstable disposition and incapable of remaining faithful for any length of time either to the same policies or the same men—on the contrary it is clear that he remained loyal to the same party and the same line of policy that he had chosen from the beginning, and indeed he was so far from forsaking these principles during his lifetime that he deliberately sacrificed his life to uphold them.[64]

However, Demosthenes' career does show him to be a man who changed allegiances and policies at the drop of a hat as he strove to make a name for himself, lending weight to Theopompus' criticisms of him.[65] He took on politically charged cases, such as those against Androtion in 355 and against the law of Leptines in 354, for self-serving reasons, using them to attract the attention of powerful politicians like Eubulus. The notoriety he gained from them fed his growing political ambitions. His first political speeches of 354 to 351, dealing with foreign policy issues from the Peloponnese to as far afield as Thrace, were largely in line with the program of the fiscally cautious and pacifist Eubulus. Their failure, however, almost cost Demosthenes a public career, as his *On Organization* of 350 suggests. Then Philip's expansionist actions in the north provided Demosthenes with the means to realize his ambition. His policy of resistance, however, was costly, involving as it did repeated calls to the people to fight Philip in the north, and led to a split with Eubulus. The *Olynthiacs* of 349–348 finally allowed Demosthenes to get the better of Eubulus in the Assembly, and his political influence quickly accelerated, as evidenced by his role in the Peace of Philocrates of 346. The success of his *On the Peace* in the same year reinforced where his political future lay: resisting Philip. From then on he focused solidly on defying the king, making Macedonia out to be as great a threat to Greece as the Persians had been. However, as Demosthenes' personal power increased, his cynical exploitation of Philip gave way to a genuine desire to defend Athens and Greece against the king's unwavering advance south.

Demosthenes, therefore, was certainly an opportunist in the manner in which he championed the rights of the wealthier citizens

---

[64] Plutarch, *Demosthenes* 13.1–2.

[65] See also T. T. B. Ryder, "Demosthenes and Philip II," in Ian Worthington (ed.), *Demosthenes: Statesman and Orator* (London: 2000), pp. 45–89.

and advised measures to improve Athenian finances in his early speeches. Yet as the threat from Philip intensified he rebelled against Eubulus' cautious foreign policy, which he believed dangerously exposed Athens, and endeavored to spur the people to action before it was too late. To this end, he deliberately put forward proposals that he knew would make him unpopular and subject to attack. Therein lies the patriot. For example, his call in *On Organization* and in the first and third *Oynthiacs* to divert the money in the theoric fund for the war effort was loathed and potentially exposed him to legal indictment. He was even more roundly censured for his policy of effecting an alliance with Athens' enemy Thebes. Aeschines devoted a significant portion of his speech *Against Ctesiphon* to denigrating Demosthenes for the harm that alliance caused Athens. Demosthenes also risked unpopularity with his demand in the fourth *Philippic* to ally with Persia, the reverse of his stirring rhetoric in *On the Symmories*. Finally, in addition to his persistent criticisms of the people to act rather than simply debate, he lambasted his opponents for pandering to the public in order to maintain their popularity and influence.

Demosthenes therefore chose to subject himself to criticism and at times ridicule, which is a testimony to his conviction that his policy to fight Philip was the needed one—and to his patriotism. His anti-Macedonian strategy, though myopic, could not be faulted for its intention; in fact, it was the only practical one that anyone could have suggested to overwhelm Philip.[66]

Demochares' argument that his uncle had "advised the people to adopt many other excellent measures and of all his contemporaries he performed the best public actions in the cause of liberty and democracy" was the reverse of Aeschines' claim, half a century earlier in 330, that Demosthenes had never advised the Athenians responsibly and that his opposition to Philip led to the Greek defeat at Chaeronea in 338 and the imposition of Macedonian rule. However, the jurors sided not with Aeschines but with Demosthenes at that time, not least because they sympathized with the stance he took towards Philip. In 280, with the benefit of half a century of hindsight, the people likewise accepted that Demosthenes had acted properly for "the cause of liberty and democracy."

[66] Sealey, *Demosthenes*, p. 219.

AFTERLIFE

Demosthenes' reputation as an orator slumped in the generations after his death because philosophers in particular disliked his politics and maintained he was dishonest.[67] Roman rhetoricians, however, thought differently—as is clear from Cicero, who titled his famous speeches against Mark Antony the *Philippics* and who was profoundly influenced by Demosthenes' style.[68] Demosthenes' rhetorical reputation increased substantially in the mediaeval and early modern periods. He became one of four classical authors, together with Virgil, Homer, and Cicero, who were the cornerstone of a western classical education after the Renaissance.[69] His life and especially death were also an inspiration for later artists. Félix Boisselier's magnificent early-nineteenth-century painting *The Death of Demosthenes* is one such example (on the cover of this book).

Demosthenes' name also became synonymous with good public speaking—not merely speaking, but having a superior style of delivery that is persuasive and memorable. In 1959, the British politician Enoch Powell gave a speech about the Hola Camp massacre in Kenya, which was later described as having "all the moral passion and rhetorical force of Demosthenes,"[70] and in 2008 Senator Barack Obama was called a "new Demosthenes" by a political pundit.[71] Even

---

[67] See C. Cooper, "Philosophers, Politics, Academics: Demosthenes' Rhetorical Reputation in Antiquity," in Ian Worthington (ed.), *Demosthenes: Statesman and Orator* (London: 2000), pp. 224–245; see also Carlier, *Démosthène*, pp. 277–286, Lehmann, *Demosthenes*, pp. 18–28, L. Pernot, *L'Ombre du tigre: Recherches sur la réception de Démosthène* (Naples: 2006), pp. 68–97.

[68] See above note with C. W. Wooten, *Cicero's Philippics and their Demosthenic Model* (Chapel Hill: 1983). See also Cicero, *ad Att.* 1.16.12, Horace, *Odes* 3.16, Juvenal, *Satires* 12.47, Seneca, *Con.* 10.5.6 for echoes of Demosthenes' criticisms of Philip.

[69] Carlier, *Démosthène*, pp. 286–293, P. E. Harding, "Demosthenes in the Underworld: A chapter in the *Nachleben* of a *Rhetor*," in Ian Worthington (ed.), *Demosthenes: Statesman and Orator* (London: 2000), pp. 248–257. Further on Demosthenes' posthumous reputation as an orator: C. D. Adams, *Demosthenes and His Influence* (London: 1927), Carlier, *Démosthène*, pp. 277–304, Lehmann, *Demosthenes*, pp. 220–228, Pernot, *L'Ombre du tigre*, passim.

[70] By the former British Chancellor of the Exchequer Denis Healey: D. Healey, *The Time of My Life* (Harmondsworth: 1990), p. 146.

[71] Gideon Rachman, "Obama and the Art of Empty Rhetoric," *The World* (international affairs blog), *Financial Times*, February 26, 2008, http://blogs.ft.com/the-world/2008/02/column-obama-and-the-art-of-empty-rhetoric/#axzz1rehzS9Sm.

Demosthenes' self-imposed regimen to overcome his speech defects inspired subsequent generations of speakers and therapists. Winston Churchill struggled for years to overcome a bad lisp and stammer, as did King George VI. In the early nineteenth century John Thelwall, the first person in England to undertake serious work on speech pathology (to use the modern term), founded a school to help correct people with speech impediments, so that from them "might start forth some new Demosthenes, to enlighten and to energize the rising generation."[72]

For some years after his death, then, Demosthenes was praised more for what he had written than what he had done, thanks to the failure of his anti-Macedonian policy. His patriotic stance eventually led to his political rehabilitation. He came to be seen as an example of how best to serve a country when faced by dire external threats, and others in similar situations throughout history took heart from him.[73] Take the case, for example, of Thomas Wilson, an adviser to Elizabeth I of England, who was also the first person to translate Demosthenes' extant speeches into English. In 1570, as the threat from Philip II of Spain grew, Wilson borrowed Demosthenes' arguments in his *Philippic* and *Olynthiac* speeches and his critique of the Athenians' war efforts to build a case against the Spanish king and influence Elizabethan foreign policy. Where Demosthenes encouraged the Athenians to side with Olynthus and keep it as a buffer against Macedonia, Wilson argued that the Netherlands were England's Olynthus, a necessary buffer against Spain. Anyone who still doubted the threat from Spain was silenced eighteen years later when the Spanish Armada set sail.

Still, Demosthenes' posthumous reputation had its vicissitudes depending on historical circumstances. In the nineteenth century, for example, he suffered another reversal of fortune, because of Hegel's philosophy of history and the philosopher's dislike of the fourth-century polis and his admiration of autocrats like Alexander.[74] The Nazi era, however, led to another rehabilitation, during which in the 1930s Winston Churchill likened himself to Demosthenes and

---

[72] J. Thelwall, "Historical and Oratorical Society at Mr. Thelwall's Institution," *Monthly Magazine* 28 (1809), pp. 152–157.

[73] Harding, "Demosthenes in the Underworld," pp. 258–266.

[74] On this period, see Carlier, *Démosthène*, pp. 293–298.

Hitler to Philip.[75] In more recent history the pendulum has swung the other way to focus on Demosthenes the rhetorician rather than the politician. Yet in our world of ordinary people standing firmly, defiantly, and bravely against tyrannies and totalitarian regimes, one cannot help but liken some of them to Demosthenes. Arguably Demosthenes is ready for another political rehabilitation.

---

[75] A. Adams, "Philip *Alias* Hitler," *G&R* 10 (1941), pp. 105–113—note the year of publication!

Ancient Coinage

1 drachma = 6 obols
100 drachmas = 1 mina
60 minas (6,000 drachmas) = 1 talent

Accurately converting ancient monetary amounts to modern is impossible. As a guide, it may be noted that in the middle of the fifth century a skilled laborer was paid one drachma per day and in the fourth century two or even 2.5 drachmas per day. In 324 Demosthenes was accused of taking a bribe of twenty talents (chapter 14), the equivalent of hiring (at two talents per day) 60,000 laborers for one day or one laborer for 165 years!

Months of the Attic Year

Hecatombaion (mid-July–)	Gamelion
Metageitnion	Anthesterion
Boedromion	Elaphebolion
Pyanepsion	Mounychion
Maimacterion	Thargelion
Poseideion	Skirophorion

Bibliography

Adams, A., "Philip *Alias* Hitler," *G&R* 10 (1941), pp. 105–113.

Adams, C. D., "Are the Political Speeches of Demosthenes to Be Regarded as Political Pamphlets?," *TAPA* 43 (1912), pp. 5–22.

Adams, C. D., *Demosthenes and his Influence* (London: 1927).

Adams, C. D., "Speeches viii and x of the Demosthenic Corpus," *CP* 33 (1938), pp. 129–144.

Adams, W. L., "Alexander's Successors to 221 BC," in J. Roisman and Ian Worthington (eds.), *Blackwell Companion to Ancient Macedonia* (Malden: 2010), pp. 208–224.

Adcock, F. E. and D. J. Mosley, *Diplomacy in Ancient Greece* (London: 1974).

Andronikos, M., *Vergina: The Royal Tombs and the Ancient City* (Athens: repr. 2004).

Andronikos, M., "The Royal Tombs at Aigai (Vergina)," in M. B. Hatzopoulos and L. D. Loukopoulos (eds.), *Philip of Macedon* (London 1980), pp. 188–231.

Andronikos, M., "Art During the Archaic and Classical Periods," in M. B. Sakellariou (ed.), *Macedonia, 4000 Years of Greek History and Civilization* (Athens: 1983), pp. 92–110.

Anson, E. M., "The Meaning of the Term *Makedones*," *Anc. World* 10 (1984), pp. 67–68.

Archibald, Z., "Macedonia and Thrace," in J. Roisman and Ian Worthington (eds.), *Blackwell Companion to Ancient Macedonia* (Malden: 2010), pp. 326–341.

Ashton, N. G., "The Lamian War—*stat magni nominis umbra*," *JHS* 94 (1984), pp. 152–157.

Asirvatham, S., "Perspectives on the Macedonians from Greece, Rome, and Beyond," in J. Roisman and Ian Worthington (eds.), *Blackwell Companion to Ancient Macedonia* (Malden: 2010), pp. 99–124.

Atkinson, J. E., "Macedon and Athenian Politics in the Period 338 to 323 BC," *Acta Classica* 24 (1981), pp. 37–48.

Atkinson, K. M. T., "Demosthenes, Alexander and Asebeia," *Athenaeum* 51 (1973), pp. 310–335.

Badian, E., "Harpalus," *JHS* 81 (1961), pp. 16–43.

Badian, E., "Greeks and Macedonians," in B. Barr-Sharrar and E.N. Borza (eds.), *Macedonia and Greece in Late Classical and Early Hellenistic Times* (Washington: 1982), pp. 33–51.

Badian, E., "Philip II and Thrace," *Pulpudeva* 4 (1983), pp. 51–71.

Badian, E., "Agis III: Revisions and Reflections," in Ian Worthington (ed.), *Ventures into Greek History. Essays in Honour of N. G. L. Hammond* (Oxford: 1994), pp. 258–292.

Badian, E., "The Ghost of Empire: Reflections on Athenian Foreign Policy in the Fourth Century," in W. Eder (ed.), *Die athenische Demokratie im 4. Jahrhundert v. Chr.* (Stuttgart: 1995), pp. 79–106.

Badian, E., "Philip II and the Last of the Thessalians," *Ancient Macedonia* 6 (Institute for Balkan Studies, Thessaloniki: 1999), pp. 109–121.

Badian, E., "The Road to Prominence," in Ian Worthington (ed.), *Demosthenes: Statesman and Orator* (London: 2000), pp. 9–44.

Baynham, E., "Antipater, Manager of Kings," in Ian Worthington (ed.), *Ventures into Greek History: Essays in Honour of N. G. L. Hammond* (Oxford: 1994), pp. 331–356.

Baynham, E., *The Unique History of Quintus Curtius Rufus* (Ann Arbor: 1998).

Baynham, E. (ed.), *East and West in the World of Alexander: Essays in Honour of A. B. Bosworth* (Oxford: forthcoming).

Bers, V., "Dikastic *Thorubos*," in P. Cartledge and F. D. Harvey (eds.), *Crux: Essays Presented to G. E. M. de Ste. Croix on his 75th Birthday* (London: 1985), pp. 1–15.

Bers, V., *Demosthenes, Speeches 50–59* (Austin: 2003).

Bianchi, E., "Nota sulla morte degli oratori nel 322 a.C.," *Prometheus* 30 (2004), pp. 129–138.

Billows, R., *Kings and Colonists* (Leiden: 1995), pp. 183–212.

Blackwell, C. W., *In the Absence of Alexander: Harpalus and the Failure of Macedonian Authority* (New York: 1998).

Blass, F., *Die attische Beredsamkeit*², 3 vols. (Leipzig: 1887–98).

Bloedow, E., "Why did Philip and Alexander Launch a War against the Persian Empire?," *L'Ant. Class.* 72 (2003), pp. 261–274.

Borza, E. N., "Fire from Heaven: Alexander at Persepolis," *CP* 67 (1972), pp. 233–245.

Borza, E. N., "The Natural Resources of Early Macedonia," in W. L. Adams and E. N. Borza (eds.), *Philip II, Alexander the Great, and the Macedonian Heritage* (Lanham: 1982), pp. 1–20.

Borza, E. N., "The Symposium at Alexander's Court," *Ancient Macedonia* 3 (Institute for Balkan Studies, Thessaloniki: 1983), pp. 45–55.

Borza, E. N., "Timber and Politics in the Ancient World. Macedon and the Greeks," *Proceedings of the American Philosophical Society* 131 (1987), pp. 32–52.

Borza, E. N., *In the Shadow of Olympus: The Emergence of Macedon* (Princeton: 1990).

Borza, E. N. and O. Palagia, "The Chronology of the Royal Macedonian Tombs at Vergina," *Jahrbuch des Deutsche Archaeologischen Instituts* 122 (2007), pp. 81–125.

Bosworth, A. B., "Philip II and Upper Macedonia," *CQ²* 21 (1971), pp. 93–105.

Bosworth, A. B., *A Historical Commentary on Arrian's History of Alexander* 1 (Oxford: 1980).

Bosworth, A. B., "Alexander the Great and the Decline of Macedon," *JHS* 106 (1986), pp. 1–12.

Bosworth, A. B., "Macedonian Manpower under Alexander the Great," in *Ancient Macedonia* 4 (Institute for Balkan Studies, Thessaloniki: 1986), pp. 115–122.

Bosworth, A. B., *Conquest and Empire: The Reign of Alexander the Great* (Cambridge: 1988).

Bosworth, A. B., *From Arrian to Alexander* (Oxford: 1988).

Bradford Welles, C., *Diodorus Siculus 16.66–95*, Loeb Classical Library 8 (Cambridge, MA: 1963; repr. 1970).

Brougham, Lord, "Dissertation on the Eloquence of the Ancients," in Lord Brougham, *Works* 7 (Edinburgh: 1856).

Brunt, P. A., "The Aims of Alexander," *Greece & Rome* 12 (1965), pp. 205–215.

Brunt, P. A., "Euboea in the Time of Philip II," *CQ²* 19 (1969), pp. 245–265.

Brunt, P. A., *Arrian, History of Alexander*, Loeb Classical Library 2 (Cambridge: 1983).

Buchanan, J. J., *Theorika* (New York: 1962).

Buckler, J., *Philip II and the Sacred War* (Leiden: 1989).

Buckler, J., "Philip II's Designs on Greece," in W. R. Wallace and E. M. Harris (eds.), *Transitions to Empire: Essays in Honor of E. Badian* (Norman: 1996), pp. 77–97.

Buckler, J., "Demosthenes and Aeschines," in Ian Worthington (ed.), *Demosthenes: Statesman and Orator* (London: 2000), pp. 114–158.

Buckler, J., *Aegean Greece in the Fourth Century BC* (Leiden: 2003).

Buckler, J., "A Survey of Theban and Athenian Relations between 403–371 BC," in J. Buckler and H. Beck (eds.), *Central Greece and the Politics of Power in the Fourth Century BC* (Cambridge: 2008), pp. 79–84.

Buckler, J., "Sphodrias' Raid and the Evolution of the Athenian League," in J. Buckler and H. Beck (eds.), *Central Greece and the Politics of Power in the Fourth Century BC* (Cambridge: 2008), pp. 79–84.

Buckler, J., "Plutarch on Leuctra," in J. Buckler and H. Beck (eds.), *Central Greece and the Politics of Power in the Fourth Century BC* (Cambridge: 2008), pp. 111–126.

Buckler, J., "Alliance and Hegemony in Fourth-century Greece: The Case of the Theban Hegemony," in J. Buckler and H. Beck (eds.), *Central Greece and the Politics of Power in the Fourth Century BC* (Cambridge: 2008), pp. 127–139.

Buckler, J., "Thebes, Delphi, and the Outbreak of the Sacred War," in J. Buckler and H. Beck (eds.), *Central Greece and the Politics of Power in the Fourth Century BC* (Cambridge: 2008), pp. 213–223.

Buckler, J., "Philip II, the Greeks, and the King 346–336 B.C.," in J. Buckler and H. Beck (eds.), *Central Greece and the Politics of Power in the Fourth Century BC* (Cambridge: 2008), pp. 233–253.

Buckler, J., "A Note on the Battle of Chaeronea," in J. Buckler and H. Beck (eds.), *Central Greece and the Politics of Power in the Fourth Century BC* (Cambridge: 2008), pp. 254–258.

Burke, E. M., "A Further Argument on the Authenticity of Demosthenes 29," *CJ* 70 (1974), pp. 53–56.

Burke, E. M., "*Contra Leocratem* and *De Corona*: Political Collaboration?.," *Phoenix* 31 (1977), pp. 330–340.

Burke, E. M., "Eubulus, Olynthus, and Euboea," *TAPA* 114 (1984), pp. 111–120.

Burke, E. M., "Lycurgan Finances," *GRBS* 26 (1985), pp. 251–264.

Burke, E. M., "Athens after the Peloponnesian War: Restoration Efforts and the Role of Maritime Commerce," *Class. Antiquity* 9 (1990), pp. 1–13.

Burke, E. M., "The Looting of the Estate of the Elder Demosthenes," *Class. & Med.* 49 (1998), pp. 45–65.

Burke, E. M., "The Early Political Speeches of Demosthenes: Elite Bias in the Response to Economic Crisis," *Class. Antiquity* 21 (2002), pp. 165–193.

Burstein, S. M., "*IG* II^2 653, Demosthenes and Athenian Relations with Bosporus in the Fourth Century B.C.," *Historia* 27 (1978), pp. 428–436.

Calhoun, G. M., "Demosthenes' Second Philippic," *TAPA* 64 (1933), pp. 1–17.

Carawan, E. (ed.), *The Attic Orators* (Oxford: 2007).

Carey, C., *Aeschines* (Austin: 2000).

Carey, C., "Epideictic Oratory," in Ian Worthington (ed.), *Blackwell Companion to Greek Rhetoric* (Malden: 2007), pp. 236–252.

Carey, C., M. Edwards, and Z. Farkas, "Fragments of Hyperides' *Against Diondas* from the Archimedes Palimpsest," *ZPE* 165 (2008), pp. 1–19.

Cargill, J., *The Second Athenian League* (Berkeley: 1981).

Cargill, J., "*IG* II^2 1 and the Athenian Kleruchy on Samos," *GRBS* 24 (1983), pp. 321–332.

Carlier, P., *Démosthène* (Paris: 1990).

Carney, E. D., *Women and Monarchy in Macedonia* (Norman: 2000).

Carney, E. D., *Olympias, Mother of Alexander the Great* (London: 2006).

Carter, J. M., "Athens, Euboea and Olynthus," *Historia* 20 (1971), pp. 418–429.

Cartledge, P., *Agesilaos and the Crisis of Sparta* (Baltimore: 1987).

Cartledge, P., *Alexander the Great: The Hunt for a New Past* (London: 2003).

Cawkwell, G. L., "Aeschines and the Peace of Philocrates," *REG* 73 (1960), pp. 416–438.

Cawkwell, G. L., "A Note on Ps.-Demosthenes 17.20," *Phoenix* 15 (1961), pp. 74–78.

Cawkwell, G. L., "Demosthenes and the Stratiotic Fund," *Mnemosyne* 15 (1962), pp. 377–383.

Cawkwell, G. L., "Aeschines and the Ruin of Phocis in 346," *REG* 75 (1962), pp. 453–459.

Cawkwell, G. L., "Notes on the Social War," *Class. & Med.* 23 (1962), pp. 34–49.

Cawkwell, G. L., "The Defence of Olynthus," *CQ^2* 12 (1962), pp. 122–140.

Cawkwell, G. L., "Demosthenes' Policy after the Peace of Philocrates I and II', *CQ^2* 13 (1963), pp. 120–138 and 200–213.

Cawkwell, G. L., "Eubulus," *JHS* 83 (1963), pp. 47–67.

Cawkwell, G. L., "The Crowning of Demosthenes," *CQ²* 19 (1969), pp. 163–180.

Cawkwell, G. L., "The Foundation of the Second Athenian Confederacy," *CQ²* 23 (1973), pp. 56–60.

Cawkwell, G. L., "The Peace of Philocrates Again," *CQ²* 28 (1978), pp. 93–104.

Cawkwell, G. L., "Epaminondas and Thebes," *CQ²* 22 (1978), pp. 254–278.

Cawkwell, G. L., *Philip of Macedon* (London: 1978).

Cawkwell, G. L., "Philip and Athens," in M. B. Hatzopoulos and L. D. Loukopoulos (eds.), *Philip of Macedon* (Athens: 1980), pp. 100–110.

Cawkwell, G. L., "Notes on the Failure of the Second Athenian Confederacy," *JHS* 101 (1981), pp. 40–54.

Cawkwell, G. L., "Athenian Naval Power in the Fourth Century," *CQ²* 34 (1984), pp. 334–345.

Cawkwell, G. L., "The Deification of Alexander the Great: A Note," in Ian Worthington (ed.), *Ventures into Greek History: Essays in Honour of N. G. L. Hammond* (Oxford: 1994), pp. 293–306.

Cawkwell, G. L., "The End of Greek Liberty," in R. W. Wallace and E. M. Harris (eds.), *Transitions to Empire: Essays in Honor of E. Badian* (Norman: 1996), pp. 98–121.

Christ, M., "Liturgical Avoidance and the *Antidosis* in Classical Athens," *TAPA* 120 (1990), pp. 13–28.

Christ, M., *The Litigious Athenian* (Baltimore: 1998).

Christ, M., "The Evolution of the *eisphora* in Classical Athens," *CQ²* 57 (2007), pp. 53–69.

Clemenceau, G., *Démosthènes* (Paris: 1926).

Cloché, P., *Démosthène et la fin de la démocratie athénienne* (Paris: 1957).

Cook, B. L., "Athenian Terms of Civic Praise in the 330s: Aeschines vs. Demosthenes," *GRBS* 49 (2009), pp. 31–52.

Cook, M. L., "Timokrates' 50 Talents and the Cost of Ancient Warfare," *Eranos* 88 (1990), pp. 69–97.

Cooper, C., "Philosophers, Politics, Academics: Demosthenes' Rhetorical Reputation in Antiquity," in Ian Worthington (ed.), *Demosthenes: Statesman and Orator* (London: 2000), pp. 224–245.

Cooper, C., "Demosthenes: Actor on the Political and Forensic Stage," in C. J. Mackie (ed.), *Oral Performance and its Context* (Leiden: 2004), pp. 145–161.

Cooper, C., "Forensic Oratory," in Ian Worthington (ed.), *Blackwell Companion to Greek Rhetoric* (Malden: 2007), pp. 203–219.

Cooper, C., Ian Worthington, and E. M. Harris, *Dinarchus, Hyperides, Lycurgus* (Austin: 2001).

Daitz, S. G., "The Relationship of the *De Chersoneso* and the *Philippica quarta* of Demosthenes," *CP* 52 (1957), pp. 145–162.

Davidson, J., *Courtesans and Fishcakes* (London: 1997).

Davies, J. K., "Demosthenes on Liturgies: A Note," *JHS* 87 (1967), pp. 33–40.

Davies, J. K., *Athenian Propertied Families* (Oxford: 1971).

Davies, J. K., "The Tradition about the First Sacred War," in S. Hornblower (ed.), *Greek Historiography* (Oxford: 1994), pp. 193–212.

Depuydt, L., "The Time of Death of Alexander the Great," *Welt des Orients* 28 (1997), pp. 117–135.

de Ste. Croix, G. E. M., "The Alleged Secret Pact between Athens and Philip II Concerning Amphipolis and Pydna," *CQ²* 13 (1963), pp. 110–119.

Develin, R., "From Panathenaia to Panathenaia," *ZPE* 57 (1985), pp. 133–138.

Develin, R. and W. Heckel, *Justin: Epitome of the Philippic History of Pompeius Trogus* (Atlanta: 1994).

De Voto, J., "The Theban Sacred Band," *Anc. World* 23 (1992), pp. 3–19.

Dmitriev, S., "Alexander's Exile's Decree," *Klio* 86 (2004), pp. 348–381.

Dobson, J. F., *The Greek Orators* (London: 1919).

Donnelly, F. P., "A Structural Analysis of the Speech *On the Crown*," in J. J. Murphy (ed.), *Demosthenes' On the Crown: A Critical Case Study of a Masterpiece of Ancient Oratory* (New York: 1967), pp. 137–144.

Dorjahn, A. P., "Demosthenes' Ability to Speak Extemporaneously," *TAPA* 78 (1947), pp. 69–76.

Dorjahn, A. P., "A Further Study on Demosthenes' Ability to Speak Extemporaneously," *TAPA* 81 (1950), pp. 9–15.

Dorjahn, A. P., "A Third Study on Demosthenes' Ability to Speak Extemporaneously," *TAPA* 83 (1952), pp. 164–171.

Dorjahn, A. P., "A Fourth Study on Demosthenes' Ability to Speak Extemporaneously," *CP* 50 (1955), pp. 191–193.

Dorjahn, A. P., "Extemporaneous Elements in Certain Orations and the *Prooemia* of Demosthenes," *AJP* 78 (1957), pp. 287–296.

Dover, K. J., *Greek Homosexuality* (London: 1978).

Drougou S. and C. Saatsoglou-Paliadeli, *Vergina: Wandering through the Archaeological Site* (Athens: 2004).

Duff, T., *Plutarch's Lives* (Oxford: 1999).

Dunkel, H. B., "Was Demosthenes a Panhellenist?," *CP* 33 (1938), pp. 291–305.

Dyck, A. R., "The Function and Persuasive Power of Demosthenes' Portrait of Aeschines in the Speech *On the Crown*," *G&R²* 32 (1985), pp. 42–48.

Easterling, P. E., "Actors and Voices: Reading Between the Lines in Aeschines and Demosthenes," in S. Goldhill and R. Osborne (eds.), *Performance Culture and Athenian Democracy* (Cambridge: 1999), pp. 154–165.

Edwards, M. J., "Le palimpseste d'Archimède et le nouvel *Hypéride*," *Comptes Rendus de L'Académie des Inscriptions* (2010, II avril–juin), pp. 753–768.

Efstathiou, A., "The 'Peace of Philocrates': The Assemblies of 18th and 19th Elaphebolion 346 B.C.," *Historia* 53 (2004), pp. 385–407.

Ehrhardt, C., "Two Notes on Philip of Macedon's First Interventions in Thessaly," *CQ²* 17 (1967), pp. 296–301.

Ellis, J. R., "The Date of Demosthenes' First *Philippic*," *REG* 79 (1966), pp. 636–639.

Ellis, J. R., "The Order of the *Olynthiacs*," *Historia* 16 (1967), pp. 108–111.

Ellis, J. R., "Population-transplants by Philip II," *Makedonika* 9 (1969), pp. 9–17.

Ellis, J. R., "The Stepbrothers of Philip II," *Historia* 22 (1973), pp. 350–354.

Ellis, J. R., *Philip II and Macedonian Imperialism* (London: 1976).

Ellis, J. R., "The Dynamics of Fourth-Century Macedonian Imperialism," *Ancient Macedonia* 2 (Institute for Balkan Studies, Thessaloniki: 1977), pp. 103–114.

Ellis, J. R., "The Unification of Macedonia," in M. B. Hatzopoulos and L. D. Loukopoulos (eds.), *Philip of Macedon* (Athens: 1980), pp. 36–47.

Ellis, J. R., "The First Months of Alexander's Reign," in B. Barr-Sharrar and E. N. Borza (eds.), *Macedonia and Greece in Late Classical and Early Hellenistic Times* (Washington: 1982), pp. 69–73.

Ellis, J. R., "Philip and the Peace of Philokrates," in W. L. Adams and E. N. Borza (eds.), *Philip II, Alexander the Great, and the Macedonian Heritage* (Lanham, MD: 1982), pp. 43–59.

Ellis, J. R. and R. D. Milns, *The Spectre of Philip* (Sydney: 1970).

Engels, D., *Alexander the Great and the Logistics of the Macedonian Army* (Berkeley and Los Angeles: 1978).

Engels, J., "Anmerkungen zum 'Ökonomischen Denken' im 4. Jahrh. v. Chr. und zur wirtschaftlichen Entwicklung des Lykurgischen Athen," *MBAH* 7 (1988), pp. 90–132.

Engels, J., "Macedonians and Greeks," in J. Roisman and Ian Worthington (eds.), *Blackwell Companion to Ancient Macedonia* (Malden: 2010), pp. 81–98.

Erbse, H. "Über die Midiana des Demosthenes," *Hermes* 84 (1956), pp. 135–152.

Eucken, C., "Reihenfolge und Zweck der olynthischen Reden," *Museum Helveticum* 41 (1984), pp. 193–208.

Errington, R. M., "Samos and the Lamian War," *Chiron* 5 (1975), pp. 51–57.

Errington, R. M., "Arybbas the Molossian," *GRBS* 16 (1975), pp. 41–50.

Errington, R. M., *A History of Macedonia*, transl. C. Errington (Berkeley and Los Angeles: 1990).

Faklaris, P. B., "Aegae: Determining the Site of the First Capital of the Macedonians," *AJA* 98 (1994), pp. 609–616.

Faraguna, M., *Atene nell' età di Alessandro: Problemi politici, economici, finanziari* (Rome 1992).

Faraguna, M., "Alexander and the Greeks," in J. Roisman (ed.), *Brill's Companion to Alexander the Great* (Leiden: 2003), pp. 99–130.

Fisher, N. R. E., "*Hybris* and Dishonour," *G&R²* 23 (1976), pp. 177–193 and 26 (1979), pp. 32–47.

Fisher, N. R. E., *Hybris: A Study in the Values of Honour and Shame in Ancient Greece.* (Warminster: 1992).

Fisher, N. R. E., *Aeschines, Against Timarchos* (Oxford: 2001).

Flower, M. A., *Theopompus of Chios* (Oxford: 1994).

Fontenrose, J. E., *The Delphic Oracle, Its Responses and Operations, with a Catalogue of Responses* (Berkeley and Los Angeles: 1978).

Fowler, H. N., *Plutarch's Moralia*, Loeb Classical Library 10 (Cambridge: 1936; repr. 1969).

Fredricksmeyer, E. A., "On the Final Aims of Philip II," in W. L. Adams and
E. N. Borza (eds.), *Philip II, Alexander the Great, and the Macedonian Heritage*
(Lanham: 1982), pp. 85–98.

Fredricksmeyer, E. A., "Alexander and Philip: Emulation and Resentment," *CJ* 85
(1990), pp. 300–315.

Fredricksmeyer, E. A., "Alexander the Great and the Kingship of Asia," in A. B.
Bosworth and E. J. Baynham (eds.), *Alexander the Great in Fact and Fiction* (Oxford:
2000), pp. 136–166.

Fredricksmeyer, E. A., "Alexander's Religion and Divinity," in J. Roisman (ed.), *Brill's
Companion to Alexander the Great* (Leiden: 2003), pp. 253–278.

Fuller, J. F. C., *The Generalship of Alexander the Great* (repr. New Brunswick: 1960).

Gabriel, R. A., *Philip II of Macedon: Greater than Alexander* (Washington: 2010).

Gabrielsen, V., "The *Antidosis* Procedure in Classical Athens," *Class. & Med.* 37
(1987), pp. 99–114.

Gabrielsen, V., "The Number of Athenian Trierarchs after ca. 340 B.C.," *Class. & Med.*
40 (1989), pp. 145–159.

Gabrielsen, V., "Trierarchic Symmories," *Class. & Med.* 41 (1990), pp. 89–118.

Gabrielsen, V., *Financing the Athenian Fleet: Public Taxation and Social Relations*
(Baltimore: 1994).

Gibson, C. A., "The Agenda of Libanius' Hypotheses to Demosthenes," *GRBS* 40
(1999), pp. 171–202.

Gibson, C. A., *Interpreting a Classic: Demosthenes and His Ancient Commentators*
(Berkeley and Los Angeles: 2002).

Gilley, D. L. and Ian Worthington, "Alexander the Great, Macedonia and Asia," in J.
Roisman and Ian Worthington (eds.), *Blackwell Companion to Ancient Macedonia*
(Malden: 2010), pp. 186–207.

Golden, M., "Demosthenes and the Age of Majority at Athens," *Phoenix* 33 (1979),
pp. 25–38.

Golden, M., "Demosthenes and the Social Historian," in Ian Worthington (ed.),
Demosthenes: Statesman and Orator (London: 2000), pp. 159–180.

Goldstein, J. A., "Demosthenes' Fine and its Payment," *CJ* 67 (1971), pp. 20–21.

Goldstein, J. A., *The Letters of Demosthenes* (New York: 1968).

Goodwin, W. W., *Demosthenes, Against Meidias* (Cambridge 1906; repr. New York 1979).

Goodwin, W. W., *Demosthenes, On the Crown* (Cambridge: 1953).

Green, P., "Politics, Philosophy, and Propaganda: Hermias of Atarneus and His
Friendship with Aristotle," in W. Heckel and L. A. Tritle (eds.), *Crossroads of
History: The Age of Alexander the Great* (Claremont: 2003), pp. 29–46.

Greenwalt, W. S., "The Search for Arrhidaeus," *Anc. World* 10 (1985), pp. 69–77.

Greenwalt, W. S., "Amyntas III and the Political Stability of Argead Macedonia," *Anc.
World* 18 (1988), pp. 35–44.

Greenwalt, W. S., "Polygamy and Succession in Argead Macedonia," *Arethusa* 22
(1989), pp. 19–45.

Greenwalt, W. S., "Macedonia, Illyria and Epirus," in J. Roisman and Ian Worthington (eds.), *Blackwell Companion to Ancient Macedonia* (Malden: 2010), pp. 279–305.

Griffith, G. T., "Philip of Macedon's Early Intervention in Thessaly (358–352 B.C.),"
*CQ*² 20 (1970), pp. 67–80.

Greenwalt, W. S., "Athens in the Fourth Century," in P. D. A. Garnsey and C. R.
Whittaker (eds.), *Imperialism in the Ancient World* (Cambridge: 1978), pp. 127–144.

Greenwalt, W. S., "Philip as a General and the Macedonian Army," in M. B. Hatzopoulos and L. D. Loukopoulos (eds.), *Philip of Macedon* (Athens: 1980), pp. 58–77.

Gunderson, L. L., "Alexander and the Attic Orators," in H. J. Dell (ed.), *Ancient
Macedonian Studies in Honor of C. F. Edson* (Thessaloniki: 1981), pp. 183–192.

Gwatkin, W. E., "The Legal Arguments in Aischines' *Against Ktesiphon* and Demosthenes' *On the Crown*," *Hesperia* 26 (1957), pp. 129–141.

Habicht, C., *Athens from Alexander to Antony*, trans. D. L. Schneider (Cambridge:
1997).

Hajdú, I., *Kommentar zur 4. Philippischen Rede des Demosthenes* (Berlin: 2002).

Hall, E., "Lawcourt Dramas: The Power of Performance in Greek Forensic Oratory,"
BICS 40 (1995), pp. 39–58.

Hall, J. M., "Contested Ethnicities: Perceptions of Macedonia within Evolving
Definitions of Greek Identity," in I. Malkin (ed.), *Ancient Perceptions of Greek
Ethnicity* (Cambridge: 2001), pp. 159–186.

Hall, J. M., *Hellenicity: Between Ethnicity and Culture* (Chicago: 2002).

Hamilton, C. D., "Philip II and Archidamus," in W. L. Adams and E. N. Borza (eds.),
Philip II, Alexander the Great, and the Macedonian Heritage (Lanham: 1982), pp.
61–77.

Hamilton, C. D., *Agesilaus and the Failure of Spartan Hegemony* (Ithaca: 1991).

Hammond, N. G. L., *Epirus* (Oxford: 1967).

Hammond, N. G. L., *A History of Macedonia* 1 (Oxford: 1972).

Hammond, N. G. L., "The Victory of Macedon at Chaeronea," in N. G. L. Hammond, *Studies in Greek History* (Oxford 1973), pp. 534–557.

Hammond, N. G. L., "Training in the Use of the Sarissa and its Effect in Battle,
359–333 BC," *Antichthon* 14 (1980), pp. 53–63.

Hammond, N. G. L., "The Kingdom of Asia and the Persian Throne," *Antichthon* 20
(1986), pp. 73–85.

Hammond, N. G. L., "The Battle between Philip and Bardylis," *Antichthon* 23 (1989),
pp. 1–9.

Hammond, N. G. L., "The *Koina* of Epirus and Macedonia," *ICS* 16 (1991), pp. 183–192.

Hammond, N. G. L., "The Various Guards of Philip II and Alexander III," *Historia*
40 (1991), pp. 396–417.

Hammond, N. G. L., "The Archaeological and Literary Evidence for the Burning of
the Persepolis Palace," *CQ*² 42 (1992), pp. 358–364.

Hammond, N. G. L., *The Macedonian State* (Oxford 1992).

Hammond, N. G. L., "Literary Evidence for Macedonian Speech," *Historia* 43 (1994),
pp. 131–142.

Hammond, N. G. L., *Philip of Macedon* (London: 1994).

Hammond, N. G. L., "Philip's Innovations in Macedonian Economy," *SO* 70 (1995),
pp. 22–29.

Hammond, N. G. L., "The Location of Aegae," *JHS* 117 (1997), pp. 177–179.

Hammond, N. G. L. and G. T. Griffith, *A History of Macedonia* 2 (Oxford: 1979).

Hammond, N. G. L. and F. W. Walbank, *A History of Macedonia* 3 (Oxford: 1988).

Hansen, M. H., "The Theoric Fund and the *Graphe Paranomon* against Apollodorus," *GRBS* 17 (1976), pp. 235–246.

Hansen, M. H., "How Many Athenians Attended the Ecclesia?," *GRBS* 17 (1976), pp. 115–134.

Hansen, M. H., "The Athenian Assembly and the Assembly-Place on the Pnyx," *GRBS* 23 (1982), pp. 241–249.

Hansen, M. H., "Political Activity and the Organization of Attica in the Fourth Century B.C.," *GRBS* 24 (1983), pp. 227–238.

Hansen, M. H., "The Athenian 'Politicians,' 403–322 B.C.," *GRBS* 24 (1983), pp. 33–55.

Hansen, M. H., "*Rhetores* and *Strategoi* in Fourth-Century Athens," *GRBS* 24 (1983), pp. 151–180.

Hansen, M. H., "The Number of *Rhetores* in the Athenian Ecclesia, 355–322 B.C.," *GRBS* 25 (1984), pp. 123–155.

Hansen, M. H., "Two Notes on Demosthenes' Symbouleutic Speeches," *Class. & Med.* 35 (1984), pp. 57–70.

Hansen, M. H., *The Athenian Assembly in the Age of Demosthenes* (Oxford: 1987).

Hansen, M. H., *The Athenian Democracy in the Age of Demosthenes*[2] (Norman: 1999).

Hanson, V., "Epameinondas, the Battle of Leuktra and the 'Revolution' in Greek Battle Tactics," *Class. Antiquity* 7 (1988), pp. 190–207.

Hardiman, C. L., "Classical Art to 221 BC," in J. Roisman and Ian Worthington (eds.), *Blackwell Companion to Ancient Macedonia* (Malden: 2010), pp. 505–521.

Harding, P. E., "Rhetoric and Politics in Fourth-century Athens," *Phoenix* 41 (1987), pp. 25–39.

Harding, P. E., "Androtion's Political Career," *Historia* 25 (1976), pp. 186–200.

Harding, P. E., "Athenian Foreign Policy in the Fourth Century," *Klio* 77 (1995), pp. 105–125.

Harding, P. E., "Demosthenes in the Underworld: A Chapter in the *Nachleben* of a *Rhetor*," in Ian Worthington (ed.), *Demosthenes: Statesman and Orator* (London: 2000), pp. 246–271.

Harding, P. E., *Androtion and the Atthis* (Oxford: 2001).

Harding, P. E., *Didymos, On Demosthenes* (Oxford: 2006).

Harris, E. M., "The Date of Aeschines' Birth," *CP* 83 (1988), pp. 211–214.

Harris, E. M., "Demosthenes' Speech against Meidias," *HSCP* 92 (1989), pp. 117–136.

Harris, E. M., "Demosthenes Loses a Friend and Nausicles Gains a Position: A Prosopographical Note on Athenian Politics after Chaeronea," *Historia* 43 (1994), pp. 378–384.

Harris, E. M., "Law and Oratory," in Ian Worthington (ed.), *Persuasion: Greek Rhetoric in Action* (London: 1994), pp. 130–150.

Harris, E. M., *Aeschines and Athenian Politics* (Oxford: 1995).

Harris, E. M., "Demosthenes and the Theoric Fund," in W. R. Wallace and
   E. M. Harris (eds.), *Transitions to Empire: Essays in Honor of E. Badian* (Norman:
   1996), pp. 57–76.

Harris, E. M., *Demosthenes, Speeches 20–22* (Austin: 2008).

Harris, E. M., C. Cooper, and Ian Worthington, *Dinarchus, Hyperides, Lycurgus*
   (Austin: 2001).

Harvey, F. D., "*Dona Ferentes*: Some Aspects of Bribery in Greek Politics," in
   P. A. Cartledge and F. D. Harvey (eds.), *Crux: Essays in Greek History Presented to
   G. E. M. de Ste. Croix on his 75th Birthday* (London: 1985), pp. 76–117.

Healey, D., *The Time of My Life* (Harmondsworth: 1990).

Heckel, W., "Philip and Olympias (337/6 BC)," in G. S. Shrimpton and D. J. McCargar (eds.), *Classical Contributions: Studies in Honor of M. F. McGregor* (Locust Valley:
   1981), pp. 51–57.

Heckel, W. and L. A. Tritle (eds.), *Crossroads of History: The Age of Alexander the Great*
   (Claremont: 2003).

Heisserer, A. J. and R. A. Moysey, "An Athenian Decree Honoring Foreigners,"
   Hesperia 55 (1986), pp. 177–182.

Heskel, J., "Philip II and Argaios: A Pretender's Story," in R. W. Wallace and
   E. M. Harris (eds.), *Transitions to Empire: Essays in Honor of E. Badian* (Norman:
   1996), pp. 37–56.

Holst, H., "Demosthenes' Speech Impediment," *Symbolae Osloenses* 4 (1926), pp.
   11–25.

Hornblower, S., *Mausolus* (Oxford: 1982).

Hunt, P., *War, Peace, and Alliance in Demosthenes' Athens* (New York: 2010).

Ingenkamp, H. G., "Die Stellung des Demosthenes zu Theben in der Megalopolitenrede," *Hermes* 100 (1972), pp. 195–205.

Jacoby, F. *Die Fragmente der griechischen Historiker* (Berlin/Leiden: 1926–).

Jaeger, W., *Demosthenes: The Origin and Growth of His Policy* (Berkeley and Los
   Angeles: 1938; repr. New York: 1977).

Jones, N., *The Associations of Classical Athens* (New York: 1999).

Jordan, B., *The Athenian Navy in the Classical Period* (Berkeley: 1975).

Kagan, D., *The Peloponnesian War* (London: 2003).

Kapparis, K. A., "The Law on the Age of Speakers in the Athenian Assembly," *RhM*
   141 (1998), pp. 255–259.

Kapparis, K. A., *Apollodoros: Against Neaira [D. 59]* (Berlin: 1991).

Karvounis, C., *Demosthenes: Studien zu den Demegorien orr. XIV, XVI, XV, IV, I, II, III*
   (Tübingen: 2002).

Keaney, J. J., "Demosthenes' Oration *On the Crown* (A Translation)," in J. J. Murphy
   (ed.), *Demosthenes' On the Crown: A Critical Case Study of a Masterpiece of Ancient
   Oratory* (New York: 1967), pp. 59–125.

Kennedy, C. R., "Demosthenes' Use of History," reprinted in J. J. Murphy (ed.),
   Demosthenes' On the Crown: A Critical Case Study of a Masterpiece of Ancient Oratory
   (New York: 1967), pp. 145–156.

Kennedy, G. A., *The Art of Persuasion in Greece* (Princeton: 1963).

Kennedy, G. A., "The Oratorical Career of Demosthenes," in J. J. Murphy (ed.), *Demosthenes' On the Crown: A Critical Case Study of a Masterpiece of Ancient Oratory* (New York: 1967), pp. 28–47.

Kertsch, M., *Kommentar zur 30. Rede des Demosthenes (gegen Onetor I)* (Vienna: 1971).

Keyser, P. T., "The Use of Artillery by Philip II and Alexander the Great," *Anc. World* 15 (1994), pp. 27–49.

Kindstrand, J. F., *The Stylistic Evaluation of Aeschines in Antiquity* (Upsala: 1982).

King, C. J., "Kingship and Other Political Institutions," in J. Roisman and Ian Worthington (eds.), *Blackwell Companion to Ancient Macedonia* (Malden: 2010), pp. 374–391.

Knox, R. A., "'So Mischievous a Beaste'? The Athenian Demos and its Treatment of Politicians," *G&R²* 32 (1985), pp. 132–161.

Kremmydas, C., *Commentary on Demosthenes Against Leptines* (Oxford: 2012).

Kurihara, K., "Personal Enmity as a Motivation in Forensic Speeches," *CQ²* 53 (2003), pp. 464–477.

Lambin, G., "Le surnom *Batalos* et les mots de cette famille," *Revue de Philologie* 56 (1982), pp. 249–263.

Lane Fox, R., "Aeschines and Athenian Politics," in R. Osborne and S. Hornblower (eds.), *Ritual, Finance, Politics: Athenian Democratic Accounts Presented to David Lewis* (Oxford: 1994), pp. 135–155.

Lane Fox, R., "Demosthenes, Dionysius, and the Dating of Six Early Speeches," *Class. & Med.* 48 (1997), pp. 167–203.

Lanni, A., "Spectator Sport or Serious Politics? οἱ περιεστηκότες and the Athenian Lawcourts," *JHS* 117 (1997), pp. 183–189.

Lehmann, G. A., *Demosthenes von Athen: Ein Leben für die Freiheit* (Munich: 2004).

Lintott, A., *Plutarch: Demosthenes and Cicero: Oratory and Political Failure* (Oxford: 2012).

Leopold, J. W., "Demosthenes on Distrust of Tyrants," *GRBS* 22 (1981), pp. 227–246.

Leopold, J. W., "Demosthenes' Strategy in the First Philippic, 'An Away Match with Macedonian Cavalry'?," *Anc. World* 16 (1987), pp. 59–69.

Londey, P. D., "The Outbreak of the Fourth Sacred War," *Chiron* 20 (1990), pp. 239–260.

Loraux, N., *The Invention of Athens: The Funeral Oration in the Classical City* (Cambridge: 1986).

Ma, J., "Chaironeia 338: Topographies of Commemoration," *JHS* 128 (2008), pp. 172–191.

MacDowell, D. M., "Law-Making at Athens in the Fourth Century B.C.," *JHS* 95 (1975), pp. 62–74.

MacDowell, D. M., "*Hybris* in Athens," *G&R²* 23 (1976), pp. 14–31.

MacDowell, D. M., *The Law in Classical Athens* (London: 1978).

MacDowell, D. M., "The Law of Periandros about Symmories," *CQ²* 36 (1986), pp. 438–449.

MacDowell, D. M., "The Authenticity of Demosthenes 29 (Against Aphobos III) as a Source of Information about Athenian Law," *Symposion* 1985 (1989), pp. 265–262.

MacDowell, D. M., *Demosthenes: Against Meidias (Oration 21)* (Oxford: 1990).

MacDowell, D. M., *Demosthenes: On the False Embassy (Oration 19)* (Oxford: 2000).

MacDowell, D. M., "Athenian Laws about Homosexuality," *RIDA* 47 (2000), pp. 13–27.

MacDowell, D. M., "Epikerdes of Kyrene and the Athenian Privilege of *Ateleia*," *ZPE* 150 (2004), pp. 127–133.

MacDowell, D. M., *Demosthenes, Speeches 27–38* (Austin: 2004).

MacDowell, D. M., *Demosthenes the Orator* (Oxford: 2009).

Mackendrick, P., *The Athenian Aristocracy 399–31 B.C.* (Cambridge: 1969).

Mader, G., "*Quantum mutati ab illis . . .*: Satire and Displaced Identity in Demosthenes' *First Philippic*," *Philologus* 147 (2003), pp. 56–69.

Mader, G., "Praise, Blame and Authority: Some Strategies of Persuasion in Demosthenes, *Philippic 2*," *Hermes* 132 (2004), pp. 56–69.

Marsden, E. W., "Macedonian Military Machinery and its Designers under Philip and Alexander," *Ancient Macedonia* 2 (Institute for Balkan Studies, Thessaloniki: 1977), pp. 211–223.

McCabe, D. F., *The Prose Rhythm of Demosthenes* (New York: 1981).

McQueen, E. I., "Some Notes on the Anti-Macedonian Movement in the Peloponnese in 331 B.C.," *Historia* 37 (1978), pp. 52–59.

McQueen, E. I., *Demosthenes: Olynthiacs* (London: 1986).

Meiggs, R., *The Athenian Empire* (Oxford: 1979).

Milns, R. D., "Hermias of Atarneus and the Fourth Philippic Speech," *Filologia e forme letterarie: Studi offerti a Francesco della Corte* 1 (Urbino: 1987), pp. 287–302.

Milns, R. D., "Didymea," in Ian Worthington (ed.), *Ventures into Greek History: Essays in Honour of N. G. L. Hammond* (Oxford: 1994), pp. 70–88.

Milns, R. D., "The Public Speeches of Demosthenes," in Ian Worthington (ed.), *Demosthenes: Statesman and Orator* (London: 2000), pp. 205–223.

Mirhady, D., "Demosthenes the Advocate" in Ian Worthington (ed.), *Demosthenes: Statesman and Orator* (London: 2000), pp. 181–204.

Mitchel, F. W., "Athens in the Age of Alexander," *G&R²* 12 (1965), pp. 189–204.

Mitchel, F. W., "Lykourgan Athens: 338–322," *Semple Lectures* 2 (Cincinnati: 1970).

Mitchel, F. W., "The Assessment of the Allies in the Second Athenian League," *EMC* 3 (1984), pp. 23–37.

Mitchell, L. G., *Greeks Bearing Gifts: The Public Use of Private Relationships in the Greek World, 435–323 BC* (Cambridge: 1997).

Mitchell, L. G. and L. Rubinstein (eds.), *Greek Epigraphy and History: Essays in Honour of P. J. Rhodes* (Swansea: 2008).

Montgomery, H., *The Way to Chaeronea* (Oslo: 1983).

Montgomery, H., "The Economic Revolution of Philip II—Myth or Reality?," *SO* 60 (1985), pp. 37–47.

Moreno, A., *Feeding the Democracy: The Athenian Grain Supply in the Fifth and Fourth Centuries BC* (Oxford: 2007).

Morrison, J. S., "Athenian Sea-Power in 323/2 B.C.: Dream and Reality," *JHS* 107 (1987), pp. 88–97.

Mosley, D. J., "Athens' Alliance with Thebes 339 B.C.," *Historia* 20 (1971), pp. 508–510.

Mosley, D. J., "Oaths at Pherae, 346 B.C.," *Philologus* 116 (1972), pp. 145–148.

Mossé, C., *Athens in Decline*, trans. J. Sewart (London: 1973).

Müller, S., "Philip II," in J. Roisman and Ian Worthington (eds.), *Blackwell Companion to Ancient Macedonia* (Malden: 2010), pp. 166–185.

Murphy, J. J. (ed.), *Demosthenes' On the Crown: A Critical Case Study of a Masterpiece of Ancient Oratory* (New York: 1967).

Nouhaud, M., *L'Utilisation de l'histoire par les orateurs attiques* (Paris: 1982).

Ober, J., *Mass and Elite in Democratic Athens: Rhetoric, Ideology and the Power of the People* (Princeton: 1989).

Ober, J., "Power and Oratory in Democratic Athens: Demosthenes 21, *Against Meidias*," in J. Ober (ed.), *The Athenian Revolution: Essays on Ancient Greek Democracy and Political Theory* (Princeton: 1996), pp. 86–106.

Ober, J., "Public Speech and the Power of the People in Democratic Athens," in J. Ober (ed.), *The Athenian Revolution: Essays on Ancient Greek Democracy and Political Theory* (Princeton: 1996), pp. 18–31.

Ochs, D. J., "Demosthenes' Use of Argument," in J. J. Murphy (ed.), *Demosthenes' On the Crown: A Critical Case Study of a Masterpiece of Ancient Oratory* (New York: 1967), pp. 157–174.

Olbrycht, M. J., "Macedonia and Persia," in J. Roisman and Ian Worthington (eds.), *Blackwell Companion to Ancient Macedonia* (Malden: 2010), pp. 342–369.

Osborne, M. J., *Naturalization in Athens* 3 (Brussels: 1983).

Osborne, R. G., "Law in Action in Classical Athens," *JHS* 105 (1985), pp. 40–58.

Parke, H. W., *A History of the Delphic Oracle* (Oxford: 1939).

Papillon, T., *Rhetorical Studies in the Aristocratea of Demosthenes* (New York: 1998).

Papillon, T., *Isocrates II* (Austin: 2004).

Papillon, T., "Isocrates," in Ian Worthington (ed.), *Blackwell Companion to Greek Rhetoric* (Malden: 2007), pp. 58–74.

Paulsen, T., *Die Parapresbeia-Reden des Demosthenes und des Aischines: Kommentar und Interpretationen zu Demosthenes, or. XIX, und Aischines, or. II* (Trier: 1999).

Pearson, L., "Historical Allusions in the Attic Orators," *CP* 36 (1941), pp. 209–229.

Pearson, L., *Demosthenes: Six Private Speeches* (Atlanta: 1973).

Pearson, L., "The Development of Demosthenes as a Political Orator," *Phoenix* 29 (1975), pp. 95–109.

Pearson, L., "The Virtuoso Passages in Demosthenes' Speeches," *Phoenix* 29 (1975), pp. 214–230.

Pearson, L., *The Art of Demosthenes* (Meisenheim am Glan: 1976).

Pelling, C., *Plutarch and History* (London: 2002).

Perlman, S., "Isocrates' 'Philippus'—A Reinterpretation," *Historia* 6 (1957), pp. 306–317.

Perlman, S., "The Historical Example, Its Use and Importance as Political Propaganda in the Attic Orators," *SH* 7 (1961), pp. 158–166.

Perlman, S., "On Bribing Athenian Ambassadors," *GRBS* 17 (1976), pp. 223–233.

Perlman, S., "Greek Diplomatic Tradition and the Corinthian League of Philip of Macedon," *Historia* 34 (1985), pp. 153–174.

Perlman, S., "Fourth Century Treaties and the League of Corinth of Philip of Macedon," in *Ancient Macedonia* 4 (Institute for Balkan Studies, Thessaloniki: 1986), pp. 437–442.

Pernot, L., *L'Ombre du tigre: Recherches sur la réception de Démosthène* (Naples: 2006).

Pickard-Cambridge, A. W., *Demosthenes and the Last Days of Greek Freedom* (London: 1914).

Poddighe, E., "Alexander and the Greeks," in W. Heckel and L. Tritle (eds.), *Alexander the Great. A New History* (Oxford: 2009), pp. 99–120.

Pownall, F., "The Symposia of Philip II and Alexander III of Macedon: The View from Greece," in E. D. Carney and D. Ogden (eds.), *Philip II and Alexander the Great: Lives and Afterlives* (Oxford: 2010), pp. 55–65.

Prestianni Gialombardo, A. M., "*Philippika* I: Sul 'Culto' di Filippo II di Macedonia," *Siculorum Gymnasium* 28 (1975), pp. 1–57.

Pritchett, W. K., *The Greek State at War* (Berkeley and Los Angeles: 1974).

Rachman, G., "Obama and the Art of Empty Rhetoric," *The World* (international affairs blog), *Financial Times*, February 26, 2008, http://blogs.ft.com/the-world/2008/02/column-obama-and-the-art-of-empty-rhetoric/#axzz1rehzS9Sm.

Radicke, J., *Die Rede des Demosthenes für die Freiheit der Rhodier* (Stuttgart: 1995).

Rahe, P. A., "The Annihilation of the Sacred Band at Chaeronea," *AJA* 85 (1981), pp. 84–87.

Rhodes, P. J., *The Athenian Boule* (Oxford: 1972).

Rhodes, P. J., "Athenian Democracy after 403 B.C.," *CJ* 75 (1980), pp. 305–323.

Rhodes, P. J., *A Commentary on the Aristotelian* Athenaion Politeia (Oxford: 1981).

Rhodes, P. J., "Political Activity in Classical Athens," *JHS* 106 (1986), pp. 132–144.

Rhodes, P. J. and R. Osborne (eds.), *Greek Historical Inscriptions, 404–323 BC* (Oxford: 2003).

Riginos, A. S., "The Wounding of Philip II of Macedon: Fact and Fabrication," *JHS* 114 (1994), pp. 103–119.

Robinson, C. A., *The History of Alexander the Great*, 2 vols. (Providence: 1953).

Roebuck, C., "The Settlement of Philip II with the Greek States in 338 B.C.," *CP* 43 (1948), pp. 73–92.

Roisman, J., (ed.), *Brill Companion to Alexander the Great* (Leiden: 2003), pp. 94–96.

Roisman, J., *The Rhetoric of Manhood: Masculinity in the Attic Orators* (Berkeley and Los Angeles: 2005).

Roisman, J., *The Rhetoric of Conspiracy in Ancient Athens* (Berkeley and Los Angeles: 2006).

Roisman, J., "Classical Macedonia to Perdiccas III," in J. Roisman and Ian Worthington (eds.), *Blackwell Companion to Ancient Macedonia* (Malden: 2010), pp. 145–165.

Roisman, J. and Ian Worthington (eds.), *Blackwell Companion to Ancient Macedonia* (Malden: 2010).

Ronnet, G., *Étude sur le style de Démosthène dans les discours politiques* (Paris: 1951).

Roselli, D. K., "*Theorika* in Fifth-Century Athens," *GRBS* 49 (2009), pp. 5–30.

Rowe, G. O., "The Portrait of Aeschines in the Oration *On the Crown*," *TAPA* 97 (1966), pp. 397–406.

Rowe, G. O., "Demosthenes' Use of Language," in J. J. Murphy (ed.), *Demosthenes' On the Crown: A Critical Case Study of a Masterpiece of Ancient Oratory* (New York: 1967), pp. 175–199.

Rowe, G. O., "Demosthenes' First Philippic: The Satiric Mode," *TAPA* 99 (1968), pp. 361–374.

Rowe, G. O., "The Charge against Meidias," *Hermes* 122 (1994), pp. 55–63.

Rowe, G. O., "Anti-Isocratean Sentiment in Demosthenes' *Against Androtion*," *Historia* 49 (2000), pp. 278–302.

Ruschenbusch, E., "Die athenischen Symmorien des 4. Jh. v. Chr.," *ZPE* 31 (1978), pp. 275–284.

Ruschenbusch, E., "Demosthenes' erste freiwillige Trierarchie und die Datierung des Euböaunternehmens vom Jahre 357," *ZPE* 67 (1987), pp. 158–159.

Ruschenbusch, E., "Die Zahl der athenischen Trierarchen in der Zeit nach 340 v. Chr.," *Class. & Med.* 41 (1990), pp. 79–88.

Russell, D. A., *Plutarch* (London: 1973).

Ryder, T. T. B., *Koine Eirene* (Oxford: 1965).

Ryder, T. T. B., "Demosthenes and Philip's Peace of 338/7 B.C.," *CQ*² 26 (1976), pp. 85–87.

Ryder, T. T. B., "The Diplomatic Skills of Philip II," in Ian Worthington (ed.), *Ventures into Greek History: Essays in Honour of N. G. L. Hammond* (Oxford: 1994), pp. 228–257.

Ryder, T. T. B., "Demosthenes and Philip II," in Ian Worthington (ed.), *Demosthenes: Statesman and Orator* (London: 2000), pp. 45–89.

Sacks, K., *Diodorus Siculus and the First Century* (Princeton: 1990).

Sakellariou, M. B., "Panhellenism: From Concept to Policy," in M. B. Hatzopoulos and L. D. Loukopoulos (eds.), *Philip of Macedon* (Athens: 1980), pp. 128–145.

Sandys, J. E., *Demosthenes: On the Peace, Second Philippic, On the Chersonesus and Third Philippic* (Cambridge: 1900).

Sandys, J. E., *The First Philippic and the Olynthiacs of Demosthenes* (Cambridge: 1910).

Saunders, A. N. W., *Greek Political Oratory*. Penguin Classics (Harmondsworth: 1970; repr. 1984).

Sawada, N., "A Reconsideration of the Peace of Philocrates," *Kodai* 4 (1993), pp. 21–50.

Sawada, N., "Athenian Politics in the Age of Alexander the Great: A Reconsideration of the Trial of Ctesiphon," *Chiron* 26 (1996), pp. 57–82.

Sawada, N., "Macedonian Social Customs," in J. Roisman and Ian Worthington (eds.), *Blackwell Companion to Ancient Macedonia* (Malden: 2010), pp. 392–408.

Schaefer, A., *Demosthenes und seine Zeit*², 3 vols. (Leipzig: 1885–87).

Schwarz, E., "Demosthenes' erste Philippika," in P. Jors, E. Schwartz, and R. Reitzenstein (eds.), *Festschrift Theodor Mommsen zum fünfzigjährigen Doctorjubiläum* (Marburg: 1893), pp. 1–44.

Scott-Kilvert, I., *Plutarch, The Age of Alexander*. Penguin Classics (Harmondsworth: 1973).

Seager, R., "Thrasybulus, Conon and Athenian Imperialism, 396–386 B.C.," *JHS* 87 (1967), pp. 95–115.

Sealey, R., "Dionysius of Halicarnassus and Some Demosthenic Dates," *REG* 68 (1955), pp. 77–120.

Sealey, R., "Athens after the Social War," *JHS* 75 (1955), pp. 74–81.

Sealey, R., "Callistratos of Aphidna and His Contemporaries," *Historia* 5 (1956), pp. 178–203.

Sealey, R., "Who Was Aristogeiton?," *BICS* 7 (1960), pp. 33–43.

Sealey, R., *Essays in Greek Politics* (New York: 1967).

Sealey, R., "Pseudodemosthenes xiii and xxv," *REG* 80 (1967), pp. 250–255.

Sealey, R., *Demosthenes and His Time: A Study in Defeat* (Oxford: 1993).

Shapur Shahbazi, A., "Iranians and Alexander," *AJAH*² 2 (2003), pp. 5–38.

Sherman, C. L., *Diodorus Siculus 16.1–65*, Loeb Classical Library 7 (Cambridge, MA: 1952; repr. 1971).

Shipley, G., *A History of Samos* (Oxford: 1987).

Shipley, G., "Between Macedonia and Rome: Political Landscapes and Social Changes in Southern Greece in the Early Hellenistic Period," *BSA* 100 (2005), pp. 315–330.

Shrimpton, G. S., *Theopompus the Historian* (Montreal: 1991).

Sickinger, J., "Rhetoric and the Law," in Ian Worthington (ed.), *Blackwell Companion to Greek Rhetoric* (Malden: 2006), pp. 286–302.

Sidebottom, H. and M. Whitby (eds.), *Blackwell Encyclopedia of Ancient Battles* (Malden: forthcoming).

Sinclair, R. K., "Lysias' Speeches and the Debate about Participation in Athenian Public Life," *Antichthon* 22 (1988), pp. 54–66.

Sinclair, R. K., *Democracy and Participation in Athens* (Cambridge: 1988).

Slater, W. J., "Pindar's House," *GRBS* 12 (1971), pp. 146–147.

Slater, W. J., "The Epiphany of Demosthenes," *Phoenix* 42 (1988), pp. 126–130.

Snodgrass, A. M., *Arms and Armour of the Greeks* (London: 1967).

Sordi, M., *La lega Tessala fino ad Alessandro Magno* (Rome: 1958).

Sprawski, S., "Philip II and the Freedom of the Thessalians," *Electrum* 9 (2003), pp. 61–64.

Sprawski, S., "All the King's Men: Thessalians and Philip II's Designs on Greece," in D. Musial (ed.), *Society and Religions: Studies in Greek and Roman History* (Torun: 2005), pp. 31–49.

Sprawski, S., "From the Bronze Age to Alexander I," in J. Roisman and Ian Worthington (eds.), *Blackwell Companion to Ancient Macedonia* (Malden: 2010), pp. 127–144.

Strauss, B. S., "Thrasybulus and Conon: A Rivalry in Athenian Politics in the 390s B.C.," *AJP* 105 (1984), pp. 37–48.

Sprawski, S., "Alexander: The Military Campaign," in J. Roisman (ed.), *Brill's Companion to Alexander the Great* (Leiden: 2003), pp. 133–156.

Sundahl, M. J., "The Rule of Law and the Nature of the Fourth-Century Athenian Democracy," *Class. & Med.* 54 (2003), pp. 127–156.

Thelwall, J., "Historical and Oratorical Society at Mr. Thelwall's Institution," *Monthly Magazine* 28 (1809), pp. 152–157.

Thomas, C. G., "The Physical Kingdom," in J. Roisman and Ian Worthington (eds.), *Blackwell Companion to Ancient Macedonia* (Malden: 2010), pp. 65–80.

Thomsen, R., *Eisphora* (Copenhagen: 1964).

Tod, M. N., *Greek Historical Inscriptions* 2 (Oxford: 1948).

Tomlinson, R. A., "Ancient Macedonian Symposia," *Ancient Macedonia* 1 (Institute for Balkan Studies, Thessaloniki: 1970), pp. 308–315.

Touratsoglou, J., "Art in the Hellenistic Period," in M. B. Sakellariou (ed.), *Macedonia, 4000 Years of Greek History and Civilization* (Athens: 1983), pp. 170–191.

Traill, J. S., *Demos and Trittys* (Toronto: 1986).

Treves, P., "La composition de la Troisième Philippique," *REA* 42 (1940), pp. 354–364.

Trevett, J., *Apollodorus the Son of Pasion* (Oxford: 1992).

Trevett, J., "Demosthenes' Speech *On Organization* (Dem. 13)," *GRBS* 35 (1994), pp. 179–193.

Trevett, J., "Did Demosthenes Publish His Deliberative Speeches?," *Hermes* 124 (1996), pp. 425–444.

Trevett, J., "Demosthenes and Thebes," *Historia* 48 (1999), pp. 184–202.

Trevett, J., *Demosthenes, Speeches 1–17* (Austin: 2011).

Tritle, L., *Phocion the Good* (London: 1988).

Tritle, L., *The Peloponnesian War* (Westport: 2004).

Tronson, A. D., "Satyrus the Peripatetic and the Marriages of Philip II," *JHS* 104 (1984), pp. 116–126.

Tuplin, C., "Demosthenes' *Olynthiacs* and the Character of the Demegoric Corpus," *Historia* 47 (1998), pp. 276–320.

Usher, S., *Demosthenes: On the Crown* (Warminster: 1993).

Usher, S., *Greek Oratory: Tradition and Originality* (Oxford 1999).

Usher, S., "Symbouleutic Oratory," in Ian Worthington (ed.), *Blackwell Companion to Greek Rhetoric* (Malden: 2007), pp. 220–235.

Vince, J. H., *Demosthenes*, Loeb Classical Library 3 (Cambridge and London: 1986).

Wallace, R. W., *The Areopagos Council, to 307 B.C.* (Baltimore: 1989).

Wankel, H., *Demosthenes: Rede für Ktesiphon über den Kranz*, 2 vols. (Heidelberg: 1976).

Waterfield, R., *Dividing the Spoils: The War for Alexander the Great's Empire* (Oxford: 2011).

West, A. B., *The History of the Chalcidic League* (Madison: 1918).

West, W. C., "The Decrees of Demosthenes' *Against Leptines*," *ZPE* 107 (1995), pp. 237–247.

Westlake, H. D., *Thessaly in the Fourth Century BC* (London: 1935; repr. Chicago: 1993).

Whitehead, D., "The Political Career of Aristophon," *CP* 81 (1986), pp. 313–319.

Whitehead, D., *The Demes of Attica: A Political and Social Study* (Princeton: 1986).

Whitehead, D., "Cardinal Virtues: The Language of Public Approbation in Democratic Athens," *Class. & Med.* 44 (1993), pp. 37–75.

Whitehead, D., *Hyperides, The Forensic Orations* (Oxford: 2000).

Wilkes, J., *The Illyrians* (Oxford: 1995).

Williams, J. M., "Demades' Last Years, 323/2–319/8 B.C.: A 'Revisionist' Interpretation," *Anc. World* 19 (1989), pp. 19–30.

Wilson, P., "Demosthenes 21 (*Against Meidias*): Democratic Abuse," *PCPS* 37 (1991), pp. 164–195.

Wilson, P., *The Athenian Institution of the Khoregia: The Chorus, The City and the Stage* (Cambridge: 2000).

Wolff, H. J., "Demosthenes as Advocate: The Functions and Methods of Legal Consultants in Classical Athens," in E. Carawan (ed.), *The Attic Orators* (Oxford: 2007), pp. 91–115.

Woodhead, A. G., "Chabrias, Timotheus and the Aegean Allies, 375–373 B.C.," *Phoenix* 16 (1962), pp. 258–266.

Wooten, C. W., *Cicero's Philippics and their Demosthenic Model* (Chapel Hill: 1983).

Wooten, C. W., "Dionysius of Halicarnassus and Hermogenes on the Style of Demosthenes," *AJP* 110 (1989), pp. 576–588.

Wooten, C. W., *A Commentary on Demosthenes' Philippic 1* (Oxford: 2008).

Worthington, Ian, "The First Flight of Harpalus Reconsidered," *G&R*² 31 (1984), pp. 161–169.

Worthington, Ian, "Plutarch *Dem.* 25 and Demosthenes' Cup," *CP* 80 (1985), pp. 229–233.

Worthington, Ian, "Pausanias II 33,4–5 and Demosthenes," *Hermes* 113 (1985), pp. 123–125.

Worthington, Ian, "The Chronology of the Harpalus Affair," *SO* 61 (1986), pp. 63–76.

Worthington, Ian, "*I.G.* ii² 1631, 1632 and Harpalus' Ships," *ZPE* (1986), pp. 222–224.

Worthington, Ian, "Greek Oratory, Revision of Speeches and the Problem of Historical Reliability," *Class. & Med.* 42 (1991), pp. 55–74.

Worthington, Ian, "The Authenticity of Demosthenes' Fourth *Philippic*," *Mnemosyne* 44 (1991), pp. 425–428.

Worthington, Ian, *A Historical Commentary on Dinarchus: Rhetoric and Conspiracy in Later Fourth-Century Athens* (Ann Arbor: 1992).

Worthington, Ian, "The Date of the Tegea Decree (Tod ii 202): A Response to the Diagramma of Alexander III or of Polyperchon?," *AHB* 7 (1993), pp. 59–64.

Worthington, Ian, "History and Oratorical Exploitation," in Ian Worthington (ed.), *Persuasion: Greek Rhetoric in Action* (London: 1994), pp. 109–129.

Worthington, Ian, "The Canon of the Ten Attic Orators," in Ian Worthington (ed.), *Persuasion: Greek Rhetoric in Action* (London: 1994), pp. 244–263.

Worthington, Ian (ed.), *Persuasion: Greek Rhetoric in Action* (London: 1994).

Worthington, Ian, "The Harpalus Affair and the Greek Response to the Macedonian Hegemony," in Ian Worthington (ed.), *Ventures Into Greek History: Essays in Honour of N. G. L. Hammond* (Oxford 1994), pp. 307–330.

Worthington, Ian (ed.), *Ventures Into Greek History: Essays in Honour of N. G. L. Hammond* (Oxford 1994).

Worthington, Ian, *Greek Orators 2, Dinarchus 1 and Hyperides 5 & 6* (Warminster: 1999).

Worthington, Ian, "Demosthenes' (In)activity During the Reign of Alexander the Great," in Ian Worthington (ed.), *Demosthenes: Statesman and Orator* (London: 2000), pp. 90–113.

Worthington, Ian, "Alexander's Destruction of Thebes," in W. Heckel & L. A. Tritle (eds.), *Crossroads of History: The Age of Alexander the Great* (Claremont: 2003), pp. 65–86.

Worthington, Ian, "Alexander, Philip, and the Macedonian Background," in J. Roisman (ed.), *Brill Companion to Alexander the Great* (Leiden: 2003), pp. 94–96.

Worthington, Ian, "The Authorship of the Demosthenic *Epitaphios,*" *Museum Helveticum* 60 (2003), pp. 152–157.

Worthington, Ian, *Alexander the Great, Man and God*, rev. ed. (London: 2004).

Worthington, Ian, "Oral Performance in the Athenian Assembly and the Demosthenic *Prooemia,*" in C. M. Mackie (ed.), *Oral Performance and Its Context* (Leiden: 2004), pp. 129–143.

Worthington, Ian, *Demosthenes: Speeches 60 and 61, Prologues, Letters* (Austin: 2006).

Worthington, Ian, "Rhetoric and Politics in Classical Greece: Rise of the *Rhêtores,*" in Ian Worthington (ed.), *Blackwell Companion to Greek Rhetoric* (Malden: 2007), pp. 255–271.

Worthington, Ian (ed.), *Blackwell Companion to Greek Rhetoric* (Malden: 2007).

Worthington, Ian, "*IG* ii^2 236 and Philip's Common Peace of 337," in L. G. Mitchell and L. Rubinstein (eds.), *Greek Epigraphy and History: Essays in Honour of P. J. Rhodes* (Swansea: 2008), pp. 213–223.

Worthington, Ian, *Philip II of Macedonia* (New Haven and London: 2008).

Worthington, Ian, "'Worldwide Empire' versus 'Glorious Enterprise': Diodorus and Justin on Philip II and Alexander the Great," in E. Carney and D. Ogden (eds.), *Philip II and Alexander the Great: Lives and Afterlives* (Oxford: 2010), pp. 165–174

Worthington, Ian, "Why We Have Demosthenes' Symbouleutic Speeches: A Note," in F. C. Gabaudan and J. V. M. Dosuna (eds.), *Dic mihi, Musa, virum: Homenaje al profesor Antonio López Eire* (Salamanca: 2010), pp. 709–713.

Worthington, Ian, "Intentional History: Alexander, Demosthenes and Thebes," in L. Foxhall and H.-J. Gehrke (eds.), *Intentional History: Spinning Time in Ancient Greece* (Stuttgart: 2010), pp. 239–246.

Worthington, Ian, *By the Spear. Philip II, Alexander the Great, and the Rise and Fall of the Macedonian Empire* (New York: 2014)

Worthington, Ian, "From East to West: Alexander and the Exiles Decree," in E. Baynham (ed.), *East and West in the World of Alexander: Essays in Honour of A. B. Bosworth* (Oxford: forthcoming).

Worthington, Ian, "The Battles and Sieges of Alexander the Great," in H. Sidebottom and M. Whitby (eds.), *Blackwell Encyclopedia to Ancient Battles* (Malden: forthcoming).

Worthington, Ian, C. Cooper and E. M. Harris, *Dinarchus, Hyperides, Lycurgus* (Austin: 2001).

Worthington, Ian and D. L. Gilley, "Alexander the Great, Macedonia and Asia," in J. Roisman and Ian Worthington (eds.), *Blackwell Companion to Ancient Macedonia* (Malden: 2010), pp. 186–207.

Worthington, Ian and J. Roisman (eds.), *Blackwell Companion to Ancient Macedonia* (Oxford: 2010).

Wüst, F. R., *Philipp II von Makedonien und Griechenland in den Jahren 346 bis 339* (Munich: 1938).

Wyse, W., "On the Use of προδανείζειν," *CR* 6 (1892), pp. 254–257.

Yardley, J. C., *Justin and Trogus: A Study of the Language of Justin's Epitome of Trogus* (Toronto: 2003).

Yunis, H., "Law, Politics, and the *Graphe Paranomon* in Fourth-Century Athens," *GRBS* 29 (1988), pp. 361–382.

Yunis, H., *Taming Democracy: Models of Political Rhetoric in Classical Athens* (Ithaca: 1996).

Index